Cholas and Pishtacos

WOMEN IN CULTURE AND SOCIETY

A Series Edited by Catharine R. Stimpson

Cholas and Pishtacos

STORIES OF RACE AND SEX

IN THE ANDES

Mary Weismantel

THE UNIVERSITY OF CHICAGO PRESS
CHICAGO AND LONDON

The University of Chicago Press, Chicago 60637
The University of Chicago Press, Ltd., London
© 2001 by The University of Chicago
All rights reserved. Published 2001
Printed in the United States of America

10 09 08 07   3 4 5

ISBN (cloth) 0-226-89153-4
ISBN (paper) 0-226-89154-2

Library of Congress Cataloging-in-Publication Data

Weismantel, Mary J.
    Cholas and pishtacos : stories of race and sex in the Andes / Mary Weismantel.
        p.   cm.—(Women in culture and society)
    Includes bibliographical references and index.
    ISBN 0-226-89153-4 (cloth : alk. paper)—ISBN 0-226-89154-2 (pbk : alk. paper)
    1. Indians of South America—Andes Region—Ethnic identity.   2. Indians of
    South America—Andes Region—Folklore.   3. Indian women—Andes re-
    gion—Folklore.   4.Sex role—Andes Region.   5. Andes Region—Race rela-
    tions.   I. Title. II. Series
    F2230.1.E84 W45 2001
    305.8'0098—dc21

                                                        2001001398

For my father, William Louis Weismantel

Contents

Illustrations

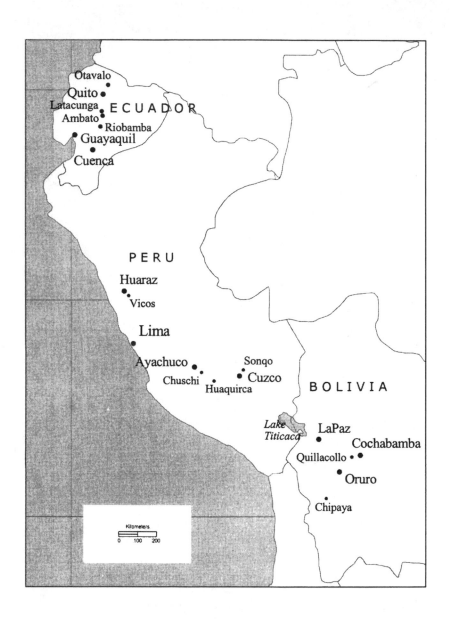

Foreword

Set in the Andes, *Cholas and Pishtacos* richly deserves the attention of several different audiences—scholars of the Andean region and Latin America, participants in cultural studies, and readers interested in social and cultural issues. Indeed, I am eager for the general public as well as scholars to read this brilliant book. Too many of us in the United States know only the superficial representations of Andean life: a picture of a llama or of a smiling Indian child playing the flute or of a coca crop that must be destroyed. Our ignorance hurts both Latin and North America. We cannot understand one without understanding the other.

The author of *Cholas and Pishtacos*, Mary Weismantel, first went to the Andes in 1982, as a graduate student in anthropology. However, she had lived in New Mexico since childhood and attended college there. Aware of the Hispanic presence in the United States, she knew families whose forebears had lived in New Mexico before the United States was a country. One of the strengths of *Cholas and Pishtacos* is the lucidity of its insights into the multiple, overlapping histories of the Americas: first that of the land itself, then of indigenous peoples, then of the European conquests (Spain conquered Latin America in the sixteenth century), then of the formation of republics in the late eighteenth and nineteenth centuries, and now of the emerging global economy. No matter how "haphazard" and "indirect" (p. 144) the connections might be between this economy and a provincial market in the Andes, they exist. Items manufactured in China and Mexico can be found next to local potatoes.

After her initial trip, Weismantel often returned to Latin America, spending long periods of time in the Andes. In 1988, she published her first book *Food, Gender and Poverty in the Ecuadorian Andes,* a well-received study of farm women, their families, and their everyday lives.

Extending her work on gender, *Cholas and Pishtacos* is the result of years of immersion in the Andes, traveling on rural buses, dwelling in small cold houses, taking in the stench and fragrance of the markets, talking to people in all their diversity, appalled by some but making deep friendships with others. *Cholas and Pishtacos* gives us what great anthropology does: a theoretical framework for understanding a culture, an account of its evolution, an analysis of its structures, and a thick description of its activities and their meanings within the culture. Crossing disciplines, Weismantel seamlessly integrates economic and cultural issues. She also wants anthropologists to be more forthcoming about the responses of their senses to a culture, to its sounds and sights and smells. Although intellectually elegant and sophisticated, *Cholas and Pishtacos* is also vivid, dramatic, *there* for its readers.

Weismantel's great project is to show the continuing power of race in Andean society. She argues that race "embeds the Andes within world history," for Andean elites assert their racial superiority to claim a place in a "global order of domination" (p. 24). Persuasively, she helps to dismantle the myth that while Latin America may be a class-ridden continent, it is free from racism. The phrase *indio sucio,* dirty Indian, and its many counterparts are casual commonplaces. Her demonstration of how race works—how a society keeps race alive, how it sutures race and class and gender together—gives us a method to apply to societies outside of the Andes.

To be sure, the Andean vocabulary of race is rich, volatile, and "hyperactive." To be sure, too, many Andeans, the *mestizos,* have a mixed heritage of Indian and European. However, the underlying structure of race is a harsh, hierarchical duality, a binary opposition between Indian inferior and white superior, Indian subordinate and white superordinate. This master binary controls a series of lesser binary oppositions between indigenous languages (such as Quechua or Aymara) and Spanish, *polleras* and "straight skirts," ponchos and suits, natives and Europeans, rural and urban, poor and affluent, primitive and modern, backward and civilized. Although she is too clear-minded to indulge in nostalgia or romanticism, Weismantel shows the human and social cost to the Andes of despising its indigenous peoples and cultures, *lo andino.* Ironically, racial prejudice against market women has helped to prevent a state treatment of the markets that might stimulate development and economic growth.

Weismantel's pathway into Andean society is the female figure of the chola and the male figure of the pishtaco, both of whom loom so large in Andean life and narratives. The chola, the market woman, is a "real person," but Weismantel explores how many, conflicted, and fragmented are the symbolic meanings that have been assigned to her and her traditional clothing of hats and the pollera (multilayered and multicolored skirts). On the one hand, postcards, tourist brochures, and billboards attempt to fix her in her costume as a regional symbol—even though many cholas now wear sweatpants and baseball caps to work. On the other hand, the cholas are a symbol for militant indigenous movements. Drawing on the ideas of Judith Butler and Bertolt Brecht, who created that famous market woman Mother Courage, Weismantel explores the market as a theater and encounter among the market women and between them and their customers. The space in which the chola performs, where women are the vast majority of the vendors, is construed as female. Occupying a swing position, the chola may be thought of as powerful and white in rural markets with her Indian customers, but she may be dismissed as an Indian in urban centers. As a female space, the market is the "raucous twin" (p. 70) of the family kitchen. Weismantel includes several vignettes about the contemptuous behavior of the upper-class housewife, often accompanied by her maid, in the market. As a public space, the chola's world contrasts to the masculine plaza, the seat of government and symbol of European power.

The pishtaco is a fantasy figure, a bogeyman. A Peruvian friend tells me that the adults would warn her that the "pishtaco" would get her if she did not behave. Such figures, if they persist in a culture, have serious meanings. The pishtaco is nearly always a vampirelike white man, who roams the countryside and plunders the fat from Indian bodies, disemboweling and dismembering and raping the Indians as he does so. Significantly, body fat was prized in indigenous cultures. Beautifully, Weismantel interprets him through Freud's theory of the "uncanny," the unfamiliar figure who is actually threatening and all too familiar. Although he is not a "real person," Andeans believe that he exists. A fearsome marauder with phallic weapons, he represents the historical destruction of indigenous peoples and their vicious cultural, economic, and sexual exploitation. The exact representation of the pishtaco has varied over time. Its origins may have been the practice of colonizing Spanish soldiers who took Indian fat to help heal their wounds. In the eighteenth century, the pishtaco appeared as a priest with a knife, and then evolved into a man on horseback or in a powerful car. During the economic crisis of the 1980s, when rural residents immigrated to urban centers, the pishtaco reappeared as the *sacaojos*, white medical technicians in dark suits who steal and dismember children. From time to time, male anthropologists have even been associated with the pishtaco. So have particularly hard-hearted cholas who assume the structural position of white men. Despite these variations, the central meaning of the pishtaco has remained stable: he is a colonizer or from the metropolitan center, he is white, he is male, he will penetrate the body of the Indian—female or male—and he will destroy and profit from the Indian.

Reading *Cholas and Pishtacos,* I was impressed again and again by how striking its individual insights and ideas are. They are assembled into a three-part intellectual structure of great integrity. Part 1, "Estrangement," maps the Andean geography of race, static in myth, fluid in actuality. Weismantel shows the constant movement of "people and things across social boundaries." The markets, bringing rurality into the heart of the city, "collapse the distance between rural Indian and urban white public space" (p. 80). So do the pishtaco stories, in which "metropolitan strangers appear abruptly in the rural heartland" (p. 80). Tragically, Andean history, which has contaminated the land with racial violence and dread, has estranged the Indians from their ancient home.

Part 2, "Exchange," focuses on the interactions within and between the races. Those in the market are complex, hybrid, improvised, and dialogic. The market women vie with one another as competitors and treat one another as friends. Their children, whether biological or taken in, are both to be loved and treated as labor, albeit labor that might someday enable them to become a partner. Other exchanges, however, are deadly, unequal, and infused with race. Weismantel argues compellingly that the exchange systems of indigenous society were morally and psychologically better than those the Europeans imposed. These earlier systems, which exist in conflict with modernity, have been harmed but not totally obliterated. Comparing traditional and modern gender relations, Weismantel tells of conversations among Indians in which they worry about men who work in the city and who then return home tense, broke, unhappy, and far more prone to domestic violence. Economically, the older systems call for the exchange of gifts; socially, they embody a vision of marriage in which men and women are far more equal sexually and in terms of property. A strong theme of *Cholas and Pishtacos* is the pervasive postconquest sexual exploitation of Indian women. Although the chola is not immune from sexual exploitation, she is freer from it than the women who go into domestic service.

Part 3, "Accumulation," is a powerful analysis of the formation of racial identity through cumulative social processes and through the accumulation of "things: our material possessions, diet, and bodily habits" (p. 193). The pishtaco signifies this accumulation, not through honest labor, but through stealing and taking from others. The white body is fed, the Indian drained. The chola, too, can accumulate wealth and possessions—a market stand of her own, her skirts, gold for her teeth, earrings, rolls of cash. However, the market exists within a parameter of male power. The wholesalers, for example, are men. The police are men. Despite her achievements, the market woman remains vulnerable.

Throughout her discussion of the chola and the pishtaco, Weismantel has told us enough about herself to let us, her readers, understand her. However, she has not been writing a confessional autobiography. She has been highly disciplined, her prose fluent but sharply chiseled. As she ends, she permits herself passages that are explicitly morally charged. From the material she has gathered she offers her readers two possibilities of human life that differ from the often dystopian modern Andean society. Both alternatives, rooted in indigenous traditions, rebuke and invert the rapacious pishtaco. One antithesis is the figure of the good father, whose honorific title is "Tayta." His phallus begets children, whom he then raises in the company of other children whom he might have taken into his home. If this good man is castrated and humiliated, the community loses its children and thus its future.

The second figure is the Mama Negra, a mythic chola, celebrated in bacchanalian festivals that the market women themselves organize and that represents their self-image as generous mothers who sustain the populace. Sardonically, Weismantel tells of one Mama Negra parade that the elite of a town have appropriated and then used to reinforce the symbols of their power. In the festivals that still belong to the cholas, a man may play Mama Negra, clad in wildly exaggerated female outfits. She becomes an androgyne, a "manly mother" (p. 242). She also carries and suckles a white child, who can signify Jesus, who will become black through drinking the Mama Negra's breast milk. Partying away, the Mama Negra transmutes the racism, economic exploitation, and misogyny the pishtaco represents into a vision of "radical democracy" (p. 258).

The anthropologist's journeys thus end in a hopeful vision. From the exchanges and toil of the chola, from her dirty and vibrant market, there might arise a new symbolic language that can articulate "social ideals" for a future that needs them as much as the Internet and capital flows from one metropolitan center to another, all haunted by their own pishtacos.

Catharine R. Stimpson
New York University

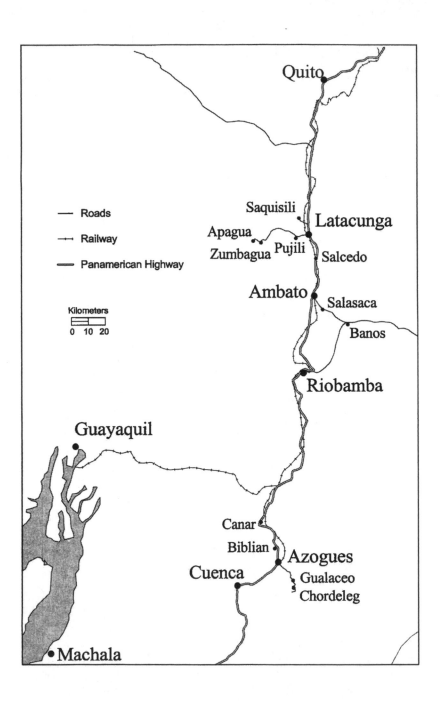

Acknowledgments

As with all scholarly work, my most profound debt is to other writers, many of whom I have never met. Their names are listed in the bibliography, but there are lots of other names in the text, where I recount conversations and events that shaped my understanding of social life in the Andes. I want to thank the people who find their names here, but I may need to apologize as well—especially since I use no pseudonyms. Despite my best efforts to be truthful, a book so devoted to telling stories comes uncomfortably close to a work of fiction—perhaps appropriately so for a book about race, something which is by its very nature simultaneously a fact and a lie, an absurd fantasy and an inescapable reality. The risks I run are familiar to novelists: I have undoubtedly misremembered and misinterpreted, and rudely revealed moments best left unrecorded. In my own defense, I can only plead a certain democracy of approach. I have treated my peers, colleagues, and friends as cavalierly as ethnographers customarily treat their research subjects.

In South America, the Chaluisa family in Zumbagua remains the touchstone of my life and of this book. My profound thanks go above all to Heloisa Huanotuñu, and to the Chaluisas, especially Alfonso, Nancy, and the *difunto* Taita Juanchu, but there are many others up in the *páramo* whom I do not forget. My time spent in Cuenca, a proud and beautiful city, was far too short, and the acquaintances made there and debts incurred too many to mention. I have especially fond memories of Lynn Hirschkind and María Cristina Cárdenas, who quickly became friends and without whose support I would have been lost. I am also grateful to Alexandra Kennedy, to everyone at the Apartmentos Otorongo and the Escuela Estrellita, and to Ann Miles for introducing me from afar to Sra. Orellana.

This book is about chance acquaintances and brief encounters, and I would like to acknowledge some of those as well. It owes a lot to the owners and staff of all the family-run hotels, restaurants, shops, and taxi stands who refused to let me — or anyone else — remain a stranger very long. Then there are the other foreigners: researchers, missionaries, development workers, backpackers, and tourists. Of all these, I would like to single out three people. In Zumbagua, the Catholic missionaries María and Mauro Bleggi, for whom my respect has deepened over the years; and in Quito, our intrepid taxi driver Julio Padilla, who took on the rutted roads of Cotopaxi and Azuay with great panache; he also introduced my daughter to Latin charm.

In the United States, my first and greatest intellectual debt is to Stephen Eisenman, my longtime companion. He is a tireless interlocutor, a tough editor, and a remorseless critic; every writer should have one like him. A special word of thanks goes to Linda Besemer and Robert Ellis, who toiled to queer my perspective on society and history. I was also fortunate to work in the intimately multiracial setting of Occidental College, an experience that indelibly changed my understanding of what it means to be white in America. I have fond memories of many people with whom I worked there: students, faculty, and staff.

Since coming to Northwestern in 1998, I have incurred a tremendous debt to Micaela di Leonardo, who has provided intellectual stimulation, friendly encouragement, and professional assistance in ways too numerous to recount — most notably by introducing me to her wonderful editor at the University of Chicago Press, Susan Bielstein. I would also like to thank my two terrific readers for the Press, Don Kulick and Patricia Zavella, for their insightful and detailed comments, as well as earlier readers, many of whom are mentioned elsewhere in these acknowledgments.

Organizing the 1997 AAA panel titled "Race in the Andes" was a critically important phase in this project, thanks to my fellow participants — Stephen Eisenman, Ben Orlove, Robert Ellis, Marisol de la Cadena, Rudi Colloredo-Mansfeld, Zoila Mendoza, Tom Cummins, Peter Gose, and Bruce Mannheim — as well as to our interlocutors from the audience. On market women, I must thank first of all Linda Seligmann, not only for her two marvelous articles, but also for inviting me to participate in an AAA panel on the topic that was the inception of my work on this book. Florence Babb and Gracia Clark, also members of that panel, have offered me much-appreciated support, friendship, and inspiration in the years since. On the pishtaco I have benefited from the unpublished writings of Andrew Orta and Stuart Rockefeller, and I would also like to thank Denise Arnold for sending me Alison Spedding's work. Nicario Jiménez, visual ethnographer par excellence, stimulated my thinking through his work, lectures, and conversations.

A few older intellectual debts also bear mentioning. My interest in the Andes began at the University of Illinois, where I was fortunate enough to study with R. T. Zuidema, Donald Lathrap, Frank Salomon, Carmen Chuquín, and Joseph Casagrande. In writing this book, I am especially indebted to Norman Whitten Jr.'s groundbreaking work on ethnicity in Ecuador; and to Enrique Mayer, who is still teaching me, most recently through a long e-mail conversation about cholos and gringos.

The real beginnings of this project go back to junior high school, when my family moved to Albuquerque and met people whose families had lived in New Mexico for longer than the United States had existed. This new education about the meaning of the word "American" continued at the University of New Mexico through the activism of politicized Chicanos and Native Americans, among whom I would like to acknowledge my father's colleague John Borrego, now at the University of California, Santa Cruz. Years later, when I moved from the Midwest to Los Angeles, those lessons came back to me. At first I found my Latino students difficult to teach: hungry for knowledge about Latin America, yet easily frustrated by material that they could not connect to their own lives. Their impatience irritated me, but it was contagious; when I attended national meetings and listened to other Latin Americanists, I was surprised to find myself just as alienated as my students. For me, too, the distance between the Andes and Los Angeles— or Chicago, where I live now—was disappearing.

On a practical note, I should thank Occidental College for the sabbaticals that enabled me to spend time reading about race, and writing; a Fulbright grant took me to Cuenca. Earlier versions of material found in this book appeared in the *Bulletin of Latin American Research* and the journal *Identities,* thanks to Peter Wade, John Hartigan, and Nina Glick-Schiller. Invitations to present earlier drafts of this work at the Universities of California at Santa Barbara and Davis, the University of Oregon, the University of Illinois at Urbana-Champaign and at Chicago, and the University of Cuenca provided welcome opportunities to receive critical commentary. Most recently, Professor Guillermo Náñez Falcón, director of the Tulane University Latin American Library, and his staff made a visit to the photographic archives delightful and profitable. I am especially grateful to Teo Allain and Julia Chambi for permission to reproduce Martín Chambi's photographs, to Fernando LaRosa for his dazzling portraits of people in the markets, and to Emma Sordo for her persistence in putting me in contact with Nicario

Jiménez. I have come to think of Anthony Burton and Jennifer Moor-house at the University of Chicago Press, known to me only via e-mail, as two friendly albeit disembodied spirits nudging this manuscript toward publication; Paul Liffman, in an act of unrequited generosity, aided in the editing process by correcting my Spanish in the sections on the pishtaco. And in the spirit of Andean reciprocity, my colleague John Hudson of the Program in Geography has placed me in his debt through a gift of labor: the two maps that appear here.

Writing a book is a lot of work, not only for the author but for everyone around her, and this one is no exception. I was helped by dear friends from Los Angeles: Arthé Anthony (wedding photogra-pher), Linda Besemer (my Best Man), Elizabeth Chin, Susan Seizer, Janet Sporleder, Catherine Brennan, and Martha Ronk. In Evanston, in addition to Micaela di Leonardo, the lively crew at the *Journal for Latin American Anthropology,* especially Heather McClure and Elisabeth Enenbach, have been wonderful companions, helping me to weather crises of all kinds. E-mail friendships with Ben Orlove and Rosemary Joyce provided welcome encouragement.

Personally as well as intellectually, my largest debt is to Stephen, who befriended my compadres despite barriers of language, culture, and cuisine; sent me off to the office on Sunday mornings when I would much rather stay home and read the newspaper; and looked after our daughter Sarah while I wrote. Thanks are also due to Sarah herself, who endured all those weekend absences and proved to be a terrific ethnographer in Zumbagua and Cuenca. I must end, however, by thanking the individual who did the most to keep me writing: my dog, Nisa. She kept me on schedule by walking me to the office in all kinds of weather, falling deeply asleep at the first click of the keyboard keys—and jumping up to remind me when it's time to quit.

Introduction: Indian and White

A contrast in light and dark: the *chola* and the *pishtaco*. In South America, the image of the chola is a sunny one: a brown-skinned woman who sits in the plaza at midday selling ripe fruit and fresh flowers. Beloved denizen of the traditional Latin city, she appears in the popular imagination in a gathered skirt and a big hat, laughing and gossiping with her companions. The pishtaco, by contrast, is a creature of night: a white man with a knife, pale and terrifying. According to tales told in the southern Andes, he waits alone in the shadows along isolated country roads, searching for victims to eviscerate.

Cholas and pishtacos belong to both low and high culture: well known from folklore, they also appear as stock characters in the national literatures of Ecuador, Peru, and Bolivia. Today, these homegrown figures seem a bit outdated, eclipsed by flashier products from Hollywood and Madison Avenue. But in one respect at least, they are not so different from commercial images produced for a mass audience. Like television and movie characters, the chola and the pishtaco pretend to be harmless fun: one arouses a nostalgic sigh or a titillated chuckle, the other a pleasurable *frisson* of fear. Yet these fantasies of brown women and white men are more dangerous than they seem, for they arouse the violent passions of a society fractured by race and sex, and divided by enormous economic inequality.

The two rarely appear together: the chola shows up as the butt of a running joke about what lies under her many skirts, while the knife-wielding bogeyman plays the lead in his own eponymous horror story. Yet in a sense, they mirror each other, telling the same story from two different vantages. For white men, the idea of the chola is suggestive, arousing pleasurable fantasies of a woman whose racial and sexual subordination make her available for almost any use. By the same token, the word *pishtaco* frightens Indians, women, and the poor, for it evokes their own vulnerability to the predations of the powerful. Together, these two figures frame a picture of Andean social life as fraught with racial and sexual anxieties—and alive with transgressive possibilities. An element of unpredictability electrifies these tales of seduction and death: in the volatile encounters between seducer and seduced, vendor and customer, or killer and victim, things do not always go according to plan.

WRITING THIS BOOK

I first went to the Andes in 1982; I have returned seven times since, for periods ranging from a few weeks to a year and half. Most of that time has been spent in the rural parish of Zumbagua, high in the *páramo* grasslands of central Ecuador, where I lived for more than a year.[1] Ten years ago I wrote a book about the farm women of that parish, their families and their everyday lives; unlike that book (*Food, Gender and Poverty in the Ecuadorian Andes*),[2] this one does not focus on one place. Instead, it ranges widely across Ecuador, Peru, Bolivia, and even the United States in order to capture the workings of far-reaching systems of race, sex, and class, only a tiny fragment of which can be seen in Zumbagua. This restless vision reflects my own travels: working in a rural area required traveling through other places, starting with the nearby cities of Latacunga and Quito. And before settling on Zumbagua as a research site, I went elsewhere—especially to small communities outside the southern city of Cuenca; and to Salasaca in the central sierra, an indigenous community bisected by the Panamerican Highway and surrounded by hostile white towns.[3] My research on food took me to markets across Ecuador and Peru, while visits to friends—usually other anthropologists—brought me to the Amazonian rainforest, to islands off the Pacific coast, and to the Peruvian Altiplano. Most of these travels were solitary ventures; in recent years I have had a companion, art historian Stephen F. Eisenman, who is sometimes mentioned in these pages.

In my student days, I adored long bus rides through little-known regions. Those many hours squeezed into small compartments with vendors and farmers, children and old people, live pigs and litters of puppies, new soccer balls and old ponchos put the lie to the image of rural Andeans as isolated autochthons rooted in their own communities. Instead, the whole region seemed to be on the move: everyone was going somewhere else, carrying things to sell, trade, or give as gifts. According to noted Peruvian literary critic Antonio Cornejo Polar, this peripatetic condition is a defining characteristic of life in the Andes.

The word *andino* (Andean), he says, long associated with an idea of Indian peasants who live and die in the same small village, actually describes a very different state of being: that of a *"migrante . . . oscilante, siempre fuera de sitio, marginal incluso cuando se establece en el centro, forastéro aquí y allá"* ("a migrant . . . oscillating, always out of place, marginal even when established in the center, a stranger both here and there"[4]) (1995 : 3).

Cornejo Polar wrote those words in an essay about José María Arguedas, the Peruvian novelist who was also the greatest of Andean ethnographers, linguists, and folklorists—a man who wrote insightfully about both market women and pishtacos. The writings of Arguedas, more than those of any other author, define Andean culture. Reading him today, Cornejo Polar finds that for all its effusive love for indigenous culture and language, and for the rural landscape, Arguedas's work is permeated with a sense of displacement that ultimately characterizes the Andean condition. This book is about that Andean estrangement, which, like Arguedas, I locate in the racial schism that runs through the continent like a volcanic fault line.

To map that divide requires moving back and forth from the city to the country, and from wealthy neighborhoods to poor ones. (I am reminded of the Colon-Camal bus in Quito, on which many years ago I began each trip up to Zumbagua. I caught it on Avenida Colon near my nice little hotel in a then-elite neighborhood, and got off at the end of its long and twisting route an hour later in the raucous, dirty Camal market far to the south. There, at the terminal near the Camal, I boarded a second bus, a big fast one that took me down the Panamerican Highway to Latacunga. In Latacunga, it was at another market, El Salto, that I found the battered old vehicles that braved the steep, hazardous road up into the breathtaking beauty and abysmal poverty of Zumbagua.)

As Cornejo Polar also observes, to write about a region so continually in motion necessitates a fluidity of languages and voices, in keeping with the Andes' own exuberant multilingualism (9). The *lenguas oprimidas*[4]—the "oppressed" Native Andean languages—of Quechua and Aymara battle with their Castillean conqueror in this book, as they do in life. But because I intend it to be perfectly accessible to those who do not know the Andes, this text makes no demands on the monolingual English reader. In Arguedas's literary works, other languages and other dialects push their way into the Spanish text; here, a different kind of intertextuality is at play, disrupting ethnography's usual empiricism. Rather than limit myself to describing what I saw with my own eyes, I juxtapose my own knowledge with the words of other ethnographers, and with other genres altogether—novels and poems, photographs and assemblages. Each of these demands its own form of interpretation, and offers a different kind of truth. My claim to the reader's trust thus rests not on my singular authority as eyewitness but on my ability to construct a credibly intersubjective narrative about a particular social world. Unlike a modernist ethnography or novel, here the author's vision is not panoptic but partial and multiple.

This book is a purely idiosyncratic view of the Andes nonetheless. And for all its wanderings, it remains firmly rooted: in ethnography, and in Zumbagua. Its topics and themes originate in my experiences in that parish: pishtaco stories gripped me because I had learned how much Indians have to fear from whites; the life story of Heloisa Huanotuñu, a Zumbagua tavern owner, first prompted me to wonder about the ambiguities of the word *chola*. Still, like many another anthropologist, I have found that a picture of life in one place is no longer adequate even to describe that place: this book can no more afford to stay in the Andean countryside than can the young people who were born there.

Instead, it follows two figures who are never at home: the chola and the pishtaco. Each represents the dynamic tension between Indian and white, women and men—and between myth and reality.

CHOLAS AND PISHTACOS

Everywhere in the Andes one sees women selling food and drink: the produce vendor with her oranges or potatoes, the cook who serves up soup and rice, the female butcher and brewer.[5] In sleepy little villages, rows of women sit on the ground with their wares spread out before them. City markets are big and crowded: the wealthiest women have permanent stalls that resemble regular stores, filled with noodles, canned goods, sundries, and candies, while the poorest vendors work as unlicensed *ambulantes,* walking the streets with their wares, keeping a watchful eye out for the policeman.

Today, most of these women wear jeans or sweatpants, T-shirts or baseball caps, but some still dress in the traditional garb of the market woman: a distinctive hat and an enormous full skirt called a *pollera*. Such clothing has long been an integral part of the folkloric tradition of each region of the Andes, for the characteristic local style of dress and speech of the cholas imparts an unmistakable color and flavor to city life.[6] Indeed, some cities are famous for their cholas. In Cuenca, a lovely colonial city of southern Ecuador, women flash by on the narrow streets wearing snowy white straw hats and enormous felted skirts of brilliant, almost psychedelic hues of orange and pink; the same skirts, spread out to dry on the banks of the Tomebamba River that courses through the city, make a patchwork of color dear to every Cuencano's heart. Peruvians know the famed cholas of Cuzco, once the Inca capital, by their tall white hats, big skirts, and flashing earrings, while Bolivians recognize a chola *paiceña* (from La Paz) by the little bowler that sits rakishly atop her head.

Market women have a contradictory reputation. With their huge skirts and audacious hats, they have long been associated with flamboyant speech and outrageous behavior. But they also evoke a more tranquil past, in which women in gathered skirts and shawls sitting placidly on the ground or trudging along with a heavy basket, hawking their wares in a loud sing-song, gave the city a more human face. Today, schoolchildren read stories and memorize poems about cholas written by now-deceased local men of letters, while entrepreneurs from the tourist industry reproduce the vendors' romantic image on postcards and travel brochures.

This pleasing picture is not as innocent as it seems. The word *chola,* which literally describes a racial category between Indian and white, has many demeaning connotations. When I told people in Cuenca that I was there to learn about cholas, everyone had an immediate response. The elderly director of the municipal library, Dr. Lloret, was delighted to recall the famous story of "La Cusinga," an eighteenth-century *chola Cuencana* whose love affair with a Frenchman precipitated an international crisis.[7] Later, at a public forum, he reminisced with pride about his own youthful sexual conquests of such women, whom elite men consider their racial inferiors. One of the librarians, a briskly efficient woman in her thirties, was moved to recite sentimental verses from the city's theme song, "La Chola Cuencana," with its intertwined themes of idealized femininity and regional pride. Jacinto Flores, a local taxi driver, insisted categorically that the word *chola* had no negative meanings in Cuenca. But he chuckled wickedly when I asked him about the title of a recent song that had gained some local notoriety: "Cholo-Boy." This popular local slang term refers to working-class youths who go to New York to earn money for their families—as he himself had done—only to return home with empty pockets and bad habits. The phrase connotes urban vice, linguistic and cultural admixture, and bodily corruption, just as does the older feminine form, *chola.*

The pishtaco, in contrast, evokes violence and fear—and racial whiteness. In Peru and Bolivia, people love to scare one another with tales about this terrible bogeyman, known in Peruvian Spanish as the pishtaco, in Quechua as the *ñakaq,* and in Aymara as the *kharisiri.*[8] Under all these names, this creature attacks unsuspecting Indians and then drags them off unconscious to secret caves, where he hangs them upside down and extracts their body fat. He offers a scathing portrait of outsiders, for he is said to be a foreigner, a white man.[9]

The pishtaco originated in the folklore of rural Indian communities, but he is phenomenally popular in all walks of Peruvian life. In 1951, folklorist Morote Best published "El Degollador (Nakaq),"[10] the result of a project conducted in the highland departments of Ayacucho, Apurímac, and Cuzco. Out of the hundreds of people interviewed, his team encountered no one who had not heard of the pishtaco. Indeed, total strangers were eager to tell detailed stories about the loathsome "Slasher" (*Degollador*), recounting "the most varied actual cases of deaths" at his hands (1951:70).[11] Four decades later, filmmaker Gabriela Martínez Escobar repeated the experiment for her video *Ñakaj* (1993). Standing on a street corner in her hometown of Cuzco, asking about pishtacos, she likewise failed to find anyone who didn't have a story to tell.

Scholars like to chronicle these macabre tales as much as storytellers love to tell them: they record each ghastly detail with evident delight. In 1969, another Peruvian folklorist, Juan Antonio Manya, recounted the story of an Indian trembling with fear as he was drawn inescapably toward the ñakaq. The magical attraction was so strong, Manya reports, that "sparks of fire" flew out of the victim's eyes in response to the killer's hypnotic gaze.[12] Twenty years later, an American writer, Julia Meyerson, included a pishtaco story in her memoir of the year she spent in the Andes with her husband, anthropologist Gary Urton. When a stranger reveals himself to be a ñakaq, she tells us, "awesome changes" come over his body, transforming him from a handsome man into a dreadful monster whose "hair stands on end," "stomach becomes engorged," and "knees swell" (1990:155).

Market women exist, and pishtacos do not. But this common-sense statement belies the slippery relationship between myth and reality. The women who sell roast pork and boiled corn are real, but the notion of the chola—dark-eyed temptress, dirty Indian, and symbol of the nation—is almost as fantastic as that of the white bogeyman. And while ñakaqs may not exist, rural people have sometimes been provoked to real violence by their fear of them, turning upon those they suspect in gruesome acts of collective punishment. The unreal figures of the chola and the pishtaco hover above everyday life, distorting actual relations between people and recasting them in their own strange image. Under their influence, ordinary people seem alien: a woman with a pile of vegetables is monstrously eroticized as a chola, while a green-eyed stranger with a camera is perceived as a bloodthirsty ghoul. The consequences of such transformations are rarely benign.

As a folklorist, Morote Best set out to collect fables, but his respondents wanted to talk about things they had actually witnessed: the persecutions of individuals accused of being pishtacos. They also spoke of their own fears of falling under suspicion (1951:70). Foreign scholars, too, are soon terrified in earnest by the ghost stories they initially found so delightful. More than one researcher has fled in fear of his life, as the rumors about his nocturnal killing sprees spun out of control.[13]

According to anthropologist Marisol de la Cadena, the fantasy of the chola also does real harm. Produce vendors in the city of Cuzco bitterly resent the term. "Sixty year old Lucrecia Carmandona, a yucca and potato vendor" told de la Cadena that "the high society of Cuzco . . . despise us. They call us 'those cholas,' they insult us; they think we are thieves and whores" (de la Cadena 1996:31). With its power to slander, the word *chola* is not a careless pleasantry, as local men pretend; nor is it just a colorful phrase when used by poets, or a value-free ethnic category when employed by social scientists.

Chola racializes produce vendors, turning attention away from the women's occupation and onto their bodies, which it sexualizes in order to degrade. As cholas, market women become the butt of dirty jokes—and the target of sexual aggression. Even their livelihood is endangered by this unwholesome image: because the imaginary chola body is unclean, the unsanitary conditions of the produce markets seem perfectly natural. The act of naming thus leads to other kinds of acts, affecting not only how the markets are perceived, but how they are managed. When politicians promise to "clean up the markets," they have no intention of providing the kinds of infrastructural development that would create healthier and more pleasant places to work and to shop. Rather, their rhetoric plays upon white fears, leading to demands that markets be controlled like other nonwhite parts of the nation: with violence, harassment, and intimidation. Race provides an alibi for the filth and crime that plagues the markets, making these problems seem to emanate not from political neglect of a vital sector of the economy, but rather from the innate unwholesomeness of those who work there.

Naming someone a pishtaco or a chola, then, or simply invoking these figures through a story or song, brings to life a garish and distorting set of racial and sexual myths that invite physical violence and instate material oppression. Manya's description is all too apt: creatures like the ñakaq really do cast a hypnotic and dangerous spell. Cholas and pishtacos electrify social intercourse with supercharged racial and sexual imagery. The ñakaq's sharp blade and dreadful deeds depict whiteness and masculinity as powerful and threatening, while the representation of a nonwhite woman with dirty hands and exposed buttocks renders her pitiful and absurd. But women and Indians sometimes use these rumors and jokes to poke holes in the armature of white and masculine domination; it will be up to the reader to decide who has the last laugh.

Throughout this book, I return again and again to three words that matter a great deal in Zumbagua, but that have been out of favor in books about the Andes for some time: "race," "Indian," and "white." A few words to explain my use of those terms—and one other—are thus in order.

KEY WORDS

RACE. "The problems of 'race' . . . are of only peripheral significance in Spanish America," wrote Pierre van den Berghe and George Primov on the first page of their 1977 book *Inequality in the Peruvian Andes.* Indeed, it is often said that the Americas are divided in two: northerners obsessed by race, and southern societies divided by class but free of racial prejudice. Many residents of the United States look longingly across the border at Latin America and the Caribbean, convinced that people there have somehow erased the legacy of white savagery against Africans and Native Americans that scars us so deeply.

But when I went to South America, I saw racism that was deeply entrenched, overt and unapologetic. I remember stopping to eat at a dirty and unpretentious open-air restaurant in Latacunga one afternoon. When a man in a poncho came in and sat down at a table with his small son, the irate owner, a tall skinny woman in her sixties, drove them from the building with kicks and blows, screaming racist curse words that no one had taught me in Spanish class. I was even more stunned by what followed. The man got up off the ground, gathered up the boy, and leaned back into the restaurant, his feet carefully planted on the sidewalk outside. In a high-pitched singsong, he begged humbly to be allowed to buy food he could eat in the street; the owner took his money and piled up meat, potatoes, and rice on two china plates, which she carried over to him. He held out his poncho, and she dumped all the food directly onto the cloth, telling him that he was now behaving like a good *longuito* (Indian).

Back in the United States, I looked for authors who, like me, questioned the myth of Latin America's racial democracy. I found out that in the 1960s, many anthropologists—including my own advisor,

Joseph Casagrande—had written about the kind of racism I had seen (Casagrande 1981). Anthony Oliver-Smith, for example, wrote that

> The Indian of the sierra is considered by local mestizo elements to be biologically and socially inferior. . . . Every aspect of contact with the mestizo demonstrates to the Indian his supposed inferiority; and his participation is . . . restricted in . . . such vital areas as land tenure, commerce, religion, and civil authority (1969:364).

Indeed classic anthropological studies of race in the Americas had been written during those years, including Julian Pitt-Rivers's "Who Are the Indians?" (1965), Marvin Harris's *Patterns of Race in the Americas* (1964), and Magnus Mörner's *Race Mixture in the History of Latin America* (1967).

By the time I started graduate school in the 1980s, though, Latin Americanists were no longer talking about race. Recognizing the spurious biology and false history on which all systems of racial stratification are based, they had concluded that the conflicts they witnessed were not really about race after all.[14] The social reality of racism in Latin America continued unabated; but scholars talked about it as something else—usually class or ethnicity.[15]

In Bolivia, for example, a people called the Yura suffer at the hands of local elites who "base their claim to high social status . . . on their supposed descent from Spaniards" (Rasnake 1988:44). In Peru, too, towns like Quinua and Huaquirca are bitterly divided between a small group of townspeople and the numerous inhabitants of the surrounding rural areas, with the former ruthlessly exploiting the latter, and justifying their actions in explicitly racist terms. But in otherwise excellent ethnographies, Roger Rasnake (1988), William Mitchell (1991), and Peter Gose (1994b), who wrote about these three regions respectively, concur that there is no racism in these towns. They argue that although locals make recourse to the language of race, the absence of a biological basis for local prejudices precludes anthropologists from describing these systems of inequality as racial.[16] In Huaquirca, for instance, "many of the putative 'Indians' have Spanish surnames and genes bequeathed to them by priests who passed through the area in previous centuries. Others are illegitimate or downwardly mobile offshoots of notable families who lost the means of distinguishing themselves from commoners" (Gose 1994b:xii).

But there is nothing uniquely Latin American about this state of affairs. The transparent baselessness of white claims to natural superiority in the Andes does not differentiate them from those made by racists elsewhere—including the United States. As Marvin Harris wrote in 1964,

Now it just so happens that all of those people in the United States who are certain that they are whites and not Negroes, and all those people in Peru or Ecuador who are certain that they are mestizos and not *Indios,* or vice versa, are whistling through their hats. . . . All racial identity, scientifically speaking, is ambiguous. Wherever certainty is expressed on this subject, we can be confident that society has manufactured a social lie in order to help one of its segments take advantage of another (55–56).

Race, then, is a fiction—just like cholas and pishtacos. But in the Andes, and throughout the Americas, it is a social fact of great salience nonetheless. Race naturalizes economic inequality and establishes a social hierarchy that spans the continent. Within specific social contexts, it operates not merely as a negative principle—the ritual casting of aspersion upon one's putative inferiors—but also as an expression of confidence that seals every successful consolidation of property and power with the name "white."

Just as race connects regions of the Americas, so it embeds the Andes within world history. Andean elites use their assertions of racial superiority to claim membership in a global order of domination.[17] In the isolated, unimportant places about which most ethnographers write, such claims to white superiority are tremendously important. They allow bus drivers, shop owners, mayors, and schoolteachers in tiny communities high in the mountains to rewrite the misery they inflict upon their rural neighbors into yet another triumph of the white race. Thus the most contingent and ambiguous of local victories is reimagined as the inevitable outcome of a conflict of global dimensions, preordained not merely by history but by nature itself.

In the 1990s, just as had happened in the 1960s, a new wave of social theorists (and activists) demanded that we return to the study of race.[18] By pretending that race does not exist, they maintain, we simply connive in its continued power.[19] In this book, I look closely at the racial hatreds condensed within the figure of the ñakaq, and the racial privilege encoded in the construction of the chola. Such scrutiny will not reinforce the false claims to superiority advanced by racists everywhere; it is intended, instead, to eviscerate them.

WHITES. I use the word "white" throughout this book, although it is a term rarely used to describe those who claim racial superiority in Spanish-speaking countries.[20] Rather than refer to themselves as *blancos,* white Latin Americans may call themselves "educated," "cultivated" (*culto*), or well-mannered; as Marisol de la Cadena points out, the Cuzqueños who called themselves the *gente decente,* the "decent people," were those "who in censuses appeared as 'blancos'" (1996:116). Elites also choose names like the "good" people (*gente de bien*), the *vecinos* ("neighbors," i.e., town-dwellers rather than rural folk), even the "notables" or the "nobles." Foreign researchers who adopt these terms from local use in their own writings do not always appreciate how explicitly racial their meanings are.[21]

Social scientists speak of racially superordinate Latin Americans as *mestizos* (or *ladinos* in Central America) rather than as whites. There are several reasons for this; one is the belief that populations in Latin America are in fact more racially "mixed" than those of Europe, the United States, or Canada. But as Harris observed, there are no "pure" races, in the Americas or elsewhere. Another understandable but misleading assumption is that the word *mestizo* (or its Quechua equivalents, *misti* in the Southern Andes and *mishu* in Ecuadorian Quichua)[22] always retains its original meaning of "mixed." In the abstract, most Latin Americans will indeed agree that *mestizo* and *ladino* refer to racial admixture, and that their national populations are composed of a tiny white minority, a mestizo middle group, and blacks and Indians at the bottom. However, in actual practice within specific social contexts, there is no intermediate or "mixed" racial category: race operates as a vicious binary that discriminates superiors from inferiors. In one context, a group of Indians look with equal mistrust upon a bureaucrat of mixed Bolivian parentage and his boss, whose parents were both born in Europe. In another, the wealthy, jet-setting super-elites of a nation like Bolivia or Peru may sometimes differentiate themselves as "whites," "Europeans" or *criollos* in comparison to the mestizo middle classes. But they are far more likely to denigrate the latter, not as "mestizos" but as "Indians," pulling the circle of whiteness inward toward themselves rather than diluting the racial binary with a third term. Thus in the classic Ecuadorian novel of class and race relations, Jorge Icaza's *Huasipungo,* when the daughter of a landowning family takes a lover with a less than illustrious surname, her father curses the seducer indiscriminately as an "Indian" and a "cholo"—although by most people's reckoning, he would be neither (1953:13).

Historian Jeffrey Gould has traced the progression of the word *ladino* in Nicaragua. In colonial times, it designated an Indian who had adopted the customs of Spaniards; by the end of the nineteenth century, this sense of "Hispanicized Indian" had almost completely disappeared. Instead, two other meanings predominated. In the first, *ladino* referred to "all intermediate strata between Spaniard and Indian, including mestizos and mulattoes, as well as to 'former' Indians." But in parts of the country with "an overwhelmingly indigenous population," the word had a different meaning. There, *ladino* simply meant "non-Indian" (1998:75). Charles Hale finds the same contrast between the "broad definition" of *ladino* in contemporary Guatemala as "people of mixed Indian and European descent" and the word's everyday usage. In practice, he says, Guatemalan ladinos have insisted on "a rigid, absolute divide between themselves and indigenous peoples" since at least the nineteenth century (1996:55, n.1).

Gould, too, says that by the beginning of this century, although *ladino* was sometimes used "in national contexts" to mean "mixed race," not so in predominantly Indian areas. There, its meaning had consolidated as "the binary opposite of Indians"—the meaning it still holds today. In contrast to Indians, ladinos consider themselves white (136). Nor was the distinction simply ethnic:

> Indeed, the locally salient meaning of ladino implicitly referred to the existence of a "ladino race." Thus, for example, the civil and ecclesiastical birth records in the Central Highlands of Nicaragua at the turn of the century list members of the "casta indígena" and the "casta ladina." (1998:75)

The relationship between ladinos and Indians was summed up by a Jesuit priest in the 1870s, who wrote that "hatred of the races consumed the people. . . . Hostile confrontations happened between Indians and ladinos . . . thefts, wounded men, dead men" (quoted in Hale 1998:72).

This is a stark binary indeed, its boundary marked with hatred and violence—and with corpses. The same line divides Indians and mestizos in the Andes. In the eyes of Indians, it is an unambiguous fact that Andean mestizos constitute a racial community as defined by Etienne Balibar: a group who utilize "forms of violence, contempt, intolerance, humiliation and exploitation" in defense of their racial privilege (1991: 17–19). In everyday acts and language, mestizos do not acknowledge partial similarity to those they stigmatize as Indians. Rather, they posit themselves as the absolute and inimical opposite of the Indian—that is, as whites.

INDIANS. Race, then, is fundamentally binary: white and nonwhite, superior and inferior.[23] Many Latin Americans and Latin Americanists will object that this definition does not apply south of the Rio Grande; Latin American elites have often claimed that the proliferation of racial categories within their societies exempts them from charges of racism. This book rejects that argument, asserting that social life in the Andes is fundamentally a matter of Indians and whites. Just as the struggle with racism in the United States was long referred to as "the Negro Problem," so too the Andes confronts "the Indian Problem."[24] And, as in the North, the real problem—the white problem—escapes attention.

Most scholars writing about the Andes are careful to talk about "indigenous people," rather than about "Indians," because of the negative connotations of the word *indio*. I talk about Indians here because it is precisely this word's negative connotations and its implications for Andean society that I wish to describe. This strategy has been adopted elsewhere—one might think, for example, of the complicated history of other slurs—Chicano, black, queer—reclaimed for oppositional purposes. The hateful word *indio*, too, has been reappropriated by those who would use its shock value for antiracist ends. Recently, the authors of an edited volume on indigenous uprisings in Ecuador titled their book *"Indios"* (Almeida et al. 1992);[25] twenty years earlier, Peruvian revolutionary Hugo Blanco said,

> My *tayta* [father] did not like to use the word *Indian* because it is the whip that the mestizos use to beat us, and for that reason among ourselves we say *runa*. He was certainly astonished when I used the term *Indian*. I tell him, yes, that it is precisely the whip, the whip we have wrenched from the landlord's hands to brandish before his very eyes. . . . [I]t has been as Indians, and with our Quechua, that we have raised ourselves up and trampled on them; and in the same way we have used the poncho, the bare feet, and the smell of coca. . . . As the *tayta* José María [Arguedas] says, yes, we are liberators for everyone. We, who have been more humble than burros; we, who have been spat upon. Yes, *tayta*, in a word then, we, the *Indians*. (1972:131)

In avoiding the word "Indian," scholars risk indulging in what Ruth Frankenberg calls a "power-evasive strategy" that allows whites to avoid confronting their own discomfort with questions of race (1993). This book attempts to make the edifice of race more, not less, visible—and so to begin the work of dismantling. I am not interested in making yet another attempt to describe indigenous people. Rather, I want to expose the dialectic of Indian and white: a racist system that, like capitalist modernity itself, is divided into two halves that do not make a whole.

Words for "Indian" are abundant in the Andes. As Gould says about Nicaragua, "The sheer quantity of colloquial expressions for 'Indian' . . . pointed to both the social distance between the groups and the elevated degree of anxiety that such distance provoked among the ladino minority."[26] The intensively negative associations of the word *indio* continually generate a need for euphemisms. In the Andes, people are notoriously unwilling to use racial terms of any kind as self-descriptors, to the despair of survey-takers. Sometimes, class terms stand in for racial categories, as when governments and intellectuals promulgated the use of the word *campesino* (peasant) to refer to rural Indians. Today, thinking in terms of class has come to be equally unpopular among the highly educated (and Americanized); such people now speak of *indígenas* rather than *indios* when they want to be polite.

In Zumbagua, older, illiterate residents, whose Spanish was otherwise broken and ungrammatical, surprised me by the care with which they paused to utter multisyllabic terms of self-reference, which collided awkwardly with the rest of their vocabulary: "*Nosotros los naturales,*" "*los autóctonos de aquí*" ("We the natives," "the autochthons of this place"). These were dignified performances, usually constructed to frame statements about injustice: we who were never allowed to attend school, we who have been treated worse than dogs . . . I was told these things most often when I was still a stranger in the parish. When old people realized that I could understand their speech (which, even when they spoke Spanish, was so heavily influenced by Quichua as to render it unintelligible to most outsiders), they recited these phrases to me solemnly, as though imparting a lesson. I was made a messenger, entrusted with carrying their protests out into unknown worlds.

Later, when I began renting my little one-room house from the Chaluisas, the family with whom I would live for the next year, I heard the other kind of words for Indians—the ones in daily circulation. Quichua-speaking mothers, driven to distraction by their children, larded their reprimands with a few choice Spanish words: "*¡Longo sucio, indio mudo!*" ("Dirty Indian, dumb Indian!") In Zumbagua, long an hacienda where Indians labored as *huasipungos* (peons bound to the land), whip-bearing overseers had introduced these racial curses into the vocabulary.[27] The few remaining descendants of those overseers, such as the white woman who was my first landlady in town, never referred to the parish residents except as *longos* or *longuitos*—a synonym for "indio" so powerfully negative it can only be translated into English as "nigger." Unlike the latter term, which has been driven underground in the United States in the last thirty years, many Ecuadorians use the word *longo* frequently and without compunction, whether or not they are within hearing distance of people they consider to be Indians.[28]

There are other epithets for Indian as well. In Quinua, Peru, Mitchell tells us, *chutu* was a favorite (1991 : 81). As we shall see, cholo/a often functions as a synonym, uttered with all the vitriol that could ever be attached to the word *indio.* For hatred is often there, perhaps most visible in the fact that indio and its synonyms are almost never heard alone. The most common phrase in which the word appears is *indio sucio* ("dirty Indian"); indeed, the very concept of an Indian is strongly associated with dirt and disease.[29] The word is often linked with animal names, as in "Indian mule," "Indian sheep," or "Indian dog." There are various ways to say "stupid Indian"; *indios mudos* and *indios brutos,* for example, are phrases so common as to be clichéd. Rasnake remarks that mestizos typically refer to the Yura as *indios brutos,* adding needlessly that this is "a grave insult in Bolivia" (1988:44).

In Zumbagua in the 1980s, this racist language had become internal to the indigenous community, filtering into everyday conversations, jokes, and commentary as part of the taken-for-granted reality of social life. Such references to "dirty Indians" and "stupid longos" coexisted oddly with other ways of speaking and thinking, in which these racial categories had no salience. In these latter contexts, such markers of indigenous identity as living in the parish, speaking Quichua, and wearing hats, ponchos, and sashes were part of a *habitus,* either unnoticed or positively valued.[30] The context of utterances that actually used words like *indio* or *longo,* in contrast, was an explicit or implicit awareness of the racism that makes being Indian a very bad thing. These words were uttered in anger or frustration, either against one another or as part of a sharp-edged critique of Ecuadorian society.[31]

This knowledge colors speech about race in Quechua as well as in Spanish. *Runa* is the Quechua word for a human being; as in many other languages, this term is used to describe a native speaker of Quechua as well. *Runa* thus inevitably becomes a cognate for "Indian"— and so becomes contested territory. Hugo Blanco, quoted above, refers to a contrast between *runa* and *indio* in which the former, like the Spanish *indígena,* asserts a positive meaning in contrast to the negatively weighted *indio.* Colloredo-Mansfeld describes a similar situation in the politically aware region of Otavalo in the 1990s. "'Indio,'" he says, "connotes a crude way of life, poverty, and irrationality," whereas both *indígena* and *runa* signal "the historic legitimacy of a culture and people" (1996:193).

Indigenous activists thus often use the word *runa* when they name their organizations, a strategy that NGOs and government agencies have been quick to mimic. Some anthropologists, too, have invested this word with an almost magical power to overcome the negative connotations of *indio.* The most eloquent statement of this position in Andean anthropology is found in Catherine Allen's elegiac ethnography of Sonqo, Peru.[32] For Allen, the word *Runa* evokes a powerfully non-Western cultural landscape: "to chew coca . . . properly, according to traditional ceremony, is to be a *Runa,* a 'real person' . . . to affirm the attitudes and values . . . of indigenous Andean culture."[33]

Allen portrays the monolingual world of the rural Quechua as isolated from the abrasively multicultural, racially divided world of Peruvian cities and towns; the latter is glimpsed only in the book's epilogue, where it appears as an unpleasant vision of the Sonqueños's future. But even within Sonqo, people are aware that the larger society that surrounds them is harshly, even violently, prejudiced against those who call themselves *Runa.* Those racial meanings, however occulted, nevertheless weight the word. When *Runa* expresses the emphatically positive associations that Allen details, it must do so in knowing defiance of Peruvian society: it is less innocent than oppositional.

In Ecuador, *runa* is far more likely to carry the explicitly negative connotations of *indio* than in the world Allen describes. Rudi Colloredo-Mansfeld heard Otaleños translate *indio sucio* (dirty Indian) into Quichua literally, as *mapa runa* (1998:196). Otavalo is somewhat anomalous, a place in which, because of the tourist trade, some indigenous people have acquired wealth and sophistication, and indigenous culture is generally looked upon more positively than elsewhere.[34] Cotopaxi Province, where Zumbagua is located, is quite different: Indians here are very poor, and the racial history of the region is uniformly ugly.[35] In Cotopaxi the word *runa* has exclusively negative connotations, in Quichua and Spanish alike.[36]

For example, when I spoke of the Quichua language as *runa shimi,* as Quichua-speakers elsewhere do, I was quickly silenced, as though I had said something offensive. "We speak *Inga shimi,*" people in Zumagua insisted: the language of the Incas, not the language of Indians.[37] I was initially surprised to hear the word *inga,* for Zumbagua was never part of the Inca empire, and people there do not identify with Incas as ancestors. I gradually realized that in local Quichua *inga* frequently functioned as a euphemism for *runa,* much as *autóctono* did for *indio* in local Spanish.

This reluctance to use the word *runa* to modify *shimi* is not surprising. In Cotopaxi Spanish, *runa* is often used as an adjective to describe anything foul, ugly, coarse, or of poor quality. Like *longo,* the Spanish racial epithet for which it may be considered a local cognate, *runa* sounds just like "nigger." And just as in my white Missouri childhood, when casually offensive expressions like "nigger-rigged" were all too common, Spanish-speakers in Cotopaxi have coined compound words using *runa.*[38] A misshapen mongrel, for example—what speakers of some dialects of American English might call a "Heinz 57"—is a *runa perro,* a "runa dog." This kind of usage has penetrated Cotopaxi Quichua as well. I remember when Berta, a teenager at the time, painted her house bright blue on a whim, using some leftover aniline dye (intended for coloring cloth or yarn).[39] The pigment adhered poorly to the white plaster; surveying the streaky, uneven results, she laughed ruefully and said, "Well, I've got myself a runa house now!"

The central sierra of Ecuador has an especially grim history of race relations. But even in the Peruvian Department of Cuzco, where Sonqo is located, *Runa* does not stand alone. It takes its meaning from the contrast to *misti* (Allen 1988 : 24, 27–28). The meaning of this Quichua variant on *mestizo* is made clear by Peter Gose in his sensitive discussion of social conflict in Huaquirca, a community not far from Sonqo: the best definition of *misti,* he says, is " 'powerful other' " (1994b:21).

If *misti* denotes power, it is a power Indians hate and fear. Gose describes *misti* as an epithet "usually spoken with a certain venom"; and as with its alter, *indio,* this one word cannot contain all the racial hatred it invokes. Thus *misti* has spawned a more vituperative synonym, *q'ala* (literally, "naked" or "peeled," a derogatory reference to the fact that whites, unlike Indians, appear in public with their heads uncovered, and without a poncho or shawl [Gose 1994b:21; Isbell 1978:67]). Dialectical variants on this term appear throughout the Quechua-speaking Andes, including Zumbagua, where the local word for "naked," *lluchuj,* is used in exactly the same fashion (Weismantel 1998 : 7). According to Rasnake, the Bolivian Yura likewise denigrate whites as *q'aras* (1988 : 44; see also Abercrombie 1998 : 46). In Central America, Gould lists several insulting synonyms for *ladino,* and adds that "the Indians of Boaco referred to any official authority as a *chingo,* a colloquial expression for 'naked'; it also meant a special breed of tailless dog" (Gould 1998 : 72). In the Andes, just as "Indian" turns into "dirty Indian," *q'ala* too is often coupled into yet more damning combinations. Gose records two, *q'ala misti* (naked *misti*)[40] and *q'ala kuchi* (naked pig) [1994b:22].

" 'Misti,' " says Gose in his ethnography of Huaquirca, "is one of the first words an anthropologist . . . is likely to hear on entering a small town" in the Peruvian Andes (1994b:21). As though that were not bad enough, in his article on the pishtaco he assures his readers that every foreigner in rural Peru will soon hear himself described not only as a pig, but as a pishtaco (Gose 1994a:297).

The fact that even anthropologists (a group composed mostly of North Americans, Europeans, and metropolitan South Americans, many of whom are themselves the children of European immigrants) are described as mistis should dispel the last doubt as to the binary logic of race in the rural Andes. For if social scientists have been quick to describe local elites as mestizos, it is surely in the conviction that the authors of the study are themselves the real whites. After all, unlike the small-town petty bourgeoisie they call mestizos, these professionals are members of an international metropolitan class who can claim symbolic whiteness not only among the rural poor, but anywhere on the continent. Local elites agree, readily ceding their own claims to whiteness in the presence of a university student or professor, whether Latin American or foreign.

To Indians, however, this distinction is relatively unimportant. Foreigners—a category which often includes Latin American visitors as well—are gringos, but they are members of the same race as local whites. In Otavalo, Colloredo-Mansfeld overheard adults "scold their children for calling me a *mishu*" (1996:193). In Zumbagua, people tried to shield me from abrasive racial language, but I heard the word *mishu* directed at whites who were out of hearing range. When a Yugoslavian friend named Misha came for an extended visit, I learned that the word applied to gringos as well. The family was horrified when he introduced himself. Over his objections, they insisted loudly and repeatedly that his name was really "Miguel"; and like Rudi, I heard them reprimand their children for following Misha around whispering his name to others—who inevitably reacted with scandalized disbelief.[40]

In sum, the rich vocabulary of race elaborates upon, but does not disguise, the vicious binary of Indian and white. Racial terminology builds up around the social breach like layers of old scabs and new seepages over an unhealed wound. As each polite euphemism becomes tainted with the same derogatory meanings that infected the old one, speakers try to cover up the injury with new inventions. The other side of this process is the enthusiastic adoption of novel curse words to convey old hatreds. This hyperactive linguistic production marks an ideological site that generates other kinds of violence as well. As the perspicacious Nicaraguan priest commented, the racial divide in Latin America is littered not only with words, but with thefts, wounds, and corpses. This is the terrain inhabited by the ñakaq; as Gose observed, pishtaco, too, can be just another synonym for white.

But what about the chola? This term fractures the binary racial system described above. Cholas are, by definition, at once Indian and white: the very embodiment of the notion that Latin American racial categories overlap, or lack clear boundaries. In the 1960s, U.S. scholars and activists became aware of the influential writings of Brazilian intel-

lectuals such as Jorge Amado and Gilberto Freyre, who had long pro-
claimed their nation a "racial democracy" in which all colors were embraced.[41] Carl Degler, who won a Pulitzer Prize for his 1971 book
comparing the United States and Brazil, coined the expression "the
mulatto escape hatch" to explain Latin racial tolerance.[42] According to
Degler, "when demographic factors encourage miscegenation, the resulting mixing of the races" erodes racism by "encouraging additional
miscegenation as well as diluting interracial hostilities" (245). Influenced by similar intellectual movements in Mexico, Peruvian leftists
likewise celebrated the Andean chola as the symbol of a nation built on
mestizaje.[43]

Almost from the outset, however, these beliefs have met with skepticism. Brazilian scholars have since convincingly documented the
fact that racism in their country is as complex, systematic, and wide-
reaching as in the United States.[44] Moreover, new theoretical work on
race calls into question the underlying assumption of a "natural" racial
prejudice that pervades Degler's writings.[45] Nevertheless, Degler's challenge remains: Latin American and Caribbean racial systems entertain
the notion of intermediate categories while those of the United States
and Canada do not. In the Andes, people use mixed race categories like
cholo/a and *zambo/a* all the time.[46] But does the existence of these categories really mitigate the effect of the white/nonwhite binary?

In fact, race does not appear any less powerful—or less brutal—
when viewed from the perspective of those whom others call *cholas:*
quite the opposite. As we shall see in chapter 3, the ambiguous location
that market women occupy in Andean racial hierarchies is no comfortable "buffer zone," as Degler imagined. In the words of U.S. poet and
essayist Gloria Anzaldúa, mixed-race women live on a "barbed wire
fence." They know—perhaps more intimately than anyone—that the
meeting place of the races is "*una herida abierta,*" an open wound, where
the subordinate race "grates against the other and bleeds" (1987:3). In
the Andes, the category of chola does not ease or erase racial conflicts:
it reveals—perhaps even exacerbates—them.

It also brings to the fore hidden sexual contacts between the races
that racial purists would rather forget, and so exposes the racial dimension of sexual oppression in the Andes. Race mixture in the Americas
has only sometimes been the result of free choices made by blacks and
Indians; more often, access to the bodies of nonwhites has been part
and parcel of white male privilege. Indeed, sexual privilege—and the
lack of it—is so deeply inscribed into the history of race in the Andes
as to make it impossible to talk about one without thinking about the
other.

SEX. In the course of researching this book, I read again and again about employers raping their maids. In the story of the pishtaco, I heard the collected rage of generations of Indians robbed not only of their health and their lives, but of their sexual and reproductive rights as well. These tropes of the boss and his maid, the pishtaco and his Indian are shaped by gender—the topic of much recent writing about Latin America—but they are also about sex. Relatively little has been written about sex in the Andes, a lacuna partly explained by the distortions of our racial unconscious, in which blacks appear hypersexualized, while Indians seem childlike and without desires.[47] In this warped mental map of the continent, the Caribbean and Brazilian coasts exude a steamy sexuality, while the Indian interiors of Guatemala, Peru, or Bolivia do not. Climate amplifies this effect: in keeping with nineteenth-century positivist geography, the tropical lowlands are imagined as erogenous zones, while the cold highlands seem—frigid. In reality, social life in the Andes, like anywhere else, is suffused with sexuality, its expressions and its repressions. It is, after all, the homeland of the lascivious chola and the insatiable pishtaco.

Of course, "sex" has two meanings: it refers to a bodily practice—having sex—and to a physical state—having *a* sex. This linguistic ambiguity is a tacit admission of the ragged boundary between processes of becoming and states of being, as Judith Butler argued in her influential book *Gender Trouble* (1990). Butler collapses the two meanings of the word "sex," insisting that they are one and the same; I follow her lead here, for it closely parallels the argument I make about race. Just as we cannot know the sexed body apart from its cultural gendering, so too there are no races before racism (Wade 1993c). Furthermore, the mixed-race, sexually ambiguous chola and the hypermasculine, hyperwhite pishtaco demonstrate just how impossible it is to separate our sex from our race.

The pishtaco typifies the kind of noxious masculinity described as macho: violent, aggressive, and hyperphallic, he is a restless nocturnal wanderer with an insatiable need for new victims. He does not, however, conform to North American views of the macho as a working-class mixed-race latino; quite the reverse. People in the Andes picture him as a white professional; indeed, he is the quintessential foreigner from Europe or the United States. The ñakaq is whitened by his sexual aggressivity, and masculinized by virtue of his whiteness.

In the case of the chola, racial ambiguity spills over into her sex, making it, too, a tangle of contradictions. Many of the sexual and gender practices I encountered while researching market women flew in the face of stereotypical images of Latin America as homophobic and patriarchal, and of its women as traduced and submissive. A successful market woman in Cuenca showed me photographs of her gay son, now living in New York, and recounted to me tearfully their last night together, when they lay down in the same bed and caressed each other and cried all night, "just like lovers." I read about two market women in La Paz who lived together as partners, and raised a daughter who called them both "mother"; I also discovered that my own godchild, Nancy Chaluisa Quispe, had acquired a second mother as well.[48]

Thus the stereotype of the chola as a colored woman routinely taken advantage of by men is fractured by other realities—and other images. Market women contest this caricature, but not by presenting themselves as asexual virgins. Rather, they marshal other, more aggressive stereotypes in their own defense: the gender-neutral ideal of the good worker, and that most potent symbol of Latin womanhood, the all-powerful mother. The image of the chola displays other kinds of potency as well. As an Indian who is part white, she also becomes a woman who is part man; indeed, like the pishtaco, some cholas wield a phallus. But their claim to masculinity and to whiteness does not imply that to be an Indian woman is inadequate. Rather, it asserts a state of nonwhite femininity so powerful it can eclipse and even incorporate its alter.

THE PLAN OF THE BOOK

This book has three parts, each composed of two chapters. The topic of the first part is "Estrangement." Here, Freud's essay on the uncanny provides a key to the terror inspired by the pishtaco, and to the alienated racial and sexual map of the Andean social landscape. Chapter 1 is about the geography of race, which makes the cities white and relegates Indians to rural life; in Martín Chambi's photographs of Cuzco taverns, we see one of the few social spaces where the two meet—with the chola as cicerone. In chapter 2, Mary Douglas's notions about dirt help us locate the produce market within the sexual map of the city, in which domestic space is feminized and public space made masculine; we also meet some market women, among them the formidable Sofía Velasquez of La Paz.

Of course, neither Indians and whites nor women and men actually live in isolation from each other: material needs and physical desires drive them to seek each other out, and give rise to a series of exchanges, verbal, visual, physical, and material. But these imaginary yet influential geographies ensure that when people do meet, they do so on uneven terrain. The second part, "Exchange," analyzes these destabilizing effects of race and sex on social intercourse. Chapter 3 uses Judith Butler and Bertolt Brecht to read the theatrical exchanges that take place in the produce markets, where vendors use language and costume in performances calculated to provoke the crowds—and entice them to buy. Chapter 4 highlights the ugly underside of the exchange relationship by returning to the pishtaco, who forces his partners to give up everything they have. Mauss's theory of the gift and Rubin's notion of the sex/gender economy allow us to understand the political ideals behind these stories, which express outrage at forcible unequal exchange, whether financial or sexual.

Finally, the last part turns to "Accumulation": the processes that maintain and reproduce racial and sexual inequalities over time. In chapter 5, the wood and papier-mâché constructions of Ayacucho artist Nicario Jiménez tell the political history of Peru through a series of vignettes involving pishtacos. Turning to the stories themselves, a close reading of the pishtaco's body lets us see things that are normally invisible: the race of whites, and the sex of men. Chapter 6 turns from what is hidden to things exuberantly displayed: in festivals sponsored by Ecuadorian market women, cross-dressed figures, intoxicating breast milk, and displays of money and food make raucous public statements about the nature of wealth, pleasure, and power—and provide an antidote to the deathly ñakaq.

Part One

ESTRANGEMENT

....

CHAPTER 1

City of Indians

The image of the open-air market is one of timeless tranquility. But in reality, the daily work of buying and selling embroils vendors in every new convulsion of the economy. In recent years, although the markets are as busy as ever, the buyers have less money to spend, prices are always rising, and itinerant vendors, many of them recent immigrants from rural areas, crowd around the perimeters, exceeding the number of regular sellers—and even the number of customers. The pishtaco, too, albeit a creature of myth, changes with the times. In colonial stories, he was a knife-wielding priest searching for human fat with which to forge his church bells. Pishtacos dressed in friars' robes are seen to this day, but in the twentieth century he adopted new costumes as well. At first, he dressed as an hacendado (the wealthy owner of an hacienda); more recently, as a foreign engineer or a Peruvian soldier. And as Indians have moved to the cities by the hundreds of thousands, the ñakaq has gone with them—both in his original guise and as a new urban bogeyman, the evil medical technician known as the *sacaojos*.

Talking about pishtacos is one means by which people in the Andes explore a recurrent fantasy of modern life: that of the stranger who brings romance, fame, or fortune. Through the ñakaq, Andean popular culture expresses a skepticism about these chance encounters, for while these moments do indeed sparkle with opportunity and danger, we arrive at them unequally armed. Nor do we ever really meet as strangers: from the very beginning, we recognize each other by the indelible markings of race, sex, and class—and, as the ñakaq reminds us, this knowledge makes us afraid.

These are tales of estrangement. Ideologies of race and sex blind us to our common humanity, creating in us instead obsessive anxieties about imaginary lacks and alienating differences. We thus become estranged not only from each other, but from ourselves and our society. In the Andes, this estrangement begins with disconnection from the land itself: it is difficult to make the landscapes of South American nations a source of self-love, or of national pride, when they are so deeply contaminated by race.

WHITES IN INDIAN COUNTRY

Writing in 1972, Eric Wolf and Edward Hansen defined the difference between Indians and whites in spatial terms. Indian communities in Latin America are "so many little cultural islands, each a stronghold of a traditional way of life . . . striving to keep outside interference at bay," while "creole" communities consisted of individuals who were "oriented toward the outside" (72–74). Although progressive in intent, their words echo stigmas long attached to Indians, and to the places where they live. At about the same time that Wolf and Hansen's book was published, Ecuadorian high school students were reading the following passage in the textbooks provided to them by their government:

> those primitives who . . . came to live within the confines of the Spanish cities . . . evolved quickly. But those who remained in the countryside . . . stagnated; and it is there, bound to the earth, that they vegetate still. (Cevallos García 1974:118, cited in Stutzman 1981:62).

One might argue that such images belong to the past. Blatant racism of the sort found in Cevallos García's text has disappeared from children's schoolbooks; in academic circles, Wolf's notion of the "closed corporate community" has largely fallen out of academic favor.[1] Postmodern geographers emphasize hybridity and border-crossings, and find territorial boundaries increasingly irrelevant.[2] But according to political scientists Sarah Radcliffe and Sallie Westwood, authors of a recent study on place, identity, and politics in Latin America, "racialized imaginative geographies" continue to circulate widely. Whether among academics or illiterates, policy makers or ordinary citizens, the working classes or the "largely 'white' elites," the link between region and race remains firmly embedded in Latin American thinking.

In the Andes, they found, rural life is uniformly "pictured in a 'commonsense' way as backwards, uneducated and poor"—and as Indian. When Radcliffe and Westwood interviewed residents of Ecuador's Cotopaxi Province,[3] they were careful to identify respondents as residents of either urban or rural areas, and by race as "white," "mestizo/cholo," "indigenous," or "non-attributable." These distinctions proved immaterial: everyone told them that whites lived in cities, Indians in the country. Comparing their results with similar studies elsewhere, the authors concluded that throughout the Andes, "'race' is regionalized, and regions racialized" (1996: 109–12).[4]

Within this "imaginative geography," the Indianness of rural places keeps them backward, isolated—and dangerous for whites. Echoing the kinds of North American anxieties crystallized in the movie *Deliverance,* Andean urbanites express fear of unknown rural areas, where they expect to be met with an uncomprehending hostility that can easily turn violent. When I first began traveling out to Quichua-speaking communities in rural Cotopaxi and Tungurahua provinces, Ecuadorians from the cities were appalled. They filled my ears with horror stories about the dangers of walking alone in such places, and recounted bloody histories of tax collectors stoned to death, visitors killed, trucks overturned and their drivers robbed and beaten. The Indians hate strangers, city dwellers warned me, especially whites. If they feel like it, they'll kill you just for walking into the countryside, just for straying beyond the town square. Your body will never be found, and no one will ever admit to having seen you. A taxi driver from Latacunga, taking me up to Zumbagua with some trepidation, explained that whites like himself fear Indian revenge. When robbing or raping an Indian, he said, it was important to know where they were from, and to avoid that area afterward. "They know how to take care of themselves," he said, gesturing toward his own throat as though with a knife.

His casual mention of white predation against Indians explains something of the far more profound fear with which Indians regard whites—and their insistent desire that outsiders should stay away from indigenous territories. In Indian communities throughout the Andes, tales of white marauders are commonplace; they range from the readily documentable to the completely fantastic. Francisca Jerez of Salasaca found a political charter in tales of white predation. The tight political organization of Salasaca during her childhood, she recalled, had its origins in nightly patrols organized to protect Indian livestock from local whites. Frustrated by the studied indifference of the provincial police force, the previously fractious and divided Salasacas were finally provoked into working together in self-defense against the incessant thievery of their neighbors, who claimed the right to take anything of value—animal or human, animate or inanimate—from the Indians. Whites acted in the secure knowledge that the courts and police of the province would never recognize Indian protests against a white man, no matter how egregious the offense.

These fears are embodied in the ñakaq: pishtaco stories often begin with the dangerous moment when a stranger appears on Indian land. From this perspective, it is the white stranger, not the Indian, who suddenly reveals an incomprehensible propensity for violence.

The Stranger

An old man from the countryside around Ayacucho, Peru, on his way back from milking his cow, met up with a pishtaco. The pishtaco, who looked and spoke like a foreigner, inquired about the local schoolteacher, wanting to know when he might arrive home, and what days he worked. "*¡Que susto, pues, mamay! ¿Cómo, pues, habré contestado?*" [Well, what a fright! How could I ever have answered him?] recalled the old man in 1987. "I didn't say anything. I just answered him in Quechua" (Vergara Figueroa and Ferrúa Carrasco 1989:130). When the stranger wanted to pay him for his trouble, the old man emphatically refused the money; finally, the stranger thanked him and left.

The old Indian explained his terror to the interviewers by pointing out the man's foreignness, his big overcoat that undoubtedly concealed knives and guns, his long hair, and his enormous boots. He recognized this gringo immediately as the pishtaco who had recently killed a young pregnant woman and a deaf-mute, removing their body fat and sending it back to his own country. Similarly, a younger woman from the same region, interviewed a few days later, remembered recognizing a stranger seen from a distance: "He was certainly a pishtaco: he had a knife, his face was bearded, foreign, with a wool cap, he was huge and he made me afraid" (131).

One knows a pishtaco, then, because he is a stranger and he makes one afraid. Most scholars writing about the ñakaq have associated this strangeness with racial whiteness. "In the vast majority of the tales" told in Ancash, Peru, wrote anthropologist Anthony Oliver-Smith in 1969, "the *pishtaco* is a white or mestizo male" (363). In 1991, researcher Carmen Salazar-Soler quoted a miner from Huancavelica: "'*El Pishtaku es alto no más, es gringo no más ojos azules*'" [The Pishtaco is tall, a gringo, blue eyes—that's just how he is] (14).

But other writers note that pishtacos are not always white. Bolivian scholar Alison Spedding, for example, tells of a *gordo*—a fat man—from the Yungas region, who fell asleep while traveling to La Paz atop a truck loaded with passengers and produce. Next to him was an old man, who got off the truck while the gordo slept. Days later, as the fat melted from his body, leaving the previously healthy gordo weak and dying, he realized that his unknown companion—although of the same ethnic group as himself—had been a *kharisiri* (the Aymara term for a pishtaco) [n.d.*a*:1–2].[5]

These chilling tales of the unknown stranger who kills by stealing fat prompt one to ask what nightmarish experiences could give rise to such macabre inventions. To many observers, the answer is obvious: the creation of the pishtaco is a response to the horrific treatment that Indians have received from whites since the Conquest. Anthony Oliver-Smith spent the summer of 1966 in Ancash collecting stories about the pishtaco. The "nocturnal murderer of Indians" was described to him as "a white or mestizo male"; these tales, he said, had been "nourished" by "the most important social relationship of the Andes—the dominant mestizo and the mistreated Indian." He saw the Ancash myth of the pishtaco as instrumental, not merely reflective: this "institution of fear" maintained the social distance between Indians and whites, and united the Indian community in the face of the "mestizo threat" (1969: 363–64).

In recent years, Peruvian intellectuals such as Juan Ansión and Eudosio Sifuentes have found in pishtaco stories a key for understanding the violent events of their nation's history. This grotesque foreigner, with his close ties to politicians and the military, strikes them as an apt personification of the violent and unequal relations between Peru and the United States, and between the rural highlands and the nation's capital. (*"Dicen que el presidente, ese Alan, los manda,"* the old man said about ñakaqs.)[6] Some U.S. scholars, such as anthropologist Nancy Scheper-Hughes, also see the pishtaco in this light. Scheper-Hughes cites the Andes as one among many places—Brazil, Ireland, South Africa—where one hears stories of foreigners who murder and mutilate. To her, this is a transparently global phenomenon triggered by global inequalities (1996, 2000).

But not everyone who works in the Andes would agree. Peter Gose writes that pishtaco stories express a deep-rooted fascination with blood sacrifice, a theme that permeates myth and ritual in the southern Andes. "The ñakaq," he asserts, is not "a representation of the evils of capitalism" but rather an "amoral" expression of the fascination that powerless people feel when contemplating the ability of superordinate beings—whether gods or local white men—to devour the weak. Far from offering an "economic analysis" or an "ideology of political resistance" to exploitation, he asserts, Indians actually use the story of the ñakaq to "articulate an erotico-religious desire" for their own destruction (1994a:309). The ñakaq, then, is an emblem of Thanatos.

His words suggest that we are looking at something deeply entrenched in the primary psychic processes—something not to be explained by culture or political history. But if human fears and desires are in one sense universal, they are also shaped by our experiences. Even the writings of Sigmund Freud can be read both for insights into human psychology and as a historical record of the emotional lives of the Victorian bourgeoisie. Daniel Boyarin reads *The Interpretation of Dreams* as historiography (1997:34); Terry Castle does the same with Freud's famous essay, "The Uncanny."[7] This essay, written in 1919, explores the universal human fascination with death; but it also offers us a delicately rendered portrait of a psychosocial terrain peculiar to the writer and his contemporaries. The centerpiece of the essay is a masterful interpretation of a popular German ghost story, E. T. A. Hoffman's *Sandman*. In his reading of small details about the imaginary killer's appearance and the scene of the crime, Freud draws us a map of German bourgeois fears and hatreds, and especially of the alienating terrain of the patriarchal family, with its distant and threatening father.

The Freudian unconscious, says Lévi-Strauss, is empty of content: it simply imposes order upon "inarticulated elements which originate elsewhere—impulses, emotions, representations, and memories" (1963:326). In the Andes, one source of these troubling representations and memories is race. Following Freud, we can see in the elusive but recurrent whiteness of the ñakaq evidence of something deeply disturbing—so much so that even while the tale exposes certain fears, it tries to shield others from view. In Hoffman's monster, Freud found a palimpsest of anxieties and animosities: beneath the frightening figure the author dares to describe is the barely discernible outline of another, still more nightmarish character, too terrible to bring fully to light. In the shape of the pishtaco, too, one can discern unmentionable truths about the Andean geography of race, half-hidden beneath an already disturbing social terrain.

Freud begins his essay with a common observation: the peculiar sense of dread aroused by figures like the pishtaco—the feeling called in German *unheimlich,* and in English "uncanny"—arises when one confronts something unfamiliar.

The German word unheimlich is obviously the opposite of heimlich, heimisch, meaning "familiar," "native," "belonging to the
home," and we are tempted to conclude that what is "uncanny"
is frightening precisely because it is not known and familiar
(1963:21)

Thus the pishtaco, an unknown white man, represents what is alien to
Indians. When such a figure appears in an unexpected or incongruous
context—deep within an indigenous community, for example, where
outsiders are rarely seen—the uncanny effect is greatly increased. The
ñakaq's strangeness is the more striking against the heimlich backdrop
of one's native ground.

One of my most unsettling discoveries when I first went to the
northern Andes in 1982 was that I terrified small children. In the
Ecuadorian province of Tungurahua, I visited the Quichua-speaking
comuna of Salasaca. As I walked down footpaths lined with agave
plants, little figures occasionally appeared running happily down the
path ahead of their mothers, or else dawdling contentedly behind. Suddenly looking up and seeing my strange form, they ran in terror to
bury their faces in their mothers' skirts. It was no mere shyness that
overtook them; their bodies became rigid with shock and fear, and
many were too frightened even to cry out. More often than not, their
mothers would gather them up and run away too, leaving me, mortified, in full possession of the right-of-way.

I attributed the children's terror to repugnance at my weird appearance—my excessive height and my glasses, jeans, and hiking boots. I
looked ugly to them, I thought, almost monstrous. My thoughts echoed those of German art historian Fritz Kramer on African perceptions
of Europeans (1993:ix). Arguing against those who saw African sculp-
tures of white men as political statements, Kramer insisted that the exaggeration and unexpected juxtapositions found in this art contained
no message beyond the utter inability of African artists to read the
white stranger's body. Bereft of any social context within which to
interpret the eyeglasses, hats, or facial expressions that they render in
weirdly exaggerated form, these artists distorted what they saw not
from any conscious motive, but simply because what is utterly unfamiliar cannot be imitated. If the artist "isolates the hidden and ordinary
and raises it to the point at which it is identified as monstrous" it is
because he perceives Europeans with an "uncomprehending eye."

For Kramer, monstrosity is the result of incomprehension. Kramer,
then, is thinking along the same lines as Freud's predecessor, the Ger-

man aesthetician Jentsch, who explained the uncanny as the product of "a lack of orientation in an unknown environment" (Freud 1963:21).[8]

Andean ethnohistorian Nathan Wachtel, writing about the kharisiri, seems to follow Jentsch and Kramer's line of reasoning as well. When a spate of kharisiri accusations swept the Bolivian Chipaya, Wachtel found them to be evidence of a tragic disorientation, brought on by a social environment changing beyond recognition. Returning to a community in which he had long ago done research, he listened in horror as an indigenous acquaintance and erstwhile employee poured out a tale of being hounded by kharisiri accusations until he feared for his life. His terrors were not unfounded: another local man, "a full-fledged member of the indigenous community," had been burned to death in 1983 in the nearby town of Orinoca as a suspected kharisiri. These indigenous men had brought down the wrath of their neighbors by seeming to be too much immersed in the world of whites. Elsewhere in the Andes, too, pishtaco accusations are directed "*al extranjero o al autóctono que lo corteja demasiado*" [at the stranger, or at the native who courts him too assiduously] (Rivière 1991:25). Wachtel, doubting his own safety as well as that of his friend, concluded sadly that these wild suspicions and their violent aftermath signaled the end of Chipaya culture as he had known it. The entire phenomenon was "certainly a symptom of a profound crisis: the intrusion of modernity into the heart of Andean communities threatens the very roots of their identities" (1994:xx).

Wachtel's thesis, however, like my own initial assumption, does not withstand scrutiny. The notion that the presence of whites—or of Indians who want to be white—is a disorienting novelty in the rural Andes flies in the face of historical reality. American anthropologist Andrew Orta writes that kharisiri accusations among the Bolivian Aymara are neither novel nor uncommon (1997). In Peru, as well, compilations of Andean folklore from earlier in the century include many tales of Indian pishtacos.[9] More broadly, Orta underscores the oddly ahistorical approach that Wachtel, generally a meticulous scholar, brings to the question of the pishtaco. Indigenous Andean culture today, Orta writes, does not retain some "original boundedness" only recently violated by a newly intrusive modernity. Rather, the Aymara have long been engaged in a "struggle to form coherent local orders" out of a social geography completely permeated by outside forces: the cash economy, the modern nation-state, the Catholic Church. Indeed, Wachtel's own insightful research has documented precisely this engagement between Andean and world history.

The pishtaco, then, has placed analysts on either side of an interpretive schism. For Orta and Gose, he is an intimate and familiar aspect of life in Indian communities; to most other scholars, including Wachtel, he is a figure of horrific otherness.[10] One must ask whether these two interpretations are as incompatible as they seem—and here Freud's analysis of the uncanny offers a first clue.

Freud found that the opposition between "unheimlich" and "heimlich" is not so clear as it at first appears. The "shades of meaning" of the word heimlich reveal it to be "a word the meaning of which develops towards an ambivalence, until it finally coincides with its opposite, unheimlich." He offers an example quoted in Grimm's German dictionary—one that could equally well apply to the dread felt by people in the Andes. "'At times I feel like a man who walks in the night and believes in ghosts; every corner is *heimlich* and full of terrors'" (quoted in Freud 1963 : 30).

The pishtaco, too, reveals a curious convergence of the familiar and the unknown. In the opening stories above, the old man immediately recognized a foreigner looking for the schoolteacher as the evil being who had recently killed two people in his neighborhood; the young woman recognized a stranger seen from a distance as a pishtaco. Employing the perfect tautology of myth, both speakers knew the pishtaco precisely because they had never seen him before. Upon recognizing him, they became afraid—and it was by their fear that they recognized him. Freud, struck by similar circularities, concluded that uncanniness is exactly so: an experience of the strange that is strangely familiar. And in this convergence, he immediately recognized the return of the repressed.

Far from being unknown, the dreadful figure that haunts us is something once known, but now deliberately hidden—*estranged*—from conscious awareness. This "secret nature of the uncanny," says Freud, explains

> why the usage of speech has extended *das Heimliche* into its opposite *das Unheimliche;* for this uncanny is in reality nothing new or foreign, but something familiar and old—established in the mind that has been estranged only by the process of repression. (47)

To Wachtel, the kharisiri represents a foreign world inimical to Indian society; to Orta, because he is not always foreign, he must be neither an enemy nor a stranger. Neither author considers the possibility that Freud suggests: that the pishtaco is not so much strange as estranged—a part of one's social universe, but terrifyingly alien nevertheless. For all their differences, Wachtel and Orta ultimately share a frame of reference in which culture is unitary: Indians and whites either inhabit separate spheres, or there is no boundary between them at all. They thus fail to come to terms with a social world so deeply divided that its members can frighten one another by their strangeness, yet so inexorably unified that they know one another intimately. A model that could interpret this dialectic between horror and familiarity would have to encompass not merely cultural difference, but also the vicious epistemology of race, which makes neighbors appear as monsters to one another. Only with such an understanding can we begin to place the social geography of the Andes within the larger topography of the American continent.

Though the pishtaco's peculiar traits have some cultural specificity, he is strikingly similar to racial bogeys elsewhere in the Americas. "As a child I did not know any white people," recalls African-American writer bell hooks: "They were strangers, rarely seen in our neighborhoods." Movement from one place to another was highly charged with racial meanings. In the town center, whiteness appears natural, and blackness out of place. The "all-black spaces on the edges of town" were different. They were "a location where black folks associated whiteness with the terrible, the terrifying, the terrorizing. White people were regarded as terrorists, especially those who dared to enter that segregated space of blackness" (hooks 1997:170). In the black child's imagination, the estranged geography of racial segregation took human form as a white intruder, striding through the only part of town where she felt at home.

The Indian children who ran from me in Salasaca, I soon realized, did not actually find in me an unreadable strangeness. My sudden appearance was both frightening and familiar: just as I found it impossible to see their ragged clothing and big black eyes except through the lens of advertisements from charitable relief organizations, they too looked at me with knowing eyes. References to encounters with violent and malicious whites abound in all the genres of oral culture with which they were familiar—jokes, riddles, songs, ghost stories, and historical tales—allowing even a child to recognize my arrival as just one more skirmish in a long-standing, ongoing conflict.

Wachtel and Orta misrecognize Aymara responses to "the terrible, the terrifying, the terrorizing" intrusion of whiteness. Wachtel envisions a war of annihilation between autochthonous natives and invading Europeans; Orta only "messy entangled spaces" within which notions of assimilation and resistance are meaningless (1997:4). The pishtaco, however, is operating on a different kind of terrain. Multiple entanglements do indeed bind Indian and white inextricably together in the Andes, as Orta contends; but racial antagonism continues to erect boundaries between the two. The political geography of race creates separations that are both unreal and fiercely defended.

Orta rejects the language of "insulation/rupture" as inappropriate to the Andes (1997:4), but in my experience indigenous communities have an overwhelmingly strong sense of their territory as intact and closed to outsiders. "It's funny, just standing here talking to you like this," one man commented lazily to me in Zumbagua. "In the old days, a stranger like you, we would never have spoken to you. We would have just killed you and dumped your body into the arroyo, and then when your friends came looking for you, we wouldn't say anything." He looked over at me to see if he had succeeded in making me nervous and then laughed. "In the old days. We were afraid then; but not anymore." But in fact, I had had stones thrown at me in Zumbagua, and curses hurled at me in more places than I could remember. I know anthropologists who have been thrown out of the communities where they hoped to work, or threatened with violence by the husbands and fathers of women they wished to interview.

After establishing myself as a *comadre* of the Chaluisas, I, too, was protected by the community against hostile outsiders. When I was attacked by armed white strangers while within the boundaries of Zumbagua, local people went after the malefactors with the intention of killing them. "If only we had caught them, we would have done what they did to that taxi-driver who robbed someone from Casa Quemada," said my old friend and comadre Heloisa, a gleam in her eye that I had not seen there before. "We would have tied them up, doused them with gasoline, and set fire to them."

Economic and political events in recent years have both strengthened and weakened these impulses toward violent closure. In *Painting Tourists,* Aaron Bielenberg's recent documentary film about the growing local industry of making folk paintings in the Zumbagua region, a young man from the neighboring community of Quilotoa poses beside the spectacular volcanic crater lake of the same name.[11] "We welcome the foreigners," he says insistently. "They will be treated well here. It's not like the old days. No one will beg for money, no one will throw rocks. We want them to come, to enjoy our beautiful land and our native customs. They should come from everywhere" (Bielenberg 1998). At the same time, however, there is a growing number of political incidents in which indigenous communities—including this one—seal off their boundaries in direct challenges to the nation of Ecuador, explicitly embracing the very notion of ethnicity as a territorial absolute that Orta claims is untenable.

As I returned to Ecuador throughout the 1990s, I sometimes found the highways into indigenous areas blocked by homemade check-points. In the rugged areas surrounding Zumbagua, boulders of enormous size are rolled onto the highways during national strikes in which indigenous organizations participate, and every vehicle is scrutinized before it is allowed to pass. The Panamerican Highway itself was blocked in 1992 by the tiny indigenous community of Salasaca, which straddles the highway between the major city of Ambato and the resort town of Baños. Women and children sat atop barricades and successfully faced down tanks sent by the military.

Rudi Colloredo-Mansfeld has documented recent incidents of vigilante justice in northern Ecuador strikingly similar to those that upset Wachtel. He makes a direct connection between such self-policing within communities and the erection of checkpoints at the their edges. He sees both as evidence of a hardening resolve to wrest self-determination—and territorial autonomy—from a nation-state that serves only white interests. According to Colloredo-Mansfeld, these grassroots movements are occurring largely in defiance of the national indigenous leadership, which has embraced a liberal "multicultural" vision rather than one of racial autarky. In 1998, a small Quichua community outside Riobamba gained national attention when it insisted upon judging and punishing two accused thieves without outside interference from the Ecuadorian police or judiciary.[12] In keeping with Colloredo-Mansfeld's analysis, this act of judicial resistance also involved the assertion of physical boundaries: all roads into the community were blocked with boulders and burning tires. Indian political demands have always included the cry for land; this urgent desire is inspired not only by the need for farmland, but by the tactical necessity for defensible space. As we shall see in chapter 4, the long history of sexual violence against Indians gives another, deeply felt dimension to the right to land, linking the defense of territory to the ability to protect one's own body from forcible violation.

If both Indians and whites share the "racialized geographies" described by Radcliffe and Westwood, they do so not as passive inheritors of an outmoded way of thought, but because of an urgent need to defend the physical and ideological spaces they inhabit. In the racialized vision held by Andean whites, the Indian is a disloyal "enemy within" the nation-state. Norman Whitten has documented expressions of this idea in Ecuadorian political rhetoric, following its permutations through successive presidencies. He captured an especially telling incident in 1972, when then-president Rodríguez Lara—a landowner from the Zumbagua region—responded to a question about the loss of indigenous land rights with the words, "There is no more Indian problem. We all become white when we accept the goals of national culture."[13] Within a nation governed by an ideology of unrelenting assimilationism, Whitten notes, black and Indian residents are not only "ethnically tagged as nonnational," but also as "nonnational*ist*" (Whitten 1981:14). To speak of someone as Indian is specifically to define that person as incapable of membership in the body politic, and hence to exclude him or her from participation in it—thus freeing the state to act solely in defense of white interests.

Indians, in turn, tell one another stories in which white men who enter Indian land, even if apparently friendly, are lethally dangerous—as are those Indians who serve white masters. Within the racialist ideologies embraced by whites and Indians alike, there is nothing especially surprising about the notion that the ñakaq is a racial alien and an enemy. But the dream of a new racial segregation is as chimerical as the apparent strangeness of the pishtaco. What ultimately renders the ñakaq uncanny is the lurking suspicion that the knife-wielding killer might not, in fact, be a stranger at all.

In his analysis of "The Sandman," Freud argues that by making this lethal and mysterious figure a stranger, E. F. A. Hoffman allows his audience to avoid a deeper and more frightening truth. In fact, says Freud, the killer is someone intimately known to his victim, Nathanael: he is none other than Nathanael's own father. The terrifying sense of being stalked originates in the suppressed fears and hatreds that a youth feels for his parent. Unable to admit these feelings, the youth insists that his stalker is unknown to him. The figure's true uncanniness lies not in its lethal intentions but in its unnerving refusal to stay fixed in the shape of a stranger; instead, his face, his voice, even the objects that he holds in his hands hint at a resemblance that cannot be admitted into conscious awareness. Freud quotes a famous phrase of Schelling, who says of the uncanny that it is "something which ought to have been concealed but which has nevertheless come to light" (quoted in Freud 1963:47).

The pishtaco belies a similar instability: conceived as a picture of the racial enemy, his image constantly threatens to resolve itself into something more intimate. In the Andes as elsewhere, a sense of uncanniness originates in the creeping realization, unavoidable yet impossible to acknowledge, that the murderer is not really a stranger at all. In this case, it is not the ideology of the German patriarchal family that is threatened, but a pan-American set of beliefs about race. Neither white people nor white forms of social interaction are really foreign to any part of the Andes, however remote; but for Indians, overt acknowledgment of this fact would dismantle the desperately necessary fiction of territorial autonomy. In a social world that seems hostile and threatening, the willed imposition of a racial geography creates a defensible space.

Wachtel is not wrong to look for military metaphors to understand the kharisiri. Like low-intensity warfare, racial conflict drags on in the Andes, flaring up in incidents small and large. But no one can really claim that the struggle between whites and Indians is between alien invaders and an autonomous nation. More apt is the metaphor of civil war, in which neighbors—even brothers—periodically turn against each other in an enmity born of old and bitter memories. Indians and whites in the Andes confront each other not as autochthon and alien, but with the lethal familiarity of estranged kin.

The pishtaco is often pictured as an enemy. He has been seen in the guise of every political foe Andean rural people have faced over the centuries, from the foreign priests of the colonial period, to nineteenth-century hacendados who engaged peasant communities in bitter land disputes, to the Peruvian militias sent to rout out Senderistas in the 1980s. But the very wealth of uniforms that the ñakaq has at his disposal reveals the depth of Indian familiarity with this particular enemy.

Retelling the story of the pishtaco alerts listeners to the fact that enemies still walk the land, but his ubiquitous presence is also an implicit admission of past defeats—and existing dependencies. Behind the myth of the pishtaco as political enemy is the reality of economic interdependency. Political exigencies impel rural people to create a map of walls and boundaries, but economic needs and desires lift every barricade. The pishtaco himself sometimes engages in commercial transactions with his victims, stealing their money even as he takes their lives. And if rural people fear the pishtaco, there are other white strangers whose arrival they eagerly await: the *negociantes* [traders] who seek out remote rural communities in search of agricultural products to buy, and Indians to sell to. These vendors, and the wholesalers and truck drivers who come with them, often seem just as white, alien, or scary as any pishtaco—but it is their absence, rather than their presence, that is most feared.

Familiar Figures
Tales of the pishtaco describe an encounter between two solitary figures in an empty landscape, but most interactions between rural people and white outsiders occur in a crowd. The tempo of rural life is one of quiet isolation among kin, interrupted by sudden but predictable im-

mersions into lively sociability with strangers at the fair. The markets create a constant pulse of people, drawing farmers to the urban centers and sending traders of all sorts out to the peripheries to sell and to buy. Rural fairs in adjacent parishes rotate throughout the week, while larger provincial towns hold them every day. The vendors move from one market to another; some women travel the seven days in an endless circuit.

In poor rural areas like Zumbagua, the market is evanescent. The Zumbagua *fería* comes into being each Saturday morning only to vanish completely before the following day. In places such as these, vendors weekly construct the entire marketplace and then dismantle it again, taking it away with them on the trucks and buses that brought them there, and that will carry them to the next town. Each woman marks her territory in the predawn hours, carving out the market bit by bit from the amorphous space of the plaza. As the square fills up with buyers, it is the stable figures of the market women amid their makeshift stalls that anchor the shifting crowd, providing both destinations and reference points within the constantly moving mass.

In his 1989 travel book, British writer Henry Shukman describes a visit to a southern Peruvian market so small that he witnessed its entire making and unmaking. Traveling with ten market women from the town of Taraco, he was dismayed when they arrived at their destination to find "not the least sign of anyone else nearby." "Had the market been cancelled today?" he wondered, only to realize that his companions had brought it with them.

> The women clambered out and I helped them with their sacks. Immediately they began spreading out sheets and blankets on the ground. . . . Then from the silent huts . . . from all around, it seemed, black figures started appearing. . . . So it continued, more and more Quechuas arriving, until the whole space in front of the church was filled. (1989:139)

Returning to the market after a short hike, he is disconcerted again: "By now it was already tailing off . . . The Chola women were tying up their sacks and folding away their blankets. I was back in Taraco by noon" (141).

This market takes place on Quechua territory, yet it is a white space. Once it exists, local residents find themselves treated as aliens and racial inferiors when they enter its temporary boundaries. To Shukman, the contrast between Indians and cholas was striking. The Quechua-speaking customers

squatted down in front of the Cholas, on the far side of the
sheets . . . took their bundles from their backs and opened them
up. They would put three or four cupped handfuls of grain or
beans out on the Cholas' sheets; who, sitting upright, surrounded by their bags, would throw over two oranges, or some
dried pimentos, or some sweets, whatever the Quechua wanted.
Sometimes the Quechua would say something quietly before she
picked up her goods. The Chola, perhaps having retained an orange in her hand, would shake her head and click her tongue.
The Quechua would put out half a handful more of grain; and the
extra orange would be dropped in front of her. (1989:139–40)

Shukman saw a marked imbalance in power between buyer and seller:
"It was, as ever, the Chola's market. They sat unmoved among their
produce, merely waiting" (140). The farm women, in contrast, struck
him as nervous and unassured, moving from vendor to vendor and
never speaking above a whisper.

The much larger Zumbagua market in central Ecuador boasts a far
more heterogeneous group of sellers, and more sophisticated buyers as
well. But here too, race estranges Indian customers from the outsiders
who have come to sell to them. When I studied the market in the
1980s, I found that local people were more intimidated by some vendors than others. The vendors of dry goods, for example, were

middle aged women whose businesses are fairly prosperous and
require substantial initial investment. They are imposing and self-
important people, quick to anger and to verbal abuse. "Indians"
approach them timidly and are frequently rebuffed. The goods
for sale here—rice, cooking oil, sardines—are associated in the
minds of indigenous buyers with the ethnic whiteness and superior class status of the seller (Weismantel 1988:74–75).

People who sell in these markets are assumed to come from the city to
the country, and so carry with them an aura of whiteness—even if the
"city" in question is only the nearest small town, or another rural area.
Their presence brings with it a promise and a threat, offering the allure
of all that is cosmopolitan, luxurious, and modern—and making rural
folk, with their empty pockets, dirty clothes, and poor Spanish, feel
inadequate and vulnerable. Temporary though it may be, the weekly
market creates a hole in the middle of Indian territory from which
non-Indian eyes look out and see their racial inferiors. For local people,
the secure feeling of being at home is rendered suddenly insubstantial—and the image of life in the white towns yet more seductive.

This uneasy mix of anxiety and desire has a mirror image in the city, where produce markets open up a space in the middle of urban life that is appealingly rustic and agricultural, but also dirty and dangerous. Its unruly appearance and organic nature offers an obvious contrast— even a welcome relief—from the concrete and steel grid that otherwise composes the cityscapes of Lima, La Paz, and Quito. But by the same token, the people and products of the market seem out of step with modern city life, an anachronism that is inevitably interpreted in racial terms. The same buyers and sellers who look frighteningly white to their Indian customers appear to city-dwellers as "dirty Indians." Here, too, they are intruders and racial aliens who do not belong within the domain of all that is modern, civilized—and white.

INDIANS IN THE CITY

In the summer of 1997, the journal *Abya Yala News* put the provocative title "Indian City" on its cover. Many metropolitan South Americans find the contemporary and historical truths behind these words to be anathema. Andean notions about urban life owe much to Europe, where, in Raymond Williams's words, "On the city has gathered the idea of an achieved centre: of learning, communications, light," whereas the country appears "as a place of backwardness, ignorance, limitation" (1973:1). Despite a heritage that includes pre-Columbian as well as Western forms of urbanity, the residents of the Andes have come to associate not only cities but civility itself with Europe. The tropical landscapes and indigenous populations of the Andes that lie outside the bounds of urban life are perceived as actively inimical to it. The "achieved centre" protects the whiteness of its residents; they, in turn, must defend their cities against the surrounding countryside and its nonwhite inhabitants.

But Indians have always been part of urban life;[14] recently, they have made their presence felt in unaccustomed ways. Well-to-do residents of La Paz bemoan a city "taken over" by market women. White Limeños lament the enormous *pueblos jóvenes* [young towns] that have sprung up on its outskirts, populated by immigrants from the highlands who have invigorated and Andeanized a city smug about its cultural and spatial distance from the impoverished highlands. And in Quito, a series of enormous, well-organized marches since 1990 have brought thousands of self-proclaimed "Indians" from the rural peripheries into the center of urban power. Each capital is being remade into a visibly Indian city. To whites, the cities themselves seem disturbingly in motion, roiling the racial geography on which ordered life depends.

Peruvian intellectual Mario Vargas Llosa pictures the city of Lima as slowly being strangled by Indian immigrants from the highlands. He writes of a "gigantic belt of poverty and misery" wrapped around the capital, squeezing the "old [white] part of Lima more and more tightly" (Vargas Llosa 1993b:513, cited in Ellis 1998). This imagery remaps the presence of the nonwhite in Peru: traditionally described as an inert "Indian stain" [*la mancha india*] stretching across the highlands far from the nation's capital, it is suddenly on the move, an active threat advancing upon the metropolis.

The upheaval in Limeño society caused by the arrival of hundreds of thousands of political refugees from the highlands during the 1980s seems unprecedented, but one might equally well argue that it is only the acceleration of a well-developed trend. In 1950, José María Arguedas included "the provincial person who migrates to the capital" as a "recent" addition to the cast of characters in Peru's "big towns." The incursion of immigrants into Lima "began quietly," he writes, but "when the highways were built it took the form of a headlong invasion" (1985:xiv). Other writers place the turning point elsewhere, in 1872 for example, when the city removed its colonial walls (Cornejo 1997). Raymond Williams finds each generation of English writers from the seventeenth to the twentieth centuries mourning the "recent" contamination of rural life by big-city mores. In the Andes, exclamations over "recent" rural incursions into civilized society can likewise be traced from the present back to the very founding of Spanish cities on sites already home to Indian populations (1993:3 and passim).

The produce market has long been perceived as a site where the city's racial defenses are especially vulnerable to attack.[15] American anthropologist Linda Seligmann, author of a pair of penetrating articles about market women, describes the Cuzco market approvingly as "the crucial intersection between rural and urban sociospatial environments" (1989:695). Civic leaders have been less enthused: in the first half of the century they condemned the same market as a locale subversive of urban culture (de la Cadena 1996:121). And if the markets constitute a threat to civil order, so too do the women who work there. Market vending is a venerable occupation in the Andes, yet vendors, like prewar European Jews, carry the stigma of racial outsiders despite their centuries-long presence on the urban landscape.[16]

The dictates of racial geography estrange the chola from the city, making market women into strangers even in the towns and cities where they work and live. But there is another side to the image of the chola—and of urban life as well. The city is the bastion not only of whiteness, but of modernity; indeed, the two concepts are inseparable.

Modernity, however, is a demanding space within which to dwell; the discontent that it so notoriously produces gives rise to a concomitant fascination with a past that seems forever lost. The city, writes Raymond Williams, is regarded as "a place of noise, worldliness and ambition," while "On the country has gathered the idea of a natural way of life: of peace, innocence, and simple virtue" (1973:3). A longing for these virtues drives the tourist industry, giving rise to rosy images of traditionally dressed women selling flowers and fruit. The same desires complicate the ideology of race, so that even the dirtiness attributed to Indians can be romantically viewed as a closeness to the earth (Orlove 1998). The fundamental geography that places the nonwhite outside of modernity, however, stays the same.

Like the Indian, then, the chola is idealized as well as denigrated; the disequilibrium caused by this contradiction animates an image that is otherwise static. For if the pishtaco is a character in a narrative—masculine, active, instrumental—the chola seems rather to be sitting for her portrait: she is feminine, passive, even monumental. But when artists and writers try to compose a lovely representation of the chola, they are inevitably troubled by conflicting perceptions of their chosen subject matter: she appears to them as both a racial outsider and as the cherished emblem of regional or national culture. This uncertainty expresses itself spatially in the simultaneous desire to bring the chola close and to push her away, lest she contaminate the urban center and its inhabitants.

Argentinian novelist Julio Cortázar, writing about photographs of women vendors in Peru, fills his essay with metaphors of distance (Offerhaus and Cortázar 1984). These black-and-white photographs, shot from the window of a train traveling across the altiplano, push their subjects away from the viewer, both physically and emotionally. The women look away from the camera, either unaware of it or trying to evade its gaze; they are strangers to the photographer, and they remain so. In his essay, Cortázar places himself still further away: he is looking at these pictures, he tells us, in his Paris apartment on a snowy evening, listening to the music of Stan Getz. Like de Certeau in *The Writing of History*,[17] Cortázar interprets this distance between a writer and his subjects as both racial and temporal. "I am her future," he writes of a sleeping infant cradled in its mother's arms, depicted in one image, "as she is my past." To Cortázar, the difference between a wealthy white man and a poor brown female is great enough to overturn the more obvious temporal relationship between himself and the child—namely, that an infant embodies a future the middle-aged man will never see.

Cortázar uses a handful of photographs of women he has never met to outline a synthetic vision of world history. While this history is brought into focus by his words, the women and children who provide the occasion for his meditations recede from sight. They are no longer actual people, but mythic figures. What Cortázar does with these pictures of market women—and he represents a long-standing modern tendency—exemplifies the process of myth-making as defined by Roland Barthes in his essay "Myth Today" (1973).

We can assume, as Barthes does in his analysis of the photograph of a black man in a French uniform, that the pictures in Cortázar's possession would have quite specific and variable meanings for someone who knew the vendors by name. Each of these women's lives has, in Barthes's words, "a fullness, a richness, a history . . . a geography, a morality" that is known to themselves and to those around them. In order for Cortázar to make their images into representations of abstract notions (of "poverty," of "Latin America," of people trapped in "the past"), he must empty them of these meanings, thus converting the signs of ordinary speech into signifiers—forms—of myth. "[A]s the form of myth," Barthes writes, the image "hardly retains anything" of the "long story" that once made it unique: it must "leave its contingency behind; it empties itself, it becomes impoverished, history evaporates, only the letter remains" (115). Once all of its original "richness" has been put "at a distance," Barthes explains, "its newly acquired penury calls for a signification to fill it" (118). Emptied of its own history, the image of the market woman is "at one's disposal": it becomes the myth-maker's "accomplice," ready to serve Cortázar's thought.

Mythic images of market women invoke a place and time outside of normal existence, or at least beyond the viewer's immediate experience. This aura of unreality makes the pictures reassuring: one need not confront the difficult realities of individual lives because Cortázar has written the narrative for us, telling us what these women "mean" and obviating the necessity to know their names. He invites us to share his own, securely privileged position in looking at them. But while Cortázar's anodyne account of women vendors is successful to a certain extent, other narratives, other histories, other meanings lurk beneath the surface, making the myth not only unreal but uncanny.

Dirty Indians

Shukman describes a nighttime visit to the Bolivian capital of La Paz:

> The streets are full of lights and confusing surges of people. Everywhere there are women sitting on the pavement selling things, each one with her kerosene lamp. . . . I turn down one narrow

street made even narrower by stalls which leave room for only a rivulet of bodies between them. . . . Behind the wide counters stand Chola women, only their shoulders and heads visible over the produce spread before them. (Shukman 1989: 111)

Every Andean town and city that he visits is filled with women selling things. Upon entering the Bolivian mining town of Oruro, he remembers, the apparent tranquility is broken when

suddenly you see a vendor standing at the side of the road, and another, and now there are side streets running off the road and at every corner a boy or a young woman with a tray of cigarettes and sweets. The intermittent houses congeal. Market stalls spring up along the street and thicken as you near the centre until all the streets are lined with stall after stall and behind every stall sits a Chola woman. The city is given up to marketing. (63)

These scenes are permeated with a sense of unease. The ubiquity of the street seller renders Andean cities "confusing" and unpredictable: importuning strangers appear "suddenly," market stalls "spring up" unexpectedly, lining the narrow streets and surrounding the passerby in a claustrophobic embrace. Having "given itself up" to marketing, the city seems to have lost its familiar angular form and been rendered unpleasantly liquid: side streets "run off," bodies form a "rivulet," the houses "congeal," and the stalls "thicken" until one reaches a city core that consists of nothing but cholas.

This market is not a fixed locale, but an active verb: not markets but *marketing* is everywhere in La Paz. In this, Shukman captures a reality of the markets: their existence depends less on permanent buildings than on incessant economic activity that claims and defines the urban spaces it occupies. The physical form of most marketplaces—sprawling vernacular architectures squeezed into the already-existing structures of the city—is assembled piecemeal by the women who sell there each day or each week. Outdoor markets and street fairs are composed of nothing more than the stalls occupied by more successful women, the cloths spread out on the ground by those with fewer resources, and the crowds that both these attract. When a fortunate group of vendors wins government recognition, the spatial patterns already in place are mimicked by municipal builders, who erect the large roofed shed that houses an officially sanctioned produce market.

But Shukman's queasy vision of market vending as an uncontrollable force overrunning Andean cities is motivated by more than the sprawling growth of marketing activities; something about the markets, and the women who work there, taps into a complex of hidden anxieties. One source of these fears is sex—the topic of chapter 2—and another is race.

Market women buy from farmers to sell to city women, or take factory-made items into the countryside to sell to rural people. In the Andes, this movement between city and country is inevitably translated into racial terms: the women who sell these goods are cholas. In the city of Cuzco, once the capital of the Inca empire and today surrounded by indigenous communities, the markets where rural products are sold have an undeniably Indian air. Residents of this city readily collapse "chola" market women and rural "indios" into an undifferentiated group of nonwhites. In the exchanges of insults that Linda Seligmann recorded in the Cuzco markets in the 1980s, well-to-do customers repeatedly called the market women "dirty Indians."

Edmundo Morales, author of a wonderful (and extravagantly illustrated) book about that most traditional of Andean foods, the *cuy* or guinea pig, found that few educated residents of the Andes shared his enthusiasm for eating in the open-air stalls around the markets, where roast cuy is a specialty. "In Ecuador, Bolivia, and Peru, the class conscious urban mestizos and whites try their best not to come in direct contact with the rustic, simple and illiterate country people," he writes (1995:41–42). Many bourgeoisie avoid the markets, sending their house servants to do business there; the well-to-do only occasionally venture into the markets to make their own purchases. These rare forays are in search of amusement more than bargains: these shoppers approach the markets as though playing tourists in their own hometowns.

Stephen's attention was riveted by one scene in the Riobamba market, where a wealthy woman with an aggressively neo-1960s look—bleached blonde hair, leopard-patterned tights, and cat's-eye sunglasses—was shopping for a dinner party. She had brought her servant with her to do the actual purchasing, giving rise to a complex buying process that involved repeated consultations between the shopper, her list, and her maid, and between the maid, the vendor, and the *cargador* (porter) hired to carry the purchases back to the car. Such scenes are increasingly rare; when the lady of the house does her own shopping, she is likely to prefer the stale but sanitized products of the *supermercado* to the fresh goods obtainable in the public plaza. Large U.S.-style supermarkets have invaded upscale neighborhoods throughout Latin America, providing spacious air-conditioned premises within which the well-to-do shopper need not come in contact with the urban poor.[18]

The desire to flee the plaza for safer havens is not just a matter of prejudice: the markets can indeed be dirty, unpleasant, and even dangerous. María Cristina Cárdenas, a professor of literature from the University of Cuenca, greeted my proposal to give a public lecture about *la chola andina* with enthusiasm, and made many insightful comments about the meaning of the *chola* for Cuencanos. But later, over tea in her stylish Art Deco apartment, she made a humorous "confession": she herself abhorred the markets. "Those women terrify me," she told me facetiously in her charming, high-pitched voice. "I have gone for years without a piece of fresh fruit in the house for fear of having to approach one of them." I had no idea whether she was telling the truth; all I could see was that she was poking gentle fun at my gringa enthusiasm for working-class Latin America. An American friend of Dr. Cárdenas later interpreted this comment to me as an oblique reference to her frustration at no longer feeling safe in public places. In recent years, as Cuenca's crime rate has risen, the professor has too often been subjected to verbal harassment, pickpocketing, and petty crime in the streets and plazas where she once moved freely. Like many residents of Andean cities, she resents her increasing confinement within the relative safety of her apartment.

Despite this reality, the city in which this professor lives is closely identified with the image of the markets and their denizens; indeed, much of Cuenca's success in luring tourists depends upon the glowing images it presents of "La Chola Cuencana." This "Chola"—a totally modern fabrication built upon Spanish colonial foundations—was not originally intended for tourists, but as an expression of regional pride on the part of the city's elite, as were other cholas throughout the Andes. At about the same time that Cuzco poets began to write about the cholas of highland Peru, Ecuadorian poet Ricardo Darquea Granda began to pen verses about La Chola Cuencana—and continued to do so for many years afterward (Lloret Bastidas 1982: 271–77). The politics of the two were very different: Cuzco's fascination with the chola is inextricable from the leftist political movement associated with José Carlos Mariátegui, whereas Darquea's chola comes directly from the conservative nineteenth-century Indianist traditions Mariátegui despised. In both cities, however, writing about cholas served one common goal: the creation of an evocative symbol to represent a regional identity. The cholas of Cuenca and Cuzco were deployed by regional elites, against the central governments of Peru and Ecuador, who created or appropriated symbols of national culture as part of their bid to direct wealth and power toward the national capital, and away from its provincial rivals.

Whether intended for internal or external, national or local consumption, the symbolic transformation of the markets from urban

blights to picturesque civic attractions requires the creation of a reassuring psychological distance between the viewer and the women on
display. This movement can be temporal or spatial, or it can simply be
a matter of making real women into figures of myth and fantasy; however it is accomplished, the geography of race both mandates and fa-
cilitates the operation.

The Picture Postcard

On a postcard sold in the Municipal Airport of Cuenca in 1998, a pair
of barefoot women in full, brightly colored *pollera* skirts are shown sitting on the ground. One faces the camera while the other shows her
back, revealing two thin braids tied together at the ends, making a
black V across the bright oblong of her sweater. Their hands weave hats
from fine straw. These hats are famous: misnamed "Panamas" in English (in Spanish they are *sombreros de paja toquilla,* after the straw used
in their manufacture), they once supported a flourishing export trade
that provided stylish summer headgear for men throughout Europe and
the Americas.

In the postcard, finished hats are everywhere: piled up beside their
makers, and perched on the women's heads, where they confer a stately,
masculine air that contrasts with the profusion of petticoats below. The
setting is at once rural and commercial, apparently an outdoor marketplace in some tranquil countryside; but the postcard is sold as a representation of Cuenca, Ecuador's third-largest city and the major metropolis of the nation's southern highlands.

The caption on the back of the card says simply, "*Las típicas cholas Cuencanas,*" obligingly translated into English immediately below:
"Typical cholas of Cuenca." The women's delicate feet, manicured
hands, and soft, rounded arms belie any thought that they "typically"
weave hats and haul them barefoot to market, but the problem is less
one of false advertising than of mistranslation. "Típica" does not imply
the ordinary so much as the exemplary: rather than "typical" cholas,
these women embody the "type" of the chola, who in turn "typifies"
the city of Cuenca. It does not matter that these particular women do
not ordinarily weave hats, sit on the ground, or sell *artesanías* in the
market; in donning brightly colored skirts, figured shawls, twin braids,
and white hats they assume a role that represents the essence of traditional Cuenca.

Primed by these images, tourists eagerly seek out Cuenca's markets—as they do open-air markets throughout the Andes or, for that
matter, across the globe. Shukman notwithstanding, most travelers
adore the incongruities of the urban market, where the people and

products of the countryside take up a temporary but exuberant residence at the heart of town. Throughout the older and working-class quarters of Andean cities, open-air markets spill out from their designated squares into surrounding streets, burying the sharp contours of the city grid beneath the colors, smells, sights, and sounds of the surrounding agricultural areas: piles of red peppers and green cabbages, the braying and clucking of animals, even the metallic smell of fresh blood and the shiny skins of dead fish.

For visitors from Europe, Canada, and the United States, this lively display is a delight. The dissonance between the homogenized prettiness of the postcard chola and the far more heterogeneous experience of the market itself does not trouble them. Strangers in a strange land, they happily consume the most contradictory images of the Andes; indeed, these very incongruities can be taken as signs of a tropical laissez-faire that contrasts pleasantly with the more rigid northern societies they have temporarily left behind.

The legions of middle-class entrepreneurs employed in the tourist industry are far more cognizant of the ironies inherent in their work. "La cholita" of the marketplace with her baskets of fruits and flowers, one of the most venerable characters of Andean folklore, has also become one of the most marketable. As tourism expands in otherwise contracting economies, such antiquated images become the only attractions capable of luring enough scarce foreign currency to shore up the faltering prosperity of the middle class. The tourist industry thus offers a Faustian bargain to its members, who hope that by selling romantic images of underdevelopment they can make it vanish.

Cuenca wants tourists, and it believes that cholas will bring them. Approaching the city by car, drivers are greeted by billboards in the form of an enormous smiling Chola Cuencana; the walls of every hotel, travel agency, and craft shop are adorned with poster-sized versions of scenes like the one on the "Las típicas cholas Cuencanas" postcard. But the city is less sanguine about actual markets. Contradictory impulses push and pull at the Andean cityscape: urban development plans "cleanse" city centers of dirty and unruly popular phenomena such as street vending (Jones and Varley 1989), even as the foreign appetite for exotica and antiquities brings fragmented memories of long-gone cholas into upscale commercial locales. In some Andean cities, the waitresses in hotel dining rooms wear bright polyester costumes that mimic those once worn by market women. In Cuenca, silver filigree earrings, embroidered blouses, woolen shawls, and pollera skirts lie on the shelves of expensive boutiques like flotsam washed up after a shipwreck, stained and tarnished by the dirt and sweat of the women who once wore them. The imagined chola who presides over these locales is an antique: she lives in the distant past, except as a memory.

In Cuenca, rumors of the chola's demise are at least somewhat premature. While the traditional garb of the chola is no longer de rigeur for working-class women, I found it impossible to go anywhere in the city in 1997 without seeing women in tall straw hats and brilliantly colored skirts. They stride through the crowded streets and marketplaces, and can be glimpsed riding in the back seats of passing taxis, perusing the shelves of the shiny new supermarkets, or waiting in line cheek-by-jowl with the tourists at the money exchange (cf. Miles 1994). My last hour in Cuenca after a visit in December 1997 was spent in the airport restaurant, where middle-aged women dressed in elaborate chola finery waited expectantly for their Americanized daughters and sons, flying in from New York or Miami to visit home.

Middle-class Cuencanos and foreign tourists alike find the presence of these old-fashioned figures in such settings incongruous, even laughable. In the minds of those who wish them to be merely folkloric, "cholas" should be neither modern nor mobile. For tourists, to travel to a distant land and see an exotic figure is rewarding; to find the same person at the airport imperils the very rationale for travel. Educated people in the Andes, too, enjoy the image of the chola as rustic and antique far more than that of a chola wielding a credit card. The middle and upper classes, whether foreign or Andean, strive to contain the chola within a genre that Renato Rosaldo calls "imperialist nostalgia," in which white colonial societies of the recent past are imagined as "decorous and orderly," in implicit contrast to the conflict and chaos of our own times. These historical fantasies, he writes, invite the audience to enjoy "the elegance of manners [that once governed] relations of dominance and subordination between the races" (1988:68).

Myth today, says Roland Barthes, exists in the service of the bourgeoisie: it naturalizes their distinctive point of view. In actuality, cholas have often been associated with working-class political militancy, as in the cook's strike in La Paz in 1935, when the municipal building "was filled with cooks and cholas" (Gill 1994:32) fighting for their right to bring produce onto the city's buses. But the chola of myth, such as Darquea's Chola Cuencana, is a figure emptied of any personal or political history. This chola has been exoticized in an attempt to produce "a pure object, a spectacle . . . [who] no longer threatens the security of the home" (Barthes 1973:152). Contemplating such an image,

all that is left for one to do is to enjoy this beautiful object without wondering where it comes from. Or even better: it can only come from eternity: since the beginning of time, it has been made for bourgeois man . . . for the tourist (151).

These mythic cholas have their roots in the eighteenth and nineteenth centuries, when painted and written images of cholas, Indians, and blacks expressed similar fantasies of a world in which the lower classes—and races—keep to their places. But the romantic image of the chola has also been used to radically different political ends. The *indígenista* and *neo-indígenista* movements that swept Latin America from the 1920s to the 1960s created their own cholas, not in order to escape from the political conundrums of modernity, but as a radical intervention that might resolve them. One artist, Cuzco photographer Martín Chambi, told a reporter in 1936 that he made his pictures of nonwhite Latin Americans to overturn the prevalent beliefs that "Indians have no culture, that they are uncivilized, that they are intellectually and artistically inferior when compared to whites and Europeans." [19]

Chicheras and Chicherías

In 1927, Chambi took a picture showing four women seated at a wooden table, variously titled *Las señoritas en la chichería* (The young ladies in the chicha shop) or *Damas Arequipeñas en chichería* (Ladies from Arequipa in the chicha shop). [20] Both captions express the incongruity of the scene: the ladies are fashionably and expensively dressed, while the setting, a chichería, is a drinking establishment for the working class. At the time this picture was taken, chicherías ringed the market squares. These businesses were operated by women brewers (*chicheras*), who made the thick Andean corn beer known in Spanish as *chicha*. (Today, chicherías can still be found in some parts of the Andes, but similarly small and grubby establishments selling cane alcohol [*trago*] have, for the most part, replaced them.) [21]

Chicherías are humble places, sometimes a permanent building with a courtyard, but often just a tiny windowless room equipped with the bare minimum of furniture. In place of a sign, the chichera hangs a small flag outside the door, indicating a freshly brewed batch of chicha ready for drinking. The ease with which this strip of cloth can be removed allows the occasional brewer to convert her living room temporarily into a bar, and then to turn away new customers when the chicha is gone. The simplicity of the icon also says something about the patrons of such establishments, who in their heyday earlier in the century would almost certainly have been illiterate.

The well-dressed young women in Chambi's photograph bear little resemblance to the manual laborers one might expect to find in such a place; yet there they sit, their manicured hands grasping the enormous thick glasses in which chicha is customarily served. The girls' bobbed haircuts bring a dash of flapper fashion to the mud-walled room, but their feet are placed awkwardly, as though they were worried about dirtying their white stockings or their elegant shoes. Nonetheless, they mime a festive attitude: two of them hold up their glasses in a toast, while the third—her mouth clamped tight as though she might otherwise burst out laughing—proffers a tin of sardines to the viewer.[22] The objects around them only heighten the sense of awkwardness: a ceramic jug and a chicken seem perfectly at home on the dirt floor, but the women's silk hats, which they have placed beside them, perch incongruously on the adobe bench.

In this photograph, as elsewhere, Chambi displays an acute class and cultural sensibility. Before coming to Cuzco, he had worked for the fashionable photographer Max Vargas in Arequipa, where he made studio photographs of the city's middle- and upper-class families (these young ladies were, perhaps, acquaintances from those years who had come to visit him in his new home).[23] In Cuzco, he continued to work as a studio photographer, recording the young bourgeoises of the city in their accustomed poses: grouped together holding their tennis rackets, garbed in elaborate gilded costumes for Carnaval, or wearing imported finery to a social dance. He took other kinds of photographs as well. His postcards, an important part of his business, helped establish the canon of touristic images of the Andes—the Incaic ruins, the brooding mountains, the lonely Indian playing a flute. Many other photographs were made without commercial intent; he himself believed that his most important legacy would be the photographic record he left of Cuzco's architectural heritage (Ranney 1993:11). But the photographs that most compel our interest today are the thousands of portraits he made of ordinary Cuzqueños. Together with his society photographs, these constitute a comprehensive photographic history of Cuzco society between 1920 and 1950.

Chambi's work invites comparison to two better-known, slightly older European contemporaries, Eugène Atget and August Sander, both of whom left distinctive photographic portraits of the cities in which they lived—Atget of Paris, and Sander of Weimar Germany. Like them, Chambi captured the life of the city by photographing people from all walks of life. His oeuvre includes not only the wealthiest and poorest members of Cuzco society, but everyone in between, like the *Schoolboys playing cards on the outskirts of Cuzco* (1928), or the uniformed policeman holding a young street urchin by the ear (*Policia de Cusco*, 1924).

In Chambi's portraits, the things that surround a person—the details of their clothing or the object held in the hand; the design of a piece of furniture or the treatment of a floor or a wall—evoke a way of life in all its cultural and historical specificity. The clothing depicted in *Popular Musicians,* photographed in 1934, for example, express the subjects' unmet aspirations and incomplete assimilation. Three of the men wear identical suits, leather shoes, and ties, while the fourth wears only sandals, a ragged sweater, and an ill-fitting pair of pants with holes in the knees. Even the men in suits cannot disguise their membership in the "popular" rather than the educated classes: their clothes are well-worn, and the man on the far left has unbuttoned his jacket to reveal an Indian *chumbi* (woven sash), not a leather belt, holding up his trousers.

These photographs heighten the viewer's awareness of the appurtenances of class and race that demarcated Cuzco society in the first half of the century; the eye, thus educated to perceive congruences between costume and setting, is doubly confounded to find them so mismatched in *Señoritas in the chichería.* We might be tempted to dismiss this photograph as merely playful: a sly sense of humor shows itself in much of Chambi's work, and frequently finds expression through unexpected incongruities and double entendres, as in the 1932 photograph of *La Torera* (a dashing young matador who is actually a woman), or the 1933 portrait *Brothers* (three of whom are dressed identically as peasants while the fourth wears the cowl and rosary of a monk).

But while it is not without humor, *Las señoritas in the chichería* records not a silly prank but rather an aspect of a political movement of which Chambi himself was a part. In the Peruvian highlands of the 1920s, when a party of *damas* from Arequipa elected to visit a Cuzco chichería, they were engaged in more than a bold escapade outside of their usual class milieu. In saluting Chambi's camera with a glass of chicha, these young women announced their allegiance to the *indígenista* movement sweeping the Andes, and their willingness to imbibe the true spirit of Cuzco—a spirit that, according to the precepts of the movement, could only be found among the working-class and nonwhite residents of the city.

When *indígenismo,* one of the most important intellectual movements of modern Latin America, was in its heyday, Cuzco was one of its most active nuclei. Groups of artists and intellectuals gathered for fervent discussions in which the affirmation of autochthonous culture, the defense of the Indian against injustice, and the glorification of the pre-Columbian past all found eager audiences. As in Mexico, it seemed possible at that moment to envision a new society based upon a fusion of socialist internationalism and regional culture. José Carlos Mariátegui's famous *Siete ensayos de interpretación de la realidad peruana* (Seven essays on Peruvian reality), published in 1928, provided the charter for these ideas; in Cuzco, writer José Uriel Garcia carried Mariátegui's banner. Martín Chambi, although barely educated—and, unlike the other indígenistas, born an Indian—was an intimate of the circles in which these ideas were discussed. One participant later recalled Chambi's studio as "an authentic 'Bohemian Embassy'" where writers, painters, newspapermen, and musicians regularly met (López Mondéjar 1993 : 22).

Chicha was an important symbol for Andean indígenismo, not least because its rich history offered meanings that could finesse the movement's internal fissures. Native to the Andes, this corn-based beverage had nationalist and anti-imperialist appeal; as a beverage of sacred importance to the Incas, who had used it in religious and political rituals, it was one of the few direct links between the present and the pre-Columbian past; as the drink of the working man, it was a natural emblem of class solidarity. Perhaps most importantly, the social and ceremonial significance that chicha still held in Indian communities enabled it to stand for a putative indigenous communism, the existence of which would be a touchstone of leftist political belief throughout much of the century.

If chicha was significant, the chichería, too, was vitally important to indígenista and especially neo-indígenista thinking. An outpost of rural and Indian culture in the city, the chichería was a place where residents of the urban Andes—and by extension, the modern nation-state they represented—could seek spiritual and cultural replenishment. Mariátegui's close associate Uriel referred to the chicherías evocatively as "the caves of the nation."[24] Along with chicha and the chichería came the symbolism of the chichera herself. When he visited Cuzco, Mexican indígenista Moises Sáenz was moved to call the Andean chola "the literal symbol of nationalism."[25] Even more so than in the vendors of fresh produce, the butchers and fishmongers, or the women who sell cooked food, indigenísmo found in the chichera the new ideal of the chola.[26] If the chichería was the birthplace of the nation, the chichera was its mother.

Mariátegui decried the nineteenth-century literary tradition he called "Indianist," in which the motif of the Indian—and the chola— was exploited as a nostalgic idealization of Peru's colonial past (Kristal 1987 : 4). The new indígenismo that he championed would recuperate these images in the service of a truly democratic vision for the nation. At century's end, however, the history of the chola does not reveal such a clear progression; rather, a plethora of different cholas compete in the

contemporary Andean imagination. Her image is employed just as frequently in the service of colonialist nostalgia as it was one hundred
years ago; and so, too, are variations on the neo-indígenista appropriation of the chola as a symbol of the nation.

In going to the taverns and drinking chicha, the educated young
women whom Martín Chambi knew declared their willingness to consider themselves symbolic daughters of the chichera, embracing a notion of national kinship that could cross racial and class boundaries. The
indigenist and socialist movements that inspired them have today fallen
out of favor, but the chola retains her power as a populist symbol. In
Bolivia, nascent political parties, ambiguous in their ideologies but eager to play upon nationalist and socialist traditions in their bids to represent "the ordinary Bolivian," have made much of the imagery of
chicha. Their posters depict smiling cholas and enormous *puños* (the
vessels in which chicha was traditionally brewed); they hold their rallies
in chicherías, and hire young women dressed as "cholitas" to appear at
every political event (Albro 2000).

The pervasiveness of the chola as a cliché of Andean identity is en-
sured by governments committed to the relentless promulgation of
national and regional loyalties. In Bolivia, *La Chaskañawi,* Carlos Medinaceli's 1947 novel about an ill-starred romance between a university
student and a chola, has been required reading for many years in the
public high schools.[27] In Ecuador, the state-sponsored presses of
Cuenca's "Casa de Cultura" published Darquea's many poems on the
subject as late as 1970, long after Cuenca's younger poets had abandoned his florid style for the rigors of modernism (Lloret Bastidas 1982:
277). Indeed, his anachronistic style creates a perfect vehicle for a sentimental and nostalgic image of traditional Cuenca.

In 1997 a lonely expatriate burst out in a long, enthusiastic e-mail
on an Ecuadorian listserv, expressing his wonderment at entering a
park in the United States and hearing the familiar strains of "La Chola
Cuencana." "Come to New Jersey!" he exhorted his fellow exiles,
"Here you will really feel at home." This may seem the ultimate in
postmodern geography, but such displacements are integral to the
operation of the myth. Walking through the park, this exiled South
American can see the youths playing volleyball and the food vendors
cooking traditional delicacies. But he cannot locate the source of the
song, or even be sure exactly what he hears. It comes to him "*de repente,
remotamente . . . los compases de una vieja melodia nuestra . . . chola cuencana?*" [now and again, remotely . . . the verses of an old melody of
ours . . . the "Chola Cuencana"?].[28]

For Andean romantics of earlier decades, too, distance was part of the chola's charm. The most conservative visions, such as Darquea's, situate her in her own mythic sphere, far away from the white spectator. In contrast, the radical young "Damas Arequipeñas" were eager to leave the white world and enter that of the chichería, where they drank in the smoky atmosphere and imbibed the thick corn beer. In recording their venture, however, Chambi depicts it as falling far short of a total immersion in working-class life. The tentative and partial nature of the damas' engagement with the scene becomes obvious if we compare them to another woman with a glass of chicha in her hand, the *Mestiza de Cusco con vaso de chicha* (1931).

The "mestiza de Cusco" is a massive woman in an enormous pollera, who faces the camera calmly, a large tumbler of chicha balanced easily within her broad fingers. She is seated outdoors, perhaps in the courtyard of the chichería, or on the street outside its doorway. Unlike the first photograph, which emphasizes the incongruities between clothing and setting, Chambi's camera here seeks out a series of resonances among the surfaces of the body and the place. The heavy fabric of the woman's pollera skirt is as densely textured as the weathered adobe walls behind her back; the curling strands of wool escaping from the rough cloth are echoed by the straw scattered over the cobblestones beneath her feet. Whether she is the chichera herself, or only a patron, Chambi represents this woman as an integral part of the scene.

Not only the surfaces but the shapes and gestures of the women's bodies in the two photos create different relationships to the setting. The body in the pollera is at rest; gravity pulls it down unresisting into the place where she sits. The folds of the skirt flow uninterruptedly over her legs and down to the ground. The señoritas' clothing, in contrast, prevents them from being at ease, despite their attempted jocularity. Their bodies are held erect, the limbs arranged to resist contact with the surfaces around them; the girl who holds open the tin can uses only the tips of her fingers. Their clothing dictates the terms of their relationship to the world around them, as English critic John Berger observed about bourgeois clothing in the photographs of August Sander. The tailored suit, Berger says, is a costume "made for the gestures of talking and calculating abstractly" (1980:38). In Chambi's photograph, too, the women's clothing allows them to speak "abstractly" of their enthusiasm for the chichería, but not to be at home there.

The ladies from Arequipa are tourists in the chichería, searching for a momentary experience of cultural authenticity that they might take back—in the form of a memory or perhaps a photograph—to the white neighborhoods in which they live. In the indígenista vision, the chicherías, like the markets, are cut off racially and temporally from the rest of the city. They remain isolated enclaves of Indianness encircled by an urban space that remains correspondingly white. Their status as mythic locales also estranges them from the city around them: they are dark "caves" into the pre-Columbian past, within which the white cosmopolitan can seek a fleeting respite from an oppressive present. Supplanted by this insidious racial geography, the leftist desire to create a modernity that was both Indian and white failed to take root.

In Cuenca today the image of the chola serves starkly conservative visions of Andean history, which look not to an imperfectly imagined multiracial future but backward to the more rigid social hierarchies of the past. Within these imagined geographies, the spatial and temporal distinctions between cholas and whites are clearly demarcated. While foreigners and expatriates are happy to associate market women with Cuenca, a city they locate far away in the retrogressive world of highland South America, the wealthy Cuencanos known locally as *los nobles* prefer to displace them into the countryside. When I gave a public lecture at the University of Cuenca, a small group of the city's elite attended, dressed in imported French fashion but very much there to represent traditional Cuenca. Afterward, they stood up to deliver a series of short impromptu speeches about the nature of the Chola Cuencana (some of which made the younger generation of Cuenca scholars who shared the platform with me wince in dismay). The audience of assembled students, many of them daughters or granddaughters of women who had worn the pollera, listened silently.

Dr. Antonio Lloret Bastidas, the city's historian—the most elderly and most distinguished of the four—spoke first. He thanked me graciously for my talk, but begged to correct a few errors, among them the notion that the Chola Cuencana was actually from Cuenca. Every woman wearing a pollera on the city streets was a country woman, he insisted, briefly come to town to sell some farm produce or to make a few purchases. It was clear that for him, her rural origins were crucial to the chola's folkloric charm—and, ironically, to her ability to represent the city. The pollera-clad woman selling the fruits of her own land refreshes the soul of a place that might otherwise be without one. At the turn of the century and for a few decades afterward, Cuenca's export economy expanded, buoyed by an international demand for "Panama" hats. The city's elites were justly proud to inhabit a truly modern city, home to beautiful new buildings that could rival those of Europe or the United States; at the same time, they also celebrated the existence of a rich and highly visible local culture. To Lloret, this dual identity had its own geography, in which the fashionable districts in the heart of town were home to a sophisticated metropolitan life, while the rural hinterlands were the strongholds of Cuenca's own regional traditions. The Cholas Cuencanas moved back and forth between the two, adorning and enriching the modern city with the fruits of the countryside: not only agricultural products, but their own rustic femininity as well.[29]

The two women who accompanied him, despite being of his generation, begged to differ with this masculine point of view. Many servant girls and market women, they reminded him, had lived in the city all their lives without ever dreaming of wearing anything but a chola's hat and pollera skirts. The fourth member of their party, a middle-aged man, attempted to broker the dispute between his elderly relations by suggesting that although some cholas may have taken up residence in the city as adults, all had been born and raised in the country. The women immediately pooh-poohed this idea as well, reminiscing with great pleasure about named houses in the center of town, inhabited by the wealthy cholas of a generation ago. These "matriarchies" of mothers, sisters, and daughters had been renowned for their high-heeled shoes, ikat-dyed shawls, and silver filigree earrings—and for their commercial acumen as well.

When I spoke to the market women themselves, they too contradicted Lloret's interpretation. Inside the Mercado 10 de Agosto, a municipal market in the center of town, every woman immediately and emphatically identified herself and her coworkers to me as Cuencanas: "We are from here, from the city, of course"; "I am a Cuencana, as you see me"; "*Aquí nació la Chola Cuencana*" (It is here that the Chola Cuencana was born). Most had inherited their professions, and sometimes even their stalls, from mothers, aunts, or grandmothers who were likewise born in the city. Rosa Loja, for example, who sells garlic, shallots, and rocoto peppers, has been a market vendor for forty-four years. Her mother was a *frutera,* a seller of fruit, in the now-defunct Mercado San Francisco.

She and the other *socias* (members) of the 10 de Agosto hold a contempt bordering on loathing for the women who come in from the outlying rural communities to sell. Without a booth or a license, these vendors are unwanted interlopers in the eyes of the Cuenca saleswomen—and this illegitimacy is unquestionably linked to their rural origins. When I took a photograph of one of these itinerant vendors (a woman wearing a strikingly beautiful rural version of the pollera and shawl) the Cuencanas were visibly affronted. In Cuzco, Martín Chambi, himself a migrant from the tiny rural hamlet of Acopía, understood these distinctions well. He identifies the woman wearing the pollera as being "de Cuzco," and, like the market women of Cuzco interviewed by de la Cadena, he eschews the word *chola,* describing his subject as a *mestiza.*

The idea of the chola as being from somewhere else serves needs that are specific to the racial elite. This displacement allows conservative and well-to-do residents of Cuenca to broker a self-identity at once metropolitan (signified by their stylish imported clothes) and local (signaled by their detailed knowledge of traditional chola clothing, which older elite women recited to me with great expertise and enjoyment). In frequent, rueful references to a growing cosmopolitanism on the part of the cholas' daughters, who are joining the diaspora of Cuenca's young to the United States, the city's "nobles" blame the collapse of their own local hegemony on this new working-class transnationalism. In shortcutting the spatial hierarchies between rural and urban, periphery and metropolis, young migrants also abrogated traditional structures of privilege.

If conservative elites decry the disappearance of women in polleras, others of their class are more upset by their persistence. As the image of the living past, the sight of a woman in a Panama hat can serve as a catalyst for disillusionment with the nation. On the Web sites, chat rooms, and listservs that cater to the international diaspora of computer-literate Ecuadorians, nostalgic desires to sing songs about cholas, or to eat traditional market foods such as roasted *cuyes,* occasionally find expression. These are rare interludes, however, among an almost constant flow of critical analyses of the endemic political corruption, economic inefficiencies, and cultural blockages that prevent young professionals from returning home. For the highly educated, whose ambitions for themselves and their nations have been frustrated by the region's seemingly insuperable financial problems, the continual existence of open-air markets, and of women who dress like cholas, can seem like simply two more indicators of a collective inability to progress.

For working-class residents of Cuenca, the chola's traditional clothing likewise elicits bitter meditations on the region's economic woes. "We are forgetting the pollera," said a young woman who wore blue jeans to her job as a hotel maid. "All everyone can think of is buying an airplane ticket to the United States. There is nothing here for us now."[30] Far from representing a backward culture or a stultifying poverty, to their eyes the chola's thick wool skirts, handmade hat, and silver jewelry symbolize a vanished prosperity and self-respect once available to the working classes. A woman selling masks for New Year's Eve, for example, was delighted to be asked about cholas. She evinced a great deal of pleasure in pointing out women dressed in polleras and Panamas, pinpointing specific neighborhoods around the city from which these women came and discussing the many positive associations that such clothing held for working-class Cuencanos. But when I asked her why she did not wear the pollera herself, a deep bitterness emerged. "I can't afford to," she said, and began to deluge me with figures.[31] She knew exactly how much each item in a traditional chola outfit cost, and contrasted these large sums angrily with her own earnings from seasonal items like the masks, or the underwear she sells the rest of the year. Her grandmother had worn the pollera with pride all her life, but she would never be able to do so.

If the professional classes and ordinary Cuencanos are both disillusioned with their city, they differ sharply in their understanding of the problem—and of the effects that their actions have upon it. The deeply held racial prejudices of the professional classes distort political and economic policy in the Andes. Peruvian development theory holds that market vendors and the so-called informal economy within which they operate constitute an impediment to national well-being (Babb 1989: 178–81). The Buechlers remark on the frequent sociological description of market vending as "informal" or even "illegal," when in fact, "in Bolivia, as well as Peru, selling in the market is among the most regulated economic activities" (1996:223). De la Cadena found that rhetorical accusations of price-gouging in early and mid-century Peru led to price controls upon market vendors far more severe than those inflicted upon other sectors of the economy (1996: 128), an observation echoed by Babb (1979:177–81) for the late twentieth century. Babb further comments on the degree to which these controls limit the ability of market women to sustain themselves economically. Thus this segment of the population, perceived as nonwhite and hence as a special threat to the nation, has long suffered disproportionately from state intervention—even while being perceived as dangerously out of control and operating beyond the purview of the state.

This desire to hold market women responsible for the failures of the national economy is exacerbated in periods of economic crisis. Stories about the rising price of the *canasta familiar,* the basic family food budget, are a regular feature of daily newspapers and nightly televised news in Cuenca; although reporters sometimes speak with market women, they are more likely to feature outraged customers making accusations of price gouging. In 1998, newspaper and television interviews regularly featured interviews quoting "ordinary citizens" or "mothers" who blamed market vendors for rising prices.

Customers' long-standing—and sometimes well-founded—suspicion that they are being cheated in the markets makes the vendors useful targets for governments anxious to deflect close examination of their own policies. General Hugo Banzer Suárez, the notorious president of Bolivia, having adopted economic policies that redistributed income upward throughout most of the 1970s, was adept at directing public hostility onto the purveyors of food, playing upon both popular and middle-class fears in speeches characterizing cholas as wealthy exploiters.[32] De la Cadena notes that periods of rapid but unequal economic growth also foster populist resentments against the market women:

> Starting in the 1940s, the economy of the city of Cuzco witnessed unprecedented commercial growth due to its gradual transformation into an international tourist center. . . . [This period] was dominated by official populist rhetoric which was generally phrased as the need to "reduce the cost of living to benefit the less privileged sectors." . . . [Market women] became the prime targets of price control efforts and were constantly accused of "raising the prices of the articles of greatest necessity." (1996:128)

Ironically, these beliefs about the markets and the women who work there are themselves a force preventing development—or at least this is the conclusion reached by the authors of a USAID-sponsored policy study of Ecuador. They were baffled by the state's refusal to provide basic infrastructure and sanitation for the produce and meat markets that feed most of the country's residents. This policy, coupled with uniformly repressive management and legislation, prompted the authors to conclude that so perverse a strategy could only be explained by "a deeply ingrained bias" toward the markets and those who worked there (Tschirley and Riley 1990:193 and passim).

Indeed, in the municipal records kept by the city of Cuzco, the city fathers describe their self-appointed task of controlling market women as more of a moral than a prophylactic obligation. De la Cadena notes some signal examples from the years 1940–60:

> Benedicta Alvarez "who sold chicha at a prohibitive price" was fined because "it was necessary to moralize using sanctions." . . . Similar treatment was meted out to a woman who sold trout, "so that she will learn not to offend the municipal police, the buyers, and the neighborhood." (de la Cadena 1996:128)

Finally, this antipathy to the markets has inspired their actual physical destruction. The Mercado Central in Huaraz, focus of Florence Babb's research between 1977 and 1987, was abruptly demolished by the municipal government without warning, "left," as Babb's goddaughter wrote her in a distraught letter, "as though there had been another earthquake" (1989:ix). This is not a new strategy; in the archives of the Museo Crespo Toral in Cuenca, I found correspondence from 1917 and 1918 that proposed similar solutions to the problems posed by market vendors. The owners of a row of stalls that offered fresh meat and cooked grains for sale had applied to the Consejo Cantonal asking for help in ameliorating the difficulties they faced in keeping their products clean and protected from the elements. The council sent a deputy to investigate their complaints; he reported that conditions were indeed horrific (in keeping with hygienic theories of the time, he especially expressed concern that "miasmas" from a trash-filled aqueduct might be contaminating the meat offered for sale). His recommendation? The vendors must be compelled to abandon these stalls—newly constructed to meet the escalating demands of a prosperous and growing city—and return to the sites they had previous occupied (Museo Crespo Toral 1917–18:307).

In these examples, the estrangement of race amounts to a kind of delusion. Racial anxieties propel a drive to control the markets, rather than to develop them; this move, so antithetical to the economic theories professed by the professional classes, inhibits the growth of a lively sector of the economy, and so hinders the very development they so fervently desire.

Displacements

The symbolism of the chola as icon of hopeless underdevelopment colors Cortázar's experience of looking at pictures of Peru, discussed above. The yawning distance between his comfortable expatriate life and the dusty train tracks where the women sit with their wares occasions in him a sense of ineradicable difference from the poor of Latin America that saps his political will. He sees weakness, shame, sadness, and hunger emanating from the women photographed, whom he describes as "immobilized" by the camera and by the hopelessness of their lives.

Race estranges us from women represented in this way; looking at them enhances our whiteness even as it drains theirs away. Ultimately, the viewer becomes self-estranged as well, feeling like Cortázar that a sense of unreality is seeping into the middle-class room that was comfortable and secure only moments before: the *heimlich* made *unheimlich* by the secret history of race. The photographer, Cortázar believes, has brought these pictures to him already emptied of history, ready to be written about as myths. And yet the more he describes their silence, the more he finds himself the victim of morbid emotions, suggesting a repressed fear that these unknown women may retain the power of speech after all. Vargas Llosa fears that Indians in the city will slowly strangle its white neighborhoods; tourists like Shukman occasionally find themselves fleeing markets that threaten to overwhelm them. How much more frightening when a wealthy and successful man discovers that, after abandoning South America to immerse himself in the utterly European modernity of Paris (complete with snow outside the window and the most cosmopolitan of music on the stereo), a handful of poor women from a continent away still have the power to haunt him? When these women, despite being first "immobilized" by a French-woman's camera, and then subjected to the efforts of a masterful writer intent upon rendering them "weak," "sad," and "ashamed," nonetheless show signs of animation—of a will and a life not accounted for in Cortázar's vision—the effect is not only frightening but uncanny.

The chola as a silent image, viewed from afar, always fading into the past: the estranged quality of this vision is made more obvious if we contrast it to the lively verbal portraits of market women and chicheras provided by an Indian. Gregorio Condori Mamani was a porter in the Cuzco market; his "autobiography," based on interviews, was published in 1977.[33] Like Martín Chambi, Condori Mamani was born in a small village of highland Peru (the former in 1891, the latter in 1908); both men traveled extensively in the highlands before settling in Cuzco later in life.

Unlike the famous photographer, Gregorio remained unskilled, illiterate, and poor; from his vantage point, the women who run chicherías, or who sell cooked food at their stalls in the market, appear as powerful allies in a world made hostile and dangerous by race. In contrast to the anonymous cholas who people the writings of elites, when Condori Mamani reminisces about a woman who helped him many years before, he insists that the listeners recording his story write down her name: "Señora Todalinda Baca. . . . Even now I still remember her name; she was a good person, the owner of a chichería in Pampa del Castillo."[34]

An orphan and a vagabond, Gregorio often found himself penniless and alone in a strange city; in these situations, he invariably looked for a produce market or a chichería. These are the fixed points from which he can orient himself, gaining his bearings in the confusing maze of city life. Freed of the white need to decenter these "Indian" places, Condori Mamani locates them as the city's heart. The chichera and vivandera know everyone, of every race and class; they can find a newcomer a job, a place to live, or a traveling companion, using their many connections to the city and its rural hinterlands to bring strangers together.

At one point, released from prison after serving nine months for the theft of a sheep he did not steal, Condori Mamani finds himself in a strange town:

> I was a stranger there in Urcos, and nobody knew me, so in order to find out if there were any travelers going to Cuzco, I went into a house where there was a little flag displayed, indicating chicha for sale. There I bought five centavos of chicha. It was a lot, two full pitchers. . . . I invited the owner of the chichería to drink one and I drank the other. Since she accepted my invitation, I told her that I was a stranger in town and had just gotten out of jail, and that I wanted to know if there might be people traveling to Cuzco with whom I could cross the Rumiqulqa Pass. (1977:61; 1996:68)

The chichera helps him to find a group of other rural men who likewise need companions in order to brave the bandit-infested mountain passes, and so he makes his way safely home.

In this tale, we glimpse a radically different racial map of the Andes. Here, the chichera is firmly placed in the center of urban life, her tavern a hub where alienation and estrangement give way to security and friendship. Seeing and being seen are important here, but gazes are exchanged, rather than moving unilaterally from white male viewer to nonwhite female object. If the chichera attracts attention, she also looks at, and looks after, the men who seek her out. White men gaze upon the chola and pass judgment on whether her appearance pleases; or like Cortázar, they are moved to meditate upon the emotions the sight arouses within themselves. Condori Mamani seeks out the chicheras not so much to look at them but in hopes of seeing the city through their knowing eyes.

In Martín Chambi's photograph of the "mestiza de Cuzco," too, we are made aware of the woman from the chichería as someone with an active and intelligent gaze of her own. She is seated; her free hand is at her side, fingers together; her mouth is closed; her eyes are half-shut against the bright sunlight. Nevertheless, her body and face engage the viewer. Unlike most people sitting for their photograph in the Andes—including many of Chambi's subjects—her posture is not rigidly formal, nor does her face wear a solemn mien. She looks directly at the photographer, her expression calm but faintly quizzical; her gaze does not project anxiety or modesty about her own appearance, but rather a frank curiosity about the appearance and intent of those who would look at her.

And indeed, Chambi explicitly saw his subjects as witnesses to Andean history. In a sharp reversal of the relationship between silent and speaking subjects in Cortázar's essay, Chambi described his photographs as "graphic testimonies" that had the power to silence him, their maker, since the images were more "eloquent" than his words. His exhibitions, like courtroom trials, were to be a public display of "evidence" that could transform the viewers, in turn, into "impartial and objective witnesses" whose "examination" of the evidence would lead them to discover new ways of thinking about Indians.[35] Cortázar, in contrast, needs the women in Offenhaus's photographs to remain mute, so that he can speak for and about them. He notes the averted eyes, the bowed heads with which the women greet the camera—in fact, it is only in the inadvertently revealed nipple of a sleeping mother that he finds an "eye" staring at him, albeit a "blind" one (Offerhaus and Cortázar 1984:21).

Barthes says that in rendering an actual person into an empty form, myth never completely suppresses its earlier meanings, which continue to serve as

> an instantaneous reserve of history, a tamed richness, which it is possible to call and dismiss in a sort of rapid alternation. . . . It is this constant game of hide-and-seek between the meaning and the form which defines myth. (1973:118)

Cortázar, too, wishes to believe that racial myths can control the histories they have appropriated, "calling and dismissing" them at will. But like Shukman—an avid consumer of every racial myth about cholas, who nonetheless finds their reality deeply disquieting—he finds that "the game of hide-and-seek" is not so easily won.

The disquieting effect of these mythic cholas casts doubt upon another aspect of Barthes's interpretation: his assumption that the operation of myths and dreams is the same. Because it appropriates images from actual experience, thus freeing them from their original moorings to rework them within an entirely new system of signification, myth acts like dreams or neuroses within a Freudian semiology—an analogy also made by Lévi-Strauss (1963; Barthes 1973:119–20). But in Freud's essay on the uncanny, we see dreams and fantasies working *against* the propagandizing function of myth. These disturbing visions attempt to reinstate meanings at the individual level that myth will not allow within the collective unconscious. In the tale of the Sandman, Nathanael witnesses frightening scenes involving his father, but the mythology of German patriarchy tells him that the only emotions he can feel for this man are love, trust, and respect. The disquieting imagery of his dreams unseats the father as a mythic figure of good and allows other meanings, derived from the boy's actual family history, to emerge. The uncanny effect is the product of the fierce force of repression, which prevents these social meanings from free expression. They reveal themselves only in nightmares, as things that are both dead—killed by the myth of father love—and alive—born of the boy's own memories.

Myth, says Barthes, is a cannibal, feeding upon history like a vampire on a half-dead corpse: "One believes that the meaning is going to die, but it is a death with a reprieve; the meaning loses its value, but keeps its life, from which the form of the myth will draw its nourishment" (118). This metaphor is strikingly reminiscent of stories about the uncanny, which revel in the imagery of the undead: the corpse that opens its eyes, the silenced tongue that suddenly begins to speak. The more we strive to repress the other meanings that lurk behind symbols such as the chola, the more they return to haunt us, drained of blood but still trying desperately to tell us something. Like the pishtaco for rural Indians, the chola unsettles whites where they should most feel at home. These figures are put to use in myths about the distance between the races; but secret intimacies gnaw away at the boundaries we have been so careful to erect.

....

CHAPTER 2

City of Women

"But why," asked Dr. Lloret, the historian, "have you insisted upon writing about the cholas of the market? The cholas from the country-side were very innocent and very beautiful in my youth, and the cholas who worked as servants in the great houses of Cuenca were absolutely delectable. But the cholas of the market—these women are *groserías*" (grossness itself). In Cuzco, too, the educated classes call market women "vulgar" and "grotesque"; throughout the 1940s and 1950s, their very presence in the city was written about as a public "scandal" (de la Cadena 1996:131). Unlike the peasant girls who stay in their country homes, or the house servants who submit to their employers' wishes, women who sell in the markets undergo a disturbing transformation in men's eyes.

Following Mary Douglas, we can read a kind of moral hygienics in this response. To the elites, the insalubrious conditions in which market women labor appear as the ostensible signs of a dirtiness—a *grosería*—that originates in the women themselves, whose existence violates "the ideal order of society" (Douglas 1966:3). An unsettled racial identity is one source of the chola's offensiveness: Indians when visible in the city, whites among the Indians, they seem as anomalous as the swarming eels and flying quadrupeds condemned by Leviticus (Douglas 1966:41–57).   45

As Seligmann said of Cuzco's cholas, the "boundaries of this social category are ill-defined in terms of race, class, ethnicity, or geographic locus" (1989:695). But not in terms of sex: the gender of the word *chola* is clear and unambiguous. Yet the "offense against order" (Douglas 1966:2) committed by the women of the plaza—the *placeras*—is as much about sex as about race.

SEXING THE MARKET

The Andean marketplace is sexed female. Men drive the trucks, buses, and taxis that move sellers and products in and out of the market, and they control the wholesale end of the business, where most of the money is made. Yet by far the largest numbers of people who work in the market are vendors, and almost all of these are women. In the 1980s and 1990s, the central markets of the city of Cuenca, as well as in smaller surrounding towns such as Gualaceo and Chordeleg, at least 90 percent of the vendors of fresh and cooked foods were women, while female ownership of the prized interior stalls approached 100 percent. Similar patterns occur throughout the highlands. Bromley found that 85 to 95 percent of the retailers of fresh fruits, vegetables, meat, and fish in the highland Ecuadorian markets in the early 1970s were women (1981). Blumberg and Colyer, too, estimated that 85 percent of the vendors in the Saquisilí main market in the late 1980s were women (1990:255), numbers that I can confirm for all of the major markets of Cotopaxi Province throughout the 1980s and 1990s. In Peru, women constituted 70 percent of all vendors in metropolitan Lima in 1976 (Bunster and Chaney 1985) and 80 percent of all sellers in the Huaraz market in the 1980s (Babb 1989:3). In Bolivia, this occupation has been "almost exclusively" female throughout the latter half of the century (Buechler and Buechler 1996:223).

The sex of the market offends not by blurring categories but by violating them. Like Douglas's "shoes . . . on the dining room table" or her "cooking utensils in the bedroom," women at work in the plaza, despite being such a familiar sight in Andean cities, are still "matter out of place" within white sexual ideologies. "Dirt," says Douglas, "is the by-product of a systematic ordering and classification of matter, in so far as ordering involves rejecting inappropriate elements" (1966:35). The markets, of course, are notoriously dirty—but as Douglas observes about systems of hygiene, the perception of uncleanliness involves symbolic as well as practical judgments. The unwashed children, the little piles of garbage, the muddy walkways, the grimy utensils, the women's dirt-caked hands arouse sensations that both exceed and explain what we see. The dirtiness of the markets—and their excitement—comes partly because they violate a cultural order in which the public sphere is masculine, while feminine realms are enclosed and hidden away from the intrusive eyes of strangers. The market woman is an indecent figure who arouses rumors of sexual anomaly: the sight of her muscular torso, or a glimpse of naked legs under the big skirt, is invested with unsettling meaning. Like race, sex creates a geography of estrangement, the boundaries of which require their own forms of policing, to which the jostling bodies of the produce market offer an immediate challenge. Safety, for women, is always a matter of sex.

The teachers and administrators who welcome foreign exchange students to Andean cities inevitably include lectures on gender etiquette among their orientation materials: women should not dress provocatively, go anywhere with strange men, or be seen out-of-doors unescorted after dark. The young women from Europe or the United States who are the targets of these admonitions are uniformly dismayed to find their lives so much more circumscribed than those of their male fellows. None of the female students, of course, hear anything in these lectures that they haven't heard before—fear and shame curtail women's freedoms everywhere. But as they begin to move about Andean cities, they are often taken aback by the speed with which lessons about sexual protocol are enforced by stray males on the prowl. On foot or in cars, idle men entertain themselves by harassing and teasing lone women who pass by; if no one else is in sight, their behavior can quickly turn menacing. Foreign women carry the stigma of sexual wantonness, and so are especially likely targets; but others are at risk too.

Rudicindo Masaquiza, a folk art dealer from Salasaca, told me years ago about the routine harassment that women from his community endure when riding the crowded buses to Ambato, the nearby provincial capital. Throughout the Andes, travelers who are considered Indians are forced—as blacks once were in this country—to sit in the back of the bus, and, when those seats become filled, to stand in the aisles. The men and women of Salasaca are often obliged to stand, for their dress is as unmistakable as it is beautiful: flat panels of densely felted wool in monochrome black or white, draped with brilliant cochineal-dyed oblongs of magenta or purple.[1] For women, the indignity of being denied a seat carries an added burden, since standing exposes them to the relentless groping that is a favorite pastime of mestizo male riders. Rudi's ex-wife, Francisca Jerez, has a small pickup truck now to carry her to her job as a high school teacher; but she has not forgotten the harassment she endured as a graduate student, riding the bus to the University of Ambato.

As Rudi explained to me, mestizo men often put an especially unpleasant racial twist to this form of harassment. A favorite game is to try and put one's hands inside an Indian woman's clothing, even ripping open her blouse if possible. But those who indulge in this pastime like to tell one another—within the other passengers' hearing—that their intent was not sexual harassment but simple thievery: they were just "finding out if there's any money in there."[2] This intimation that the Indianness of Salasaca women's bodies renders them repugnant to the touch is not especially credible; but it is an effective insult nonetheless. The men who ride these buses—poor country bumpkins in shabby clothes, with accents that betray their Quichua-speaking grandmothers—will be treated like Indians themselves when they arrive in the city. On the way there, they make the most of this fleeting opportunity to humiliate women less white than themselves.

Whatever their race, almost all women are vulnerable to some variation on these embarrassments. City girls may be taught to blame themselves, because "good" women belong in the home; on the street and in the plaza, they feel out of place and ill at ease. They travel across public spaces like moving targets, sometimes hopeful of earning men's admiration, always fearful of attracting their ridicule or abuse. Unlike men, women rarely loiter in public. Like a black man in a white neighborhood, they move quickly, purposefully. I'm only here temporarily, their body language says; I have a gender-appropriate destination.

The incompatibility between femininity and public space is, of course, inflected by race and class. For the most part, working-class women have not been afforded the protection—or suffered the imprisonment—of seclusion within the private domain to the same extent as elite and middle-class women. Ethnicity, too, changes how South Americans think about women's mobility. The contrast between Indian and white attitudes was brought home to me in the Hispanic fishing communities of coastal Ecuador in 1983 and 1984. I was living in Zumbagua then, but I occasionally left the high *páramos* of the Andes to visit archaeologist Tom Aleto and his wife Karen Elwell on the island of Puná. There, I was shocked to discover that women rarely left their homes. Accustomed to the sunburned farmwomen of Zumbagua, who spent most of their waking hours among the sheep and the barleyfields, I could not comprehend the lives of women who used chamber pots inside their canebrake houses rather than risk being seen out-of-doors unaccompanied by a man. (In Zumbagua, women working or walking in public places squat down unashamedly to urinate beside the path, just as the men turn their backs to do the same. It is a surprisingly modest act for those who wear Indian clothing: the women's full skirts cover them from exposure just as the men's long ponchos do.)

Anthropologists, cognizant of these differences, no longer claim universality for the women:men::private:public paradigm; but this does not make it everywhere irrelevant. Among its first proponents were anthropologists studying the gendered social geographies of the Mediterranean, where the long-standing association of women with domesticity continues to be the subject of contestation and reaffirmation.[3] In Latin America, where the dominant cultures are Mediterranean in origin, feminists continue to struggle with this aspect of their heritage, finding it to be a source of both strength and oppression. In her influential essay "Democracy for a Small Two-Gender Planet," Mexican anthropologist Lourdes Arizpe surveys a wide range of politically active women, including "Bolivian peasant[s] . . . Chilean trade unionists, mothers . . . in Argentina . . . and the women leaders of the poor neighborhoods and shanty towns in São Paolo, Lima, and other Latin American cities" (1990:xvi), and finds one underlying commonality: all of these women struggled to gain access to the public life of their societies. Regardless of class, race, or nationality, Arizpe asserts, the opposition between a feminine private domain and the masculine outside world is fundamental to the social geography of the continent.

Arizpe goes on to provide an illuminating analysis of political activism at the end of the century; but the gendered geography from which she begins is not as universal as she claims. Her Latin America does not include the long-established dominance of women vendors in thousands of produce markets across the Andes—as well as in some indigenous regions of Arizpe's own Mexico.[4] That such a large, old, and well-established institution could remain invisible to educated women like Arizpe, allowing her to speak unconditionally of Latin America as a society without public spheres for women, illustrates just how anomalous the market is within dominant sexual geographies.

The Two Plazas

Gender is deeply inscribed in the plan of the Latin city, which exalts the difference between public and private. Traditional homes are often walled, turned inward to protect family life within a generous but totally enclosed space. Public life occurs within a city plan dominated by a central square, typically bearing a name like "Plaza de Armas," "Plaza de la República," or "Plaza de la Independencia." Encircled by the palatial halls of government, this central space bespeaks a Mediterranean legacy stretching back to the city of Athens in the sixth century B.C.E., where the *agora* was celebrated as the heart of the *polis*. The Latin American city plaza recalls the Western classical tradition deliberately and self-consciously, but also idiosyncratically: the Plaza de Armas is distinctively American even in its use of European antecedents.

The evocation of ancient Athens is one layer in a palimpsest of histories, each consolidating an image of gloriously triumphant European masculinity. In addition to local histories, the form of the plaza reinscribes two particular military victories on every Latin city: the originary conquest by Spain, and the later founding of the modern Republics. For Imperial Spain, establishing the central plaza was crucial to the new geography of power, whether they were founding a new city or simply rededicating existing architecture in the service of Europe.[5] In the nineteenth century, the creole founders of the new Andean states did not erase this first conquest, but rather consolidated and further Americanized it. They did so with the help of two newly forged ideological tools: a strengthened and modernized form of patriarchy, and the triumphant consolidation of scientific racism.[6] As a physical representation of these victories by and for European men, the Plaza de Armas defines itself against those it excludes: Indian leaders dethroned and banished to the peripheries of empire, Africans deracinated and forced into slavery, and women of all races disenfranchised and contained within houses and convents.

The central plaza is designed to present a visually overwhelming image of the power of the state, the glory of the wealthy, and the honor of men. It is clean and barren and masculine, an open space surrounded by the closed and forbidding architecture of state power. But the Plaza de Armas is not the only plaza to be found in Andean cities. They also boast another plaza: the messy and feminine space where the produce markets are held. Here, rather than the empty formality of the masculine plaza, every available space is filled with impromptu constructions and crisscrossed with ephemeral passageways. In its haphazard functionality and enforced intimacies, this is a public place that mimics the informal spaces of domestic life. Here, the architecture is decidedly vernacular: small in scale and open-walled, these structures invite the passerby to look, touch, and taste.

In rural towns, these two different plazas occupy the same space: once a week the market takes over the civic plaza, temporarily redefining its purpose. Larger cities try to keep the two spaces separate, designating specific squares, streets, and buildings around the periphery of the city as officially sanctioned markets, and sending the police to cleanse the main plaza of vendors and *ambulantes*. Everywhere, public authorities are perpetually at work to contain the constant, organic growth of the markets within spatial and temporal limits, and so to protect the city's public persona.

Public life derives its masculine air of importance, its celebratory sense of dignified display, from its contrast with the secluded world of the family. Market women play havoc with the gender of the city, breaking down this opposition with activities that undermine the plaza's self-importance, making low comedy of high drama. In this plaza, the atmosphere is redolent with the smells of food and cooking, as well as of the refuse heap and the abattoir. The sight of bloody carcasses and dirty potatoes, the loudspeakers extolling Jesus or toilet paper, the bustle of women cooking dinner, washing dishes, emptying the slop bucket—all of these bring the mundane and even the unmentionable into open view.

The markets are filled with women, and with women's work; at the same time, their aggressive colonization of public space makes them distinctly unfeminine. Entering such a contradictorily gendered space heightens one's awareness of one's own sex; it is a different place for men than for women.

Men in the Market

The market is made up of individual stalls, row upon row piled with fresh food. Whether the display of produce is simple or elaborate, at its center sits the market woman herself, a rounded vertical form rising from flat rectangles piled with goods. Repeated again and again across the open expanse of the plaza, or under the enormous metal roofs of the municipal market building, these female bodies take on an almost architectonic function. Seligmann writes of the vendors in the outdoor markets in Cuzco that

> They occupy crucial space in more ways than one. They spread out their numerous cotton or velveteen skirts and wares around them and sit, ignoring the uproar of crowding, often covering their faces from the sun with their hats, which have tall, white, stovepipe crowns and wide black or colored bands. (1993 : 194)

Stationary in the midst of the tumult, these pivotal figures give the market its shape and purpose.

Men's writing about the markets, like their portraits of market women, reveal a variety of responses to the experience of a space both nonwhite and female. In 1949, American anthropologist George Collier and his Ecuadorian colleague Anibal Buitrón created a beautiful book of black-and-white photographs of the Andean town of Otavalo.

The accompanying essay was written in a conscious attempt to create an international identity for the town as a tourist destination—which it has, indeed, become. Their description of the market is superficially inviting:

> In the early-morning sunlight each market is a swirl of color a formless pattern that fills the square like the morning tide. Dark-red ponchos, wine-purple, deep-blue, mixing with magenta shawls, cherry-red . . . electric-blue and emerald-green shoulder cloths, white hats . . . , blouses embroidered with bright . . . colors, the flashing red of coral and gilded beads. (19)

Upon reflection, however, the reader may detect a curious emptiness in this text. The authors' marketplace is oddly disembodied, full of colorful clothing but apparently without any actual women and men to inhabit the ponchos, shawls, blouses, and beads they so lovingly describe. Like Cortázar in chapter 1, they speak from a distance: not only are they creating this image of the market for an imagined English-speaking audience who will come from afar, but they describe the market as though seen from above, in an aerial photograph. Despite their claim to a thorough knowledge of the people and the place, this is the distanced voice of an authority both white and male—not the familiarity of an intimate.

A journalist's recent encounter with Bolivian market women shows what can happen to the male traveler who ventures closer. When a female friend brought Eric Lawlor, author of *In Bolivia: An Adventurous Odyssey through the Americas' Least-Known Nation,* to the La Paz markets, he had a series of alarming encounters. His rising sense of panic culminated when he accidentally knocked over a pail of *refresco* (fruit drink) belonging to one of the vendors. "The woman glared with such ferocity," he recalls, "that, before I quite knew what I was doing, I had pressed all my money into her hand and fled" (1989:31–32).

The most intimidating figures are those of the well-established *vivanderas,* who evince a total equipoise even when confronting wealthy foreigners. Unlike recent migrants and the perennially poor—who trudge down the streets with their merchandise strapped to their backs, balanced on their heads, or held in their arms—these merchants sit comfortably in one place. In country markets, or in the market squares at the edge of town that cater to rural customers, the vendors sit in long lines on the ground, their wares spread out before them on blankets. More upscale, centrally located plazas have tables and booths. Inside civic buildings, the stalls are more elaborate still; many resemble small shops, their merchandise arrayed on tall shelves. The most successful vendors of all move out of the market into the buildings adjacent to it, renting rooms that they convert into shops, restaurants, and bars. Most of the small businesses crowding the streets around the market belong to entrepreneurs who began by selling in the markets, and who still depend upon the custom of clients who do business there.

Since they sell to a regular base of customers, established vendors rarely call out to strange passersby; instead, they wait for their buyers to come to them. Travel writer Henry Shukman was made more uncomfortable by these older women than when accosted by aggressive younger vendors on the streets outside. When he entered the municipal market building of a small town on the Peruvian altiplano, he was stung by the silent stares of the sellers. They seemed indifferent to him; even their clothing—"absurd, wide, ballerina-like skirts and derby hats"—expressed an apparent unconcern with attracting masculine desire that he found frankly terrifying. Upset by their unreadable expressions as they gazed upon him, appalled by the absence of other men, he hastened to leave. "[T]hey didn't want me here," he writes, apparently astonished at the notion (1989: 53).

I was initially surprised by the hyperbolic quality of Shukman's prose: describing this scene, he calls the women "witches, guardians of an arcane religion, a cruel moon-worship" (53). Reading travel accounts by other authors, however, I found that he is not alone in describing the daytime market scene in terms usually reserved for midnight horrors. Eric Lawlor, too, enacts a childish revenge upon the La Paz women who upset him by representing them as nursery villains. They are

> a row of crones stooped low over steaming caldrons. . . . In one of the caldrons, the owner had placed a stick, which she twirled back and forth between her palms like someone making fire. The concoction in her pot began to froth. Was it my imagination, or did she cackle? *I'll get you, my pretty. And your little dog too.* (1989:31–32)

Seeking pleasurably masculinist adventures and tropical exotica, these young men encounter instead women they find repulsive and menacing. In their texts, market women fill the innocent male passerby with a sense of dread the more unsettling because its exact origins remain obscure to the writer himself. In short, they describe the male experience of the markets as uncanny. This public visibility of the female form, on display not for male delectation but for other purposes entirely, presents a symbolic inversion of the dominant sexual order that some find profoundly unsettling. The sight of so many women so completely at ease in a public sphere of their own making creates a corresponding unease in some masculine visitors. Constrained by the bold gaze of a myriad of women, they find themselves unexpectedly self-estranged by the sudden loss of a hitherto unquestioned privilege: the freedom to move about in public with relative unself-consciousness.

Entering the markets with hesitation, such foreigners leave with the uncomfortable sensation that people are laughing at them. This uneasiness can translate into a suspicion that one has been fleeced: accusations of financial chicanery abound, even when, as is often the case, prices are fixed. In 1997, after my traveling companion, Stephen, and I had been in Cuenca some weeks, he encountered an American acquaintance leaving the 10 de Agosto market on Christmas Eve. My compadres had introduced Stephen to the pleasures of eating fresh fava beans in Zumbagua, and he in turn had encouraged this man, a retired engineer with wide-ranging interests, to try some favas himself. When Stephen met up with him, the engineer immediately launched into a long harangue about his frustrating experiences in the market, which his daughter, who had spent many years in Latin America, tried in vain to stem. The vendor, mindful no doubt of governmental price controls, had refused to bargain with a stranger. "But I had just seen her giving one of her regular customers a better deal," he fumed.

"Dad," responded his daughter hopelessly, "It was only a thousand sucres' difference—that's less than twenty-five cents."

"That doesn't matter," he responded through clenched teeth. "It's the principle of the thing. She was making a fool out of me, and I wasn't going to stand there and take it. Not with everyone staring at me to see what I was going to do next."

When he stopped to buy beans, this tall, gray-haired Midwesterner undoubtedly attracted attention, speculation, and commentary. Tourists often come to the produce markets to gawk, but—having nowhere to cook raw products, and fearing to eat the cooked items—they rarely make a purchase. Local men, too, can find shopping in the markets unnerving. When I said good-bye to Rosa Loja, the rocoto seller mentioned in chapter 1, she interrupted our conversation to wait on a woman in a hat and pollera, who was making a few purchases accompanied by her young daughter. The two entered into an extended discussion of the merits of Sra. Loja's merchandise, punctuated by the occasional exchange of small amounts of produce and cash. Sra. Loja began pulling out small caches of items not on display. "I've been cooking these myself lately," she said, showing her customer some small tubers. "I boil them in the morning—it doesn't take as long as you might think—and I eat a few handfuls hot, before I get on the bus to come here. You should try them, they're really good." She spoke to the woman in the pollera warmly, as an equal and an intimate—although they did not appear to know each other well.

Nearby, a man in a well-worn suit was pricing potatoes, his wife in tow. He seemed unused to the market, and looked relieved when he overheard Sra. Loja giving her customer such careful guidance. But when he took his turn at her booth, questioning her about varieties of peppers and how to cook them, he received a very different treatment. The rocoto seller looked at him with an unreadable expression, answering his questions civilly, but without elaboration. Even after he made a few purchases, she did not warm to him appreciatively—although I thought I could detect a mild pity in her response to this confused attempt to buy her attention. But as she watched his retreating back—and that of his wife, still silently following behind—I was surprised to discern a look of palpable contempt.

The problem might have been the couple's respectable but threadbare attire—his jacket and tie, her straight skirt and stockings. Disdaining a working-class identity, they nonetheless lacked sufficient wealth to intimidate or impress. Men who share the vendors' working-class identity navigate the markets with greater ease. A few men work as vendors themselves, selling side by side with the women. The truckers and taxi drivers who ferry vendors and their products to and from the markets are also at home there, eating and drinking in the markets every day, and entering into familiar relationships—including love affairs—with the women. The same is true of the wholesalers, bakers, restaurateurs, and other men who do business with market women on a regular basis. The attitudes of all these men toward the women among whom they work range from easy camaraderie to outright sexual predation. Indeed, Condori Mamani sought out market women and chicheras not only for assistance, but also on both occasions when he was looking for a wife (1996, 1977).

In markets across the Andes, I have occasionally come across an awkward scenario in which a young market woman sits at her stall but is unable to sell because her boyfriend is sitting on her lap. He affects an air of defiance and possessiveness, throwing his arm around her neck or clasping his hands around her waist. She looks alternately—or simultaneously—miserable, ashamed, and angry. Work comes to a halt in the stalls around her, as older women stare disapprovingly and girlfriends giggle at their colleague's public humiliation. Her boyfriend is acting inappropriately, but it she who will pay the price: she cannot sell until he leaves, and her reputation as a serious vendor has been greatly diminished in the eyes of the older women she longs to impress.

If class alliance can make men more at home in the market, class distinction can alienate women from one another. A very wealthy Ecuadorian woman told us about going to a well-known market for a lark. She and a girlfriend descended upon a woman selling apples, and asked to know the price; but the woman refused to sell. "Well, at first I was going to get angry, but then I realized—poor little thing, it was early in the day and she was afraid we would buy all her stock. Then what would she have done? It's not as though they go there to make money, you know. Sitting there all day with her apples was all that she had in the world to do."

Our Quiteño taxi driver, Julio Padilla, listened to my retelling of this story with interest. "I know exactly what happened," he said. "I've often seen it. Those rich women, they walk in there like they own the place, and start demanding the price of everything. But they don't even listen to the answer. They just throw down some money, grab what they want, and walk away. The women working there can't stand them, that's why they won't talk to them."

Class affiliation, then, undercuts the power of gender. A man like Julio has immediate sympathy for women who, like himself, struggle to keep their dignity in the face of upper-class arrogance. And market women are happy to sell to, talk with, and occasionally be seduced by the working-class men whose jobs bring them into the market. But there are limits. The vendors' reaction to a man who bothers a woman while she's selling show that even class allies must respect the restrictions imposed by work and sex.

In the global society occupied by the professional classes, it has become a commonplace to speak of women's success in entering traditionally masculine spheres of business and politics. But the inclusion of women—and nonwhites—as full-fledged members of such communities remains tentative and incomplete, giving rise to a popular discourse about glass ceilings and a legal wrangle over hostile environments. These architectural metaphors are apt: the buildings erected by governments, banks, and corporations are white male spaces, within which femininity and nonwhiteness are stigmas that mark the interloper. Radcliffe and Westwood did not expect the geographical specificity of one common response they received when asking residents of Cotopaxi to describe whites: "Ah, yes, those are the men in the offices" (1996:112).

In the produce markets, it is well-to-do white men who feel peripheral. Shukman complained bitterly of the inhospitality of a place which, despite being "the center of Cholo life," consigned men to "hover in the dimness outside" (1989:138). The women who work there, of course, have a very different point of view: to them, the market is not only a home—and a workplace—but also a refuge from the inhospitability of the rest of Andean social space, where men dominate and women must submit. In actuality, the markets are largely constrained and controlled by men. But the opportunities for independence and homosociality they provide, partial though they may be, create a social realm so different from the world outside that it has given rise to rumors and myths that within the patriarchal heart of the Andes lies a secret, "matriarchal" society of cholas.

"Friendships between Women"

"To be frank," Eric Lawlor confesses in his travel journal, "marketwomen unnerved me" (1989:32). One wonders, however, if he is unnerved—or unmanned. Foreign observers of a different gender react enthusiastically to the experience of being in a predominantly female world. Linda Seligmann, explaining her initial attraction to the Cuzco market as a topic of research, recalls:

> When I did my first field research in Peru in 1974, I was struck by the forceful, energetic, and at times bawdy market women known as cholas. They stood out because they appeared fearless, astute, different, and unpredictable. I could not find a counterpart among Peruvian males.

Even their rough handling of gringas like herself only increased her enthusiasm: "The cholas feigned neither humility towards rich white foreigners nor unbridled admiration for their ways" (1989:694). To the feminist academic, the predominance of women in Andean public places and the confidence with which they took on all comers offered a pleasing escape from the more familiar city streets of her homeland—masculine spaces into which women venture with trepidation.

Travelers' impressions of the Andean marketplace as a profoundly female, even antimasculine zone, are supported by those who know it well. A recent life history, *The World of Sofía Velasquez: The Autobiography of a Bolivian Market Vendor* (1996), was produced through years of collaboration between Sofía Velasquez herself and two anthropologists, Hans and Judith-Maria Buechler. Hans Buechler grew up in Bolivia, and he and his wife have spent more than thirty years doing research there, often with Sofía's assistance. In this text, composed largely of Sofía's own words as spoken to the Buechlers in interviews between 1964 and 1994, we meet a woman who has built an entire life in the markets of La Paz. Unlike the alienating sea of identical female faces described by male writers, the market in Sofía's book is a richly heter-

ogeneous territory, thickly interlaced with social, emotional, and economic meanings. She speaks with affection, antagonism, familiarity,
and irritation of many different kinds of women: her fellow vendors,
with whom she must negotiate for room to sell; the female restaurant
owners who buy her pork, eggs, and cheeses; the women who loan her
money and those who are indebted to her.

Like the women of Cuenca's 10 de Agosto market (and unlike the
impoverished recent immigrants to Andean cities who try to sell on the
streets), Sofía entered the trade with the help of a female relative. While
men—especially her brother Pedro—are never entirely absent from
the story of her life, they are far overshadowed by the dozens if not
hundreds of female partners, competitors, customers, relatives, neighbors, friends, and enemies who populate Sofía's busy world.

The working lives of many professional women are largely defined
by their relationships with men, whether as subordinates or colleagues.
In contrast, Sofía, asked about what it means to be a woman, emphasizes the everyday homosociality of the produce market:

> I see friendships between women sitting next to one another.
> They become friends or comadres. I frequently see them talk to
> one another or go and drink together. They lend one another
> money and they are concerned about what is happening in each
> other's lives. (168)

For women who work in such intimacy with other women, the home
has a different meaning than it does for those who work in male-
dominated contexts—or who do not work outside the home at all.
From the perspective of the produce market, the private home does
not appear as the one definitively and unambiguously female domain,
where women can feel secure and in control; far from it. In a radical
inversion of this gender paradigm, domestic life with husbands, fathers,
and brothers appears in market women's testimonies as an ominously
patriarchal territory controlled and dominated—often violently—by
men.

In Velasquez's account, domesticity and the market are twin mag-
netic poles pulling women in opposite directions, toward men and
away from them—although for Sófia, there was never any doubt as to
which exerted the strongest attractions. Throughout her story, two
family members stand for these opposite worlds. Her mother represents
a happily feminine life of buying and selling, while her brother Pedro
emerges as a repressive figure, forever attempting to shape her behavior
to conform to masculine ideals that Sofía does not attempt to refute,
but which she nevertheless refuses to live by. When she began her ca-

reer in the markets as an *ambulante,* carrying a tray of goods through the streets with her friend Lola, conflict with Pedro erupted almost immediately.

> [O]ne afternoon, my brother Pedro saw me selling on the street. . . . [and] said, "I will tell my sister that she is no longer my sister. It is shameful for her to be selling on the street." . . . He said that it was unseemly for me to sit in the street and that his friends would criticize him. . . . But . . . I liked to sell. Selling was pleasant. I could go and sell whenever I wanted and I was earning money. (20–21)

At this young age, Sofía's turn to marketing involved staking out her gender loyalties, rejecting male authority, and looking to other women for support. "'I won't stop, Mother,'" I told her. 'Let him go ahead and say that I am not his sister. It's fine with me. They (the other vendors) will help me.' And so I continued to sell" (21).

To her brother, and to working-class men of La Paz, it is especially inappropriate for married women to sell. Sofía repeatedly tells of women leaving the market at the behest of husbands, especially newlyweds. They often reappear, however, when family finances dictate: one of Sofía's most richly enjoyed victories over Pedro occurs when his finances take a downturn and he is forced to allow his wife to join his sister selling on the street (135).

If family life sometimes pulls women from the marketplace, it has just as often pushed them into it. This feminine workplace not only provides women with an income when male wages are insufficient; it also acts as a refuge when a home falls apart, or becomes too dangerous. Chilean anthropologist Ximena Bunster and North American political scientist Elsa Chaney, in their 1985 study of working-class women in Lima, heard many tales of domestic tragedy when they interviewed recent immigrants from the highlands. Some women had been abandoned, like Alicia, who said, "I had separated from my husband because he ran off with another woman. That was the reason I came to Lima. In the sierra I couldn't support myself. . . . I came alone." Or Edelmira, who explained, "I didn't have anything, my husband went off with another woman. I came here when I was two months' pregnant." Another woman fled "the sexual advances of her stepfather after her mother's death" (1985:40–41). American scholar Leslie Gill, who wrote an engaging study of domestic workers in La Paz, also met many young immigrants escaping family violence: "Six-year-old Zenobia Flores fled to La Paz with her mother in 1972 to escape the drunken rages of her father, who regularly beat up his wife and children" (1994:

65). Bolivian anthropologist Silvia Rivera Cusicanqui spoke with a woman who had been abandoned by her mother as a child (Rivera Cusicanqui et al. 1996:245).

Inasmuch as it provides them with a source of income, the market clearly gives women some independence. Perhaps as importantly, it places them within a collectivity of other women, one that, in the central markets, is highly organized. To a limited extent, this position enables them to pass collective judgment about what goes on within the domestic sphere, and even to intervene. When married women work in the market, their coworkers claim the right to protest marital abuse, speaking on behalf of market women in general.[7] At the least, they can offer their emotional support, as Sofía Velasquez commented: "If a man is mean they might be angry against him. If a man beats a woman they may commiserate with her" (168).

When she became secretary-general of the marketer's union, Sofía herself intervened in troubled marriages. "My secretary of organization, Rosa Espinosa, was beaten by her husband. One day, I called her husband and told him that I didn't like the fact that he was beating his wife." Speaking with the authority of her post, she informed him that his wife was not unfaithful: "Since I am a leader, I see with whom the woman is drinking." Enumerating to him his failures as a husband and provider, she berated him: "I have never seen your wife drink with men, only with Señora Nieves. And you must be aware of why she is drinking" (168).

In another case, involving a woman named Ventura, the union leadership acted less aggressively in her defense, finding some merit in her husband's complaint that she was carrying on with a client—a man who bought pigs' heads from her. They did respond to coworkers' complaints about the brutality of the beatings Ventura endured, but the story ended tragically: "We [the market women's union] dealt with the matter, but the man killed her anyway, by beating her." In the end, her friends were as helpless as coworkers elsewhere. They could only mourn: "Ventura had a friend called Máxima. . . . The day Ventura died, Máxima cried" (169).

The surface appearance of the market as an independent city of women can mislead. Relationships with men and with masculine institutions set invisible boundaries everywhere. Socially, women live within neighborhoods and extended families dominated by men; in their businesses, market women depend upon the male wholesalers, truckers, and drivers who bring them their merchandise; politically, the relentless intervention of the state wears a masculine face and uniform—that of the policeman. Policemen are among the most common—and most despised—male intruders into feminine realms such as that of the fruteras. Vendors' stories about the police and military are filled with references to physical and sexual violence that provide an uncanny echo to their tales of domestic abuse. Police-market relations in the city of Cuzco, as documented by Seligmann and de la Cadena, seem especially brutal. Seligmann was horrified by the tales of police harassment and violence she heard from Cuzco market vendors, which included sexual humiliations:

> If a municipal agent succeeds in seizing a vendor's products, it is a terrible risk for her to retrieve them by paying a fine because, more often than not, paying a fine means paying not only money but also sexual favors . . . [which the women] find morally reprehensible. (1993:201)

And just as market women attempt to defend one another against domestic violence, so too the Cuzco market women fight back against police abuse. One woman, Eutrofia Qorihuaman, told Seligmann, "We try to defend ourselves when they abuse us. . . . We all help each other" (201). Seligmann herself witnessed these defensive actions:

> the market women . . . form a united front. Some, screaming and creating confusion, assist the victim in hiding her products; others run ahead to warn other[s]. . . . Still others, by jumping onto the truck and trying to retrieve the products, will attempt to prevent agents from taking them away. (1993:201)

The police figure frequently in Sofía Velasquez's accounts of marketing in La Paz as well, but her relationship to them, while always fraught with tension, changed from conflict to cooperation as she moved up through the ranks of her trade. As young women selling without an established place in the market, Velasquez and her friends constantly fled the police. Later, she survived the notoriously repressive Banzer regime of the 1970s by alternately colluding with and deceiving a policeman charged with enforcing government-imposed rationing. Finally, as an established member of a formal market, with a municipal license and well-lubricated official connections between her own union and that of the police, her relationship with them came full circle: now it is she who calls on the officers to drive away unwanted young competitors.

Although Sofía spent only a few years as one of the illicit vendors who are most vulnerable to police violence, policemen figure in her stories as an aggressive masculine presence, individual and collective, that must be held at bay through offerings of money, food, or liquor.

She sees herself as able to avoid unwanted sexual manipulation, but others assume that her work must oblige her to give sexual favors to male authorities from time to time. When her brother Pedro discovered that she was smuggling contraband products from Peru in the early 1960s, for example, he accused her of prostituting herself to the border police as a bribe (1996: 58).

Rejecting Patriarchy

In abusing market women sexually, the police may assume that these are women already degraded through forcible sex in the past—but not necessarily in the working class and poor rural homes into which they are born and marry. Rather, it is in the middle- and upper-class homes in which Indian women are hired to work as domestics, and which often serve as entrances into a career as a market woman, that sexual abuse is widely believed to be a universal condition of employment. "The sexual harassment and abuse of household workers is one of the enduring features of female domestic service in La Paz," says Leslie Gill (1994:74).

Speaking to Bunster and Chaney in Peru (1985), and to Gill in Bolivia (1994), market women explained their choice of occupation by describing themselves as psychologically unable to bear the repressive and abusive situations they had encountered previously as domestics. Gregorio Condori Mamani's wife Asunta Quispe Huamán, a vendor of cooked food in the Cuzco market, recalled her earlier employment as a domestic with distaste. She left her first employer, who mistreated her, only to find that the husband of the next was "a real devil" who tried to rape her whenever he found her alone in the house (1977:96; 1996:113).

Elite men imagine the chola as sexually available; domestic servants fulfill these expectations, even if under duress. The notion that male employers have sexual access to female domestic workers is found everywhere, from novels to the jokes that circulate among professional men.[8] When they escape these settings, women redefine themselves in the elite male vocabulary from the "delectable" chola of fantasy to the "grosería" of a street hawker.

The knowledge that a woman selling vegetables may have come to this occupation through her refusal to be an employer's plaything or a husband's punching bag affects the image of the market woman. Andean popular culture is filled with hints of a widespread recognition that the markets allow women not only to escape from domestic settings they find unbearable, but even to reshape the politics of domestic life itself. Consider the words of Bolivian working-class men in the early 1990s, who described market women to anthropologist Robert Albro as *varonil,* or manlike (1997, 2000). More telling still are the exchanges between Cuzco market vendors and other working-class women recorded by Seligmann.

In one argument, a market woman snapped at a customer, "Watch out or I'll slap you one." The other woman replied, "And you? Who are you to have to slap me? Don't I already have a husband who slaps me? Perhaps you [formal] don't have one who would slap you" (Seligmann 1993:196). This customer flaunts her own embrace of a form of marriage that includes domestic violence. But while secure in the assumption that her own domestic arrangement is the more socially approved, she nevertheless acknowledges that the market makes other choices possible.

Asked to describe a typical "chola valluna," a populist politician in Quillacollo, Bolivia,[9] laughed and told Albro, "She . . . loves strongly . . . she'll kill you if you cross her. She'll yank you by your plumbing [*pichula*]!" [1997:16]. In Arguedas's novel *Los ríos profundos,* the chichera who leads a political protest is said to have two husbands, both *"humildes"* in contrast to their valiant spouse (1958:214–15). Even Shukman, ignorant of specific histories but sensing a general air of independence, quickly translated this lack of submission into an imagined reversal of the patriarchal order, in which market women "hold a frightening dominion over the men" of the Andes (1989:53).

The "manliness" of the market woman lies in her reputed strength of will and large sexual appetites; or it may be found in the resoluteness with which she rejects heterosexual marriage. I first became curious about the domestic arrangements of such women in Zumbagua, where I came to know two women who had succeeded in opening establishments not in the market square itself, but on its periphery. One was a tavern-owner—although not a chichera, for in this north Andean region, located well above the upper limits for growing corn, women do not brew chicha for a living. But Heloisa Huanotuñu, the owner of a small but much-frequented establishment on the edge of the square where the weekly market is held, fits the traditional image of the chola as matriarch as well as any chichera could. Well-known throughout the parish, she is a public figure, not a private housewife; within her extended family, she exerts a power and influence that has grown exponentially in the years since I first met her.

I met Heloisa in 1983 through Helena, my first landlady in Zumbagua, a white woman whose family had been employees of the hacienda until the Agrarian Reform of 1965. Helena stayed in the parish as other whites fled, working for the parish church as sacristan—a role she inherited from her father. She had great contempt for Indians, but a great love for her friend Heloisa. The two were inseparable, Heloisa's tall black-clad figure a counterpoise to stout little Helena, who always wore one of the frilly shawls that the Irish nuns had taught local women to crochet. Heloisa and Helena were well-respected businesswomen by the standards of the town, and both were popular there. Helena's kitchen, where lunch was served during the week to the teachers from the school and the nurses from the clinic, and Heloisa's bar, where indigenous farmers from outlying areas gathered to drink on market days, were central clearing houses for news, as well as crucibles where public opinion was forged.

Helena and Heloisa were the first two women I was to know well in Zumbagua, and yet they did not conform at all to the image of rural Andean women promulgated in social-science textbooks, in which heterosexual marriage is described as mandatory.[10] Neither woman had ever been married. Although they maintained separate (but adjacent) households, it was Helena who provided Heloisa with companionship, in the early morning, at meals, in the slow hours of the afternoon, and at night in bed. (In the cold mountain towns of the Andes, sharing a bed in an unheated bedroom is a common practice and, although inevitably creating physical intimacy, is not necessarily assumed to imply sexual contact. It can, however, lead to speculation and gossip—as was certainly the case among Helena and Heloisa's neighbors.)

I never heard either woman express the slightest desire for adult male companionship—indeed, quite the reverse. They spoke of the married women they knew in voices that mixed sympathy, pity, and a slight contempt. Counting up her personal triumphs and disappointments, Helena dwelt upon her ambitions for her brothers and her sons, and the lost glories of white Zumbagua society. Heloisa, daughter of a local indigenous woman, had little patience for the latter topic. Her conversational gambits included long disquisitions upon her passionate, almost obsessive love for her own mother; the intelligence and compassion exhibited by her stepfather, Juanchu Chaluisa, whom she greatly admired and respected; and her constantly revised plans for meeting the needs of her large and impoverished extended family.

I can remember them clearly, sitting on little wooden chairs in Helena's unheated, windowless, dirt-floored kitchen, talking over the events of the day. Two poor and illiterate women, no longer young, dressed in drab, dirty clothes, they nevertheless exhibited all the amused self-confidence of wealthy businessmen or society matrons. Within their milieu, they had achieved social and political recognition, what limited financial success was available, and love and companionship to boot. A graduate student at the time, I could only long for a time when I, too, might achieve such a secure position in my own world.

Far to the south in Bolivia, living in a bustling capital city rather than in a remote rural periphery, Sofía Velasquez grew up knowing women like Heloisa and Helena. As a child, Sofía was resentful of her older brothers' control over her, and quick to note that some of her friends lacked male relations. As though to foreshadow the adult relationships between women that would be so important to her later on, the first page of Sofía's life story introduces a childhood friend, Yola, who lived in an exclusively female household:

> She doesn't have a father. [Her mother] lived with a friend called Agustina Quiñones. They came from Peru together. . . . To this day, neither one of them is married and they are still living together. They are inseparable friends. (Buechler and Buechler 1996:1)

Explaining her decision to work in the market, Sofía begins by stating that she had never had any desire to marry, or to live with men. When one of her elementary school teachers, Mother Chantal, meets her as a young woman and scolds her for never having married, she answers simply, "I can't, I don't like it" (172).[11] In drawing the connection between working in the market and escaping domestic life with men so explicitly, Sofía inadvertently makes her brother's relentless opposition to her marketing more understandable. Like his sister, Pedro sees the market as the antithesis of patriarchal domesticity—and thus as a direct threat to his own attempts to control the women in his life, both sisters and wives.

The notion that the market chola has escaped a patriarchal home life is pervasive among Andean elites as well (although its opposite, the idea that they are routinely brutalized by bestial husbands, also finds expression). The cholas of Cuenca, I was repeatedly told, are "matriarchal," as is said of those of Cochabamba, Bolivia (Paulson 1996:104); de la Cadena found the same notion in romantic writings about cholas in Cuzco several decades earlier. She quotes Vallarnos, who wrote, "At home the chola exercises a kind of matriarchy. Different from the Spanish woman . . . a decorative figure . . . or the Indian woman who is the submissive servant of the husband . . . the chola is the boss of the house."[12]

In Cuenca, the notion of the chola as the epitome of Cuencana culture links the supposed matriarchy of the chola household to the vaunted matriarchies of the elites. The female descendants of famous "noble" families from the past enjoyed describing their ancestral families to me as "matriarchies." Sra. Crespo, who unlike most of her contemporaries still lived in a crumbling Beaux Arts mansion on the Calle Larga, overlooking the Tomebamba river, told me stories that, like her house, were more romantic than reliable. Listening to her reminiscences about her mother, one of a household of beautiful sisters orphaned by the death of their beloved father, a dapper widower, I began to feel as though I had taken down a book from a shelf of fiction. It was a family as female as that of García Lorca's *Casa de Bernarda Alba,* and as cursed as García Marquez's unfortunate Buendías.[13] As she went on to recount the tragic and mysterious deaths of these women's suitors, fiancés, and nephews, the stories seemed less surreal than gothic— but with a curious sexual reversal. Like the heroines of Edgar Allan Poe, it was the men in Sra. Crespo's tales who were beautiful, adored— and deceased.

Doña Lola, our landlady, although also descended from a noble family, was of a quite different disposition. Unlike Sra. Crespo, whose absorption in the past led some of her contemporaries to dismiss her as a crank, Lola had as little trouble negotiating the present as she did maneuvering Cuenca's narrow streets in her Japanese station wagon. However, both women shared a fervent idealization of the *Casas Grandes* of Cuenca's past.

To our eyes, Doña Lola had successfully created a modern version of the Casa Grande in her own home. She presided with great authority over a sprawling household composed of her husband, children, and daughter-in-law. With the help of three female employees, she also managed ten apartments, which she had built next door and filled with students and visiting faculty from the nearby university. She loved to see her tenants gathering in the late afternoon around the outdoor tables she had set up in the courtyard, for then she could descend upon us like a benevolent great lady, bearing a tray of glasses and a thermos of strong *canelazos*.[14]

But she did not share our perception of her life. Doña Lola expressed contempt for modern households, her own included, as weak and disorganized. Her role was attenuated and improvised, she felt, compared to the great houses of the noble families from which she was descended. She longed for the days when the authority of older elite women over their dependents—whether servants, children, or temporary residents like ourselves—was unchecked. To Doña Lola, it was a self-evident truth that not only the decline of her own social class, but the decay of Western civilization in its entirety, could be traced to the rise of the nuclear family.

Myths about "noble" and "chola" matriarchies arise because wealth and poverty alike create patterns of kinship and residence that do not conform to bourgeois ideals. Wealthy Ecuadorians today often maintain households in several cities—even on different continents—allowing spouses to affirm the importance of lifelong marriage without having to endure co-residence. At the other end of the spectrum, the economic independence of market women sometimes allows them to enter into heterosexual relationships on a more flexible and egalitarian footing than might otherwise be the case. Dominga, a Bolivian potato vendor, told Rivera Cusicanqui that she was pressured into marriage by her mother. She stayed in the marriage, though, because "*mi marido trabajaba, me aydaba, sabe lavar los pañales de la wawa, concinar, limpiar la casa.*" [My husband worked, he helped me, he was used to washing the diapers, cooking, cleaning the house.] Like the other vendors Rivera Cusicanqui interviewed in La Paz, Dominga spoke candidly about how the independence she had gained in the market shaped her domestic life (Rivera Cusicanqui et al. 1996:254). That these relationships have been so readily interpreted by intellectuals as a "matriarchy," or by foreigners as evidence of female "domination" over men, points to the rarity and fragility of any form of gender equality or female autonomy in a society in which sexual hierarchies are all-pervasive.

Señora Blanca Orellana is the most successful vendor I met in Cuenca, but she defers to the authority of her far less productive husband. She began her career selling cooked food to other market women, and has built her business into a small restaurant just off the Plaza Rotary, where most of her clients are the vendors, truckers, and other workers from the adjacent market. The dimly lit concrete space— subdivided into a kitchen, two small dining rooms, and a semiprivate area for the family and employees—has been made as cozy as possible, with cheery plastic tablecloths on the tables. Strangers would be unlikely to seek her out, for the restaurant entrance is off a narrow and uninviting alley. Her customers know where to find her, though, because for years she sold hot meals from a folding table set up in the mouth of the alley, facing the market across the street. In those days she rented only a tiny area inside the building for cooking and storage. Gradually building up a clientele, she began renting enough square feet for a few indoor tables, expanding bit by bit into a set of rooms that is palatial in comparison to the cooked food stalls inside a market building.

Stephen and I found her restaurant after a few false starts, following directions from anthropologist Ann Miles, who had met Sra. Orellana when conducting a survey a few years earlier. When we hesitantly introduced ourselves, the señora inundated us with conversation and with food and drink, delighted to entertain a friend of her beloved "Anita." Lively and self-assured, she peppered us with questions about Ann's health and family. But when her husband Lucho joined the table, nursing a hangover and displaying a gregariousness indistinguishable from truculence, she turned watchful and diplomatic. She intervened mildly but effectively when he wanted to open a third large bottle of beer for us—it was, after all, still morning—and waited until he left to fully unburden herself of opinions he didn't share. She might be the breadwinner, and quite likely the decision-maker as well, but he retained the trappings of male authority nonetheless.

Sra. Orellana offers us one glimpse of domestic life for market vendors, but her choices are not the only ones to be found among the women who sell in the plazas, streets, and municipal buildings. While some market vendors suffer execrable relationships with men, far different from the amiable partnership of the Orellanas, Sofía Velasquez describes such situations as "rare" (156). On the whole, vendors are more likely than other women to terminate relationships that are abusive, to seek transitory rather than permanent alliances, or to insist upon more egalitarian relationships with husbands and lovers. Furthermore, the market enables women to reject heterosexual partnerships with men completely. Florence Babb told me in 1998 that most of the women she came to know in the Huaraz market thought of life with men as an unfortunate episode from their past, thankfully put behind them.

Market women's self-imposed marginality from dominant sexual politics does not render their understanding of the home as a patriarchal space irrelevant. Don Kulick observes that such marginality can allow members of a subculture to "distill and clarify" aspects of sexuality and gender that are of profound and pervasive importance in Latin America (1997a: 582). Andean market women, like the prostitutes with whom Kulick worked, express views about sex and gender that originate in more general attitudes; looking at the home from their perspective provides an oblique angle on Andean domestic life, from which we may indeed be able to see more clearly.

The perception of the Latin home as a domain within which women live restricted—even oppressive—lives is widely held and finds frequent expression in books by and about South Americans. Robert Ellis, in an article comparing the sexual themes in contemporary books by Peruvian male authors, finds that childhood memories of well-to-do homes are characterized by an all-pervasive and terrifyingly violent paternal order (1998). The title of Wendy Weiss's doctoral dissertation sums up the domestic lives of working-class Quiteños with the phrase "Es El Que Manda" (He gives the orders) (1985).

The difference lies in whether or not one can imagine an alternative. Most women, rich or poor, resent the autocratic behavior of husbands and fathers, but in a helpless fashion. Male authors like Vargas Llosa or Cortázar write of vaguely imagined temporary refuges, such as an escape into nature or a few hours in a whorehouse.[15] In contrast, the markets are full of women who slammed the door on oppressive domestic lives and actively pursued viable permanent alternatives. This fact has not been lost on other sectors of Andean society. In the 1970s, the wealthy Bolivian girls who went away to college in the United States or Europe began coming home filled with new feminist ideas about domestic partnerships outside of marriage. Once back in La Paz, however, they found that such a move had meanings within the Andes that it did not have elsewhere. In Europe, to reject sexist domestic arrangements might seem a radical innovation; in Bolivia, it was instead a scandalous abandonment of one's class and race position. These highly educated women were choosing to live like market vendors—something far more abhorrent to their families than mere sexual experimentation. Upon returning to the Andes, most quickly put such experiments behind them and dutifully married their domestic partners (Gill 1994:87).

The produce market, then, provides the women who work there with a vantage point from which to critique, to reject, and even to transform the domestic unit that is the building block of society. This apparent rejection of domesticity explains why Pedro considered his sister Sofía Velasquez's work "shameful" and "disgraceful." Many of the women who work in the market are in fact married, like Rosa Loja, the rocoto seller in Cuenca, who describes herself with pride and satisfaction as "married to one man for forty years, and still contented." Others live in consensual unions with men; most of them are mothers; and all of them, except the truly destitute, have homes. Still, even among market women themselves, the occupation is conceived of as that of women without husbands: when choosing a leader, the women in Sofía's union agreed that their standard bearer must be "an unmarried woman who was intelligent, astute, and who knew how to fight for the union" (Buechler and Buechler 1996:138). The general public makes less benign associations: market women, even when earning money to support their husbands, fathers, and sons, evoke images of the wicked woman rather than of the good wife. The negativity that attaches to the woman of the plaza is a measure of the positive valuation given to the woman at home.

PUBLIC AND PRIVATE

The chola of the market, then, is a public scandal: a woman without a
man, working the streets. The only problem with this picture is that
the street market is less an antithesis to the domestic kitchen than its
raucous twin. The public market exists in close economic symbiosis
with the unseen interiors of the private homes that surround it. The
home and the homemaker are the market to which produce vendors
sell their daily goods: the world of the plaza exists to provide services
for the domestic sphere. "*Casera, casera,*" shout the market women to
potential customers: "homemaker, homemaker." [16]

Visitors from other countries are often charmed and surprised by the
incongruous domesticity of scenes in the market: a man sits at his sew-
ing machine, ready to patch your trousers or catch up a fallen hem; a
woman spreads a wooden table with a bright-colored plastic tablecloth
and offers to sell you anything from a Coca-Cola to a four-course *al-
muerzo,* complete with dessert. This public homeliness contributes to
the uneasy sensation of the *heimlich* turned *unheimlich* that renders the
markets uncanny for middle-class men. Reminded of a familial sphere
by the presence of cooking odors, matronly shapes, servants, and children, they find themselves at once at home and profoundly dislocated.
The comfortable spaces of the bourgeois home, and its attendant masculine privileges, are here turned inside out.

At Home in the Market

Nor is this commercial domesticity a mirage: workmen and students
cultivate special relations with particular market women, eating at their
stalls day after day, taking comfort in the familiarity of the woman's
voice, her steady supply of gossip, and her knowledge of their particular tastes and appetites. Real and fictitious family relationships abound.
Some customers are distant relatives—perhaps the son of a country
cousin, sent to the city to attend high school with a strict enjoinder to
eat all his meals "*donde su tía*" (where your aunt is). No one who eats at
a particular stall for any length of time remains a stranger; regular customers are inexorably drawn into the domestic dramas between the
women who work there, and are ruthlessly—albeit sympathetically—
interrogated about their own lives and kin.

Cooking is not the only housewifely work that market women do.
Like women who shop for their families, they bring the products of
male producers and wholesalers into a feminine realm where these can
be transformed into meals for individual families. Babb observes that
market women's labor is wrongly characterized as strictly distributive

in nature. In fact, many kinds of food processing take place in the market that would readily be interpreted as productive if done in a factory (1989:119–30). Vendors break down bulk quantities into smaller portions; shell beans and peas; peel fruit and vegetables; chop herbs; and grate onions. They even make small ready-to-cook soup packages, filled with combinations of raw legumes, herbs, and vegetables in exact proportions. Many stalls feature a single product offered in every stage of preparation, from unpeeled and dirty, to washed and sliced, to cooked and ready to eat.

Heloisa's trago shop is a case in point. She buys contraband cane alcohol in large quantities from the men who bring it up from the western jungle by mule and llama train. The little caravans arrive at her home in the early hours of the morning, and she and the men pour the alcohol from saddlebags into big plastic containers that once held kerosene. Customers occasionally buy entire barrels of the stuff for parties, or to bootleg over the mountains for resale in the white towns down below in the Interandean Valley. Most people bring smaller containers—gallon jars, empty liquor bottles—which are filled by a hose and closed with a fragment from a plastic bag. As the morning wears on, other customers appear looking for a shot to be consumed on the spot. Heloisa or another family member is ready to oblige, siphoning the liquor directly from a fifty-gallon drum into a small glass.

If work done in the market strikes economists as somehow too informal, too feminine, too unimportant to be recognized as productive, it is at the same time too commercial in nature to be properly domestic. The same activities, done inside the home, do not count as labor at all; in economic terms, they become invisible. For housewives, in fact, the existence of inexpensive market labor radically reshapes the workload within the home. Women come to the market to buy big quantities of corn already cooked into *mote* for a family dinner, or a little bag of it with hot sauce on top for immediate snacking. They may purchase a whole cooked pig or a single slice of roast pork. Enormous wheels of *panela* (turbinado sugar), dark and strong-smelling, wrapped in banana leaves, are sold in some stalls; but the vendors are happy to divide a wheel, or even to cut off a little chunk to eat like candy as you walk around.

Histories of the American consumer describe the advent of ready-to-eat foods as a recent innovation made possible by enormous technological advances. The willingness of working women and their families to eat prepackaged food, or to dine in restaurants, is described as a fundamental change in twentieth-century social life. Arizpe describes a pernicious penetration of the capitalist market into Latin daily life, usurping women's traditional functions and leaving them "empty handed" (1990:xv). These visions of history are too narrow in both class and geographical perspectives. In Latin America, the presence of the markets with their abundance of precooked foods is old, not new. Some industrial technologies have filtered into the markets: many factory-made foods are sold there; beverage stall counters are lined with electric blenders; some of the small stores ringing the market have invested in refrigerators. But for the most part, this enormous system of provisioning works through the most simple technologies possible: knives to slice and peel, ropes and baskets to carry bundles, cooking pots and wooden spoons to boil and stir. It is human labor that adds value to the products sold there.

Working-class women depend upon the ready availability of meals and ingredients from the markets; in small cities and towns this attitude extends to professional women as well. Traveling the back roads of Cotopaxi Province with a car full of Ecuadorian anthropologists, I was surprised when one passenger insisted that we drop in for lunch on an old school friend he had not seen in some time. Her feelings would be hurt, he insisted, when she found out he had been in the town and had not let her give his friends a midday meal. How, I wondered, could this unknown woman cope with a half dozen unexpected lunch guests? The market provided the answer: our hostess disappeared within minutes of our arrival, then returned to usher us in with fanfare to a dining room laden with local specialties: potato pancakes, roast pork, tomato salad, fresh corn. Beaming, she boasted of knowing all the best market stalls in town: without her, she insisted, we would never have been able to eat well in a strange place.

The willingness of market women to perform any sort of food preparation, and the eagerness of housewives and domestic servants to avail themselves of these services, mediates the boundary between the loving work of caring for a family and the paid labor of strangers. Men and children eating a meal at home consume the work not only of their own wife and mother, but of other women as well. In order to be the ideal housewife who knows how to provision her family, women must create and keep good relations with the women of the market and of the small shops that surround it. Thus even for women who do not work there, the markets demand a degree of female homosociality that customers find alternately maddening and rewarding. Market women foster affective relations with their customers, capturing their loyalty, blurring the line between business and friendship. Debbie Trujan, an expatriate American scholar who lives in Cuenca, speaks fondly of "her egg ladies," two sisters whose stall is a regular stop on her Saturday morning excursions around town. But personal relationships are always risky: when Sofía Velasquez, an "egg lady" herself, got on the wrong side of a restaurant owner who bought from her weekly, she found herself scrambling for new customers—a story to which we will return in chapter 4.

The relationship has its own arcana as well. Many a gringa who has lived in the Andes for an extended period of time recalls with pride her first *llapa:* the first time that, as a repeat customer, she earned a little "extra" scoop of flour or beans, poured into her bag after it had been weighed and the price figured. Market women who sell to Indians often keep a bag of cheap, brightly colored candies with which they llapa their customers, preferring to offer these treats rather than any of the more expensive dry goods or produce they sell. The result is a subtle insult, masked as a kindness: are these candies for the purchaser's children, or is the Indian woman herself being treated as a child? Why is it that the seller, pretending friendship, nevertheless insists that Indians—unlike their white customers—pay full price for every ounce of merchandise?

I vividly remember archaeologist Clark Erickson and his wife Kay Chandler's return to the United States after spending almost three years in a small, isolated community on the Peruvian altiplano near Lake Titicaca. They ruefully recalled to me their first attempts at creating pleasant relations with local shopkeepers. Anxious not to offend, the couple had tried to alternate making purchases between each of the two small stores that sold dry goods—the only source of food on the days in between the weekly market. The women who owned the shops, miffed that Kay had not cultivated a special friendship with one or the other of them in accordance with local mores, responded by refusing to sell them anything at all—and temporarily succeeded in turning the market women against them as well. Within a few months, however, Kay had learned to behave appropriately enough to create a completely different relationship with "her" chosen shop owner: by the end of their stay, the woman carefully tucked away specially chosen eggs and cheeses for "her" special gringa to buy. Once back home, Clark and Kay found the experience of shopping in American grocery stores completely alienating. The shopkeepers and market women of the altiplano had changed them more completely than they realized, and they found themselves unwilling—almost unable—to engage strangers in commercial transactions involving food.

From the market woman's perspective, maintaining the proper degree of intimacy with customers is among the most complicated and delicate of tasks—and the one that separates an inept vendor from a successful entrepreneur. My landlady in Zumbagua, Rosa Quispe, operated a cooked-food stall in the Saturday market there for a while, but gave it up in disgust. "It costs me more than I earn," she explained to me. "The entire family comes to the market and expects me to feed them for free, but I have to buy all my ingredients in Latacunga the day before, and there I pay cash." Successful market women, too, find the boundary between market and domestic relations impossible to maintain. What distinguishes stall-owners in the Cuenca municipal markets from amateurs like Rosa is their ability to make profit out of their personal relationships, while using their commercial ties to benefit themselves and those they care about. For the true professional, the line between public and private, commercial and familial disappears almost completely.

In the late afternoons, the 10 de Agosto market is a drowsy place. There are almost no customers. The big metal doors of the market are pulled down partway, making the interior dim and cool. Young assistants and relatives have been sent home; only the older women, owners of the stalls, lounge in them half-asleep, reading newspapers or taking naps as though in their own living rooms. They take out their reading glasses, their crocheting, and their slippers, wrapping themselves in their shawls and propping their feet up on a sack of potatoes or noodles.

If the market is literally a domestic space for these women, whose work brings them there seven days a week from the middle of the night till mid-afternoon, their homes, in turn, become staging sites for commercial and productive operations.[17] Sra. Loja, the rocoto seller, doesn't mind that her daughters have not followed exactly in the footsteps of their mother and grandmother. They sell clothing rather than food, and recently began to manufacture some items at home. "They have turned the house into a factory," she remarked with satisfaction.

In La Paz, Pedro complains that Sofía uses the family home, inherited from their mother, as a source of income. He doesn't mind that she has filled the bedrooms with boarders, as her mother had done before her. What upsets him is that Sofía rents out the courtyard to her fellow vendors as storage space. It is stacked with folding tables, portable stoves, piles of raw produce, and even—much to Pedro's disgust, and eliciting complaints from the long-suffering tenants—loads of freshly slaughtered meat.

Heloisa Huanotuñu lives in her trago shop. The counter and shelves, table and chairs serve both as her kitchen and the bar's furniture. Her bed, partly curtained with a sheet of plastic, and the small storage areas above and below it are the only semiprivate spaces within the one-room building. Much of her emotional life is centered elsewhere, in the family farmstead some distance from town, where her brothers and sisters and nieces and nephews live. She spends many hours there, cooking and eating, listening to complaints and giving advice, loaning money and demanding help. But she does not sleep there. She, too, then, has arranged working, sleeping, eating, and loving in ways that cannot readily be reduced to a single dichotomy of public and private.

Henry Shukman and Pedro Velasquez are separated by race, class, and nationality.[18] They are united, however, in their embrace of the idea that family life, the home, and domesticity should be a single unit, defined by its contrast to the public spheres of work, business, and politics. Within this gendered geography, the produce market is a dangerous anomaly. The stigma that surrounds the space of the market is part of a social hygenics intended to protect Andean home life against its dissolution. With it, as Pedro seems all too aware, could go some foundations of Andean patriarchy: the authority men claim within the family, an authority backed up, when necessary, with violence; the distinction between a masculinity at home in political and economic life and a feminine zone of secluded domesticity. Perhaps most unsettling of all is the threatened erosion of the distinction between highly valued male wage labor and the unpaid domestic labor performed by women.

Living Like Indians

In confounding the boundaries between private and public life, market women are not overturning universal or essential sexual patterns, or even innately Hispanic cultural patterns. In its long history, the Mediterranean has seen many configurations of social space, as have the Americas. The challenge they pose is rather to a separation specific to modern capitalism, which fetishizes the home as the realm of affective relations (Moore 1988:23). This brings us back from sex to race again, for it helps to explain why market women are "dirty Indians." The lives of women like Sofía Velasquez and Rosa Loja, city-dwellers who live entirely enmeshed in commerce, seem utterly different from those of the peasant farmers with whom they are often confused. Yet in their resistance to this, capitalism's central tenet, they do in fact resemble the Indian peasants who live on its fringes. To their many other violations of social decorum we can add this confusion of public and private, which manifests itself not only as a literal washing of dirty dishes in public, but also as the practice of countrified, Indian ways of life within the confines of the city.

In indigenous communities—as among the market women—homes are workplaces. Unlike bourgeois life, here Arizpe's "schizophrenia of the public/private divide in capitalist society" does not reign absolute.[19]

If the work done in the produce markets blurs the lines between the processing of food and its sale, subsistence agriculture renders the entire gamut of activities from primary production to final consumption a single continuum. In Zumbagua, "peeling potatoes to make soup is simply one of the last actions in a process that began when the earth was turned over for planting" (Weismantel 1988:37).

THOA (the Andean Oral History Workshop, a group of Aymara scholars) writes of Aymara farmwomen,

> Unlike urban or proletarian women . . . indigenous women cannot clearly separate the sphere of production from that of reproduction. Their domestic activities are intimately linked to agricultural production . . . domestic manufacture—which in the case of textiles is basically a female activity—bartering between different ecological zones, and participation in the market. (THOA 1990:160–61).

For THOA and Rivera Cusicanqui, who are highly critical of the urban white sectors of Bolivian society, this merging of productive and domestic spheres in Indian society is to be admired. Another Bolivian woman, Ema Lopez—a young Aymara maid interviewed by Leslie Gill—reached the opposite conclusions:

> Lopez works for a wealthy white family. She is very impressed by her employer's affluence and unfavorably compares her family's dwelling in the countryside with the mistress's urban home. Lopez dislikes the fact that her family sleeps in one room, which also serves as a kitchen. "At the señora's," she explains, "there is a kitchen and the bedrooms are separated . . ." She also resents her family's lack of concern for order and cleanliness. "I like everything clean, but my family's house is so disorderly . . . I always ask [my family], 'Why is this so ugly? Why do you do things this way?'" (Gill 1994:102)

To tourists visiting Latin America from Europe or the north, the line between Indians in the country and whites in the city is invisible; they see only an undifferentiated Indian/mestizo populace. Within the Andean city, however, the distinction is fiercely defended. Leslie Gill writes that for white women in La Paz, domestic order—albeit maintained with the help of Indian servants—is a crucial defense against the nonwhite masses:

> white notions of cleanliness encompass much more than basic concepts of health and sanitation. They are related to questions

of lifestyle and morality. Cleanliness means not being poor. It entails living in a home separated from productive labor and equipped with indoor plumbing. It also requires sexual restraint and morally upright behavior, which are qualities that, according to whites, the poor, by definition, do not possess. (Gill 1994: 116)

Here, a restrictive sexual code and the separation of productive work and the domestic sphere are conjoined to define what it means to be white—and by implication, what it means to be Indian as well.

Indeed, so important is the segregation of white and Indian living spaces that the thought of its erasure can produce a fear as nauseating as any sexual anxiety. Awareness of the Indian proclivity for collapsing public and private compounds the danger, for a step into the market can plunge the city-dweller not only into a nonwhite space, but into a sudden and unwanted domestic intimacy with its inhabitants. American students who spend a semester abroad in Andean cities such as Cuzco or Cuenca are often strictly forbidden by their host families to enter the produce market under any circumstances. If they obey this injunction, these commercial spaces—unlike tourist markets such as Otavalo's textile plaza—remain a mysterious zone of unknown but potent dangers.

This map of urban danger zones also illuminates the terror the pishtaco arouses in the countryside. For if the Indian home is not an isolated unit of familial consumption, it follows that indigenous public space is not an unbounded realm of anonymity. Marta Colque, an Aymara woman, reminisced about her childhood in an indigenous community in Bolivia, Punku Uyu:

> We tended the land between us, family by family. We would eat together in the fields, cooking in huge pots. During the carnivals and the Espiritu religious festival, which is our holiday, we cooked and ate together. We all went to a green field with our pots and we would eat and drink there. (THOA/Rivera Cusicanqui 1990: 154)

Here, the entire community—not only the houses, but the fields and pastures, the roads and paths—are part of an open-air domesticity, in which all members of the society are imagined to stand in kinship relations to one another. Despite the enormous inroads made by capitalist relations, rendering the image of sharing and commensuality more fictive than real, it is still an enormous shock to find a stranger boldly traversing territories that are not, in fact, public.

When Henry Shukman accompanied the vendors of Taraco to an

indigenous community on the altiplano, he wandered off from the makeshift market, enjoying the tranquil beauty of Lake Titicaca. He was soon accosted by a man waving his arms and shouting, who interrogated him suspiciously and then declared, "You cannot enter here without a permit." Shukman, mystified because he "was unaware of having entered anything," returned to the only part of the community where his presence was permissible: the temporary market (1989:141).

If Shukman failed to grasp the private nature of the Indian community, other gringos are blind to its existence as a sociopolitical entity. In Zumbagua, an enormous amount of planning surrounds the annual festival of Corpus Christi and its popular bullfights (Weismantel 1997b); as with similar events in the United States, seats in the bleachers constructed for the event must be purchased weeks in advance. But tourists who arrive at the last minute often clamber up onto the stands, ignoring the indignant shouts of those whose seats they have taken. Delighted with the unfamiliarity of what they are witnessing, they are unable to conceive of the festival as a carefully organized and rulebound event, rather than a spontaneous and chaotic happening in which anything goes.

Whether they are aware of it or not, the actions of these strangers appear to local people as egregious aggressions—even as criminal acts that invite punishment. When I took two young men, one from Chicago and one from Quito, to a festival in a smaller community outside of Zumbagua, some of the celebrants became enraged by the visitors' picture-taking activities and began to threaten them with physical violence. The situation was defused only when others in the crowd recognized me: "Lay off," they told the angry men. "Those aren't strangers—that's Tayta Juanchu's comadre from Yanatoro and her guests."

In American popular culture, entire genres of horror stories begin with the open road: the lonely hitchhiker, the ghost behind the wheel of a semi, the lurking killer who attacks young couples in parked cars. Despite a superficial resemblance, the friendly yet ominous white man who accosts an Indian walking down a path does not belong with these denizens of the public way. The horrors attendant upon the ñakaq are of a different sort: his kinfolk include the shadowy figure on the other side of the shower curtain, the man hiding in the closet or under your bed; his is the strange voice on the phone who whispers, "I know where you live." The special horror of the pishtaco is that he appears *inside* a zone that is, if not the private home of the nuclear family, nonetheless a domesticated space belonging to a community of Indians.

The pishtaco, then, insists upon treating the private Indian world as public space open to whites, and so endangers the fragile defenses of an indigenous community already weakened by the incursions of the outside world. In the cities, the female produce market threatens to create a domesticity without walls, destroying the fundamental distinction not only between public and private, but between commercial and familial relations. Their collapse of public and private makes these incursions seem uncanny and dangerous; but as violations of the estranged geographies of race and sex that paralyze the Andes, the appearance of these anomalous figures where they do not belong also invests them with all the allure of forbidden freedoms.

ESTRANGEMENT

The chola and the pishtaco are cultural inventions that use race to push people apart. Pictures of cholas crystallize a racial distance between the subject and the viewer, momentarily solidifying the notorious fluidity of Andean racial categories. In reality, the cities, like the markets, remain racial "crossroads" filled with people in motion; the white myth of the chola strives unsuccessfully to freeze the action, and so to secure racial boundaries. The Indian myth of the white bogeyman, too, intervenes when friendly white foreigners appear unexpectedly, causing local people to perceive them as monstrous.[20] Both figures express an ineluctable estrangement that residents of the Andes feel from themselves, their societies, and one another. That the end of the twentieth century finds people thus alienated should come as no surprise: a quality of estrangement has characterized the entire age, according to the writers who defined modernity.

Durkheim wrote of anomie (1951); Freud of a quality of self-estrangement that he took to be universally human, but which his interpreters have more commonly found to be symptomatic of his moment in history. Marx, too, wrote of estrangement, which he linked to modern structures of inequality. In *The Economic and Philosophic Manuscripts,* he says that estrangement (*Entfremdung*) is inescapable in capitalist society because class relations in capitalism destroy our ability to know and appreciate one another as fellow human beings.[21] Owners of capital appear "alien, hostile, powerful" to workers, who see the bosses enriching themselves at their employees' and customers' expense (1964:114). The wealthy, in turn, refuse to recognize in their workers a common humanity, reserving their sympathies for members of their own class (119).

Class difference, Marx writes, creates a world "of estranged labor, of estranged life, of estranged man" (117); in the Americas, we exacerbate these estrangements with the alienating ideology of race. Cultural imagery of all kinds is saturated with exaggerated and distorted representations of the differences between white and brown bodies—and between women and men as well. Even the relationships between human beings and material objects are estranged when things become commodities. Living in such a world, we do not feel surrounded by fellow humans, or even by tangible objects, but by alien beings incapable of sharing our own embodied experience of social life.

Although these estrangements are pervasive, inequality structures the manner in which we experience them. In the southern Andes, a chance encounter with a privileged stranger fills powerless people with such dread that they see not a man but a spectral white killer. The powerful, in contrast, upon encountering an Indian or a woman, conjure up a corporeal arena in which they are free to assert their will—even to enact depredations that exceed those licensed by class. A mutuality of mistrust, coupled with an asymmetry of power, defines each interaction before it occurs.

When these estrangements extend into landscapes and cityscapes, the resulting racial geography reinscribes itself on the body as fear: finding oneself in the wrong place is upsetting, even dangerous—and so too is the unexpected appearance of someone who doesn't belong. White men in Indian country, like women of ambiguous race who straddle the boundary between country and city, frighten the poor, who try unsuccessfully to defend their home territories against intrusion. And because they represent an unrealized potential for social upheaval, these fantastic figures threaten the security of elites as well.

The open-air markets, an implosion of rurality into the heart of the city, collapse the distance between rural Indian and urban white public space. So, too, do pishtaco stories, which begin when metropolitan strangers appear abruptly in the rural heartland. What makes these acts so troubling is not that they violate the Andean geography of race, but that they expose its unacknowledged aspects. Cholas and pishtacos—both in story and fact—reveal the relentless movement of people and things across social boundaries, driven by processes of unequal exchange that link together metropolis and periphery, commodity exchange and domestic consumption. These interconnections are as structurally integral to the geography of race as is the phenomenon of estrangement.

Part Two

EXCHANGE

....

CHAPTER 3

Sharp Trading

From the geography of estrangement, we now turn to the welter of interconnections that bind Indians and whites, women and men to one another. Exchange—economic and sexual—is the theme of the next two chapters. The previous two chapters were about impediments to motion: estrangement, distance, and barriers both real and imagined. Now we are going to see some action: exchange sets things and people in motion, propelling them toward one another. In this chapter, racial categories like the word *chola* begin as labels affixed to mannequins in a museum, but they come to life in the marketplace, where vendors use them as insults and invitations designed to provoke the passive onlooker—and her money—into active engagement.

JUST LOOKING

The city of Cuenca, once the Inca town of Tomebamba, has built a glistening new anthropology museum atop some of its archaeological ruins, one of a string of regional museums built under the auspices of the national "Casa de la Cultura." On the ground floor, visitors travel through Ecuador's past: from shell middens to Inca q'eros,[1] then on to gold-encrusted paintings of the Virgin and patriotic portraits of national heroes. The historical sequence ends at a staircase, where a sign directs the visitor to climb upward into the ethnographic present. The upper floor is laid out not chronologically but geographically: the viewer is led from the Amazonian rainforests to the coast, and thence to the Andean highlands. Each region features a series of vignettes, peopled with life-sized mannequins dressed in *traje típico* (traditional attire) and surrounded with appropriate artifacts. The exhibition is large and ambitious: Amazonian natives sit within replicas of traditional houses; in the coastal section, plaster fishermen push actual reed boats into the painted surf. The displays about the highlands are arranged to mimic the corridor of the Andes itself, traversing the nation from north to south. The sequence begins in the northern province of Imbabura, with a display featuring Otaveleños weaving textiles; then proceeds to the central highlands, represented by Indians from Cotopaxi wearing Corpus Christi costumes; and finally arrives in the southern provinces, where the figure of a Saraguro man plows a nonexistent field, using a wooden plough pulled by plaster oxen. After completing this tour of the nation as a whole, one enters the last and largest room, devoted to the city of Cuenca itself.

The room contains several clusters of figures, all depicting the same folkloric type: la Chola Cuencana. In one vignette, cholas are portrayed as vendors in an open-air market, seated on the ground surrounded by the fruits and vegetables they sell. They wear layers of brightly colored pollera skirts, and shawls with a delicate, ikat-dyed pattern and a long, elaborately knotted fringe; each mannequin is crowned with a Panama hat.[2] Another grouping features a still more elaborately dressed chola, leading a mule festooned with an exuberant display of foods and flowers; this scene represents Cuenca's famed "Paso del Niño" procession, a Christmas event honoring the infant Jesus.

While the size and prominence of the section devoted to Cuenca makes this museum unique, the form of the exhibition as a whole—a gigantic map of the nation in which each region is portrayed by a distinctive human "type" surrounded by folkloric props—is a common enough didactic tool, found in museums, schools, books, and posters.[3] One of the most elaborate examples is the museum at the Mitad del Mundo, a national monument marking Ecuador's location on the equator. Inevitably, Cuenca is represented there by the chola. The hundreds of schoolchildren from nearby Quito, the nation's capital, who are regularly brought to the museum, learn there that the two large mannequins dressed as "Cholas Cuencanas" symbolize a city far to the south, which many of them will never visit (Radcliffe and Westwood 1996:74). These folkloric figures suggest a quaint and rural place comparable to Ecuador's Indian communities, and completely unlike Quito. There is no hint here of Cuenca's own self-image as a commercial hub that rivals the capital city in importance: celebrations of cultural difference in national museums are carefully crafted to enhance, rather than threaten, the centripetal power of the state.

Selected tenets of a somewhat outdated liberal cultural anthropology serve the designers of these exhibits well: the suppression of history, the promotion of the concept of ethnicity rather than race or class, and, as Radcliffe and Westwood observe, the erasure of relationships between ethnicities. All the different groups, the cholas of Cuenca among them, are arrayed on a timeless plane of difference like species of butterflies pinned to a sheet of cardboard. The Mitad del Mundo provides a small map next to each figure, in which one discrete region has been highlighted in red; there is no overlap between the areas highlighted on one map and those shown on the next (Radcliffe and Westwood 1996:74). In the Cuenca museum, each small cluster of figures is separated from the others by walls and walkways, producing a sense of isolation enhanced by the low barriers that prevent viewers from coming too close.

An emphasis on absolute difference between populations in turn demands that the groups themselves appear entirely homogeneous. In the case of the cholas, this sameness disguises the economic heterogeneities of the actual market, where a tremendous gulf separates the prosperous women who rent stalls inside the market from the desperately poor street hawkers who circle around the outside. But then, these displays strive to excise all political or economic dimensions: they represent only "culture," a matter of folk art and festivals.

Ironically, the end result of this relentless quest to present only positive and playful images is a viewing experience more dispiriting than lively. We saw few visitors on the days that we went to the museum in Cuenca, although the library was busy with students doing research projects. In the empty exhibition halls, the mannequins seemed not so much inanimate as long-dead. Even the real objects and articles of clothing—the plough and spindle, ponchos and polleras—were rendered unreal: their individual histories of toil were opaque, like the objects archaeologists label "ritual" because their use is no longer known.

Although it is far humbler than the palatial state museums, the little museum at the shrine to the Virgen in Baños, a spa town in a warm, beautiful little highland valley, provides a quite different display of the nation. The shrine, which attracts invalids, pilgrims, and tourists, has turned its cloister into a museum devoted to the Virgin's extensive wardrobe of elaborately embroidered and decorated robes and shoes.[4] These gifts from her devotees fill several large rooms. Other rooms contain desiccated stuffed animals, warped blowguns, and dusty ceramics from the rainforest—exotica in the Sierra, for although the jungle is close by, the descent from the highlands is difficult. These rooms are tributes to Baños's geographical location at the beginning of the torturous Baños-Puyo road, a major link to the interior lowlands—and to the Virgin's special role in protecting travelers from the mudslides that make the journey so treacherous.

The covered porticoes that connect these rooms are lined with a series of glass cases displaying objects from each of the nation's provinces, including Azuay, the southern province of which Cuenca is capital. This haphazard collection reminds the viewer of the Virgin's national importance and her power to attract worshipers from every corner of the country. It also situates Baños within the nation and provides a gracious reminder that other cities, too, have their own attractions.

Perhaps because they lack scientific pretensions, these display cases provide a more heterogeneous and less racialized vision of regional difference than the professional exhibitions of the Casa de Cultura. Some contain objects that might be found in more than one province, for example, thus violating the strict segregation of regional cultures. There are references to a province's major industries and photographs of noteworthy modern buildings—aspects of life unmentioned in the folkloric version of the nation. The display devoted to Azuay does not attempt to fabricate a mythical "chola," but rather to show an array of economic and artisanal activities in which real cholas take part: the exportation of Panama hats, the mounting of the annual Paso del Niño procession, the making of ikat-dyed shawls and embroidered skirts.

The state museum in Cuenca holds many of the same items: hats, shawls, and skirts, and a Paso del Niño float. But these objects have been emptied of their material history; their only function is as symbols of ethnicity. Shorn of economic or political utility, the mannequins' actions, too, have an enforced purposelessness. The scene of the cholas in the marketplace, for example, renders commerce into a ghostly shadow-play: no money changes hands. In fact, these vendors have not been provided with any customers, and the chola's faces are frozen into unaccountable grimaces. In the designers' impulse to reduce social life to a static set of cultural clichés, we can read the outlines of a disavowed intellectual history.

"Mestiza de Cusco con vaso de chica," Martín Chambi, 1931.
Courtesy Chambi family.

Above: "Damas Arequipeñas en la chichería," Martín Chambi, 1927.
Courtesy of the Chambi family.

Below: Two indigenous women from Quiguijani, Quispicanchis, drinking together.
Martín Chambi, n.d. Courtesy of the Chambi family.

Heloísa Huanotuñu surrounded by her family, Rumichaca de Yanatoro, Zumbagua, 1997.
Photograph by Stephen F. Eisenman.

A Cuenca market in the early 1940s. Photograph by Pal and Elisábeth Keleman. Courtesy of the Latin American Library of Tulane University.

Scene from the Huaraz market, 1974. Photograph by Fernando La Rosa. Courtesy of the artist.

Rosa Loja of the Mercado 10 de Agosto, Cuenca, 1997.
Photograph by the author.

Above: Detail of a retablo by Nicario Jiménez. This middle segment of a three-tiered retablo shows the pishtaco of the 1960s, with airplane, car, and hacendado on horseback. Photograph courtesy of the artist.

Below: Detail of another retablo by Nicario Jiménez. This retablo depicts the scissors dancers of Ayacucho performing with shears and whips. Note the women in polleras. Photograph by the author.

Left: "Las gemelas": two market women of the Mercado 9 de Octubre, Cuenca, 1997. Photograph by the author.

Right: Paso del Niño parade, Cuenca, 1997. Photograph by Stephen F. Eisenman.

Paso del Niño parade, Cuenca, 1997.
Photograph by Stephen F. Eisenman.

Seeing Race

This museum is intended, among other things, as a corrective to the prejudice against Indians and blacks endemic in Andean society. And yet a covert racial message can be read in the careful phrasing of the wall texts, which do not treat all groups alike. Most of the people portrayed in the Cuenca museum are Indians, although the coastal displays do include Afro-Ecuadorians playing the marimba. Only two groups are classified as "mestizo": the cholas and some fishermen identified as "montubios." This intrusion of a mixed-race category into the world of blacks and Indians undermines the exhibition's coherence. The word "Indian" is not mentioned in the other exhibits, which rely upon ethnic/regional terms such as "Saraguro" and "Otavaleño." But in describing chola and montubio as variations on mestizo, the texts are forced to make reference to Indians as an explicitly racial category— both to explain what cholas are not, and, trickier still, to explain how they came to be. The Indians, understood to be autochthonous, need no origin story; the concept of a "mestizo," in contrast, brings the unbecoming history of miscegenation into an exhibit designed to avoid it.

Chola is meaningless outside of a set of other, contrasting racial categories: Indians, mestizos, and whites. This set of differences, unlike ethnicity, cannot be arranged as equally important locations scattered across a horizontal plane. Theirs is a hierarchical relationship, in which every name takes its precise meaning from those directly above and below it, so that a *cholo* is whiter than an Indian but less white than a mestizo. Ultimately, each is measured by its distance from the racial pinnacle: pure whiteness. The ethnographic map tries to disconnect itself from these discriminations, replacing the history of racial hierarchies with a fictional, two-dimensional space in which difference exists, but inequality does not. The inclusion of cholas and montubios transects this cultural map with the stratigraphy of race, and so abruptly introduces a suppressed third dimension. Suddenly the map of Ecuadorian ethnicities is not horizontal and timeless, but vertiginous and diachronic. Like the Andes themselves, this social landscape cannot be mapped as a featureless plain. It is scarred and bent, deeply marked by a series of volcanic upheavals—wars and revolutions, Indian rebellions and their brutal suppression—that forced it into its contemporary contours. Systems of knowledge about the Andes cannot be innocent of this violent history: however bloodless the contemporary museum's display of ethnicity, it cannot completely disguise its origins in the science of race.

Racism flourished in South America and the Andes in the nineteenth century, as it did throughout Europe and the Americas.[5] "All is race, there is no other truth" wrote British novelist and politician Benjamin Disraeli in 1847: these were, indeed, in Stocking's words, "the dark ages . . . of anthropological ideas." [6] In the writings of Gobineau and Gustave Le Bon in France, Mathew Arnold and Cecil Rhodes in Britain, and S. G. Morton and Josiah Nott in the United States, race predetermined a nation's economic, intellectual, and military vitality. It predicted as well a colonized people's propensity to civilization and a colonizing nation's likelihood of achieving imperial mastery. "The more perfected a race," wrote the fin-de-siècle French colonialist J. M. A. de Lanessan, "the more it tends to spread; the more inferior a race, the more it remains sedentary." [7]

Scientific racism reached its apogee in the late nineteenth century — a period that was, not coincidentally, one of the bleakest for Andean people of native and African origins. European scholars eagerly assisted in the construction of specifically South American racial typologies: the expansion of existing systems of knowledge to include new regions was an exciting opportunity. The trouble with Ecuadorians, wrote the French geographer Elisée Reclus, is that they are mostly *métisses,* with only a weak infusion of Spanish blood (1895:446). In Peru, scientists determined a bipartite division of the populations into *Limeño* and *Serrano;* in Ecuador, a tripartite separation into white (coastal), cholo-Indians (highland), and savages (rainforest). Peruvian physician Hipólito Uñanue published such a scheme in 1805; [8] some decades later, in his *Account of Travels in Peru, During the Years 1838–42,* the influential German geographer J. J. von Tschudi published a more elaborate version, describing no less than twenty-two racial castes in Lima alone, ranging from mulatto (white father and Negro mother) to Zambo claro (Indian father and Zamba mother) to Indio (Indian father and China-Chola mother) [1847:114]. Each caste in turn, according to von Tschudi, defines itself in opposition to its nearest neighbor. He writes, "The Mulatto fancies himself next to the European, and thinks that the little tinge of black in his skin does not justify his being ranked lower than the Mestizo, who is after all only an *Indio bruto*" (116).

There were always dissenting voices. In contrast to the profound racism of von Tschudi, who not only argued that the "Negro" skull and brain more closely resembled that of monkeys than of Europeans, but also called the movement to free black slaves in Peru "a plague to society," German naturalist Alexander von Humboldt wholly rejected what he called "the depressing assumption of superior and inferior races of man." [9] At the end of his life, he claimed that all humans formed a single community, and all had a right to freedom and respect (1840:

351). But although Humboldt's writings about his travels in the Andes gained him immense fame, his ideas about race had little influence. The intellectual project of dissecting the spectrum of human variability, isolating and labeling each "type" and then locating them precisely within one vast racial taxonomy, continued on apace.

When the British explorer C. Reginald Enock wrote his several studies of the Andean region at the end of the nineteenth century, he gave considerable attention to describing its several races. "Whilst in general terminology," Enock writes,

> the Quechuas and Aymaras are called Indians, they must not be confounded with the savage tribes of the forest, from which they are distinct in every respect. They are, in addition, generally known as Cholos, or Cholo-Indians. They have, of course, absolutely nothing in common with the imported negros of the coast, and are not necessarily dark-skinned—their complexions sometimes being relatively light—although they are beardless. They are strong and hardy in constitution, and are much sought after as mining laborers, having a natural aptitude for this work. (1908 : 143−44)

As this passage makes apparent, the pure science of race had many practical applications. For the colonial powers, it provided a means to catalog conquered peoples, and so to develop a blueprint for social engineering: mountain Cholos to work the mines, imported Negroes for the coastal plantations. As the ex-colonies became modern nation-states, scientific racism helped manage the inherent conflict between democracy and capitalism. The "natural" inequalities of race provided a ready explanation for the continued and even exacerbated existence of great economic disparities within the new societies, despite their fervent dedication to political equality. The appeal to the science of race to resolve this central contradiction can be found in the foundational writings and speeches of Simon Bolívar—and in modern South American political thought ever since.

Sexual identities were marshaled to the task as well, and not only because the natural inferiority of women was also the subject of its own new science. In Latin America, the act of sexual intercourse was likewise redefined and racialized; in this new role, it was seen as instrumental in the originary myths of conquest, and in the new nationalist mythologies of mestizaje as well. In the Andes, the word *chola* bears this heavy mythological burden, as we shall see in the next chapter.

The origins of the word are obscure; it appears to have entered Spanish early in the conquest period, and to have diffused throughout the empire; today, it has quite different meanings in the various parts of the territory that once belonged to Spain.[10] In California, for example, *cholo* has been around for a long time—but has recently gained new currency among non-Latinos as a synonym for the African-American "homeboy," a term suggestive of gang affiliation and definitively associated with urban youth culture. In the Andes, too, it can connote the urban, streetwise working-class youth; but racial meanings predominate. Here, the geography of race is incarnated by the cholo, whose body and mind are seen as loci of unresolvable conflicts between Indian rurality and white urbanity. And because this racialized body is highly sexualized as well, the female body of the chola signifies in a radically different register from the male body of the cholo—a fact that has often been lost on social scientists.

Seeing Cholos

Anthropologists have been at some pains to define the cholo, as can be seen in table 1, a handful of quotes selected almost at random from ethnographies of Ecuador, Peru, and Bolivia written during the past thirty years. Despite some variation, the central core of ideas is clear. Cholos are neither white (mestizo) nor Indian, a position more often defined in cultural or geographical than explicitly racial terms. Whiteness is Western civilization, modernity, upward mobility, acculturation, even Methodism or the cash market; it is Lima, the city, national culture. Indianness is rural, local, community. And, as we saw in chapter 1, this racial contrast is temporal as well as spatial. Cholos are moving forward: they *had been* Indian but *are becoming* white. Movement through space thus becomes movement through time, for just as produce moves between rural and urban markets, so too the vendors are seen to move toward whiteness. In reality, this racial identity would be better expressed as an oscillation, for vendors appear Indian to whites, and white to the Indians; a person who works in both rural and urban markets may literally move back and forth from one identity to the other. But in the social science literature, this movement is conceived in Darwinian terms, as unidirectional, evolutionary, and inevitable: the cholo is an Indian who approaches—but never achieves—whiteness.[11]

Despite their desire to define this contrast in ethnic rather than biological terms, many authors find it necessary to refer to race, however obliquely: indigenous origins, Indian descent, Indian background. In a 1972 doctoral dissertation, Leslie Brownrigg felt comfortable using the phrase "racial mixture." By 1997, Deborah Poole still needed the concept; but, writing for an audience that was not only wider than Brown-

Table 1　A Sampling of Academic Cholos

Doughty 1968

"a people . . . increasingly influenced by modern Western civilization as mediated by Lima. Yet they are inevitably bound, in various degrees, to their respective local and regional traditions. It is this ubiquitous . . . human being who has been popularly and scientifically referred to as the *cholo* . . . a person who is neither Indian nor mestizo in a cultural sense."

Brownrigg 1972

"Cholo, chola, cholita . . . a term denoting Indian background and racial mixture. . . . [M]arginal individuals born and raised in an Indian context but who have personally acquired Hispanic speech, dress, economic roles, and lifestyle. . . . Indians . . . if they adopt modern dress . . . come to be labeled 'cholos' or 'chazos' outside the community—a recognition of their special status as well as a mockery of their inexact attempt to acquire the national culture."

Isbell 1978

"cholos, . . . sometimes used in a derogatory fashion to refer to upwardly mobile people who have neither become fully integrated into the dominant society nor fully shed their peasant identity."

Guillet 1979

" . . . cholo, a term that signifies an aggressive acculturated peasant."

Lehmann 1982 (from the glossary of an edited volume)

"cholo: Person of Indian descent, but, by virtue of cultural adaptation and economic position, above the mass of *indio* peasants in social status."

Skar 1982

"The complete transformation from Indian to *misti* may occur over several generations. A first generation Indian may only partly make the transformation thus becoming a *cholo*—an intermediate category."

Crandon–Malamud 1991

"The term cholo varies in usage . . . but on the southern altiplano it refers to those Aymara who have entered the cash market. . . . In Kachitu, however, cholos happen to be mostly Methodists. Perhaps because that is the case, Kachituños are reluctant to use the term in town where it is considered derogatory."

Turino 1993

"*Cholo*. A word that is used relatively to refer to people in social transition from indigenous to mestizo identity. It is sometimes used to refer to rural highlanders in cities; it can be a term of disparagement when used by people of the upper classes to refer to highlanders."

Poole 1997

"*Chola* refers to a woman of indigenous origins who has adopted urban or Spanish clothes and who may or may not be of 'mixed race.' In modern usage, *chola* (or *cholo*, masculine) usually carries a derogatory or insulting connotation."

---

rigg's but that had grown more critical in the intervening years, she found it necessary to distance herself from the phrase by using quotation marks.

If scholars have moved from a racial to a cultural definition of the chola, popular opinion—both Andean and foreign—remains firmly fixed in a racialist conviction that cholas are physically different from whites, and that this difference is immediately visible. Tourists from Europe, Canada, and the United States think of market women as a racial group different from themselves and from middle-class residents of the Andes. Some told me that the women were "Indians" (this from newcomers, and from people who hadn't read any books about the Andes). Others, better informed, welcomed the opportunity to show off their new vocabulary: they called them "cholas"—a word that they earnestly explained to me in overtly racial terms. When I asked my informants why they identified the women who sold in the plazas as "Indians" or "cholas," they would inevitably reply, "Just look at them!"

These beliefs echo those held by residents of the Andes. Doña Lola's teenaged son, despite his criticisms of Cuenca society as racist, unhesitatingly told us that the cholas of Cuenca are not white. When I asked him how he knew this, he, too, replied with great conviction, "Just look at them!" Especially with the slight laugh and offhand gesture that accompanies it, this phrase has a double meaning that reveals the duplicity of race itself. The command to "look" sounds like a simple appeal to empirical evidence: the market woman's race is a visible, and hence incontrovertible, fact. With a slightly different intonation, though, the exhortation to "Just *look* at them!" is no longer a call for objectivity, but an invitation to enjoy another's abjection. It asserts that the object of vision is somehow laughable or shameful, even degraded.

The hollow claim to empiricism offered by race becomes apparent if one obeys the injunction to "just look at" market women. The more I looked, the less I could see the racial indicators that were so readily apparent to others. Indeed, the more time I spent looking at market women across the highlands of Ecuador and the Andes, the more I realized that this group of people shared only one physical characteristic: heterogeneity. Market women are brown-skinned, black-skinned, and fair-skinned; they have straight hair, nappy hair, and wavy hair. Mostly, they look like the other working-class people of their city or region. Sometimes, as with the many Afro-Ecuadorian produce vendors in Otavalo, a town renowned for its Indians, the markets reveal hidden facts about the rural populations surrounding an urban area. But wherever they are located, the markets, with their high proportion of migrants and itinerant merchants, are inevitably home to a far more diverse group of people than is usual in the Andes. Only in the neighborhoods of the very wealthy does one find a greater cosmopolitanism, for the movements in and out of those parts of the city are international rather than transregional.

Zumbagua, a rural parish high up in the páramo, is a place where people really do look pretty much alike as far as clothing and coloring are concerned. The Saturday market there is a kind of ethnic fair, which introduces different kinds of people—European backpackers in their unisex clothing, Otaveleño men with their long pigtails, even a black-skinned man from Esmeraldas—to a rural population largely unfamiliar with them. The permanent residents of the little neighborhood around the market square, too, are more varied in appearance than is the rest of the parish. Enter one building adjacent to the square and you may find a beautiful and well-liked Afro-Ecuadorian woman cooking meals for sale; she has lived in the parish for years and founded a family there. Another woman in the same line of work has reddish hair and freckles—traits so anomalous in that black-haired, brown-skinned world that she considers them to be disfigurements.

In Cuenca, too, the markets are populated with people whose clothing, hair, or skin color betray exotic origins. It is one of the only parts of the city where one sees indigenous people from the province of Azuay itself: Saraguros and Cañaris show up as occasional customers, although not usually as sellers. Among the vendors, one occasionally sees a style of dress or hears an accent from far away. A fruit stall in the market at the Plaza Rotary, for example, was run by sisters from Chimborazo Province, dressed in their characteristic blue *anaku* skirts, densely woven sashes, and long strings of tiny orange beads.[12] They carried on a quiet conversation in Quichua with one another even while they spoke to customers and other vendors in the distinctive Spanish of Azuay. A friendly woman selling photographs in the city park showed her African ancestry in the texture of her hair and the shape of her face—a great rarity in the southern highlands.

This internal variation is overshadowed by similarities: the women of each market have their distinctive style, treasured by tourists and locals alike as emblematic of the cultural—and racial—distinctiveness of the region. As a result, the racial significance of the word *chola* varies from place to place. In Cuenca, a city that prides itself on its European heritage, the racial associations of the word are subtle, whereas in other highland cities, such as Cuzco, the chola is unambiguously perceived as an Indian. In the lively cultural context of La Paz, cholas are often described as urban Indians, a phrase that elsewhere in the Andes is a non sequitur. Coastal cities like Lima and Guayaquil saw a more complete extirpation of indigenous populations and a concomitantly greater involvement with the African diaspora during their colonial histories; market women (and working people in general) there are more likely to be seen as black or mulatto than Indian—although they still may be referred to as "cholas."[13]

Indeed, as I discovered in Cuenca, the question of the market woman's race is inextricably linked to regional identity. Older Cuencanos believe that the rural residents of Azuay are inherently different from urbanites, but unlike Doña Lola's son, they insist that these differences are not attributable to Indian origins. They maintain adamantly that the cholas of Cuenca, like the city's aristocracy, are a direct import from Spain unblemished by racial admixture. Until recently, according to this vision, the small towns and rural areas around the city were exact replicas of a long-vanished European pastoral.

Working-class residents of the city expressed to me a different but not wholly unrelated point of view. They absolutely refused to entertain the idea that the word *chola* has negative connotations. When I pressed the issue by insisting that elsewhere in the Sierra the word is taken as a racial slur, maids, taxi drivers, and market vendors politely suggested that I did not understand Cuenca. What people thought in faraway Riobamba, Latacunga, or Quito was absolutely without relevance to the southern highlands. Implicit in these statements is a racial discrimination between the "white" southern highlands and the "Indianness" of the rest of the Sierra—a distinction that, in the discourse of well-to-do and ambitious Cuencanos, plays a part in the rivalry between Cuenca and Quito as centers of international commerce.

Despite this cherished regional identity, the wealth of racial epithets in daily use suggest that Cuencanos hardly find themselves free of non-white undesirables. Asked by an eager student of Spanish what words one should call out if one's purse were to be snatched by a thief in the market, Doña Lola thought for a moment, then astonished her questioner by replying not with textbook responses such as *"Alto!"* or *"Socorro!"* ("Stop!" or "Help!"), but with the following: "Well, you must shout out, *'Longo sucio! Hijo de puta!'"* ("Dirty Indian! Son of a whore!")

Despite the supposedly unimpeachable European origins of the Chola Cuencana, every middle- or upper-class Cuencano to whom I spoke was emphatic that no one from a "good" family could marry someone related to a chola. As an expatriate Cuencano explained to me via e-mail before I went there, "Everyone in Cuenca will tell you how proud they are of their Cholas Cuencanas. But just let one of their sons bring one home with him as the girl he wants to marry, and that little *morlaquito* [slang term for Cuencano] will find himself out in the cold. You won't hear anything about the lovely traditions of the cholas then." And indeed, my landlady, asked how she would respond if a son or daughter wished to date the child of a chola, retorted unhesitatingly, *"Mijo, porque te metes con esa longa?"* ("Son, why mess with that Indian?")

Thus among white Ecuadorians, the difference between Indians and cholas disappears completely when either is linked or compared—even hypothetically—to whites. Tourists, too, find the market women of Cuenca indistinguishable from Indians. The travel literature on the city is liberally sprinkled with references to cholas, and here again one finds confusion as to whether the chola is, or is not, an Indian. Some authors identify the "Cholas" of Cuenca, like cholas elsewhere, as being of mixed race. Sometimes they append a clarifying note explaining that a chola is more Indian than a mestizo, or is a "mestizo in which the Indian dominates." Alternatively, market women may be described as Indians "ruined" or "contaminated" by exposure to city life. Standing in the midst of the congestion and filth of the city, they have lost the purity and nobility associated with Native Americans; but surrounded by dead chickens or dirty potatoes, the products of Indian hands, they have scarcely achieved racial whiteness in exchange.

Cholas and Cholos

In its mixture of biological and cultural language, and in its endless regional variation, the meanings of the word "cholo/a" seem hopelessly muddled. In 1977, Pierre van den Berghe and George Primov published *Inequality in the Peruvian Andes: Class and Ethnicity in Cuzco,* which would become one of the most widely cited studies of ethnicity in the Andes. Using a few objective criteria, especially language and clothing, the authors attempted to cut through the welter of ethnic terminologies in use among academics and ordinary Peruvians alike in favor of a simple dichotomy: all Cuzqueños were either Indians or mestizos. Only two kinds of people defeated their attempt to impose sociological order. One was a small band of leftist intellectuals, who deliberately donned Indian attire as a political statement and taught themselves a highly academic Quechua. For the authors, this tiny group was only superficially a problem: the high social status of its members made the notion of classifying them as Indians preposterous, despite their linguistic and sartorial pretenses. With hindsight, the authors' readiness to jettison their own analytical apparatus, designed to overcome racial prejudice, in favor of "common sense" knowledge is all too telling. But at the time, the conundrum posed by the students' attempts at speaking Quechua and wearing ponchos was deemed inconsequential.

A more significant problem was posed by "a large class of women . . . often referred to as cholas . . . who are urban by Peruvian definition, and who frequently engage in market trading" (120). These confounding individuals clearly were "not Indians," but the authors hesitated to classify them as mestizos either. Despite the dry language, one can almost hear the scientist's frustration at a phenomenon that eludes categorization. Between the rural Quechua-speaking Indian and the urban Spanish-speaking mestizo steps a group of people more urban than not, yet more Indian than not; bilingual yet preferring Quechua, a highly stigmatized language, over the prestigious language of the conquerors. And they are women.

Throughout their work, van den Berghe and Primov ignore gender, assuming that all ethnic categories come in two sexes, like animal species, and that in academic discussions of ethnicity, the masculine can safely be used as the default. The anomaly presented by the vendors, then, is not only ethnic: it also momentarily forces women into the picture and pushes men briefly into the background. The authors note in passing that it is only the women who pose a problem: their husbands fit easily within the criteria for "mestizos." But they do not develop this observation.

More recently, other authors have had a great deal to say about the asymmetry that sex introduces into racial categories. Marisol de la Cadena quotes rural Peruvians who say, "*Las mujeres son mas indias*": women are more Indian (1995). Joel Streicker, in a subtle and incisive analysis, finds that white and black masculinity are conceived quite differently in rural northern Colombia; moreover, different sexual behaviors on the part of the same individual are described as either white or black (1995). Carol Smith writes that gender transects racial categories in nationalist mythologies of mestizaje throughout Latin America, which depict "Spanish/criollo and mestizo men . . . [as] active, predatory, virile"; Indian and mestiza women as "fertile, chingada, disloyal"; and Indian men as "powerless, emasculated" (1996:157). Recent studies by Diane Nelson (1998) and Abigail Adams (1998) comment on the sexualized rhetorics of racial politics in Guatemala. There, ladinos use sexual humor to disparage a Maya woman, Nobel Prize–winner Rigoberta Menchú, and rumors about affairs with white women to discredit prominent Maya men.

In the Andes, the word *cholo* is clearly gendered, as Seligmann pointed out in 1989.[14] Although the total range of meanings of *cholo* and *chola* may be roughly the same, so that they can operate simply as male and female versions of each other in specific contexts, the pattern of usage for each word is strikingly different. Burkett captures a typical image of the male cholo when she describes him as "drunk, bumbling, meek, and not very bright."[15] One of the most interesting discussions of this disparaging sense of the term was written by Peruvian sociologist Aníbal Quijano, for whom the male *cholo* exemplifies urban pathology: an embittered, unbalanced, and violent social character, the very type of Durkheimian anomie induced by the loss of traditional mores (1980).

The feminine inflection *chola* shows up less in urban sociology than in the lyrics of corny songs: "*Ayyyy, mi cholita linda*" ("Oh, my beautiful cholita"). The marketplace chola, with her traditional costume and her basketful of fruits and vegetables, has become a colorful type not unlike the "Baiana" immortalized in camp by Carmen Miranda.

As images, then, the male cholo represents an unpleasantly destabilized present, the female chola a vanishing yet unchanging past. In real life, though, cholas are more easily identified than their male counterparts. In her 1972 study of ethnicity and class in Cuenca, Leslie Brownrigg conducted a series of photo apperception tests, in which city residents were asked to identify the ethnicity of individuals through photographs. Her results are strikingly gendered. Photographs of certain women—especially women shown working at such occupations as selling bread or butchering meat—were almost universally identified by her informants as "cholas" (1972:77–122). In contrast, only one ambiguous photograph of a group of men elicited the word "cholos"— and even then, most respondents chose other terms: "indio," "chato," [16] "del pueblo" (of the people), "del clase bajo"(of the lower class), "pobre" (poor), or "campesino" (peasant) [84].

Nevertheless, eager to arrive at a systematic (and gender-neutral) compilation of results, Brownrigg placed this photograph, together with the photographs of women identified as "cholas," in a general category "cholo." [17] The other photographs of men in her *cholo* category had never been described as cholos by any Cuencano (1972:82– 84, 113–16).

These responses suggest that the word *cholo* simply struck Cuencanos as an inappropriate way to describe an unknown man in a photograph, whereas calling an unknown woman a *chola* was unproblematic. Informal address is different: people of many different social classes call one another *cholo* as a teasing or endearing form of address. This can only happen, however, when the interlocutors share the same social background. Indeed, to call someone of the same sex *cholo* without fear of causing offense affirms a racial status identical to one's own—and this in itself contributes to the effect of establishing intimacy. [18] When aimed at a poor man, *cholo* sounds very different: it becomes the most cutting of curse words. The father in Jaime Bayly's 1994 novel about middle-class Lima routinely uses *cholo* and *chola* to address or refer to his social inferiors; the effect is very ugly. In one scene, he becomes enraged upon learning that an elderly newspaper salesman sold his son a dirty magazine; as he sets out to confront the man, he utters the ominous words, "*Ya se jodió conmigo ese cholo maricón.*" ("That faggoty cholo has fucked with me now" [24]). His horrified son, fearful that his father will beat up the old man, hears the epithet correctly: as a denigration and a threat.

We have now pulled words like *cholo* and *chola* down off the museum walls and out of anthropology textbooks, and taken them out into the streets. Here, although they pretend to describe what we see when we look at someone, they say more about how we talk to—and about—one another. Rather than unambiguous descriptions, they are multi-vocal instruments of social intercourse. In one context, *cholo* expresses contempt; in another, it establishes intimacy; in a third, it promises violence. This language pulls people toward one another and pushes them apart; gender and sexual tensions detach the words themselves, so that *chola* and *cholo* no longer mean the same thing. This volatility makes these terms singularly inappropriate as fixed categories for social science. But the same qualities make them perfect tools for the women of the produce market, who inhabit a social world just as mobile—and just as unequal—as the linguistic universe mapped out by the words *cholo* and *chola*.

ACTING UP

Long ago, a wrinkled old market woman in Ambato presented to me, with great ceremony, a tiny wrinkled apple from her own apple tree. Eating its too-soft flesh and feeling distinctly like a character in a fairy tale, I wondered what it meant. Moved for some reason by our conversation, she had suddenly pulled it out from behind the goods she had on display; she said it was too precious to sell. I didn't understand: raised in the cold north, I hadn't yet realized that apples are rare in the tropics, where they are difficult to grow.

Ambato, a big, rapidly growing city in the middle of the Ecuadorian highlands, is memorable to me mostly for truck exhaust and traffic noises. Nonetheless, it calls itself the "city of fruits and flowers," a phrase meant to evoke the lovely neighborhoods where the well-to-do live, as well as the large, active produce market in the town center. More especially, the name recalls the fact that on the broad plains that surround this city, it is possible to grow fruits and flowers of European origin—such as apples. Ambato is lower and warmer than the highland Indian towns perched on the high slopes of the mountains, where only native crops like quinua and potatoes, and a few hardy European imports such as sheep and barley, can survive. And Ambato is higher and cooler than the lowland jungles, hot and damp, where savages and wild animals live and only tropical fruits grow. This temperate location is associated with civility: it evokes Europe—and racial whiteness. The woman who gave me the apple believed that its taste could communicate this identity. With it, she would impart to me something of her own racial identity, embodied in her Spanish surname, her fuzzy crocheted shawl—and the warm sunny yard of her house with its apple tree. With this apple, I think, she hoped to woo me from my decision to go and live with the Indians in the cold, dusty hills where the only fruit is the hard native cherry called *capulí*.[19]

Apples from Ambato, garlic from Riobamba, trago from Angamarca: the products of each region have their special qualities. In their materiality, these foods make a sense impression: they are hard or soft, heavy or light, stinky or sweet—and so are the people who handle them. In the eyes and the noses of their customers, market women are as strong or delicate, perfumed or odiferous as their wares. Sitting in a tavern in a cold, highland town, the narrator of José María Arguedas's *Los ríos profundos* listens to the voices of the women who sell trago (made from sugar cane) and is reminded of "another landscape": "the warm country" of lower altitudes, where sugar cane grows. When the women sing the *huaynos* of their childhood, he hears "the heavy, tranquil rain falling on the cane fields."[20]

As the Panamerican Highway goes from Ambato to Quito, it passes through Latacunga; just outside town is a crossroads where the highway meets up with a big road from the hot, humid coast. When the interprovincial buses slow for the stoplight there, the vendors crowd around the windows. In the high voices of highland women, they cry out that they have *allullas* for sale, letting their voices linger on the sounds: "Ah—zhhhhuuuu—zhhhhaaaas!" The very word *allullas* signifies the region doubly, for its two *ll*'s highlight the characteristic highland "zh," which is very pronounced in the central provinces. To the groggy passengers, those soft, buzzing *zh*'s signal their arrival in the Sierra just as much as the cold gusts of air blowing into the bus. A few years ago, when the economy permitted such small indulgences, everyone rolled down their windows to purchase the bland, crumbly pastries—some to eat now, and a big bag to take home.

For the traveler, places, tastes, and voices mingle together. When the buses go down the steep western slopes toward Guayaquil, they stop at a similar crossroads in the lowlands, where the hot, sticky riders buy mangoes and sugar cane, and colas sold from ice buckets that sweat in the heat. The rapid, indistinct Spanish of the coastal vendors, who "swallow their words," is as rich and soft as the flavor of the mangoes. And in Latacunga, that "zh" melts in the ear like the warm lard soaking through the paper wrapper of the allulla and onto one's fingers, so comforting on a drafty and unheated bus.

One can talk this way in South America, where people enjoy mixing sentimentality and sensuality, but to write like this in English is to risk ridicule—or worse. Anxious to disavow exoticist writers of the past, ethnographers these days assiduously avoid expressing sensual enjoyment of the places where we work. Indeed, anthropology, once the relentless diarist of minutiae, now avoids the systematic recording of sense impressions, beset by an almost puritanical fear of admitting that they matter to us. Instead, symbolic anthropologists expose the pernicious political implications of such descriptions in the work of earlier writers. Economic anthropologists, too, express distaste for conventionally romantic portrayals, in which the sensuality of fruits and flowers serve to gloss over the long hours, hard work, and desperate circumstances of the women who sell them.

Florence Babb, for example, opens her book about the Huaraz market with a lively and enjoyable evocation of her first entrance into the market building, when she unwittingly stumbled upon a celebration honoring the market's patron saint; but she quickly asserts that these impressions were false and misleading. The market's "array of stimuli to [the] senses" is only a "distraction": the vendors' appearance as "picture-postcard figures with full skirts, broad-brimmed hats, and long braids" belies their true significance: "in fact," they "underwrite the Peruvian national economy" (1989:2).

This discrimination between appearances and hidden truths is inapposite. The sights, sounds, and smells of the marketplace are as much material facts as the contributions market women make to the Peruvian economy. And if some writers have evoked the sense experience of the material world in order to justify or excuse inequality, it has been just as crucial a part of the oppositional visions of justice and freedom offered by authors like Arguedas. Concrete relationships between people and things are, after all, the stuff of which both poverty and wealth are made; in the markets, injustice is embodied in the conflict between the sensory perception of abundance and the knowledge that one has no money to buy. Nor can we ignore our sensual relations to one another—the pleasure we take in the voices, the touch, the sight, the smell of other people—for these give solace and sustenance, even in the direst of circumstances.

Babb and Seligmann begin by describing what first drew them to the markets: big, bold women, loud and laughing; an intoxicating mix of voices and bodies, people and food, strong smells and bright colors. Like other ethnographers, however, they quickly move to a more distanced stance; and it is there, withdrawn from sensory knowledge, that they begin their analysis. This book takes a different tack, immersing itself in the evidence provided by the senses, and building its argument from there. For in the places where women in polleras sell onions and noodles, race and sex are produced as much through colors and textures, movements and voices as through words and ideas.

Naming Market Women

Today, the task that van den Berghe and Primov set themselves—to fix and classify every inhabitant of the ancient city of Cuzco by ethnicity—seems not only impossible but downright silly. *Inequality in the Peruvian Andes* is dated by its assumption that the authors can serve as impartial judges, coolly evaluating the messy give-and-take of social life from a vantage point above the fray.[21] Some ten years later, in 1989, Linda Seligmann would write about Cuzco in a very different vein: the ambiguous ethnicity of the city's market women was no longer a problem, but rather a refreshing antidote to otherwise stultifying social hierarchies. Nevertheless, she too fixes these women in place with a name: they *are* cholas.

Seligmann mentions in a footnote that her assertion contradicts what the women themselves had to say:

> Informal surveys and observations show that the term *chola* is rarely used as a form of self-identification except in joking exchanges when it is a form of endearment combined with condescension or in exchanges of insults. In fact, no single encompassing term of self-identification . . . exists, so far as I know. (1989:704n.7)

In 1989, the women's own opinions weren't supposed to matter very much: it was the social scientist's job to come up with an ethnic label, regardless of local practice. But by 1993, when Seligmann published her second article, such authorial omniscience had fallen from favor, and notions of hybridity challenged the idea of clear-cut ethnic categories. This later article begins by cautioning that *mestizo* and *cholo* are "inadequate" as "descriptors of social categories"; what makes these words matter is not their utility in social science, but their use in the give-and-take of everyday social life (188).

By 1996, Marisol de la Cadena would go even further, in an indirect critique of Seligmann's earlier work. Social scientists err, says de la Cadena, when they call the women "cholas": since the vendors themselves dislike the word, and prefer to be called "mestizas," mestizas is what they *are*.[22] The authority to name has come full circle: now, the research subjects' own words are given all the weight once granted only to those of the scientist—including the power to discount the latter's opinions.

In the end, however, this disagreement between Seligmann and de la Cadena, like the one between Orta and Wachtel discussed in chapter 1, presents a false dichotomy. Despite its power to insult, the use of the word *chola* to describe women who work as produce vendors, chicheras, butchers, and cooks is not an imposition by foreign anthropologists, nor the fantasy of literary writers: all Cuzco knows them as cholas. But neither does this word have the absolute definitional power with which social scientists sought to invest it: as van den Berghe and Primov had observed in 1977, it is too freighted a term to serve as an objective description of anyone (128–29). What is needed is an analytical framework that encompasses all these insights.

We might start by asking what people in the markets do call themselves, since everyone agrees that they do not use *chola* in that way. Market women and their peers identify one another through metonymies: terms that identify women by the things they sell, the clothes they wear, or the place they work. Vendors are called *vivanderas,* from the word *víveres* (provisions, groceries); *fruteras* if they sell fruit; *verduleras* if they sell greens; if they work out-of-doors, they may be called *placeras,* women of the plaza. Women who wear the distinctive clothing of a market vendor are said to be *de pollera* (literally, "of the pollera"), in contrast to women in "Western" clothing, who are *de vestido,* from the Spanish word for "dress."

All these terms focus on material aspects of the women's lives, giving them the names of the things that surround them. Vendors categorize their customers along similar lines, as when Teofila, a fruit seller, explained to de la Cadena that

> Mujercitas [Indians] never eat chicken; on special occasions they buy menudo. . . . In February when their own harvest runs out they buy handfuls of potatoes. . . . Mestizas buy second or third category beef meat, maize, wheat, chuño, potatoes, onions. Damas [ladies] buy chicken, first-rate meat, potatoes and fruit of the valley. "Gringos" [the foreign workers of the development institutions] buy lots of fruit, vegetables and chicken. (1996:135)

These taken-for-granted references to the material life of the market—its physical spaces, the foods for sale there, the clothing worn by its inhabitants—contrast sharply to recent ethnographic writing, which finds physical descriptions morally bankrupt, or factually misleading. Paralyzed by the discredited politics of "the gaze," anthropologists have become reluctant to analyze what they see. And indeed, a short history of how scientists have looked at market women seems to validate this mistrust.

Turn-of-the-century studies of race in the Andes, such as Chervin's 1908 tome on the physical anthropology of Bolivia, were explicitly visual: scientists and amateurs alike compiled enormous photographic catalogs of human "types," which inevitably included pictures of women labeled as "cholas" (Poole 1997:134–37). The fabrication of these curious artifacts was motivated by a kind of scopophilia, a desire to scrutinize the nonwhite body; as with pornography, the development of this fetishistic practice was made possible by the new technology of photography.[23]

A century later, we still define our projects against those earlier scholars, whose beliefs we now find repellent: thus van den Berghe and Primov's insistence in 1977 that race does not matter in the Andes, and their deliberate obliviousness to the phenotypical details that obsessed Chervin. Nevertheless, these anthropologists are still *observers:* they keenly scrutinize the city of Cuzco, discounting what its residents say about themselves in favor of what their own eyes tell them. The contrast between their approach and that of de la Cadena is profound, for in the years between 1977 and 1996, ethnography became infused with the dialogic sensibility championed by James Clifford and others (Clifford and Marcus 1986).

De la Cadena records what market vendors said, but not what they looked like—nor the material qualities of their speech and gesture. Unlike previous scholars, she gives the vendors' statements more weight than any other form of evidence: when they say that they dislike the word *chola,* they convict the neo-indígenistas of racism and misogyny. The other piece of evidence against the Cuzco intellectuals is their predilection for depicting the bodies and voices of cholas real and imagined: their very attention to the physical qualities of these women is cause for suspicion.

Her case is convincing. But if foreign scientists and native romantics enjoyed looking at cholas too much, and for the wrong reasons, we do not rectify their errors by refusing to look at all. The market women's anomalous location on the social map might seem to be a projection on the part of elites and outsiders, but it is also a product of what the *women themselves* do and say. Indeed, in the testimonies de la Cadena collected, the vendors returned often to the topics of food, clothing, and speech. Unlike the anthropologist, they find that these, too, speak. As the women talked to her, they were giving more than one kind of testimony: even while they rejected the idea that they are cholas so emphatically in their referential speech, they may have been saying something quite different in the indexical statements made by their polleras and their hats.

Costumes and Accents

Market women struck van den Berghe and Primov as ethnically anomalous because of two things: clothing and language. Other anthropologists' efforts to define the cholas' indeterminate racial category, too, are replete with references to costume and speech. Dress figures often as a metaphor in their writings, as when Isbell refers to those who have not "shed" their peasant identity. Any discussion of ethnic categories in the Andes inevitably begins by detailing the sartorial differences between Indian and white clothing in a particular region. The contrast in skirts, earrings, shawls, and hairstyle must be cataloged precisely, before the reader can comprehend how it is that the chola's dress expresses a racially indeterminate status.

Thus in Latacunga, Indians wear their hair in a single bundle, the *huangu,* tightly wrapped with woven ribbons until it is as rigid as a stick.[24] White women, in contrast, cut their hair and have it styled in a salon if they can afford it, or treat it at home with bottles and boxes of store-bought chemicals. The chola hairstyle differs from both: stereotypically, the woman dressed de pollera wears her hair in two thin braids tied together at the end with yarn. This tripartite system— perms, braids, huangus—is largely invisible to outsiders, but familiar to any local resident.[25] Variations on the pattern are common—and highly expressive. Thus when white women dress up as "cholitas" in civic parades, the pinning on of false braids is an essential part of the costume—and the subject of much laughter and silliness.[26] An Indian woman may braid her hair to go sell in the market (although she often opts for one braid, rather than two), while an urban market woman who sells mostly to white customers may cut and curl her hair. People notice: the first time a vendor appears with her new hairdo, her compatriots in braids may well scorn the change as an affectation and an affront.

Styles of speech, too, indicate a person's race and class, as I learned for myself. After spending time in Zumbagua, my voice, accent, and intonation patterns when speaking Spanish began to resemble those of a Quichua-speaker. When people could see me—an obvious gringa— they usually found this hysterically funny;[27] but on one occasion I got an inkling of what it can mean to sound like an Indian. Having been invited to the house of a wealthy Quiteña, I showed up at her address and was confronted by the tall, forbidding walls and locked gates necessitated by the city's high crime rate. When I spoke rather hesitantly into the intercom, my hostess interrupted me harshly and told me to go away immediately and never come back. Hearing my awkward, Quichua-inflected Spanish, she had mistaken me for a recently fired employee returning to beg for another chance.

The speech of cholas, it is said, is neither Indian nor white. Brownrigg describes the market women who have "permanent posts" in Cuenca's markets as the possessors of "a characteristic speech pattern, a high pitched, ungrammatical Spanish" that evokes the "stylized falsetto" of the monolingual Quichua-speaker (1972:95).[28] But, she says, the Cuenca cholas do not speak as Indians do: "An Indian, whatever his dress or customs, speaks a heavily Quechua-accented Spanish . . . distinct from the speech of city *cholos*," while the latter, whatever their clothing or occupation, "share a singsong Cuenca accent" (107). (As elsewhere, she has generalized an observation about women into a statement about "cholos.")

In the southern highlands, servants in elite households were once famed for their elegant clothing—and their aristocratic manner of speech. Brownrigg, who was in Cuenca in the late 1960s, was able to interview women who worked in the city's "Casas Grandes":

> Servant women attached to aristocratic households, whose *chola* costumes are almost a livery of their occupation, may imitate the speech of upper-class women, another distinctive "sung" Spanish. The gentility in speech and manners of such traditional servants is truly charming. Their speech, like that of upper-class women, is said to be danceable. "*Cuando se habla una Cuencana, la gente se pone a bailar*"—When a Cuencan woman speaks, people begin to dance. (Brownrigg 1972: 107–8)

Cholas' distinctive clothing and language enraptured poets and philosophers. Moises Sáenz spoke admiringly of the chola "singing half in Spanish half in Quechua," and "her fluffy petticoats of boiling colors." Cuzco poets lauded "your round skirts and your blouse of percale," "your two braids" like "two vipers along your back," "your fourteen skirts and your pure wool shawl." In Cuenca, too, verses were penned about the chola's pearl and filigree earrings; her embroidered underskirt, as "incendiary" in its effect on the poet as in its bright hue; and of course the hat made of toquilla, "tilted to one side as though winking" at her admirer, its whiteness "turning your brown face into a flower."[29]

These evocative phrases hint at the inadequacy of social scientific descriptions, especially those that characterize chola style as a simple mixture of Indian and white. Market women's clothing certainly borrows articles from both these other vocabularies. In Latacunga in the 1980s, some women secured their skirts with a sash, like an Indian, and then covered the upper half of their bodies with a white woman's crocheted shawl. But the most noteworthy elements in dressing de pollera are items not found in other women's clothing, Indian or white: the distinctive hats, the special jewelry. Even absent these specific items, de pollera clothing is too dramatic to impress the viewer as a mere muddle of borrowed identities; it is unmistakably sui generis. Indeed, what makes the vendors' clothing distinctive in some regions is its very excesses: where everyone wears hats, none is as tall and white, or as tiny and curvaceous, as a chola's; where Indian women wear polleras too, the pollera of the market woman is bigger, brighter, shorter, more multilayered.

Shops near the market in Cuenca display ikat-patterned shawls dyed in brilliant, almost psychedelic hues of pink or chartreuse, and thick wool skirts in even brighter hues. I stopped in one store to admire tiny, sequin-studded polleras made for the Baby Jesus. I had first seen this distinctive form of ritual cross-dressing in Baños. Among the clothing on display in the shrine were gifts sent by worshipers from the southern highlands: finely made matching sets of embroidered skirts and straw hats for the Virgin and Child. Back in Cuenca, the shop's owner and her daughter were friendly and loquacious; they themselves dressed de vestido, but they showed off their young seamstress, who wore lavish polleras like the ones for sale.

Despite being a "traditional" garment, the pollera is highly susceptible to trends and fashion fads. (As are indigenous garments: in the early 1980s, velours and terry cloths were all the rage in Zumbagua women's shawls, but not so a few years later.) In 1981, Sofía Velasquez "explained the attributes of the ideal pollera for a fiesta" to the Buechlers. According to the La Paz fashions of the day, such a skirt should be "made from a thick, textured, acrylic velvet, named 'chinchilla' . . . Because of the thickness of the material, such a pollera had to be sewn by hand with three, rather than the more usual four, pleats." Chola jewelry, too, had its own "intricacies" into which one must be "initiated." The heavy pearl earrings with floral motifs were decorative, the Buechlers report, but they were also important markers of prestige; women invested their savings in them, confident that they would keep their value better than the inflation-prone Bolivian currency (1996:7).

Even more so than polleras and earrings, hats identify their wearers as ready to trade. Traveler's sketches from the past century show vendors wearing huge, showy toques.[30] Today, Cuzco's tall white stovepipe, Cuenca's "sombrero de paja toquilla," and the Paiceña's tiny "sombrero hongo" (bowler, lit. "mushroom hat") still command attention. To the cognoscenti, the quality of a woman's hat marks her success at her trade. In Cuenca, a famous maker of fine straw hats has two showrooms: a shop at street level that features the stiff, white-painted hats favored by cholas, and a studio upstairs that caters to tourists, where the hats are soft and straw-colored. But his apprentice confided to me that the downstairs room is little-frequented, for fewer and fewer women can afford to buy hats of that quality.

In Bolivia, the true chola paiceña wears not just any bowler but a real Borsalino. (In one of the ironies of the postcolonial world, the "Italian" Borsalino is no longer made in Italy: when Italian men stopped wearing hats, the factory closed its doors in Europe and moved operations to the altiplano, home to thousands of loyal female customers.)[31] Hat styles change, too, as the Buechlers discovered in 1975, when they decided to buy chola outfits for their daughters—and received another lesson from Sofía. "The hat, we learned, had to be light gray, to correspond to the latest chola fashion, the crown had to be high and the hat relatively small, so that the hat could be worn at a jaunty angle and with the combed back hair showing above the forehead" (7).

The first descriptions of market vendors' clothing that appear in my field notes are from Latacunga, where I watched the festival of the Mama Negra, described in chapter 6. The festival is sponsored by the women of the big market of El Salto, who march alongside the costumed performers during the parade down the streets of the city. The performers' outfits were certainly eye-catching, but the festive garb of the sponsors attracted attention as well. Their homburg hats were brand-new, the plush carefully brushed, with jaunty little feathers sticking up from the hatbands. Their knee-length skirts were gathered into knife-edge pleats and embroidered at the bottom with metallic threads; their underskirts, in contrasting colors and borders, peeked out from below. Above, they wore shiny blouses, fuzzy acrylic sweaters, and shawls with long, silky fringes.

Fifteen years later, Stephen and I watched women de pollera march in another parade, Cuenca's Paso del Niño. Here, the colors and fabrics

were far more exuberant: the polleras were canary yellow, brilliant orange, or scarlet, and the straw hats were dazzling white, tall and stiff,
adding inches to the women's height. Most beautiful of all were the
ikat-dyed shawls, many of them antiques brought out for the occasion
and worn with pride and ceremony. The bicolored woven designs were
of birds, animals, or flowers; other, more elaborate patterns—including baskets of fruit, letters, and numbers that spelled out place names
and dates, and the escutcheon from the Ecuadorian flag—had been
knotted into the long fringes. Newer shawls were chartreuse or hot
pink, the older ones pale blue; in some, the knotted designs had been
picked out in brightly colored metallic threads.[32]

In both parades, feet caught my attention. Unlike white women
in the Andes, who teeter on the highest of spike heels in rainbow colors, the vendors wore dark, dressy little pumps, severe and almost masculine in style.[33] A feminine vanity showed itself nonetheless, for these
were the tiniest possible shoes into which the feet of a stout matron
might be squeezed. Hemmed at the knee, their skirts allowed a co-
quettish display of ankle and calf—and created an imbalance between
the large, heavily clothed upper halves of their bodies, and their lower
legs.

On those occasions, we saw women de pollera dressed in their finest;
but even on ordinary days, market women's clothing calls attention to
itself—as do their voices. Vendors of different products each have their
own distinctive musical call, of which the allulla seller is only one. When
I first came to the region, I stayed in a small hotel in Salcedo overlooking
the market; early each morning, long before dawn, I would begin to
hear the vendors' different calls. "Escooooobas! Escooooobas!" boomed
a man who walked the streets, his voice swelling and fading as he passed
my window: "Brooms! Brooms!" The women who sold lupins came
later, and settled in one place, their voices sweet and mocking: "Chochos! Chochos!" they twittered.[34]

Saenz liked the chola because she "speaks in a loud voice, a little vul-
garly," and indeed, market women are famously loud and verbally aggressive. This attribute has sometimes been overemphasized. Although
Andean market vendors are certainly willing to engage in a verbal scrap
when offered the opportunity, they are part of a highland cultural
world noted for a quiet, "closed" (*cerrado*) demeanor stereotypically described as "melancholic." In many markets, the really serious conversations about price take the form of quiet, insistent, almost secretive
negotiations. A customer returns again and again to a stall, waiting until
there are no other customers, to murmur her best offer, or a vendor pur-
sues a reluctant buyer down the street, tugging on her clothes and whis-

pering in her ear. In Zumbagua, the loudest vendors are not the women from the highlands, but the male fish sellers from the coast, who

> yell and shout at passersby, . . . cajoling, threatening, begging, and teasing them to buy. They keep up a constant loud sales pitch and try with their boisterous, irrepressible sallies to get a retort from the soft-spoken "Indians" they despise. (Weismantel 1988:75)

Collectively, all these voices make a lot of noise: the auditory experience of the market is a disorienting hubbub of people talking, whispering, laughing, and shouting—a constant hum punctuated with louder voices. In Otavalo, Collier and Buitrón recall "a ventriloquist whose doll laughs and talks to his audience, selling a marvelous medicine guaranteed to close any wound" (1949). Pablo Cuvi speaks of "the shouts of a woman advertising the Bristol Almanac that shows the new moon and the old moon" at the Latacunga market (1988:50). Shukman offers an evocative reminiscence of his entrance into La Paz at night. He arrives in darkness, approaching from a distance: the city first makes its presence known through the "shouts of vendors and hagglers in the streets" falling upon his ears "loudly" and "thickly." "Even without seeing it," he comments, "I could hear that La Paz is the largest permanent market on the Altiplano" (1989:111).

Individual interactions in the markets can be lively. Accustomed to doing fieldwork in indigenous communities like Zumbagua, where it can be difficult to initiate conversations with strangers, I was unprepared for the Cuenca market women, who were totally unafraid of me and quick to speak their minds. When I told the women from whom I bought fruit that I didn't have a blender—the favorite appliance of South Americans—they expressed not only amazement but scorn. After chiding me energetically and engaging in a thorough-going attack on the thoughtless Cuenca landlords who would claim that an apartment without a blender could be described as furnished, they settled in to interrogate me in exhaustive detail about the contents of my kitchens in both Cuenca and the United States.

In December, when I brought back photographs I had taken the previous July, young women snatched them impetuously out of my hands, pushing me out of the way and yelling to one another to come and look. A senior market woman, curious to see what was causing all the ruckus, descended in stately fashion from her stall and held out her hand for the photos. The gang of girls subsided immediately, according her all the respect that I had not merited. Once she had looked, smiled, and nodded appreciatively at me in regal fashion, she too began shouting loudly to other senior women around the building, reporting on what she had seen: "She took a photograph of the Orellana sisters! And one of poor Blanca Mendoza, who is in the hospital now."

In clothing and language, the market vendor has a singular presence. Like the boldly printed words on an advertisement, or the gaudy colors of a circus performer's costume, this is a display designed to stand out in a crowd. In fact, women in the produce market can often be seen showing off, acting up, trying to draw a crowd. "[V]endors and clients alike make private exchanges into public performances to gain the sympathy, support, and at times derision, of the general public," says Seligmann (1993 : 189). The atmosphere is that of a theater, not a museum or a laboratory—and it is in theories of performance, not in racial typologies or catalogs of ethnic types, that we will find ways to interpret the language, clothing, and gestures to be found there.

Performing Race
The word "performance" immediately brings to mind the influential writings of feminist philosopher Judith Butler. Butler's theory of performativity, first expressed in her 1990 book *Gender Trouble,* swept through the humanities and social sciences with gale force. It knocked down creaky constructions of ethnicity like van den Berghe's and breathed new life into identity politics, now understood as a contest of tactics and maneuver, rhetoric and play rather than of essence and being. Identity, Butler says, is not an epistemological fact at all, but an ongoing, improvisational performance, which takes shape through the "mundane signifying acts of linguistic life" (144). These acts, not language itself, are what matter, because language is not "an exterior medium . . . into which I pour a self": there is no singular, stable identity behind the representations.

Butler's work relies upon that of earlier queer theorists, who became fascinated with gender behavior intended to mislead: transvestism, or cross-dressing.[35] These analyses are oddly reminiscent of anthropological discussions of cholas, for in relying so heavily upon sartorial clues, ethnographers unwittingly echo the language of the transvestite. Anthropologists who want to explain what *chola* means begin by describing all the items of dress and manner that distinguish an Indian from a white, as I did above in describing styles of hair. Cross-dressing, too, must start from a familiar vocabulary that enables spectators to read a clothed body as either female or male: there can be no crossing without lines to cross.

Early readings of transvestism emphasized the contrast between what is seen (the gender of the dress) and what is hidden (the sex of the body).

Descriptions of cholas, too, refer to an Indian body incompletely disguised as white. But gender theorists have become more nuanced in their analyses of the difference between passing and drag—a helpful distinction when thinking about cholas.

Passing—whether racial or sexual—is a signifying act that attempts to con the viewer into misreading the relationship between the clothing and the body; if it is successful, the error may never be discovered. In the Andes, where prejudice against Indians is rampant, there is ample motivation for trying to pass—and plenty of examples of failure. Every day country boys put away their ponchos and purchase polyester clothes in rural markets; when they arrive in the city, however, their newly purchased outfits earn them only derision for their outlandish and outmoded styles. Such boys are teased as "chagras"—hicks.[36]

Anthropologists looking at cholas have seen them as chagras: since the chola's clothing does not really mime that worn by whites, writers describe what they see as a kind of poor copy, an inexpert attempt to look completely white. The implication would be that, like those country boys, cholas do not understand the dressing code well enough to put on a convincing performance. But although market women's clothing mixes items of Indian and white, it is hard to read in it a failure at "de vestido" costume. Why not just put on a dress?

A comparison with queer theorists' analyses suggests that drag might be a better analogy. Passing tries to avoid detection, but drag invites it: we laugh at the burly man in high heels and frilly lingerie because he is so obviously *not* what he pretends to be. This kind of sexual cross-dressing is common in Andean folk performances. In the 1980s, the costumed skits and dances performed in Zumbagua on Corpus Christi included a short play about marriage, featuring a man and his cross-dressed "wife." The pair danced, fought, and mimed copulation, eliciting gales of laughter from Tayta Juanchu, Heloisa's step-father.

In such performances, there is no attempt to disguise the fundamental incongruities between body and clothes: the gender "mistake" is clearly—and intentionally—on display. In the United States and Europe, contemporary drag performances abandon even the pretense of cross-dressing; instead, they combine articles from both male and female sartorial vocabularies, creating a clothed body that offers a proliferation of contradictory signs, confounding the viewer's ability to "read" the performer's sex. These performances more closely resemble the costumes of the women who sponsor floats in Cuenca's Paso del Niño or Latacunga's Return of the Mama Negra. They, too, make no attempt to convince onlookers that they are "really" either Indian or white; and like a straight audience at a drag show, viewers equipped with only two racial categories find themselves frustrated in their desire to read a unitary race into what they see.

A famous non-Western example of cross-dressing, the Native American *berdaches* or two-spirit people, offers another comparison.[37] In his classic study, Walter Williams did not find "men dressing like women," but rather bodies draped in layers of male and female clothing:

> Pete Dog Soldier . . . is remembered as having worn a woman's breastplate, shawl, and undergarments, but always men's pants. . . . A nineteenth-century Kutenai . . . was remembered as wearing "a woman's dress, below the bottom of which his masculine-type leggings were visible." (Williams 1986:74)

Such mixed messages have the effect of disrupting our belief in a unitary identity for the body underneath. If it were just a dress, there might really be a man underneath; if the clothing were clearly mestizo, the woman underneath might be simply an uppity Indian. But if the clothing is itself layered, multiple, subject to more than one reading, the body that inhabits it might turn out to be equally complicated. In this sense, too, we might liken the chola's clothing to a drag performance. To attempt to pass as white would be to admit to white racial superiority; to fail at the attempt would inadvertently admit racial inferiority. But to intentionally occupy a position in between is a brazen disruption of the binary categories themselves.

But surely, one might object, a market woman is nothing like a burlesque artist: the skirts and hat she wears to work are her real clothes, not a costume. Butler, however, refuses to accept the naturalness of anyone's clothing, or their identity; and indeed, in the Andes dressing *de pollera* is always a conscious choice. Susan Paulson and Pamela Calla describe a rural Bolivian potato farmer who spends most of a day "cooking, serving, digging, harvesting and sorting potatoes," occupations that identify her as an indigenous campesina.

> In the late afternoon, however, her identity shifts. . . . Faustina hurries back to her patio where she wets and combs her hair, rebraiding it with shiny hair pieces and brightly colored tassels. She quickly changes into her best market clothes; the *transportista* is due at 6:00 to load the potatoes, and if he thinks she is some dirty Indian he'll cheat her. . . . She spends the night in the back of the truck, bouncing along on the bags of potatoes. . . . Arriving at the Cancha market before dawn, Faustina arranges her produce in a market stall rented by a cousin who lives in the city. She is

careful not to intrude on the space of the neighboring chola vendors, as they resent her presence, calling her a clumsy campesina.
Nevertheless, in her short pink pollera and tight lace blouse glit-
tering with plastic pearls, Faustina competes successfully for the
attention of passing customers. (Paulson and Calla 2000: 3)

Even women who wear the pollera daily, and whose credentials as
"chola vendors" no one could question, wear it as a matter of choice;
other vendors, including those whose mothers wore the pollera their
entire lives, dress de vestido instead. Similarly, some women put on the
pollera for the first time as an adult, having dressed differently as a child.
Their descriptions of making the change show that the completed outfit is as deliberate a construction as any showgirl's.

Sofía Velasquez is one such woman: having grown up dressed de
vestido, she planned her transformation for a long time. Her reminiscences about her first appearance in a pollera are strikingly reminiscent
of sexual transvestites, who often try out their new personas at costume balls before making a daytime appearance. Sofía adopted a similar
strategy. She joined a dance troupe in which all the members perform
in color-coordinated polleras. She bought the same outfit as the other
women, practiced with them, and appeared in public with them; but
when the other women returned to their de vestido outfits the next
day, Sofía left her pollera on for good. As she explained to the Buechlers, joining the troupe gave her an excuse "to purchase the expensive
clothing and jewelry of the properly dressed chola" (1996: 171).

A more common story, perhaps, is that of the Indian girl from the
country who decides to make the change. One such woman, Lucrecia
Carmandona, told her tale to Marisol de la Cadena. As a young girl,
she began working for a white couple as "an Indian servant." Her "pa-
trona" had a garden on a small plot of land; one of Lucrecia's jobs was
to sell the vegetables at a nearby market. With this experience, she began to plan her transformation into a full-time produce vendor. She
used her wages to acquire the "typical" white hat and apron of a market
woman—clothes that she kept carefully hidden from her employers.
"'Neither of these [the hat or the apron] I wore when I was in the
house. They did not want a mestiza as a servant, they wanted an Indian,'" she told de la Cadena. When she was fifteen, and "already knew
how to sell, and could be a mestiza," she ran away to the city of Cuzco,
where she bought "a basket and a few bananas."

> "Walking up and down the streets, with my basket, my apron and
> my hat, I was still learning how to be a mestiza, I was not one yet,
> and people did not consider me totally one. I was not a servant

any more, but I was still working in the streets. Now people consider me a mestiza, a very good mestiza. I have a permanent stall in the market place, I have good clothes, but I had to learn a lot before this." (de la Cadena 1996 : 33)

We see in this statement Butler's concept of "iteration": a successful performance must be rehearsed many times before it appears "natural." But the appearance of naturalness through iteration is only one of the things people do with identities: Butler also speaks of playfulness, innovation, and improvisation. Lucrecia desires nothing more than to convince others—and herself—that her new identity is real; but other women, in other contexts, prefer to contradict themselves and to tease and mislead others. Indeed, such contradictions and misdirections may be inscribed in the very costume in which Lucrecia so earnestly discovers her new identity.

This, says Butler, is a good thing, for it is by "causing trouble," by playful disruption, that restrictive labels are best attacked. "Laughter in the face of serious categories," she says, "is indispensable for feminism" (1990 : vii–viii). De la Cadena misses this potential for subversive laughter in her earnest interrogations—but market women do not: irony and double entendre are their stock-in-trade. The Cuzco vendors sounded sincere in what they said about being called "cholas" to a sympathetic scholarly interlocutor, and they have ample cause for real bitterness. But they are not always so serious; and besides, they are ill-placed to complain about racial and sexual slurs, for when it comes to insults and epithets, market women have few peers.

In 1993, Linda Seligmann wrote about an amazing series of arguments she recorded in the Cuzco markets between vivanderas and their customers. The insults are rich and inventive: in the space of just a few minutes, one vendor calls a wealthy woman a "stinking dame," a "prostitute," and a "pig with lice eggs between her thighs" (Seligmann 1993 : 192–93). The use of metaphor is also striking: one woman turns racial difference into a difference between animal species when she refers to an Indian as a "smelly llama woman"; another expresses class difference in mineral terms, calling bourgeois women "women of glass," whereas she herself is a "woman of steel" (1995 : 20). The customers were no slouches, either. It was clever of the market woman to call an indigenous shopper a "llama"—an animal that, like Indians, is an "*autóctono*" or "*natural*," a "native" of the Andes. But the woman responded with a far more pointed insult in the same vein, calling the vivandera a "mule woman" (1993 : 197). An animal halfway between a donkey and a horse, born of forcible interspecies miscegenation and unable to mate, the mule evokes some ugly meanings of the word *chola* that will be explored in the next chapter.

Seligmann points out that it is in contexts such as these that one actually hears words like "Indian," "chola," and "mestiza" in the market: not in serious statements of self-identity, but in verbal contests and performances where they are momentarily seized upon, then tossed aside. The vendors treat race words as useful expressions to be stockpiled for future performances—indeed, as an arsenal of epithets for deployment in future battles.

They also use racial and sexual images of themselves to attract customers. Selling the products of Indian labor to urban buyers, vendors market their own autochthony; when they hawk industrially produced foods to rural customers, they show off an urban sophistication that makes their merchandise more desirable. They can be warm and womanly, the image of the mother you never had; or reassuringly masculine in response to a timorous femininity ("These are the best in the market! Buy them—you won't be disappointed"). The potato seller who donned her "short pink pollera and tight lace blouse," described above, is a case in point:

> She plays up her Mizque identity; Mizque potatoes are known for their quality. She converses merrily with male customers and jokes with them in Spanish; important traits of urban mestizo manliness are established through flirtatious relationships—as well as sexual encounters—with indigenous women. With urban housewives, however, Faustina ingratiates herself . . . with humble poses and phrases sprinkled with Quechua. She knows that by emphasizing her Indian ethnicity she can better please clients whose own sense of identity (whiteness, educatedness, cleanliness, female purity) depends on their superiority to her. (Paulson and Calla 2000 : 3 − 4)

Each little drama demands a different performance. A woman must flirt with one customer and flatter another, defend herself from an abusive cop, berate a tardy *cargador,* show appropriate interest in another vendor's gossip. Rapidly alternating between moods and dialects, the woman in the pollera might be hard put to explain when she is expressing her "true" self and when she is "just" acting. Is the machine-gun Quichua loaded with coarse Spanish curse-words that she fires at a slow-moving porter her "real" speech, or is it the polite Spanish filled with flowery Quichua endearments with which she addresses her customer? To women trying to make a living in the raucous, lively environment of the market, this question is irrelevant—possibly even meaningless. Indeed, it may be that what annoys market women when elite men call them cholas is not only the connotations of this particular word, but even the assumption that their identity can be captured by any one word. In the market, racial identities are not unitary or even hybrid, but infinitely prolific.

Dialogues

In the United States, discourses of identity insist upon its naturalness: if not biologically innate, a credible claim to an ethnicity or sexuality must originate in some kind of essential truth, deeply felt and fervently espoused. In contrast, the race and sex at play in the market make no attempt to disguise their artifice or their evanescence. The "llama woman" and the "mule woman," the "woman of glass" and the "woman of steel," not to mention the "pig with lice eggs between her thighs" are utterly fantastic. The inventions of a moment, their very absurdity is designed to enrage one's opponent, as well as to amuse and delight an audience of fellow vendors and passersby. In a sense, Butler's work is not as perfectly germane to this setting as it initially appeared, for its main thrust is to make us question apparently "natural" performances; these are nothing of the kind. To interpret the exuberant theatricality at play in the markets, we may be better served by a theory expressly dramaturgical. Nor is it difficult to decide where to look, for to mention the words "theater" and "market woman" together must immediately call to mind the greatest theorist of the modern stage, Bertolt Brecht. After all, Brecht created the most famous market woman of the twentieth century: Mother Courage.

As a playwright and director, Brecht's approach differs in one crucial regard from that of social scientists and philosophers: he analyzes method. He does not want to know why other people did what they did. He wants to know how to do things himself: how to use speech, clothing, and gesture to create an effect. And because his theater is explicitly revolutionary, he is especially interested in whether a particular kind of performance might actually change the people who witness it. In his analyses, then, we can find some very specific tools for understanding market women's performances—and the reactions of their audience.

Like Butler, or the vendors themselves, Brecht values subversive humor. In the opening of *Mother Courage and Her Children*, for example, he lampoons the notion of identity. Asked by a soldier to present her identity papers, Courage responds by "rummaging in a tin box"; she then offers him, in rapid succession, the pages of a missal "to wrap cucumbers in"; a map for a place she's never been; and proof that her dead horse is free of hoof and mouth disease. "Is that enough paper?" she queries (1955:27).

Here we can find a first principle about method. Brecht's method of attack is a fast-paced exchange of words, in which the soldier's stiff language provides a springboard for Courage's wit. Asked for a license, she offers her "honest face" and protests that she wants no rubber stamp on it; when the soldier, incensed, demands if she is "pulling his leg," she turns his cliché into an obscenity, insisting that she is not "pulling anything of his." He says the army needs discipline; she retorts, "I was going to say sausages." This adroit substitution of useful things for empty symbols depends upon a particular rhetorical form: dialogue.

Like Mother Courage, market vendors in the Andes are at their best in verbal give-and-take. Negotiations, arguments, flirtations, and gossip are the stock-in-trade of the market, as they are of the playwright. Social analysts have repeatedly observed that vendors dislike making straightforward statements of self-identity when asked point-blank; indeed, they claim to be unable to do so. And yet, as Seligmann notes, the language of race is heard everywhere in the markets—but only in dialogues that are not about identity at all. Like Mother Courage, the vendors seem to find things like cucumbers, sausages, and sex more important.

The fundamental place of dialogue in the market is revealed through one surprising fact: people come to the produce markets in search of certain kinds of conversations as well as for food and drink. Seligmann writes of wealthy women who emerge from their chauffeur-driven cars, immediately get involved in an acrimonious dispute with a vendor, and leave without making a purchase. It is hard to avoid the conclusion that these dames came expressly to have an argument, like characters in a Monty Python comedy sketch. In a very different vein, Gregorio Condori Mamani goes to the markets and chicherías whenever he needs companionship, information, or assistance—even when *looking for a wife*. In these episodes, buying a glass of chicha or a hot meal is just an excuse to start a conversation with a woman de pollera.

The dialogues in the produce market appear particularly freewheeling, a kind of no-holds-barred discourse that draws attention—and customers—because it is unique to this particular locale. Nineteenth-century travelers to Lima commented in their letters home on the contrast between "the raucous public market where mulatas sold their goods" and the private gardens of the city's elite families, "inner sanctums" of peace and tranquility (Poole 1997:96). This same contrast is replicated today when a woman enters domestic servitude. Once she leaves the market, the loud, vulgar voice she had as a vendor is muted, if not silenced completely.

In the early 1980s, Tom Miller found silence, not "danceable" speech, to be the hallmark of the Cuenca domestic. While researching the Panama hat industry, he was befriended by a hat wholesaler named González, who invited him along on a purchasing trip. As they drove out to Biblián, a small town known for both cholas and hats, Miller noticed another passenger in the car.

> A woman sat in the back seat the entire trip as if she wasn't there; she didn't say a word, nor was she spoken to. . . . I motioned to her, mouthing silently: "Who's that?"
>
> "Oh, her." González seemed surprised . . . "That's my servant," he said, at once answering the question and dismissing the subject.
>
> "What's your name?" I asked her later.
>
> "I'm the servant," she replied.
>
> I introduced myself. "And you are—" I said, hanging the sentence in midair.
>
> "—*para servirle,*" she answered. At your service. (1986:142–43)

It is a common enough phrase, and yet her deft use of it to avoid telling him what he wants to know is reminiscent of the quick verbal wit of the vivandera. Nevertheless, the contrast between this self-effacing presentation and that of the women in the plaza could not be more complete.

An incident recorded by Seligmann illustrates this difference perfectly. When an exchange between a butcher and her well-to-do customer turned into a heated argument, the butcher began insulting the buyer loudly and fluently in Quechua. The woman turned to ask her servant (who had accompanied her to carry the packages) what was being said, but the domestic only shook her head and feigned ignorance. In the presence of her employer, she defended herself with silence. Even suppressed speech might be punished: in 1932, a Bolivian employer dragged her maid into court for "perverse" and inaudible "muttering" (Gill 1994:27).

Women selling produce seem to suffer no such constraints; indeed, the freedom with which Cuzco vendors insult members of the city's elite is remarkable. However, the apparent anarchy of the market is a carefully fostered illusion, for a motivation far stronger than self-expression shapes the vendors' speech: they are there to sell vegetables.

At the chapter's beginning, we saw that museum displays empty the market of meaning when they suppress its economic aspects; we must be careful not to repeat the mistake with our theatrical metaphor. And this, of course, is where Brecht is so very useful, for his theater is never merely entertainment, nor does he ever forget the material needs that drive his characters. If the designers of ethnographic displays hope to paper over the fault lines of their societies, Brecht wants to expose them. He wrote *Mother Courage* expressly to provoke our reaction against the nature of market exchange: its cruelties, its inequities, its inherent contradictions.

Every conversation in the market is structured by inequality. If small-time vendors sometimes work as domestic servants, big market women are often employers; and as bosses, they have a terrible reputation. Condori Mamani has bad memories of working for market vendors who paid him only in food, or for a place to sleep: the work was grueling, the accommodations poor, and the verbal abuse incessant. Zenobia Flores, a runaway, was

> taken home by a chola woman, who saw her crying and walking aimlessly down a street, and for a year Zenobia worked for this woman, grinding chilies into powder and selling in a small dry-goods store. She was never paid and frequently went hungry, and the woman eventually abandoned her on a street corner. (Gill 1994:63)

Nor are such abuses limited to wage relations. Buying and selling, too, is riddled with antagonism and exploitation—tensions that underlie the daily dramas of the market.

Brecht's dialogues expose the conflict that lies at the heart of exchange: a series of duplicitous and soul-rending negotiations drive the plot of *Mother Courage and Her Children* to its devastating end. Frederic Jameson comments on how unusual the playwright is in this regard: whereas other writers depicted class conflict as hostilities between workers and owners, Brecht wrote about business and market exchanges, too, "as a ferocious struggle between two eternally hostile groups" (Jameson 1998:69). The engagements between produce vendors and their customers are simultaneously seductions and fencing matches, in which each side wants something from the other but is unwilling to cede any more than absolutely necessary in return. Brecht was fascinated with this odd mix of attraction and mistrust, which he explored in the *Three Penny Novel*. He begins with the seller's antagonistic vision of the buyer:

The client normally materializes before the shopkeeper as a skin-flinted, ill-intentioned, mistrustful individual without any needs at all. His attitude is unequivocally hostile. He perceives the seller, not as a friend and counsellor, prepared to help him in every way, but rather as a two-faced and evil person who is out to seduce and deceive him. . . .

And then introduces the necessary obverse. Perhaps, the seller thinks, he has "misperceived and misrepresented" the buyer:

he may be better than he looks. It is only tragic experiences in the bosom of his family or in business life that have made him closed and mistrustful. At the very core of his being there persists a quiet hope ultimately to be recognized for what he really is, namely, a buyer of grand proportions! He actually wants to buy! He needs so very very much! And when he has no wants, he is miserable! So he really wants to be persuaded that he needs something. He requires instruction! [38]

Behind the humorous exaggeration in this caustic portrait, we can grasp something of what drives the vendors' performance: they must not only persuade but "instruct" the buyer in his own secret wants. Like Brecht's seller, they are locked into a relationship of real and imagined desires with their buyer. If the most successful vendors continually reconfigure themselves as the fascinating opposite of their interlocutor, as Faustina did, it is in hopes that the buyer in turn will satisfy their own desires by becoming that fantasy figure, the "buyer of great proportions."

This is where race and sex become so useful, for their binarism defines an alter who can supply what ego lacks. The white woman responds to a humble Indian, the Indian to a big white friend; the older buyer to a sweet little girl, and the younger one to mama. The versatility these performances demand finally makes the vendors' clothing comprehensible: its odd jumble of Indian and white features are like the heterogeneous musical instruments carried by a one-man band, on which the seller can play any tune she needs. But always, the vendors' willingness to satisfy one's desires is evanescent, and the exchange of identities illusory: what is real is the money and the produce that changes hands.

Just as the relationship between buyer and seller veers uncertainly between desire and antagonism, so too the politics of the market itself are inherently contradictory. "Casera, casera," market women call out hopefully whenever a white woman enters the marketplace, smiling and beckoning; a favorite fantasy of many vendors is to become the special trusted intimate of such a customer, ready to dispense not only produce but advice, sympathy, and warmth. Condori Mamani, poor and Indian, at times speaks of the vivanderas as just such confidantes— but when he remembers the women who hired him to haul their merchandise or do odd jobs, the picture is of cruelty, mistreatment, and spite. In the abstract, though, he trusts the vendors more than the bourgeoisie do. Despite the sellers' avowedly entrepreneurial aspirations, the latter see them as class enemies: despicable because they are poor, dangerous if they are not.

And indeed, if the vendors appear to other urban poor people as abusive employers and exploitative merchants, they have also been legendary figures of working-class political solidarity. Seligmann comments on "their participation in large numbers in neighborhood organizations and communal kitchens . . . Almost all of them belong to unions; and they are on the front lines of protest marches and strikes, often in conjunction with peasants and workers" (1993:202). José María Arguedas's depiction of pollera-clad chicheras and market vendors as political activists in *Los ríos profundos* was based in reality: the market women of Cuzco were infamous for "closing the marketplace and convening massively in the Plaza de Armas," just as Arguedas depicted them (de la Cadena 1996:131). "In April 1958," the year *Los ríos profundos* was published, "the market women's union contributed to the success of a general strike by kidnapping the general in charge of the local army, and forcing him to negotiate" (de la Cadena 1996:131).

Brecht built a revolutionary theatrical style out of elements taken from popular culture; policemen and politicians likewise read a political message in the costumes of the street market—and respond to the perceived threat with coercive action. At mid-century, de la Cadena found archival evidence of a concerted effort at sartorial regulation. The city fathers proposed banning the vendors' distinctive clothing—referred to in the documents as the "vestido de castilla" (Castillean dress)— altogether. The women's long braids were to be shorn, lest they come into contact with the food and contaminate it; the pollera came in for special criticism as a "favorite nesting material for bugs and filth (*inmundicias*) of all sorts, and a permanent carrier of bacteria" (de la Cadena 1996:121). Then and now, when scuffles break out between police and vendors in Cuzco, officers target the articles of clothing they find so offensive. Seligmann quotes market woman Eutrofia Qorihuaman: "The municipal agents abuse us, herding us like sheep, throwing our hats on the ground" (1993:201).

Market women fight back against such attacks, using every tool at their disposal. When the city of Cuzco passed its new sartorial code, the newspapers filled with sensational articles about their unruly response:

> Yesterday a woman called Rosa Pumayalli, a meat seller, set off a serious disturbance in the marketplace because the guard . . . informed her that she had to wear her apron and clean her belongings in conformity with the orders from the mayor's office. That was enough for Pumayalli, whose Quechua name means vanquisher of tigers. She tried to attack the guard and chased him brandishing a knife and showering him with insults from her well-supplied repertoire. (de la Cadena 1996:121)

Pumayalli sounds apocryphal, but the anxieties that market women provoked among white newspaper readers were real, for they are the products of the exchange relationship itself, which is both conflictual and duplicitous. As they do their jobs, vendors play to bourgeois fantasies about race—yet at the same time, the obvious artifice of their performances undermines bourgeois belief in their own "natural" superiority. In this, they resemble Brechtian actors more than ever, for this is what Brecht set out to do in his theatrical work: to estrange the bourgeoisie from the ideologies they hold dear.

The Estrangement-Effect

Tourist Henry Shukman reacted strongly to the outfits worn by Bolivian vendors, which struck him as acts of sartorial misbehavior:

> Dressed like absurd travesties of circus clowns and silently chewing coca leaves with their mouths agape, the women were almost sinister: their enormously wide skirts which reached only to the knees, their outrageously bright shirts and cardigans, all a blaze of colours, and above them, barely noticeable, their dark faces; and perched on top the little bowler hats. It was all an extraordinary miscarriage of western dress. The hats were not in the least practical: they were not warm, they were always several sizes too small, and they weren't even intended for women. . . . they seem like a deliberate effort to dress up, to assert a cultural identity; even to mock the foreigners who introduced the hats in the first place. (1989:32)

This passage defines Brecht's "estrangement-effect." Estrangement from ordinary vision was, for Brecht, the goal of revolutionary theater: "to make something look strange, to make us look at it with new eyes" by momentarily shocking us out of "a general familiarity, of a habit which prevents us from really looking at things, a kind of perceptual numbness." This is what happens to Shukman when he walks into the market building. He had gone to the Andes in search of the exotic, but he finds something that is strangely familiar—and thus estranging. Rather than natives dressed in ethnic garb, he is confronted with the sight of "dark" women dressed in Western clothing not "intended" for them.

His reactions seem too strong: their violation of the vestimentary code is an "extraordinary miscarriage," he says, as though justice itself, not just clothing, were at stake. They are "absurd travesties"—but of what? Whose "intentions" are violated by their hats, produced for them by artisans and factories across the Andes? He reads into their costume a deliberate subversion of the very attitude with which one chooses one's everyday garb: their clothing is theatrical, "not even practical"; they look "like circus clowns." But if they are clowns, he is not entertained: he suspects a joke and fumes at the thought that it might be at his expense.

What distresses Shukman is the apparent willfulness of the women's hats: they "seem like a deliberate effort to dress up," he says, as though he senses a conscious mockery of those who—like himself—believe themselves to be the sons of conquerors. Textile researcher Janet Catherine Berlo, too, has recently argued that there is an element of willful reappropriation in Latin American clothing styles usually described as "traditional." Scholars have typically described the use of elements from other clothing traditions in Lévi-Straussian terms as "bricolage,"[39] but Berlo takes exception to the concept.

> For many years I thought that indigenous, post-colonial Latin American textiles were prime examples of bricolage . . . [because of their] fragmented stratigraphy of influences: wool and wild cotton; acrylic and metallic yarns; indigo and aniline dyes . . . gauze and polyester; . . . embroidery and machine stitch.

She has become dissatisfied, however, with a term that she perceives as ascribing passivity, rather than active agency, to the wearers of these clothes:

> As Lévi-Strauss defined it, inherent in bricolage is the notion of making do: the bricoleur works with . . . the fragmentary and limited possibilities at hand. . . . Increasingly it is apparent to me that all of the cultural cross-currents and overlays in the textile art of Latin America are not, however, simply a "making do." They are not merely a passive, defensive response to five centuries of

> colonialism . . . the improvisations and appropriations in women's textiles are deliberate. (1990:438–39)

Having moved beyond the naturalistic assumptions of earlier writers, for whom clothing is a transparent expression of ethnicity, she calls for a new set of concepts with which to analyze the specific processes by which these "fragmented stratigraphies" are assembled. Here Brecht, who established a vocabulary to talk about method, is once again useful.

Brecht constructed his performances to create discordant impressions. The mood of the music clashes with the lyrics; the actors play their parts, but they also read the stage directions aloud; even their emotions and motivations zigzag between extremes of humor and anger, cynicism and idealism. Before long, audience members have been shaken wide awake, nerves jangling and eyes open, completely uncertain of what to expect: the very experience of theatergoing has become strange and new.

Brecht called this technique distancing *(Trennung):* a deliberate mismatch between two different elements. To achieve it, he searched for ways to hold two entirely disparate qualities together without letting them merge: they must be superimposed, yet held apart from each other, so that the audience registers the tension created by their incongruity (Jameson 1998:70). Berlo finds similar strategies in indigenous Latin American clothing assemblages:

> [I]n Maya textiles, the joins between two woven panels are often the focus of articulation and elaboration [in which] the seam is not rendered unobtrusive as it is in our apparel. Instead, it is emphasized by silk or rayon stitching of bold color and emphatic form. . . . So too, . . . seams of cultural articulation are often emphasized and highlighted. Attention is called to the diverse materials and influences that have been incorporated into the native domain. (Berlo 1990:453)

In my notes on market women's clothing, I often resorted not to "bricolage" but to one of Brecht's favorite words: "collage" (Jameson 1998:39). In a collage, a variety of items are stuck onto a single piece of paper, often in fragments, overlapping and only partly seen; as with Brecht's notion of distancing, this juxtaposition leaves their disparate origins clearly visible. In market women's clothing, too, Indian and white overlap, neither completely visible nor completely effaced.

In the Mercado Central in Huaraz, Peru, the market women's costumes divide their bodies into halves, and their clothes into layers. This assemblage can be read vertically—the top half of the body dressed in the shawls, blouses, and braids of a peasant woman, while the bottom half is covered in the skirt of an urbanite. Or from the outside in: stuffed beneath the dark, somber straight black skirt of a respectable city woman are the abundant flounces and brilliant colors of a peasant pollera.[40] This overlay of articles of clothing from different domains is strikingly reminiscent of the berdache dressing style described above. Like Pete Dog Soldier with his trousers sticking out from underneath his dress, the market women of Huaraz, with their polleras stuffed under their straight skirts, layer Indian and white apparel in a way that does not hide one or the other, but leaves both clearly visible.

But the comparison between sexual drag and chola clothing is more than just an analogy. Shukman's anxieties are about sex and gender, as well as race; in the passage cited above, he complains that the Bolivians were wearing hats "that weren't even intended for women." In the Andes, such hats no longer carry a masculine gender, but his perception of gender-bending is not entirely off the mark: the clothing of market women does sometimes violate Andean gender rules. It is not only berdaches who wear trousers under their skirts; in Latacunga and throughout the central Sierra in the 1980s, female vendors wore them as well. The muscular women who work as butchers and sellers of meat, in particular, wore trousers under their skirts and aprons on top of them; and so, too, did a mother and daughter who ran a small concession near the highway in Zumbagua. Cheerful, fair-haired women with arms and legs like tree trunks, they handled the heavy tools of their trade with ease: cases of bottled sodas and beers, axes with which to cut kindling for fuel, and heavy metal skillets and pans in which to cook *mote* (corn kernels mixed with tasty nuggets of fried pork and hot peppers).

In Latacunga in the 1980s, market women wore black plastic work boots, men's pants under a plaid skirt and an apron, a frilly blouse with a man's cardigan, elaborate earrings and a baseball cap. Yet rather than being seen as shockingly transgressive in the highly gendered world of provincial Andean cities, this outfit raised no eyebrows: it seemed that race confused the picture. Indians and whites each had their own dress codes: articles of clothing that were not appropriate for white women were worn by Indian women, and vice versa; thus the gender appropriateness of a particular article of clothing for market women was difficult to ascertain. A white woman in the Andes at that time would never wear a baseball hat or work boots, but these items were unisex within the indigenous lexicon; if market women are part-Indian, why shouldn't they wear them?

But in fact, their clothing did not obey the sexual rules for either white or Indian women. The Latacunga market women dressed very "white," and even if they had been Indians, they would still have been cross-dressers, for they routinely violated the strictest of indigenous vestimentary rules. Indian women wore a shawl called a *lliklla,* but professional market women never did; instead, they wore the crocheted shawls associated with whites. The only unmistakably Indian garment worn by the vendors was the poncho—the defining article of indigenous masculinity.

In these examples, we can see specific acts of distancing at work. Peruvian market women layer one race over another, while their Ecuadorian counterparts layer one sex over another—using race as an alibi. Like their tongue-in-cheek verbal performances, the market women's exuberant clothing styles perform race and sex as improvisational collages constantly subject to revision: they thus undermine the notion that the social order that exists, must be.

THE POLLERA AS QUOTATION

A market woman wears ordinary, machine-made clothes—a fuzzy pink sweater, a bowler hat—in novel ways. These assemblages confuse, but they do not deceive: rather, they achieve that effect of estrangement from the taken-for-granted that Brecht sought in his dissonant and distancing theatrical productions. One of his favorite techniques was "quotation"—and in this, too, Andean vendors excel. To achieve it, Brecht instructed his actors to read their lines as though they were quoting them, so that the audience is constantly made aware that the actors are not the characters they portray. At the same time, however, the actors act out their lines just as the character would. This rupture in the illusion, so that we see the actor acting without losing sight of the character, alienates the audience from their belief that people's behavior reveals their "nature" (Brecht 1963 : 138).

Whatever role they are playing at the moment—the humble peasant whose potatoes were dug up by her very own hands, the honest merchant sincerely outraged by your suggestion that her prices are high and might possibly be lowered, or your dearest friend, sacrificing her own profits in order to offer you an incredibly special deal—Andean vendors, too, quote their lines in Brechtian fashion. Even as they try to convince, they wink at you, pointing out the artificiality of the part as they play it to the hilt. Indeed, it is not uncommon for a woman to momentarily break out of the role altogether to speak to someone nearby in a completely different tone. I have even seen a woman offer an ironic commentary on her own performance—stopping to ask other vendors whether she is overplaying the part in a stage whisper that you are perfectly welcome to hear. Such playfulness is disarming: it would be churlish to accuse someone of lying when they've already indicated that they didn't really expect you to believe them.

Quotation can also take more political forms, in the "speech" of clothing as in verbal expression. It is no accident that the two sartorial problems posed for van den Berghe were poncho-clad Communists and women in polleras: the pollera is a garment with a political history. Vendors in polleras march in protest in Linda Seligmann's photographs from the 1980s, as they did in Bolivia in the 1930s. To wear this garment is to lay claim, however obliquely, to that history; and to wear it during a political action is to quote its past directly.

Today, market women's organizations are no longer hotbeds of political activism, as they once were (Rivera Cusicanqui et al. 1996:194–97). And many women have abandoned the pollera for jeans and sweatpants. But when they do march in protest—as they still do—these same women call upon the chola tradition by wearing their family's finest polleras. When university students donned ponchos and sashes and spouted archaic Quechuaisms in 1968, it was obvious that they were deliberately appropriating anachronistic forms of Indian language and garb as a matter of political choice, in a pointed critique of contemporary political economy. Blinded by race, academic observers have sometimes failed to recognize the similarities between these performances and those of politically savvy market women. In donning their grandmothers' shawls, polleras, and hats to re-create the elaborate chola costumes of an earlier generation, these women, too, employ a self-conscious archaism. Like the students in their ponchos, they are quoting rebellions of the past—the students mimicking long-dead Indians, the market vendors evoking their own forebears. In wearing clothing emblematic of a vanishing working-class prosperity, the vivanderas also make pointed reference to the exacerbated poverty that has stripped them of their clothes.

This same tactic of politically motivated quotation may be found in language as well. In Arguedas's novel, the ringleader of the insurrection exhorts the other women in Quechua to "Shout! Shout so the whole world can hear you." She leads the way, shouting out a single word that unites the crowd and impels them to action. But this word, addressed to the marchers but intended for the ears of the entire city, is not in Quechua but in Spanish: "*Avanzo!*" ("Forward!") [1958:138–40].

In Ecuador, I witnessed a far more subtle use of bilingual quotation at work in ordinary conversation. The dusty town of Zumbagua Centro sits on a site that once was the administrative center of a sprawling hacienda; the proliferation of little bars and stores that line its streets are the offspring of earlier shops run by the non-Indian wives of hacienda overseers. Some of the women who run these enterprises are the grand-daughters of those white shop-owners. Others are indigenous women who have moved into the plaza, whitening a little as they become part of the local elite; still others are outsiders, who ended up here by some odd accident of personal history. Heloisa moves easily in this social world, known to everyone and liked by many. Her clothing seems de-signed to avoid making a statement. She wears a homburg hat like an Indian, but no bright-colored shawls or underskirts. She prefers dark, muted colors, usually navy blue or black, and her pollera is neither tight like a white woman's skirts nor full like an Indian's. Her behavior, however, is as distinctive as her clothing is not: she moves quickly, speaks commandingly, laughs loudly, and loves to engage in razor-sharp repartee.

Spanish is the language of choice among these shopkeepers, al-though all of them use Quichua in their transactions with the mostly monolingual Indian women who buy their wares, and many of them speak it as their mother tongue. It is understood among them—as it is decidedly *not* in the Indian comunas outside of town—that Spanish is the better tongue, just as those few families who live full-time in the Centro are a better class of people than the "longos" who surround them. In Zumbagua, this preference for Spanish makes one white, even though none of these women, with their rural clothing, obvious pov-erty, and heavily accented Spanish, could easily pass for white or even chola in nearby Latacunga or Saquisilí.

In Zumbagua, whiteness is achieved in several ways; language is one. Residence in the town center is another. Whites attend church every Sunday rather than only at life crises. In the cemetery, a small area clos-est to the entrance boasts the large above-ground tombs of the white community, while an ocean of small wooden crosses marks the Indian graves beyond.

Finally, whiteness expresses itself in a willingness to talk about local indigenous culture in disparaging terms. Even the act of objectifying particular linguistic practices or ways of dressing or eating as "In-dian"—rather than marking anomalous and stigmatized behavior as "white," as most parish residents do—immediately places someone on the white side of the parish's racial divide.[41] Everyone who lives in the center of town is, to some extent, bicultural: as able to perform cor-rectly as the godmother at an Indian baptism as to attend a white wed-ding properly dressed. But the members of this little white community laugh openly at Indian customs, while pretending to a far greater familiarity with the ways of residents in the provincial capital, two hours' bus ride to the east, than they actually command.

Heloisa positions herself slightly differently. She moves with ease in the white community, frequently dropping the name of her natural father, a white hacienda overseer (now resident in Latacunga) who had impregnated her mother in the unhappy years before the Agrarian Reform. But everyone knows that her real loyalties lie with the rest of her family, indigenous farmers who live just outside of town. The affection that she has for them, and especially for her adoptive father, motivate her constant, subtle interventions into white conversations.

In my memories of slow midweek afternoons in those shops in the late 1980s, other women would be laughing at something foolish that an indigenous customer had done, or some drunken excess witnessed in the waning hours of the Saturday market, when customers stop buying staple goods and start purchasing shots of trago instead. Heloisa would listen, laughing loudly at the punch line just like everyone else; never once did I hear her object to a racial epithet or insult. But when she recounted her own anecdote, she always turned the sense of the story, recuperating the worth of the Indian protagonists and commenting with derision on the foibles of the white characters. It was adroitly done, so that no one could really take offense; far more so than anyone else, Heloisa, whose Spanish and Quichua are equally rich, excels at the rapid code-switching that characterize these conversations, and so was able to nuance her tales exactly. She was almost always forgiven, in part because Heloisa always seemed to be having so much fun, and invited her listeners to have fun even as she subtly mocked their pretensions to racial privilege.

These interventions are not unlike the sartorial drag discussed above. In a context where Spanish is the privileged tongue, Heloisa does far more than simply try to pass unnoticed as someone whose mother was a monolingual Quichua speaker. She subtly shifts the quotidian bilingual play of the shopkeepers in such a way as to bring its unspoken politics momentarily into conscious awareness, and thus provokes a momentary distancing from the taken-for-granted racial superiority of this little community of merchants. For just that moment, they both see and do not see themselves as the Indians see them, because they hear their own speech almost—but not quite, not "really"—as their Quichua-speaking customers do.

From verbal quotation we may turn once more to that most complicated and powerful symbol of all, the pollera—and back again from race to sex. In working-class parlance, the women who work in the markets are women "of the pollera": this garment defines them. In its enormous bulk, its voluminous folds, its bright colors, its multiplicity (one skirt worn over another), the pollera approaches self-parody: we might now ask whether it does not constitute a kind of ironic quotation of women's dress. It is unquestionably a skirt, the quintessential emblem of a woman. Yet it is sometimes worn with trousers; and even on its own (or rather, with its multitudinous underskirts) it represents a femaleness so exaggerated, so determined to draw attention to itself, that it ruptures the aura of unquestioned normalcy that surrounds women in skirts.

At a minimum, the pollera announces the rejection of certain aspects of femininity, in which dress and body language express an implicit promise to be nice, to be agreeable, to be passive. These conventions, so pleasing to men's eyes, have a frightening corollary for women: the vulnerability that marks them as ready-made victims. The wearer of the pollera offers a very different guarantee: she promises to put up a good fight. The pollera carries with it the aura not only of organized political protest, but of the knife-wielding Pumayalli.

When I tell people outside the markets that I have seen market women in trousers, they often suggest that the purpose might be as a protection from rape. This seems a sensible notion, since vendors often must sleep outside in the public square, or on buses making overnight trips across the Andes. Too, in the late afternoons as the market winds down, the plaza fills with drunks, many of whom are in search of recipients for their amorous attentions. If this is a motivation for wearing trousers, it also extends to the pollera, for women talk about it, too, as providing a kind of protection not available to those who wear other kinds of skirts.

In attempting to explain her midlife decision to adopt the pollera, Sofía Velasquez had this to say: "A woman who is *de pollera* can sit wherever she wants without having to be afraid. Someone who is *de vestido* is afraid to [sit in the street]" (173). She explained this statement by comparing her own life to that of a schoolteacher, an occupation that her own teachers had urged upon her in her youth: "I have seen what the life of a teacher is . . . People look down on you . . . I have seen a lot of vulgar things. So I said to myself that I wasn't accustomed to behave like that."

For Sofía, working in the streets of La Paz dressed as a chola provides a greater sense of control over her own sexuality than would the supposedly more respectable occupation of teaching. Her perspective struck me as counterintuitive until I compared the schoolteachers I had known in Zumbagua to the women who sold trago, dry goods, and cooked food there. The schoolteachers worked together with and for men, in whose company they adopted a hyperfeminine and flirtatious mode of behavior. Their clothing style contrived to be both respectable and provocative, with knee-length straight skirts and long-sleeved, high-necked blouses that were nonetheless tight enough to reveal the outlines of the brassieres and girdles worn below; red lipstick and high heels completed the picture.

The shopkeepers and open-air vendors, in contrast, were uncorseted; working outside in the cold air, they wore layers of skirts, sweaters, and shawls over a simple shift that served as an undergarment. (The absence of underpants among cholas is notorious in a certain class of men's humor). A few of these women dressed in an indigenous style, their enormous skirts anchored by yards of wide woolen sashes wrapped around their waists. Most of them, however, distinguished themselves from the peasant women of the area by adopting the straight skirts that signal white identity. But unlike women who work in offices or classrooms, these women wore their skirts with thick multicolored crocheted underskirts stuffed beneath them, creating a bulky profile not unlike their indigenous counterparts. These layers of heavy clothing did not disguise the unconstrained movement of breasts, bellies, and buttocks underneath. But this visibility was businesslike and matter-of-fact, the necessary physicality of a working-class body at work. The schoolteachers' attire, in contrast, offered up female body parts tightly covered and constrained, yet emphasized and offered for view.

While tending her small Zumbagua tavern alone, Heloisa Huanotuñu has certainly learned to deflect unwanted suitors. She told me that any woman can defend herself "if she has the will." This self-assurance has an invisible corollary: her trousers. Although I have never seen Heloisa wearing pants in the fifteen years that I have known her, she is nevertheless renowned for having done so. She only did it once. The occasion was a public fiesta, in which she appeared before hundreds of her assembled neighbors. In Zumbagua, festival performance is an exclusively masculine activity; there is no female counterpart to the male cross-dressers of whom Tayta Juanchu was so fond.[42] So Heloisa had to improvise her own role when she took part in the most masculine of festival activities, the Corpus Christi bullfight.[43]

I never saw her in the ring; Heloisa was already in early middle age when I began my fieldwork, and it was her teenaged brother Alfonso who "played" with the bulls. In 1985, Alfonso attracted the attention of the crowd with his bravery and skill in the ring. When I complimented him, he was pleased but quick to contrast his own successes with his sister's much greater fame: "When *she* was young, she put on trousers and rode into the ring on a big horse—it was a wonderful sight!"

"Didn't people criticize her?"

"Oh, no, not at all—not her! She could do it!"

"But other women can't."

"No, of course not—women here don't ride horseback, and they certainly don't ride with the bulls on *Corpus fishtu*. But Heloisa did, wearing trousers and a man's poncho. She's the only one."

In the eyes of her neighbors, then, Heloisa was never without her trousers—or her reputation for reckless courage in front of both the bull and the assembled crowd. Trousers and polleras thus play a certain game of visibility and invisibility on and around the market woman's body. Sometimes co-occurring, sometimes replacing each other, they are held together yet apart by the semiotics of costume in a taut "distancing." As with Indian and white clothing, the "and-and" that replaces "either-or" when transvestism becomes drag is at work here with a vengeance. The pollera—a skirt in quotation marks—is at once the most skirtlike of all skirts, and its opposite: a pair of trousers. Market women, too, are unmistakably female—but also rather masculine. In the words of one of Seligmann's interviewees, "I have seven sons. But I've also taught my daughters to be . . . *machas*" (1995:42).

Butler's critique of essentialism is directed at gender and sex, although she has also extended it to include race (1993). There is a Brechtian quality to her attacks, which undermine the notion of the individual—yet missing from her work is the earlier writer's sustained attention to matters of class. Yet it may be their class position—rather than their sex, their gender, or their race—that gives market women's performances their most subversive qualities. Their particular form of play does more than skewer the naturalistic claims of both race and sex; in their lives and work, they seem to both embrace the relentless individualism of capitalist culture and reject it.

THE MARKET AS "LEARNING PLAY"

In the 9 de Octubre market, the fruteras sit high above the aisles on a raised dais, peering down at their customers across piles of bananas, papayas, and pineapples. One beautiful and flirtatious young woman caught my companion's attention. When Stephen tried to engage her in conversation, she took him on immediately, much to the delight of the vendors standing around her, all of whom looked down on us from the same heights (and most of whom, I later learned, were her relatives). Leaning forward dramatically, she inspected his tropical linens and sunglasses, his large and expensive camera, and demanded, "So you're from Los Angeles, where they make the movies? Take my picture, then, and make me a star!"

Even without the klieg lights, she was already performing. Her audience included the customers who come and go—and the other vendors, who are always there. In our several conversations with her, she kept us off balance by switching the roles she expected us to play. At times, she showed off for us; the next minute, she turned away to her mothers and sisters to talk about us, or about something else, as though we were no longer there. We weren't her only audience—and we weren't just an audience: she also used us as her foil, her straight man, drafted willy-nilly into humorous little skits performed for other vendors' enjoyment.

Many a tourist, desiring merely to look and listen, has been acutely discomfited by the same realization: in the theatrical space of the market, everyone is on stage. Customers appear mostly as amateurs, assigned bit parts and "character roles." There is no predetermined script; rather, buyer and seller size each other up, each waiting for the other's cue before deciding which character to play. In this kind of theater, where everyone is on stage, writing the script as they go along, we can no longer assume the safe passivity found in bourgeois forms of entertainment to which we are accustomed. Judith Butler's notion of performativity is too often interpreted in the latter context, as though social life were a theater in which artist and author, audience and actors are rigidly separated. Thus although the sexual rebel challenges the scripts she has been handed, she remains securely in the spotlight, surrounded by a silent audience who pass judgment on her performance, but may not climb up on the stage. In this model of a performance without interlocutors, identity once again becomes reified—and commodified. The woman freed of constraints upon her gender and sexuality is just a shopper who can try on any of the clothes in the mall, men's as well as women's, in an individualistic quest for self-expression.

Brecht despised this kind of theater. His work was directed toward destroying the bourgeois individual, to be replaced by a radically different subjectivity. To this end, he staged "learning plays": performances without audiences, in which each actor continually changed the role he performed, so that all the parts rotated among the players. Jameson compares these to an actor's master class (1998:62–65), but a better analogy would be to grand precapitalist performances like the Mandan O-Kee-Pah, in which every member of a community put on a costume and became part of a collective enactment of myth (Catlin 1867). Andean produce markets are neither tribal rituals nor modernist experimental theater; but these examples remind us that we should not assume that the performances that take place in them are simply expressions of the self as we understand it.

When I offered to take photographs of women in the Cuenca markets, I was surprised by how few of them wanted to pose alone. My offer was immediately met with a wide smile and a shouted invitation to a nearby woman: "Come and let's have our picture taken!" In a typical scene, one woman wanted her sister in the picture, but wasn't sure how to pose. "Like twins! Like twins!" urged a younger boy excitedly, and everyone around them took up the refrain: "Yes, yes, that's it!" Both women smiled, and, embracing one another closely, faced the camera like one person with two heads.

As self-portraits, these photographs of "twinned" women are telling. Market women are aggressive, competitive individuals within a capitalist economy—and something very different. They are also kin to other women, in all the senses of merged social, material, and physical identity that kinship can carry in indigenous society. As such, they are not individuals, but rather "dividuals" who form part of a dyad, and that dyad, in turn, is one among many such (Strathern 1988).

This concept of the self formed in and through others accounts for a peculiarity of Sofía Velasquez' life history, which puzzles the middle-class reader. Her tale is a chronicle of financial and social success, but it reads nothing like a Horatio Alger story, any more than it does a conventionally feminine biography. Because it lacks any descriptions of an interior emotional life, the narrative leaves us baffled as to why she does what she does. In this text, motivation develops through interactions with others: it is in dyads, not alone, that Sofía discovers her subjective feelings—and imparts them to the reader. She tells her life as though it were the script of a play—but one absent the soliloquies through which actors from Shakespeare to soap operas communicate their characters' inner selves. Sofía's story is told through dialogues and stage directions. Read in this way, all the human drama previously lacking suddenly jumps from the page. Major dilemmas—her conflicting loyalties toward her mother and her friend Yola, or her struggles with her brother and her child's father—come vividly to life.

Her decision to become a market woman, for example, unfolds through a series of dialogues: with her mother and brother, with the nun who urges her to become a schoolteacher, and of course with her friend Yola. "Yola . . . was selling peas wholesale and she was talking about the marvelous things she did with her money. . . . she is the one who egged me on" (17–18).

Their relationship exhibits that tension between competition and sisterhood that defines market women, for they are both partners and rivals: "it was fun, because Yola and I were free to laugh and make fun of the policemen. I was no longer tied to my home. I earned good money" (20); but at the same time, "[I]t was strange. Whenever Yola got something, I had to have it too. We were in constant competition" (24).

Like Brecht's learning plays, the market is a theater where everyone is on stage: middle-class tourists try vainly to behave as mere spectators, only to be accosted, teased, mimicked—even robbed or beaten up. In this theater, the stakes are material: one leaves richer or poorer in vegetables, in cash, in friendships, and in knowledge than one entered. Not only is it impossible to remain passive and invisible; one's very self is at risk here, for a few interactions with the vivanderas may unravel the seams of identity. Visitors can find themselves estranged from their own race or sex, which suddenly seem like a not-very-convincing quotation of lines written by someone else. Indeed, the pollera embodies self-contradictions that go beyond Indian and white, or even masculine and feminine. Politically, it represents both avaricious commerce and collective struggle; the women who wear it prize the individual freedom it represents, yet identify so closely with other women that they cannot imagine being photographed alone.

The root of these contradictions lies in the nature of the exchange relationship itself. This chapter moved from a futile search for monologic statements of identity to an appreciation of the multiple and dialogic use of race and sex in the markets; in the next chapter, we turn from exchanges of words and glances to more physical forms of intercourse. The apparent free flow of words in the market partially disguises the movement of money and commodities, but the latter drives the former. The real distancing within the pollera is between two forms of material exchange: the chimera of reciprocity represented by the figure of the Indian, and the reality of unequal exchange embodied in the story of the ñakaq.

CHAPTER 4

....

Deadly Intercourse

The chola is an image, not a narrative, but there is a story behind her: the tale of a violent and unequal form of intercourse. The pishtaco, too, appears as an actor in a history of unequal exchange. Indeed, the two of them could almost be characters in the same story, about what can happen to an Indian who meets up with a white man. These stories are a tangle of sex, money, and death; capitalist culture encourages us to believe that one can separate economic exchange from relations of sex and love, but here they look like two games played by the same rules. Sex is a form of exchange, and the kind of sex people have depends upon their material relations to each other.

These particular stories are about exchange at its most radically unequal—rape, murder, and theft. We tend to reserve our outrage only for these especially egregious forms of exploitation, and otherwise to accept it as natural that one party to an exchange is enriched at the other's expense. But just as polleras and "mushroom hats" can make us question the taken-for-granted categories of sex and race, so too these tales make us look anew at ordinary acts of capitalist exchange, and to realize that our economic behavior is no more natural than the way we have sex.

This estranged glance at capitalism may be easier to achieve in the Andes than elsewhere, for here one finds memories of a very different ideology of exchange. The Incaic economy of the gift is long gone, but it still haunts the region like a five-hundred-year-old dream. In rural communities, too, peasant traditions of reciprocity, although much diminished, have not been entirely destroyed. A fading image of un-alienated social intercourse—economic, social, and sexual—provides a sharp if suppressed critique to a very different set of echoes from the past, in which whiteness and masculinity provide an alibi for acts of unrequited violence. The contest between these two forms of inter-course is fought out in historical myth: the conquest of the Americas is remembered in the Andes not only as the defeat of Indians by whites, but of women by men, and of gifts by theft.

GIFTS

I know the El Salto market in Latacunga well; it is the last stop on my way back to Zumbagua, where I pause to shop for food before embark-ing on the two-hour trip up from the city into the páramo on a wind-ing and dangerous road. I am a curiosity in the plaza, a foreign woman who buys in large quantities, like an Indian: eight loaves of bread, sixty bread rolls; four pineapples, two papayas; forty tangerines, ten avoca-dos; two kilos of blackberries, six of tomatoes. Arriving at El Salto on days and times when there are few customers, I am conscious of be-ing a public spectacle, visible for a great distance across the enormous square. The vendors of grains sit on the ground rather than using tables; when I bend down to ask the price of dried corn or fava bean flour, the women stare up at me in surprise, and make me repeat my unexpected requests.

Upon arriving in Zumbagua, visibility changes to secrecy. These days, I arrive by taxi rather than by bus, Stephen at my side. Children and adults swarm around the vehicle, embracing us and eagerly offering to carry all the bundles into the house. We immediately begin handing out oranges and bread rolls to every child we see; but I am expected to observe the rules of gift-giving, and so to somehow manufacture a se-ries of private interludes with each adult. These are the moments when packages are surreptitiously handed over with a sidelong glance and a little mumbled directive that "this is for you" or "for you and your children," or "perhaps you will take this up to your parents next time you visit them." The bags and baskets disappear, never to be mentioned again in my presence; indeed, it behooves me to exit as soon as possible after handing them over, to give the recipients the opportunity to open them up, inspecting and exclaiming over the sweaters and baby clothes, shoes and toys.

In better times, so strictly observed were the niceties of gift-giving that I never ate a morsel of the food I delivered. After hauling in a hundredweight of fresh fruit and vegetables from the tropical and temperate regions below, I could rest assured that nothing would cross my lips except the foods that grow in the cold thin air of the parish: a bland regimen of barley gruel and potato soup, roast guinea pig and boiled mutton. I would at least have enjoyed watching them eat the pineapples and berries—rare and precious treats—but even this was simply not allowed. In recent years, however, tidbits of tomato and fresh *ají* peppers—my gifts to them—have begun to show up in my bowl, tangible signs of the pall of poverty and sadness that has descended on the house. This inability to preserve the rigid requirements of giving and receiving is bitter to me; the foods I once longed for now taste of Taita Juanchu's death, Compadre Alfonso's unemployment, and Comadre Olguita's deep, unshakeable depression.

These days, the family desperately needs what I bring them; but even so Alfonso and his sisters Heloisa and Clarita work hard to subordinate each narrowly material transaction to the entirety of a multistranded relationship that cannot easily be defined. They want each letter detailing their spiraling needs, each tearful request for a loan to be the briefest of interludes within long hours of playfulness, sociability, and mountains of food—and are never so frustrated as when a tooshort visit abbreviates the rituals of sociality.

Calculated in cash, my gifts are much larger than their countergifts; but our meetings take the form not of charity, but of the constant exchange of incommensurate things: cooked meals for raw foods, hospitality for goods. And, indeed, I have more often been shamed and overwhelmed by their insistent desire to give, than irritated by their constant need to receive—even as I recognize that in the calculus of the gift exchange, the two movements of goods—toward them or toward me—are ultimately identical. However acute the crisis of the moment, my Zumbagua family is always less concerned to meet it than to somehow increase my total long-term emotional indebtedness, and so to keep the channel of compadrazgo open and the flow of gifts steady. And despite the tremendous inequality in our means, they have been astoundingly—frighteningly—successful: I will never even the score, never feel that I have done enough to repay them.[1]

The Gift Economy

In 1950, Marcel Mauss published his "Essai sur le don" (Essay on the gift), in which he outlined the structure of a gift economy. In societies characterized by this form of exchange, he said, economic intercourse takes the form of "acts of politeness"; these rituals underscore the fact that each transaction is only a small part "of a much more general and enduring contract" involving every aspect of social life. He commented on the peculiar tension between free will and obligation that characterizes the gift: "these total services and counter-services are committed to in a somewhat voluntary form by presents and gifts, although in the final analysis they are strictly compulsory" (1990:5).

Some twenty years later, a series of brilliant economic analyses by scholars interested in the Andes, among them Maurice Godelier (1977), Nathan Wachtel (1973), and most notably John Murra (1975), wedded Mauss's insights to Marx's. They made a conceptual link between Andean precapitalist intensive agropastoralism as a mode of production, and reciprocity—the gift economy—as a form of exchange. One result was a new understanding of the Incas, who famously began their relations with a newly conquered people by showering them with gifts. This once-puzzling form of imperial largesse could now be interpreted as a forcible jump-starting of the exchange relationship, which thus immediately established an inescapable obligation on the part of the new subjects toward their lords.

The same paradigm also stimulated a burst of field studies analyzing contemporary Andean forms of reciprocity, most notably in the collection edited by Alberti and Mayer in 1974. Scholars found twentieth-century rural Andean communities balancing two competing economic systems, each of which had its distinctive form of exchange.[2] Subsistence agriculture depended upon the reciprocal exchange of labor, which was enshrined within rituals that constituted a system of "acts of politeness" of just the sort outlined by Mauss; the cash economy, in contrast, was built up of nakedly economic exchanges between strangers. Indigenous Andean culture, then, was not just a superstructural matter of rituals and folklore, stories and songs, but an entire social fabric of economy and morality.

At the same time, a group of women scholars, among them Billie Jean Isbell, Catherine Allen, and Olivia Harris, began to define what they saw as a peculiarly Andean sex/gender system, based upon a principle of "complementarity," just as the indigenous economic system was one of reciprocity.[3] Building upon R. T. Zuidema's structuralist analysis of Inca kinship (1977), which posited a system of parallel or dual descent (women inheriting from women, and men from men), they argued for a far greater degree of sexual equality in the Andes than one might find in peasant societies in the Old World. In many parts of the Andes, women inherited land and property equally with men, rather than being jural minors—perhaps as a residue from the ancient dual descent system, unacknowledged in the Napoleonic legal codes of the Andean republics.[4] Throughout the region, gender roles were highly flexible, and marriage was based upon equal economic contributions from women and men, rather than on female dependency.[5]

In Zumbagua, I found that marriage did not involve the fusing of capital and productive resources, but rather the partnership of individuals and families who exchange gifts of labor and things, while retaining a fundamental economic independence.[6] Everyday interactions between spouses were ritualized as gifts: when a woman offered a bowl of soup to a hungry husband, it was a formal prestation enacted with strict propriety. Bourgeois culture idealizes a family life governed by generalized reciprocity; this ideology of boundless love creates ill-defined exchanges filled with unresolved guilt and resentment. The movement of material goods within indigenous families, in contrast, was marked by a mannered courtesy at once more distant and more generous than the casual intimacies of middle-class life. Relations not only to one another but to the material world were altered as a result: things appeared not as fetishized objects of individual desire but as the products of other's labor and so as symbols of social interdependence.

In the cities, well-to-do parents giggle with pleasure when their children speak their first words, reaching toward a thing and uttering its name—"*nana*" (banana), "*'sito*" (*osito,* my teddy bear)—or just saying "I want" or "mine." Zumbagua families delight in other kinds of utterances. Rather than expressing a relationship between the developing ego and an inanimate object, their children speak the name of a relationship between themselves and another person, through which they receive things they need and desire: "*'Pagui,*" they say (from "*Dyulsulupagui,*" thank you, may you be repaid).[7] Just so, they will not speak of eating, but of being fed; and they will take a further stumbling step toward maturity when they begin to share their own food with a still younger child in small awkward rituals already marked by a certain formality.

From the moment that academics first delineated the features of the indigenous culture of the gift, they have fiercely debated its importance and its future. Economic anthropologists disagreed about the relative autonomy and significance of reciprocal exchange systems, and the speed and completeness with which market systems were making inroads upon them. Similarly, if the indigenous sex/gender system had once been more egalitarian than its European and Asian counterparts—a point upon which not all scholars agreed—it was today deeply inter-penetrated with misogynist and patriarchal influences from Hispanic American culture.[8]

Like Quechua and Aymara, the *lenguas oprimidas* or oppressed tongues of Indians, the language of the gift is muted today, drowned out by voices speaking of bargains and rip-offs, easy money and raw deals. Yet despite its diminished importance as economic practice, reci-procity survives as an ideal within Latin American intellectual life, where it offers a powerful reproach to the profound and violent in-equalities of everyday life among whites. No writer has used imagery derived from indigenous Andean culture—*lo andino*—as a critique of present-day Andean society to greater effect, or had a keener under-standing of the radical implications of indigenous systems of exchange, than Peruvian writer José María Arguedas, the great champion of Que-chua language and culture.

The market woman Doña Felipa in *Los ríos profundos,* like Bertolt Brecht's itinerant trader Mother Courage, represents the struggle of common people against injustices perpetrated by the powerful. A com-parison between the two shows what the Andean tradition has to offer. The existence of Quechua culture within Peru creates a different moral and political landscape than that of Brecht's Europe. Courage, travers-ing seventeenth-century Northern Europe, knows nothing beyond the competitive and isolating struggle to survive by monetary exchange. Felipa, in contrast, is the leader of a militant collectivity of market women, and reaches out toward indigenous women in an act of radi-cally anticapitalist gift-giving. She operates within a social world suf-fused with the hope represented by the indigenous gift economy, but also lacerated with the viciousness of race.

In *Los ríos profundos,* Arguedas pours all his hopes for Peru into the image of chicheras and vivanderas turned revolutionaries. Toting rifles and wearing polleras, they are the river that overruns its banks, leaping from the merchants' storehouses to the Indians' huts, and inundat-ing the city of Cuzco with the destructive and creative sexual energy known in Quechua as *tinkuy.*[9] Their revolutionary actions disrupt the normal circuits of exchange: breaking into the warehouses and distrib-uting the contents to Indian women and children, they momentarily replace the unequal exchanges that impoverish Indians with a radical redistribution of goods to those who most need them. In discussions of Andean folklore, tinkuy is defined using three different examples: a ritual battle, the tumultuous joining of two streams of water—and the act of sex. The market women's actions, too, are a battle, a flood—and a sexual challenge. Acting against the interests of the male wholesalers who are their usual suppliers, and ignoring the attempts of male priests, politicians, and soldiers to stop them, the women from the markets and the chicherías fill the hands of rural women with food. Their action allies them with rural Indians rather than urban whites; and it ruptures the unequal distribution of power that makes women dependent upon men for their material survival.

Arguedas's idealization of nonwhite Peruvians is as profoundly right as it is wrong: the actual women of the marketplace are at least as much like his Doña Felipa as they are like Mother Courage. Market women are not Indians; they inhabit the arena of commerce, rather than the moral economy of the peasant farmer. And yet their whiteness is incomplete—not because they have nonwhite mothers, but because of their relationship to the foods they sell. Like the waitresses who sing of fruit trees and peasant farms even while serving in "fly-filled caverns, those dives reeking of chicha and cane liquor," the produce vendor remains an Indian in the city.[10]

Selling Food

In the hands of market vendors, products become commodities: to Indians, these women glow with the aura of money. But they also stink like food and garbage: the strong smell of onions hangs around the verdulera; flies gather around the tavern-owner, attracted by the chicha spilled on her skirts; skinny dogs follow the butchers, lapping up the pooled blood at their feet. Whites deride market women's financial successes by making reference to their intimate relationships with farm foods. The tomato wholesaler in Cuzco whose wealth supposedly enabled her to buy a mansion was scorned as "*la reina del tomate*" (the tomato queen) (de la Cadena 1996: 132).

The foods such women sell seem to be a peculiarly primitive form of commodity, one that announces its availability and its use value in vulgar displays unlike those of more sophisticated goods. Expensive commodities appear as individuals, each one cosseted in its own display, separated from the public by plastic or glass. Their brightly colored images appear grotesquely enlarged on billboards, or miniaturized on the glossy pages of magazines. In contrast, the inexpensive objects that draw ordinary buyers into the markets are displayed not in glamorous singularity, but in an overwhelming multiplicity. Street vendors show the entirety of their merchandise, piling up their wares in large and small heaps on tables or pavement. These architectural efforts—the pyramids of oranges, ziggurats of barley, and hanging gardens of bananas—do nothing to disguise the prosaic nature of their goods: these are not luxury items, but the solid building blocks of the *canasta familiar,* the family "breadbasket."

Large-scale commerce is conducted in private, by means of a hidden network of financial arteries linking cities and towns to the fast-flowing systems of global capital. The small-scale retailing of oranges and potatoes, buckets and shoelaces requires no such reticence: rather than the silent and instantaneous movement of capital along electronic circuits, the exchange of money and goods in the Andean market is noisy and protracted. However, if the Andean marketplace thereby recalls forms of premodern commerce such as the medieval fair, neither the market nor the food for sale there represent precapitalist economic relations; indeed, this fair is a jumble of productive regimes as much as of objects. Some of the grains, cheeses, and meats are grown on tiny family-owned farms where production is organized along precapitalist lines; sometimes one can even buy cheeses or chickens directly from a member of the family that raised them. But today, many vendors buy their produce from a big wholesaler; they no longer have direct ties to producers. And some products, such as rice—the emblematic food of Andean whiteness—are produced only through large-scale commercial ventures.[11] A lot of rice is imported, but much is also grown on coastal plantations in Ecuador and Peru, in capital-intensive enterprises that combine high technology with large inputs of manual labor. Other foods—bags of noodles and bottles of soft drinks, cubes of bouillon and tubs of shortening—are manufactured in small-scale, low-tech national factories.

Beyond the fresh food stalls lie the peripheral areas that bleed out from the tightly organized central square or market building into the surrounding streets and sidewalks. A hodgepodge of mostly useful items is for sale there: tools and clothing, hair ribbons and toys, dishes and containers. The products of small-scale hand labor have all but vanished from these areas: one occasionally sees a row of ceramic pots, a handful of wooden spoons, or a pile of baskets, but most items are mass-produced and usually imported from China, Mexico, or Colombia. Vendors of all ages and sexes work here, in contrast to the central market, where older women dominate the sale of food. Some items, like tools for construction and agriculture, are sold primarily by men; others, like cassette tapes and electronic goods, are specialties of the young; still others—blankets and bedding, pots and pans—are equal opportunity items, sold by young and old, male and female alike.

In 1973, during the heyday of Marxist critiques of unequal exchange and cultural imperialism, Eduardo Galeano wrote a book with an unforgettable title: *Las venas abiertas de América Latina* (The open veins of Latin America). The flow of vital fluids from south to north that he described primarily took the form of cheap agricultural goods, their prices artificially lowered by repressive labor policies that kept workers terrorized. He saw the blood and sweat of plantation laborers pouring into the homes of the U.S. middle class in the form of sugar and bananas—exotic foods made so inexpensive that they have come to be regarded as the birthright of every American.[12] The movement of these kinds of goods has only expanded, as the development of container shipping and improved refrigeration has added shrimp and fresh flowers to the traditional "dessert crops" like sugar, coffee, chocolate, and tea. The reciprocal movement of cheap manufactured goods into Latin markets is greatly accelerated as well—although the networks are more complicated today, involving players other than the United States. The T-shirts emblazoned with misspelled English phrases and baseball caps printed with Disney characters are faux Americana, mass-produced just south of the U.S. border, even though most of the profits still flow steadily north into gringo pockets.

Anthropologists writing about the Andean rural economy today do not make the errors sometimes made by tourists, who blissfully mistake urban cholas for "real Indians," or the rapid flow of devalued currencies for premodern barter. Seemingly out-of-the-way places like Saquisilí, Riobamba, or Cuzco are not isolated from world systems of production and consumption, but rather are intimately connected to them through channels so indirect and processes so haphazard as almost to defy analysis. These markets, which today are overrun by more would-be sellers than customers, are less remnants of a vanishing precapitalist past than indicators of the instability caused by the neoliberal present (Rivera Cusicanqui 1996).

But it is also easy to err in the opposite direction and insist that any perception of oppositional economic practices in the markets is wishful thinking. The apparent difference between the jam-packed cornucopias of food and household goods on view in the markets, and the cool isolation of articles from one another and from the viewer in upscale store displays, expresses an actual discrepancy between forms of exchange. The Andean market is more than a postmodern simulacrum of medieval fairs, a dance of fetishized commodities and hybrid identities disguised as an authentic place. The women who sell in the markets handle actual food—sensual and nourishing for the consumer;

fragile, heavy, and labor-intensive for the vendor—and they provide this food through a web of dense social ties unlike the impersonal and purely competitive relations praised by free marketeers. From this curious location, surrounded by material objects, enmeshed in face-to-face relations yet battered by intangible global forces, they represent a powerful amalgam of material histories. Standing at the juncture between the gift and the commodity, use value and exchange value, they seem also to hover between freedom and unfreedom, resistance and acquiescence.

Llapas: Gifts and Money

Sofía Velasquez lives an entirely commercial life. Even after editing by the Buechlers, her story is rendered almost unreadable by its numbing reiterations of rates of exchange, deals and bargains, losses and miscalculations. She does not fit our image of how women handle money, for she is neither a sentimental weakling incapable of hard calculations nor a manic shopper unable to control her impulse to buy. Nor could she be further from the image of the overly generous and easily duped Indian, unable to understand or unwilling to participate in the hard-edged world of commerce. Sofía eats, sleeps, and breathes the arithmetic of profit and loss, which never loses its fascination for her.

Money is the currency in which Sofía evaluates her relationships with her "caseras" and "caseros," the women and occasional men from whom she buys, and to whom she sells.[13] Her idea of a perfect relationship is one that allows both parties to profit—a form of exchange normally achieved only at the expense of others outside the fortunate dyad. She recalls with great nostalgia a friendship based in petty illegality during a time of government rationing:

> first sugar and then potatoes became scarce and so we handled the potatoes as though we were thieves. . . . We would collect the money jointly and then divide it later. We would help one another. It was impossible to engage in business all alone. It was a beautiful arrangement. (55)

This was, she says, "a lovely business," made possible by the acute suffering of the country as a whole. At other moments, she speaks with great pleasure of her two sets of scales, one that weighs accurately and one that cheats—a practice she learned from her mother.

But even when only one scale is used, market women do not treat all customers the same, regardless of how carefully the government fixes and regulates the actual price per unit of specific items: the rationality of this market is a highly personalized one. Years ago, I was part of a gathering of women sponsored by the Catholic Church in Zumbagua for the purpose of baking Finados breads.[14] Each woman had purchased two kilos of flour; but as we poured our contributions into the scale, we found that while the local women had all gotten somewhat more than two kilos for their money, the foreigners—especially the nuns— had been shortchanged.

In addition to the loose hand that adds a little extra when pouring, there is always the *llapa,* the "extra" gift that lubricates the exchange. Too, market women are finely attuned to certain material qualities of the agricultural products they sell, which prevent any two objects from being of exactly equal value. Thus older produce is sold to strangers and fresh items kept for old customers; similarly, access to scarce products must be earned through long loyalty. In rural shops and markets, precious items like eggs and cheese are never openly displayed; they do not circulate freely as commodities in a limitless market, but move within circles of exchange restricted by affection, by intimacy, and by the investment of time.

Of course, business relationships between much more formal and well-capitalized enterprises also depend upon these extra-commercial factors of trust and time, reputations and habits. As a yearlong Fulbright scholar, I was granted a slightly better exchange rate at a big Quito *Casa de Cambio* than was posted on the big sign outside; and while all the tourists and backpackers lined up to do their business at tiny barred windows, I was ushered into a private office to receive my sucres. Any momentary thrill of self-importance was quickly dissipated, however, as I realized my lowly position: truly important customers, whether Ecuadorian or foreign, were whisked away to far more luxurious rooms, where the rates of exchange were still more generous.

Sofía's business depends upon her familiarity with the rituals of the indigenous gift economy. Like an Indian, she does business with relatives when she can, and uses gifts to create fictive kin when she needs them. The family in Zumbagua asked me to become their comadre wordlessly at first, through a formal prestation: bottles of liquor and Coca-Cola, roast guinea pigs and cooked food laid down outside my doorway in a sunburst pattern. Sofía, too, opens the doorway to a relationship with a present, as when she convinced one of her mother's business partners to become the daughter's partner as well: "there was a very nice woman . . . I would always buy a hundredweight can of alcohol from her for my mother's store and she took a liking to me. . . . *In order to win her over, I brought her chickens as a gift*" (55). But while she knows how to make these relationships work, she is well aware of their inherent drawbacks: the endless demands on her time and emotions, and the constant uncertainties. Describing her cheese business, in which she gives out cheeses to individual vendors on credit, she complains about the difficulties in collecting payment:

> One . . . always has to chat first. One doesn't just say, "Give it to me right away." One asks them how they are, whether sales are good. Then I tell them, "give me the money." Then they might say, "Please wait, I haven't sold the cheeses yet." For example, . . . Doña Augustina who sells baby bottles . . . I have to sit there till late to watch whether she is selling anything. . . . [T]he other day Doña Marta . . . said, "Come back at six for the rest." When I returned at nine, she had already left her stall. Then, when I went once more early in the morning, she again told me to return later. She finally paid me at noon. It's tedious. (100)

Sofía's language is simultaneously the language of intimacy—the delicate sensibilities we associate with feminine relationships, infused with jealousy and compassion, infectious laughter and acrimonious bickering—and the calculating language of the capitalist.

We see her most clearly as a creature of the gift economy—despite her incessant references to her "capital"—when she talks about the difficult process of breaking off from a casera. All the qualities of the gift relationship—its multistranded nature, the incommensurability of the items exchanged, and the protracted movement of payments and repayments—make it impossible to completely close the books. When a long-standing agreement to supply eggs to a couple who run a lunchroom goes awry, Sofía acknowledges that the restaurant owners were right to be angry when she failed to make a promised delivery. But what about all the times that she had given them all the broken eggs as a llapa? "I was a very good casera," she insists: "What other egg vendor does that?" She refuses to make up but is unable to let go: the "really good sandwiches" they used to feed her haunt her memory. "[S]ometimes I would like to go and eat some, but my pride stops me from going. I would rather send someone else to buy the sandwiches." Against the free sandwiches she once ate, she weighs the unpaid work she did balancing their books for them, since she is literate and they are not. But then again, they did send over two cases of beer when she held a retirement party for her father. In the end, this particular calculus leaves the door slightly ajar: "I think that my old casero Martin is having second thoughts. His wife . . . greets me when she sees me on the street." There is no final resolution—for all we know, she is eating those sandwiches with Martin now.

THEFTS

Within the logic of the gift, material exchanges enrich everyone and everything connected with them. Outside the Andes, in a classroom on the Xingú River in the Amazonian region of Brazil, Mariana K. L. Ferreira recorded the answers that students gave to an arithmetic problem: "I caught 10 fish last night and gave 3 of them to my brother. How many fish do I have now?" Robotki Suyá's was typical: "I gave 3 fish to my brother, so that is 10 + 3 = 13." When Ferreira objected, the boy replied, "[I]f I have 10 and give him 3, he will give me more fish when he goes fishing. So that is 10 + 3, and not 10 − 3" (Ferreira 1997:141). Indeed, she found that one of the most difficult concepts for these youths was the difference between plus and minus signs. One protested, "I know you want me to use the minus sign here instead of the plus sign, but I don't understand why. Does giving away always mean minus for you guys?" (Wenhoron Suyá quoted in Ferreira 1997:141).

The students from the jungle learned quickly, anxious to master a skill they need in their dealings with whites. "In the beginning the white men tried to finish with us using guns, whips, and diseases. Now they use numbers," said Kuuiussi Suyá (Ferreira 1997:134). While the gift economy takes reciprocity as its basic premise, mandating generosity above all, the ethos of capitalist commerce rewards those who take advantage when they can, treating partners as opponents and engaging in the game of buying and selling as though it were a war. The Suyá are aware that the trader who offers them two cruzieros for an arrow will sell it in the city for seven. To the trader, the subtraction of two thirds of his selling price from his buying price is simply rational, needing no justification other than his self-evident need to make a profit. To the Suyá, however, this transparent attempt to enrich himself at their expense is a despicable violation of the ethics of human intercourse; as such, it exemplifies to them the nature of interactions between Indians and whites.

And indeed, race underwrites the trader's actions. Infuriated when the arrow-makers respond to his offer by demanding a price as ridiculously high as they believe his to be low, he fumes, "You lazy Indians know nothing about money, about buying and selling. It's true what people say, that Indians are too stupid to learn math" (133). A favorite racial myth thus provides him with a pretext for ignoring the Indians' deliberate insult, which expressed not their ignorance of his arithmetic, but a studied rejection of it. His purposeful misunderstanding curtails the possibility of meaningful verbal exchange, just as their response had cut short the negotiations over goods.

In the Andes, unlike Amazonia, no one can stand so completely outside the logic of inequality: capitalist exchange permeates social life both within Indian communities and outside them, and reciprocity retains little autonomy. Nevertheless, in Andean economic interactions, just as for the Suyá, profit-taking is often understood to be synonymous with whiteness. The contrast between noncapitalist and capitalist exchange lies at the heart of racial difference in the Andes. More so than rural and urban, more so than ponchos and suits, or polleras and straight skirts, more so even than dark skin and light, or black eyes and blue, this is the crucial distinction. To be white is to participate in the market economy; to be Indian is to belong to the world of the gift. When Indians and whites meet, it is on the terrain of the market, the white's home ground; indeed, to successfully claim the most advantageous terms in a commercial exchange is in effect to position oneself as white.

Whiteness as Theft

Today, as in the past, the profit margin for many small-scale market sellers is extracted from the small advantage provided by racial difference, which vendors use to bully poorer and more Indian clients into accepting disadvantageous terms. Nuñez del Prado explains the effect of the rigid caste system of several decades ago on exchanges between Indians and market women:

> The Indian loses two ways: first, he receives a smaller amount of the article purchased than he is entitled to, and second, he is given a very poor price for the products he offers in exchange. For example, if eggs are sold for ninety centavos each at the market in Cuzco, the Indian will be paid twenty centavos. (1973 : 16)

Of course, who is an "Indian" in the market depends entirely upon context. A white woman from Zumbagua's markets, who calls all the local people "dirty longos" and brags to her friends of her Latacunga connections, is herself a humble Indian when she descends from the bus into the El Salto square. Making the rounds to her usual buyers and sellers, she wheedles and whispers, immediately ceding the racial advantage to the shopkeepers and market vendors of the provincial capital. Indians are routinely mistreated; but one could also say that those who allow themselves to be bullied are permitting the market women to make Indians out of them.

Indian customers sometimes respond to this treatment by labeling abusive vendors "pishtacos," and in stories, the pishtaco is sometimes depicted as a shop-owner who seduces his Indian victims through the lure of the commodity. In the ten years between 1975 and 1985, as the Peruvian community of Sonqo became increasingly involved in the cash economy, Catherine Allen began to hear tales of a new kind of *saqra,* or demonic cannibal, who appeared in the form of a vampiric entrepreneur.[15] "Nocturnal travelers, they say, [see] the hillside open beside their path to reveal a rich Mestizo store full of manufactured goods. . . . The urge to enter is nearly unmasterable, but the fool who does so" suffers a lingering death as the demonic store owner slowly extracts his hapless customer's flesh (1978 : 111). In the 1990s, Orta, too, heard stories of men lured to their deaths by a "señorita"—a young white woman—who invited them to enter a magical shop (1997).

It is hard to imagine a more radical critique of commercial exchange than this, in which profit-takers are described as demonic thieves whose secret operations suck the life out of others. In *Los ríos profundos,* José María Arguedas also condemns the ordinary workings of South American capitalism—and he borrows from both the idiom and the ideology of Andean folklore to do so. The novel opens with a portrait of evil, embodied by a wealthy old man (the *viejo*): "*Infundía respeto, a pesar de su anticuada y sucia apariencia. Las personas principales del Cuzco lo saludaban seriamente.*" [He inspired respect, in spite of his antiquated and dirty appearance. The important people of Cuzco greeted him courteously.][16] The viejo, in turn, enacts an exaggerated (*llamativa*) obeisance before the Church and its priests (1978:4; 1958:9).

Outside of Cuzco, the old man's behavior is very different: he terrorizes his *colonos,* the Indians who work for him on his haciendas. Here, we can see what is invisible in the city: the oppressive material relations upon which his urban privileges are erected. Even in Cuzco, however, the viejo's decrepit appearance offers a clue to his disrespect for the material riches of the Andes. The disrespect with which he treats his own body corresponds to his contemptuous handling of the fruits of his land—and of the Andean people who live there. "*Almacena las frutas de las huertas, y las deja pudrir; cree que valen muy poco para traerlas a vender al Cuzco . . . y que cuestan demasiado para dejárselas a los colonos*" (1958:9). [He stores up the fruit from his orchards and lets it spoil; he doesn't think it's worth taking to sell in Cuzco . . . and says it's too dear for him to leave for his *colonos* (1978 : 3).]

In these few words, Arguedas outlines a moral vision. The dirty body of the old man and his storehouses full of rotten fruit reveal a Peru so estranged from itself that it destroys its own physical and material well-being in order to shore up wholly illusory systems of wealth and prestige. The viejo treats what he has as other white Peruvians do the natural and cultural wealth of their nation: unable to sell it to whiter and more developed nations, or to find any value in it themselves, they prefer to destroy it rather than to share it with nonwhite Peru. Arguedas presents the opposition between exchange value and use value as the difference between a destructive delusion and a hidden truth: thinking that he is harming only the Indians, the viejo is oblivious to his own corporeal and spiritual dissolution. For despite his ostentatious piety, " *¡Irá al infierno!' decía de él mi padre"* ["He'll go to hell," my father said of him (1958:9).]

Arguedas's critique of the viejo turns the tables on racial ideologues: the backwardness of Andean economies originates not in the heavy weight of incompetent, lazy, and drunken Indians who drag white society down, but in the destructive acts of whites. In an arresting image, Arguedas says that the old man shouted down at the Indians from the mountaintops *"con voz de condenado."* Translator Frances Barraclough offers us "with the voice of the damned" here (1978:4). But in Quechua mythology, the "condenadu" is not a dead soul banished to the inferno: he is a member of the undead, his restless, rotting body condemned to wander the territory he inhabited while alive. Like the viejo's body, or the fruits of his orchards, the flesh of the condenadu is putrid and loathsome. He is also very dangerous. Like the Indian trader so deeply despised by Ferreira's students—who boasted of the blonde and the speedboat he had bought with his profits, even while announcing his intention to accumulate still more women and things— the condenadu is filled with insatiable desires. He attacks the living— seducing, raping, and stealing from them—yet each of these forcible exchanges leaves him as hungry and alone as before.

The story of the condenadu preaches the morality of the gift economy. The generous parent, the faithful child, the industrious spouse end up as respected ancestors, amply fed and fêted by their descendants, the mortal body peacefully reunited with the living earth and stones of the mountain. In contrast, selfish acts—sleeping with one's daughter or father; neglecting to pour libations to the ancestors; stealing from a neighbor—will make the earth refuse the corpse and render the body of the dead unable to enjoy the gifts of food and love that it so craves. Unwilling to give in life, in death the condenadu is unable to consume.

In popular culture today, exploitative whites are condemned not as condenadus, but as pishtacos. The condenadu resembles an old-fashioned hacendado like the viejo: his orbit is circumscribed and local, and his sins are sins of the flesh, motivated by laziness, gluttony, or lust.

The ñakaq is a more modern figure: like the Indian trader, he steals in order to sell, rather than for his own use. But if he violates Indian bodies in pursuit of profit, like a white, he also attacks them sexually, like a man. In either case, he takes without giving in return.

The Sex Life of the Bogeyman

The pishtaco is a serial killer with a penchant for dismembering and disemboweling his victims; he has other bad habits as well. Andrew Orta tells of being at a Bolivian fiesta where, after a long night of drinking, the celebrants confronted a stranger among them: "his identity card was demanded, and he was viciously insulted and accused of having designs to steal women, and of being a kharikhari" (1996:18). When William Stein arrived in Ancash in 1951, locals said he was a Pishtacu—an accusation that had distinctly sexual overtones. "[P]eople believed that I was a rapist, and women were warned that sexual contact with me would . . . be painful because of the size and shape of the sexual organ." Hostile neighbors "maintained that I was making sexual use of the people I visited, men as well as women" (1961:x).

This Andean bogeyman may have more in common with his European namesake than is immediately apparent. Walter Willliams, exploring the etymology of the word *berdache,* discovered that it was part of a pair. *Bardache,* he tells us,

> originally came from the Persian *bardaj,* and via the Arabs spread to the Italian language as *bardasso* and to Spanish as *bardaxa* or *bardaje* [and to] . . . French as *bardache.* . . . The 1680 edition of *Dictionnaire francais,* for example, gives this definition: "a young man who is shamefully abused." . . . The dictionaries, however, make it clear that both *bardache* and *ganimede* refer to the passive homosexual partner. The French word *bougre* was used for the active male partner, akin to the English words *bugger* and *bougie man.* . . . In the sixteenth to eighteenth centuries . . . the terms *bardache* and *bougre* were the most commonly used to denote male homosexuality. . . . For example, in a satirical text, *Deliberations du Conseil general des bougres et des bardaches,* published in France in 1790, the author wrote, "the *bardaches* dropped their trousers, and the *bougres,* becoming erect as satyrs, took advantage of them." (W. Williams 1986:9–10)

The bardaches, we may assume, were willing partners of the bougres; not so the victims of the Andean bogeyman. He is identified as a rapist in unpublished field notes collected in 1961 as part of the famous Vicos project, where the Peruvian anthropologist Humberto Ghersi (possibly quoting an earlier observer, Norman Pava) noted that

> Alberto Torres [a local hacienda owner] had wide notoriety as a pishtaco, and was feared and avoided. . . . Vicosinos were afraid to pass his mill alone at night, and would often wait (especially women) hours for some other Vicosino that happened along, so as to have company in passing the dreaded spot. . . . According to MCV, Alberto Torres' notoriety as a pishtaco is based on his frequent molesting of Vicos women for sex purposes.[17]

An American summer school student, Harold Skalka, wrote:

> Juan said that pishtacos don't rape women—but I said, I thought one of the reasons Alberto Torres was such a big pishtaco is that he used to rape the Vicosinas. Octavio said, [pishtacos] certainly [do rape], and Juan finally agreed. He said they kill them after this.

These references to the pishtaco as rapist bring to the fore barely disguised undertones of sexual predation in more conventional ñakaq stories, which begin with a seduction: "They seem to be pleasant, friendly, handsome people, who fall in beside you smiling, chatting amiably" reports Meyerson (1990:154). Attuned to heterosexuality, Anglophone ears can hear the sexual theme more clearly if we give the neutral Spanish pronouns that describe the victim a feminine form.[18] Listen, for example, to my translation of Juan Antonio Manya's classic 1969 article on the subject:

> The Nakaq rides on horseback, wearing riding pants, elegant, dazzling, with a white cap on his head, and the horse similarly well-attired. . . . He blows a hypnotizing dust over his victim, who begins to tremble . . . and is drawn inescapably toward him. Arriving at his side, she falls on her knees and into a deep sleep; immediately the Nakaq begins to work on her buttocks, injecting a needle connected to a tiny apparatus . . . when he is finished, he slaps her, and she awakens without knowing what has happened to her, without noticeable marks on her body . . . but the damage is irredeemable, and within fifteen or twenty days she will die.[19]

Ambiguities between rape and murder likewise emerge in a long, curious tale about two brothers told to Manya by a certain Doña Satuca. According to the story, Sitticha and Jasikucha were both pishtacos, but Sitticha specialized in young boys, and Jasikucha in women.

Don Jasikucha, monstrous, fat, and clever, at once cowardly and mean, . . . [attacked] women, especially Indian women. . . . He was seen on the farm of two humble shepherd girls, wearing a leather vest, and with two little Pishtaquitos at his side, illegitimate offspring whom he abandoned, with their mothers, once he had perfected his technique of slashing throats by day and by night, in the city and in the country. Like a ravenous fiend he conquered his victims, under the cloak of love and friendship; and when he had extracted their fat he looked for pretexts to export the poor women far from home, where they died in oblivion.[20]

Founding Fathers

Nonconsensual sex is commonplace in the Andes; indeed, it is woven into the very fabric of Latin American society from the threads of poverty, racism, and male domination. This is the other form of unequal exchange that permeates Andean society, imposing an ethos of predation upon sexual intercourse as relentlessly as market exchange does upon economic transactions. In economic transactions, we reserve the word "theft" only for some kinds of unequal exchange, choosing to believe that in the other cases, the victim's losses are voluntarily incurred. Similarly, "rape" is a strong word; yet the question of free will is as fraught in sex as in commerce, and sexual encounters conducted on unequal terms abound. In the Americas, sexual inequality is exacerbated by race: Roger Bastide once said that the nature of sexual relations between whites and nonwhites "effectively reduces a whole race to the level of prostitutes."[21] This history of racialized rape is deeply inscribed onto the body of the chola, a fact well-known by her admirers.

In Cuenca, the museum exhibition isolates the "chola Cuencana" from the Indians that surround her geographically, such as the Cañaris or the Saraguros, and also from the only other people identified as part-white: the "montubios" of the coast. An observant visitor might note, however, that one oddity links the Cuencanas to the montubios: the coastal fishermen are depicted without women, just as the cholas are without men. Racially homogeneous groups are depicted as sexually dimorphic, but a sexual homogeneity is imposed upon the racially heterogeneous. On postcards and in museums, Indians and blacks are often depicted in mixed-sex groups, including married couples and families; in contrast, cholas may have children, but never male companions.

On the surface, this absence is easy enough to explain: there is no folkloric "cholo" outfit in which one might dress a male mannequin.[22]

But there is more to it than that: a quite specific racial logic governs this deployment of the sexes. As the product of interracial relations, the chola cannot be represented with both her parents: in the segregated world of ethnographic displays, there is no room for such a family. Mothers can be included in the museum of nonwhiteness, but not the chola's father—or the father of her children.

A brutally simple sexual paradigm underlies the Latin American idea of miscegenation: in the act that creates the mestizo or mulatto, the man is white and the woman is not. Or one could say, the white is male and the nonwhite is not. Two profound inequalities—between non-whites and whites, and between women and men—combine to make the bodies of nonwhite women into receptacles for white men's physical passions. According to this account of our sexual history, the mixture of races that can be read in faces and bodies across the continent is visible proof that a wealthy white man can get what he wants. Indeed, the nineteenth-century mestiza was explicitly perceived as the product of white masculine desire (Feal 1995).

Other kinds of interracial love do occur—but those love stories exist at the margins of history, while that of the race rape has the status of myth. A nativity scene deformed by racism, the story of the white man, the Indian woman, and their mestizo child is written into every epoch of Latin American history, beginning with Columbus's arrival in Hispaniola. From sixteenth-century European engravings depicting the New World as a naked woman passively awaiting her conqueror to the twentieth-century poetry of Gloria Anzaldúa, the mythic history of the continent takes the form of a narrative in which territorial claims are staked through racialized sexual violence.[23]

The antiquity of this form of violence is used to justify its continued reenactment in the present, as Peter Gose found in Huaquirca. Elite men there, known as *vecinos,* trace their right to power directly to the myth of the Conquest. In their retelling, the long and convoluted history of European imperialism is condensed into a single act of sexual violence: "the forced consummation of the lust of the Spanish conquistador for the beautiful Inca princess (ñusta) in a scenario of primordial rape" (1994b:20). This mythic rape infuses the racial language used by the vecinos with special meaning. In stigmatizing their comunero neighbors as Indians, Gose says, the vecinos excuse sexual abuse. Driven by "dual impulses of attraction and violation" for the comuneros, vecino men explain their rapacious desires by using the "image of conquest as a mythical vehicle" according to which modern social relations are simply a reenactment of that first, "primordial encounter between the Hispanic and the Indian" (19).

These sexual ideologies are part of rural history. Throughout the Andes, oppressive and exploitative systems such as the peonage that bound Indian laborers to the land—called *huasipungaje* in Ecuador, and *pongaje* in Bolivia—or the rampant *gamonalismo* of southern Peru continued well into the twentieth century. In Zumbagua, an hacienda until the mid-1960s, disobedient workers were routinely whipped, beaten, and chained. An old woman from Apagua, a community located just outside the boundaries of the old hacienda, told me that she met her husband when his family smuggled him out of Zumbagua, fearful that the next beating he incurred through his bravado would be a fatal one. Under this regime, the forced concubinage of Indians in the service of hacienda overseers, managers, and owners was commonplace; I heard many such tales in collecting Zumbagua family histories, but I never wrote about them.

Indeed, the anthropological and historical literature of the twentieth-century Andes, for all its attention to the economic and political predations of white society on indigenous communities, has been largely silent on these most gendered forms of violence. South American writers of fiction fill this void: they have explored the theme of forcible sex in terms that make the connection between race, sex, and subjugation terrifyingly clear. In the 1934 *Huasipungo,* Ecuadorian novelist Jorge Icaza begins the requisite rape scene with the hacienda owner's assertion of absolute privilege: *"Era dueño de todo, de la india también"* [He was master of all, including the Indian woman] (Icaza 1953:61). The hacendado forces the Indian to submit through a mixture of blackmail and violence, yet he is angered by the stoic silence in which she endures the violation. As he leaves, he tells her that she has now proven her racial inferiority by making love "bestially, like a cow" (62). The vicious and nightmarish logic of these words, like those of the Indian trader on the Xingú, make the victim into the author of her own abasement: it is the animality of her body, as it is the stupidity of the boys' minds, that makes these Indians into natural prey.

The twentieth century has gradually seen the bitter struggles for agrarian reform bear fruit, as revolutions in Peru and Bolivia and reforms in Ecuador eliminated the legal underpinnings of Indian serfdom. But the attitudes and practices that assume white male access to nonwhite bodies for sexual gratification remain strongly entrenched. Naked sexual violence against nonwhite women continues, as well as the thinly veiled coercion of racial prejudice, which motivates women to choose "the 'whitest' possible" men as sexual partners, hoping to brighten their children's futures by whitening their skins (Smith 1996:157).

During my second summer in Ecuador, I rented a room in Salcedo,

a pleasant market town just south of Latacunga. I liked the house—
which was big and old, with an enclosed garden—and the owners too:
a retired couple who lived alone, except for their maid and her daughter. To my Midwestern eyes, the four of them could easily have been
members of the same family. Everybody was short, stout, and lively,
with black eyes, shiny hair, and tiny feet—cute as buttons, my grandmother would have said. The owners would have been appalled by my
perceptions; they considered their own whiteness to be as self-evident
as the fact that their maid was an Indian. The only question mark in
their minds was one they had placed over the child.

The house was rarely quiet, as I soon discovered; retirement had
produced an irritating intimacy. The maid often slammed about her
tasks in a barely concealed rage, while one or both of the older people
followed her around, issuing grim but unconvincing warnings about
the ingratitude of those who could find themselves without a roof over
their head for the night. I was fascinated and appalled by this relationship, which combined deep affection with utter inequality in a way I
had not before seen.

At night, the maid and her daughter retired to their tiny cubicle
behind the washing machine, where they lay together on the sagging
single bed, listening to the radio. The retired couple, meanwhile,
settled on the sofa in the living room to watch soap operas on television. There, conversation frequently turned to the little girl. The two
of them combed through the domestic incidents of the day, assembling
new evidence of the child's intelligence, innate manners and modesty,
and refined appearance: in short, of her whiteness. These gleanings
were used to weigh the relative qualities of her parents. Each additional
proof of the girl's racial superiority to her mother, according to their
calculus, added doubly to the breeding and social worth of her father:
for a woman so low to have produced so high-class a child, they rea-
soned, the male parent must be an exceptional man indeed.

The identity of this paragon was entirely unknown to them, although they assumed he was the maid's previous employer. She had
initially refused to acknowledge that the child even had a father, claiming a sort of immaculate conception; but gradually, she became com-
plicit in their fantasy, saying nothing to disabuse them. I remember her
listening impassively as they compared her—the stupid Indian foil—
to her daughter. She liked to hear them talk so, she told me later: perhaps their belief in her daughter's innate superiority would inspire them
to pay for the girl's education.

In this family, then, illegitimacy conferred a secret whiteness upon a
child—but did not free mother and daughter from a domestic servi-

tude so total as to resemble slavery. To many readers from the United
States, the story of a half-white servant girl, the illegitimate child of her
mother's employer, who is pampered because of her heritage but not
freed, sounds weirdly archaic, like a chapter from a nineteenth-century
slave narrative. And indeed, the roots of such stories do lie in the con-
tinental history of unfree agricultural labor, which encompasses not
only the slave plantations of Brazil and the United States, but also the
hacienda system of the Andes.

In his magisterial studies of the Brazilian slave plantation, Gilberto
Freyre defined an "all-encompassing system of sexual and family life"
that he called "polygamous patriarchalism" (1946:7). In the "Big
House," the white male plantation owner ruled as absolute patriarch
over women and children of all races, as well as black and mulatto men.
Long after the "Big House" existed only as a memory, Freyre argued,
elite men like himself still inherit its racialized psychosexuality, moving
from a childhood of distant white mothers and intimately familiar black
nurses to an adulthood divided between desexualized white wives and
eroticized black or mulatto sex partners.

In his 1994 novel *No se lo digas a nadie* [Don't tell anyone], Peruvian
novelist Jaime Bayly tells the story of a disaffected middle-class youth
who first discovers his own homosexuality through the revulsion he
feels at his father's penchant for illicit sex with working-class women.[24]
To the father, these women are all "cholas"—from the family maid
whom he forcibly penetrated when he was thirteen (1994:59) to the
waitress he addresses as "cholita rica" (tasty little chola) while having
sex with her in front of his son (82). Bayly writes with more rage than
finesse, but his relentless focus on the sex act as an enactment of race
and class power takes him much further than the Peruvian left has traditionally been willing to go. In the early 1980s, the elites of Huaquirca
espoused a left-nationalist ideology and repudiated the overtly racist
gamonalismo of the immediate past; but this political volte-face had
done nothing to undermine their love of the tale of the Spanish conqueror and the Indian princess, or their use of that story to explain their
own behavior with lower-class women (Gose 1994b:20–25).[25]

A generation earlier, the neo-indígenistas likewise celebrated the
notion of a nation founded in interracial sex. While a previous group
of intellectuals had cherished the image of the pure Indian woman who
resisted the conqueror, the neo-indígenistas praised the chola for having no such qualms (de la Cadena 1996). Unlike the idealized and inaccessible white girl, the chola and the mulatta attract attention through
displays of vulgar sexuality.[26] One poem implores the "little chola,

very pretty chola" of Cuzco to "lift your skirt a little . . . show me how you like to move your buttocks." [27] What is at work here is less the championing of nonwhite women as beautiful than the fascination of a woman who is desirable because she is almost white, and available because she is not.

These erotic poems do not read as expressions of interracial amity so much as a wish to repeat the sexual violence of the past—and thus to retain the structural inequalities of the present, which secure the writer's power over the object of his desire. The poet wants to be "a hawk to seize you with my claw," and to "sack" the chola's buttocks with his "pirate hands." The image of the buccaneer, like that of the conquistador, is one that provides rape with a romantic history. In the end, then, the neo-indígenista songs of praise to lusty cholas are failures as antiracist texts, since these sexual fantasies about white men and brown women reproduce the very system of racial inequality they claim to abhor.

Sexual Exchange

Unlike other indigenistas, José María Arguedas's critique of Peruvian society encompasses more than economic and racial discrimination: in books like *Los ríos profundos,* he also gives voice to an anguished protest against Andean sexual violence. Here sexual intercourse takes the most degraded of forms: the repeated gang rape of a mentally deficient woman, as witnessed by the novel's protagonist, a schoolboy.

> *De noche . . . [l]a descubría ya muy cerca de la pared de madera de los excusados. . . . Causaba desconcierto y terror. Los alumnos grandes se golpeaban para llegar primero junto a ella, o hacían guardia cerca de los excusados, formando una corta fila. Los menores o pequeños nos quedábamos detenidos junto a las paredes más próximas, temblando de ansiedad, sin decirnos una palabra, mirando el tumulto o la rígida espera de los que estaban en la fila. Al poco rato . . . la mujer salía a la carrera . . . pero casi siempre alguno la alcanzaba todavía en el camino y pretendía derribarla.* (1958:76)

> [At night, . . . [t]hey would find her already quite close to the wooden fence around the latrines. . . . This discovery caused confusion and terror. The biggest students hit one another trying to be the first to reach her, or stood guard near the latrines, forming a short line. We younger, smaller boys, unable to leave, stayed next to the nearest walls, trembling with anxiety, unable to utter a word to one another, watching the fighting or the rigid expec-

tation with which the boys waited in line. After a little while, the
woman ran out onto the road . . . but then almost always someone
caught up with her and tried to knock her down.]

In depicting this sexual encounter as a forcible act that robs its participants of pleasure, Arguedas attacks a form of sexual intercourse that,
like capitalist commerce, destroys use value in search of a chimerical
exchange value. The woman gains little or nothing: her desire for
sexual pleasure drives her to the latrines, but what happens to her there
drives her away again. The older boys take what they want from her,
but they gain only the most impoverished and momentary of physical
pleasures, in a form that aggravates rather than relieves their emotional
turmoil. What they get instead is the fantasied achievement of a kind
of manhood that must be purchased through sexual aggression.

In *Mother Courage,* the prostitute Yvette sings bitterly of her own
introduction to sex at the hands of soldiers. "The pipes play and the
drums do beat / The foe parades down every street / And then with us
they take their ease / and fraternize behind the trees" (Brecht 1955:
45). In the Andes, too, the rape of local women by policemen, soldiers,
and prison guards is hardly an unknown occurrence. But even outside
a military context, sex is notoriously a battleground to which the participants come unequally armed. Women—as disempowered by their
gender as the terrified boys behind the latrine who are too "little" and
too "young"—often find sex with men to be an unhappy bargain
struck with an enemy. "A cook was my own foe," sings Yvette. "I
hated him by daylight / But in the dark I loved him so."

One of the most compelling social theories about such bargains is
that of American anthropologist Gayle Rubin. Rubin's essay "The Traffic in Women: Notes on the 'Political Economy' of Sex" appeared in
1975, some twenty-five years after "The Gift" was published in Paris.
It was to become as much of a classic in feminist scholarship as was
Mauss's essay in the field of economic anthropology. Rubin's "sex/
gender system" uses Mauss's theory of the gift to build a model of unequal sexual exchange. She shows how heterosexuality—which first
separates women and men through the sexual division of labor, and
then binds them together in the institution of marriage—undermines
the logic of the gift. Instead of the disinterested giving between social equals envisioned by Mauss, gender—which Rubin calls a "taboo
against sameness"—poisons sexual exchange by anchoring it in dependency rather than in free will. Other institutions, cultural and economic, enforce women's inequality, adding asymmetry to unfreedom.
For Rubin, unlike essentialist feminists, a sex act between a woman and

a man is not inherently unequal, exploitative, or violent. But compulsory heterosexuality in the context of gender inequality forces intercourse to become an unequal exchange, and so undermines its potential to be a mutually enriching exchange of gifts.

Rubin rejects theories of universal patriarchy. Like Mauss, she argues that each particular form of sexual exchange operates within a totality of social relations: not only those between men and women, but between "town and country, kinship and state, forms of property, systems of land tenure, convertibility of wealth . . . to name a few" (210). Thus the logic of sexual intercourse operating within a particular sex/gender system must be found both inside sexual exchange itself and in the other forms of economic and social exchange that surround it.

This kind of materialist analysis has too often been missing in discussions of Andean gender, which are largely motivated by a liberal desire to emphasize mutuality within marriage as the ultimate goal of feminism. Ironically, the result has been a celebration of Andean women's dependence on men, rather than of the economic independence that underwrote traditional marriages. And yet the latter made possible marital sex of a strikingly different nature than that decried by Rubin and other writers under the rubric of compulsory heterosexuality. Sex in the indigenous Andes has often been described as rough and playful, a pleasurable fight between equally matched opponents that begins with adolescents who try to steal one another's clothes, and escalates into rock-throwing, wrestling—and sex.[28] Thomas Abercrombie recalls

> a young Mamani woman [who] came to our house in search of what might be called beauty aids—the mirrors, barrettes, and large-sized safety pins that unmarried but marriageable women wear in quantity. She also, however, was bleeding from a cut on the top of her head, and we helped her wash and disinfect the wound. When we looked more closely, we noticed that she also sported a large bump, and she related that a certain young man who had been courting her had scored a direct hit with a small sling-thrown stone. Laughing about it, she reported that she thought she had landed a few shots on him, too. (1998:66)

The sex act that follows such roughhousing is itself a physical contest between equally matched opponents, in which both parties' capacity and desire for sexual gratification is taken for granted:

> [T]he sex of the child is determined by . . . [who] "wins" in intercourse. Each sex contains its embryo which is directly passed from

mother to daughter for females and indirectly passed through the wife along the male line. They believe that if the man climaxes before the woman . . . she conceives a boy. But if the woman climaxes before the man, then she "wins" and conceives a girl. (Bastien 1978:86–87)

We can see Zuidema's theory of parallel descent at work here; the egalitarian nature of these tussles are also reminiscent of what Malinowski described as *The Sexual Life of Savages*. In the Trobriands, too, amorous games and contests led up to a sex act in which a woman is as active as her partner; the Polish anthropologist was surprised to be told that women and men ejaculate in the same fashion. The Trobrianders, it would seem, modeled their sexual practices on their economic activities, making sex into a reciprocal exchange of pleasures. In a different form, so too do those in the rural Andes fortunate enough to live in communities where sexual partners meet as economic equals, whether they are unmarried lovers or spouses.[29]

Such free play vanishes when unequal exchange begins to permeate indigenous social relations, reshaping sexual relations into a more familiar—and far more oppressive—mode. When Trobriand women had sex with white colonials, they were dismayed by the expectation that they should lie passively under the male. "Many a white informant has spoken to me about perhaps the only word in the native language he ever learned, *kubilabala* . . . spoken with some intensity during the sexual act. This verb defines . . . movement during intercourse, which should be mutual" (Malinowski 1929:285).

In the late 1980s, Zumbagua men left the parish on a weekly basis to earn money in Quito, leaving their wives to care for the family's crops and animals, its children and old folks. The articulation of capitalist and domestic economies was thus moved into the heart of young families, occurring at the conjuncture of female and male roles (Deere 1976:9; Weismantel 1988). These marriages mirrored the relationship between the parish of Zumbagua itself and an Ecuadorian nation anxious to define itself as modern and white. For parish women, men constituted the only access to commodities, turning marriage into a form of dependency painfully at odds with Andean cultural norms. Ragged and exhausted, Zumbagua wives looked at the husbands whom they had to beg for spare change and saw men who were strangely whitened: fed on Coca-Cola and clothed in machine-made polyester, whisked to and from the city in buses as they joked and gossiped with their companions *in the incomprehensible Spanish language,* they had turned into aliens.

Even more troubling than this racial estrangement was a tremendous upsurge in male-on-female domestic violence. Parish people are un-surprised when husbands hit wives — or when wives hit husbands, as in the scene I once witnessed between a drunken José Manuel and his exasperated wife and sister-in-law, who rained blows on his head while he stood crying, not attempting to defend himself because he knew that they were right to be angry. The newer forms of domestic vio-lence, which occasioned much worried conversation among older resi-dents, were more gendered — and more lethal. Men came back from the city each week brutalized by their experiences there and despairing at their inability to meet their families' incessant demands for money. Drunk, broke, and tired, returning husbands lashed out in vicious at-tacks that left women battered, blinded, miscarrying, or even dead; un-married men turned their rage upon themselves, committing suicide by drinking cleaning fluids or pesticides.

When Indian women meet strangers, too, money, sex, and vio-lence are often conjoined. In Vicos, "Sometimes, Octavio said, the pishtaco pays the women 2–3 hundred soles for sexual privileges. . . . He then kills her (a process which is made easier because she is now cooperative and unsuspecting), and of course takes his money back, along with hers." [30]

The harassing young men on the bus from Salasaca, described in chapter 2, enjoy the ambiguity of their pleasures. Reaching into Indian women's clothing, they may find some quick cash, or just cop a feel. Either way, they imagine themselves licensed, by virtue of their race and sex, to take whatever is there. In their minds, an Indian woman is not the rightful possessor of either her own body or her money. Here, sex has been completely immersed in the logic of negative exchange: the woman must experience no pleasure, only loss; indeed, the men will measure the success of their venture directly through their percep-tion of how little they have pleased their partner.

Despite the North American desire to portray such sexual predation as peculiarly Latin, these proclivities define many Western forms of masculinity. The desire to define heterosexuality as perfect inequality can be found in the wealthy and self-satisfied French roués of an ear-lier age. The poet Baudelaire praised his mistress for her sweetness, her submissiveness — and her total lack of sexual enthusiasm. With a woman so completely blasé, the French *boulevardier* could enjoy sex unconcerned that his partner might gain anything in the exchange. [31]

A century and a half later, we can find another kind of one-sided sexual economy among a group of upper-middle-class young men in the United States. Peggy Sanday found that University of Pennsylvania fraternity members explicitly conceived of sex as "a commodity that is acquired by the brothers from women" (1990:56). Sexual encounters enhanced a young man's masculinity at the expense of his female partners, whose worth as individuals—and as future sexual partners—was diminished in the process. Rituals of gang rape on an unconscious victime were a central feature of party life, while in ordinary dating, time and sex were conjoined in an arithmetic of competition. In interviews, the boys quantified their sex acts to such a degree that sex sounded like factory piecework. One brother

> decided to have intercourse with thirteen new and different girls before the end of the semester. Setting quotas was the means by which he checked and evaluated his masculinity. He explained that the joy of sex was "not just the pleasure derived from the act"

but also the far more important "feeling of acceptance and approval of my masculinity which goes along with" rapidly acquiring and discarding sexual partners (115).

Arguedas saw this fetishism of the exchange value of the sex act over the physical pleasures to be enjoyed with another person as dehumanizing. Desire, beauty, and love are powerful plot elements in his novels, but the circuits on which they run resist the mandates of Andean patriarchy and heterosexuality. He replays the scenes beloved of the neo-indígenistas in a very different register. Like them, the novel's young protagonist is drawn to the "lively" quarter, occupied by "the market women, the laborers, and the porters, who did the daily work of the city"; here he discovers the chicherías, where "they played harp and violin . . . and danced huaynos and marineras" (1958:44).

The boy admires the women who work in these taverns, with their "shawls of Castilian cloth trimmed with silk" and "whitened straw hats"; he listens with pleasure to their high voices singing huaynos and watches their flirtations with their working-class customers. But this author, repulsed by the unequal couplings that so attracted the earlier generation of Andean writers, never positions his protagonist as the chicheras' lover. Instead, the boy finds pleasure as a passive witness who enjoys the fact that although the waitresses actively pursued sexual pleasure, "the [men's] struggle [to win] them was long and arduous; it was not easy to get to dance with them" (1978:45). Watching these scenes of feminine sexual agency, he finds an antidote to the other scenes to which he is a passive witness: away from the chicherías, he is troubled by images of the schoolyard rape that "filter into his dreams."

He is tormented by nightmares about "*el húmedo piso en que se recostaba la demente*" [the damp ground on which the madwoman lay down] (1958:88), surrounded by weeds and broken concrete. In his imagination, this place, like his uncle's storehouses piled with rotting fruit, is filled with an "oppressive stench." All the younger boys were similarly afflicted: *"luchábamos con ese pesado mal, temblábamos ante él"* [we struggled with this evil burden, we trembled before it] (88). After a fight in which the older boys try to force an unwilling schoolmate down onto the woman, the little ones' fears escalate. They avoid the spot where it occurred *"como si en el patio durmiera . . . un nakak"* [as though a ñakaq might be sleeping there] (87).

This narrator, who regards the sex acts of his fellow students with such revulsion, is not without passions of his own; but these are so transgressive that their sexual content remains disguised—perhaps even from the author himself. Unmoved by the young white girls to whom his classmates devote their daytime attentions, the boy develops a fascination with a powerful older woman: the chichera Doña Felipa, leader of the chola uprising. Standing in the crowd of women as she speaks, surrounded by their large and sweaty bodies, he says, "*La violencia de las mujeres me exaltaba*" [the violence of the women excited me tremendously] (1958:137). The descriptions of his male playmates are also erotic: the younger boy with a face like a flower, the older dandy who lends him a volume of Ruben Darío's poetry. His sexual desire for them is never articulated, much less consummated, but an ache fills the passages in which he describes their skin, their eyes, their hair.

In offering us such sexually ambiguous figures—masculine women and feminine boys—as the objects of his protagonist's desire, Arguedas suggests the outlines of a covert sex/gender system that breaks with the conventions of inequality, in which strong men desire weak women, and powerful whites take Indians by force. This attempt to create a space of sexual liminality parallels the book's racial geography. Arguedas's novels take place neither in rural Indian communities nor in the neighborhoods where wealthy whites live; both remain in the background, representing the two halves of a violently disarticulated society. The foreground is occupied by places and people that bridge the racial chasm: chicherías, plazas, and schoolyards; rural migrants, the urban working classes, and provincial elites.

Arguedas's critique is powerful; but so too is that contained in popular-cultural stories about ñakaqs and cholas—the source for his novels. Pishtaco stories retell the primordial myth of race rape, but here the myth serves to indict present crimes, not to excuse them.

From Noun to Verb

"The Indians call the whites . . . Pishtaco," observed Humberto Ghersi; but pishtaco "could also mean rapist." Calling pishtacos rapists and white men pishtacos might seem merely to elaborate upon a well-known social fact, but these fantastic and gruesome stories communicate an Indian perception of events that is sharply at odds with white attitudes. Men joke about "taking" cholas and Indian women all the time. In the *Léxico de vulgarismos Azuayos,* for example, Alfonso Cordero Palacios records many amusing slang terms, among them "cholero" and "chinero" (1985:113). The cholero, he informs us, *"Es el hombre muy dado a perseguir y cortejar a mujeres del bajo pueblo, de aquellas que designamos con el nombre de cholas, y entre las cuales abundan tipos de singular belleza"* [is the man given over to pursuing and wooing lower-class women, of the type that we designate with the name of cholas, among whom examples of singular beauty are abundant] and he goes on to quote a few verses of Darquea's "Chola Cuencana"; the chinero, similarly, is addicted to chasing "chinas" [another term for nonwhite working-class women]. Through the idiom of the pishtaco story, Indians refuse to get the joke; instead, they insist on recounting the ugly consequences of such pursuits, which too often end in rape, violence, and abandonment.

White tales about the ravishment of Indians exude an air of fatal inevitability, in which both victim and aggressor find that their will to resist is much weaker than the desires that emanate from their bodies; sex and race function as inescapable destinies that neither reason nor volition can overcome. Bastide writes scornfully of the myth of the "dusky Venus," by which Latin American men locate the origins of their rapacious appetites outside of themselves, in the irresistible bodies of dark-skinned women; La Malinche, too, cannot resist betraying the men of her own race, simply because she is a woman.[32]

Pishtaco stories are different. If they are not romances, neither are they tragedies, in which the protagonists discover the inevitable fates that await them. If anything, they resemble American slasher films, in which the normality of everyday life is suddenly rent asunder by events that simply cannot be happening. Horror movies focus on teens from middle-class Middle America, banking on the geography of privilege to intensify the audience's reactions: how could one so young, so white, so fashionably yet casually dressed be subjected to fear or pain? How can such typical (albeit large and impossibly clean) suburban tract houses be the scenes of such suffering, such grief? Poor and nonwhite communities have long been angered at the lack of such responses when serial killers stalk their neighborhoods. They feel keenly the geography of race that blunts other Americans' reactions to hurt and sorrow experienced on the meaner streets of the city, as though bereavements and atrocities were simply part and parcel of life for the underprivileged.

In phrasing pishtaco stories as horror tales rather than tragedies, residents of the Andes reject the inevitability of their own suffering. The rural Indians who speak of ñakaqs and kharikharis, like the impoverished city-dwellers who invented the related genre of the *sacaojos,* use these stories to insist that in their communities, just like in suburbia and small-town America, there is nothing quotidian about the violation of a human body. This genre fulfills Brecht's mandate for revolutionary theater. The spectator in a conventional theater says to himself, "It's only natural—it'll never change . . . The sufferings of this man appall me, because they are inescapable"; in Brecht's theater, he wanted them to say instead, "That's not the way— It's got to stop . . . The sufferings of this man appall me, because they are unnecessary" (1963: 70). So, too, the tellers of the pishtaco story eschew the conventions of the Andean race rape tale, which portray each new incident as predestined. Instead, these stories insist that no matter how often they occur, each individual act of sexual violence is novel, appalling—and unnecessary.

The pishtaco tale could be considered a kind of quotation of the chola story, one that estranges the audience from the ideology of racial and sexual inequality within which violations of the Indian body are acceptable, even pleasurable. The technique through which this is achieved involves a dialectical interplay between the myth and its retellings. The myth of the pishtaco was born from a thousand stories about white people, perhaps starting with the horrifying discovery that European soldiers on the battlefield were using body fat from Indian corpses as a medicine to heal their own wounded. As such stories accumulate within a people's historical memory, they coagulate into myths. Today, every community of color on the continent has its legendary whites, whether the hooded lynch mob of Southern memory or the ill-mannered buffoons lampooned in Apache jokes (Basso 1979).

Once it has taken shape as a myth, collective memory begins to react upon individual histories. It pushes people to act in particular ways, waiting behind quotidian social interactions like a prompter holding a script. Thus past lynchings serve to warn black men and white women that if desire, or even mutuality, quickens at a chance encounter, tragedy will ensue; more ominously, they instruct an abandoned white lover to exact the bloodiest possible revenge. In the Andes, the myth of mestizaje and a culture of mandatory heterosexuality act oppressively on each new coupling, forcing it into an appropriately unequal form in which someone plays the man and someone the woman, one an Indian and one a white.

But myth can serve other purposes as well. By calling the viejo a "condenado," Arguedas takes the man's actions out of a social context in which they are admired, and places them instead within a different moral universe. Ñakaq stories can do the same thing. The myth operates differently in the abstract than in specific retellings—and meaning is generated through the friction between the two. As myth, the pishtaco story tells of a generic white male enacting gruesome violence upon an Indian victim. But actual pishtaco stories do not make all whites or all males culpable, nor do they exculpate Indians and women. Rather, each version names a specific person as the agent of the crime. Don Folincio of Chinchero, for instance, who consorted with mysterious strangers at mid-century, found himself tagged with the nickname "*Papacha Folincio Ñak'aq*" (Big Daddy Folincio Ñakaq) as a result (Manya 1969:137). A gentleman of Apurímac remains unnamed in the written text but was assuredly known to those who heard the tale in his hometown, since he had been elected mayor, judge, and governor. This meteoric career, it was said, had been lubricated with quantities of human fat, which kept his mills running and polished the faces of the saints in the church (Morote Best 1951–52:74).

The name "pishtaco" can be used to accuse anyone; it introjects the nauseating fear of racial violence into a conflict, which automatically becomes more volatile. In the 1960s, Oliver-Smith reported that

> Engineers in charge of . . . agrarian reform have encountered extreme difficulties because the landlord had informed his serfs that pishtacos were coming. Local mestizos reported to me with much hilarity that they would kill a dog or a pig and leave its entrails with a blood-drenched skirt or hat on a mountain trail to convince the Indians that a pisthaco was lurking about. (1969: 367–68)

Frustrated, Oliver-Smith saw the Indians as mystified by false beliefs; but these violent threats were real. Indian dogs and pigs had already lost their lives; the next victim could be as human as the ñakaq himself.

The word can conjure up violence; it can also name violent acts that have already occurred. According to local men in Vicos, it was Indian women who first named Alberto Torres a "pishtaco." "[Torres] would rape some Vicosina, and she would be mortified to have it known that she had laid with a Mestizo, so she would publicly berate him to everybody as having tried to pishtar her." In calling him a pishtaco and making the name stick, these Vicosinas upended the myth of the chola, successfully rebutting the implication that, as Indian women, they were to blame for Torres's acts of sexual predation. And by picking up the story and repeating it, other women and men of Vicos agreed upon a single interpretation: Torres was a criminal so loathsome as to be scarcely human. Elsewhere, the field journals note that the "authorities" held Torres above the law; myth enabled the Vicosinos to pass a public judgment nonetheless.

In linking a man's propensity to sexual abuse to his race, pishtaco stories interrogate the long and often forgotten history of race and rape. "Rape," like "woman," or "whiteness," does not have a single, transhistorical definition, but rather is produced through and defined within specific historical contexts. In Latin American colonial history, the question of "which bodies can be violated and with what social impact, by whom and with what level of impunity," was key to the very definition of "white women" and "nonwhite women" (Athey and Cooper Alarcón 1993). Indeed, it may be a defining characteristic of colonialism that rape becomes a matter of race as much as of sex. The rape of a female slave in colonial Anglo-America was not a crime, nor was the rape of an Irishwoman in thirteenth-century England (T. Allen 1994:46). Even in nineteenth-century America, a woman who claimed to have been raped could find her case dismissed as laughable by a jury, were she proven to be other than white (Sharpe 1991:27).

If only white women can be raped, then deciding whether a particular act of forcible sex is either an outrageous and illegal violation of bodily integrity, or an appropriate, even amusing reaction to sexual provocation, does not rest upon the nature of the act. Instead, the act is defined by the nature of the person upon whom it was performed. Pishtaco stories reverse this causality, insisting that the act does not follow from the racial identity, but rather the racial identity from the act. For in the myth itself, the source of the violence is a white man; but in individual retellings, anyone—male or female, Indian or white—can become the pishtaco through their actions. Whiteness is not an essential quality of particular bodies, but a structural position that any body may assume.

The focus, then, is on action, not being. The word "pishtaco" actually occurs less often in the Vicos field notes than the verb "pishtar," which appears in many different Spanish conjugations—"I used to pishtar," "he got pishtared"—and in Quechua as well, in the threat, "*Pishtashunki*": "I'm going to pishtar you."[33] This transformation of a racial noun into a verb is reminiscent of the "choleando"—chola-chasing—recorded in Palacios, but it resembles the speech of other peoples of color even more. The Chicano terms "agringado" and "vendido,"[34] or Helán Page's references to some middle-class African-Americans as "whitened" (1997), define perpetrators rather than victims. Pishtaco tales, too, do more than insist that what happens to Indians should be recognized as rape; they also assert that by raping an Indian, a man proves that he is really white. Andy Orta and Nathan Wachtel heard only accusations against Aymara men, each of whom had done or become something that linked him to white society: in U.S. terms, these suspects were agringado or whitened.

These stories, then, are not about how chance encounters between a white man and a nonwhite woman inevitably lead to sex, but about an act of sexualized violence that transforms the participants into a white and an Indian, a man and a not-man. Oddly enough, the message is ultimately rather optimistic, despite the gruesome occurrences. In the end, tellers of these tales suggest that race is not really our immutable destiny; it's more like a bad habit we might yet learn to outgrow.

By the same token, these are not stories that let the powerful evade culpability. The relationship between the enormous corpus of pishtaco stories, in all their variability, and the core myth, in which the attacker is always a white man and the victim always an Indian, reminds us of how racial atrocities are actually committed. In Brecht's terms, these stories destroy the illusion of "the changeless and the eternal"; instead, each act of race rape is part of our history—something that we made, and that we can change (Jameson 1998:40). In contrast to white myths about whiteness, in which a vague and generalized guilt cannot be connected to individual acts, nor located in the present, pishtaco stories insist that oppressive race relations are daily and deliberately constituted anew through dozens of individual and voluntary acts of white predation, without which race itself would cease to exist.[35]

Masculinity as a Verb

In talking about people who like to "pishtar," storytellers insist that sex, like race, is enacted rather than essential, for the gender of both victim and aggressor varies, without changing the fundamental sexual relation. Humberto Ghersi commented in perplexity, after noting that "pishtaco" meant rapist, "But men also could be pishtared." And Harold Skalka was told, "There was a woman pishtaco in Charcas. She put on man's clothing at night."[36] Both roles—masculine aggressor and feminized victim—can be played by either women or men (whether by putting on a pair of trousers, or losing them).

These possibilities evoke attitudes toward sex and gender elsewhere in Latin America. In Brazil, doing research with transgendered prostitutes, Don Kulick encountered a sexual universe that was not composed of men and women, defined through their genitals, but rather of "men" and "not-men," defined through their actions:

> the salient [gender] difference . . . is not between men and women. It is, instead, between those who penetrate (comer, literally "to eat" . . .), and those who get penetrated (dar, literally "to give"), in a system where the act of being penetrated has transformative force. Thus those who only "eat" (and never "give") in this system are culturally designated as "men"; those who give . . . are classified as being something else . . . [as] "not men." (1997a: 580) [37]

It is not merely by having a penis but by acting in ways specified by the sex/gender system under which he lives—whether by being the one who always "eats," through repeated sexual conquest, or with violence—that a man actualizes his masculinity. In Nicaragua, says Roger Lancaster, "one's appropriate gender is defined by and through a practice (sex) that is itself defined as violent and dominating" (1992:41).

In the Andes, this violent sexuality is inextricably connected to race; it is as though whiteness brought with it a phallus. Indeed, women anthropologists working in rural communities or working-class neighborhoods of Latin America often find that their superordinate racial status brings with it a symbolic masculinity. Accustomed as a woman to being afraid of strange men, I was astounded to discover that in the rural Andes it was I who had the power to inadvertently terrify women and children. Billie Jean Isbell (1978:8) comments on how useful she found it to be able to pass from male to female and back again, depending on circumstance. When archaeologist Kathy Schreiber learned that I was investigating tales of women pishtacos, she contributed a story of her own. When she needs to clear her archaeological excavations of nosy children, she recounted in 1996, she takes advantage of the widely held Ayachucho belief that she is a ñakaq by threatening facetiously to grab one and eat it, at which they all scatter, laughing but also repeating the tale.

Some married women ethnographers avoid being accused as pishtacos—because suspicion is deflected onto their male partners. In Sonqo, Peru, Catherine Allen overheard mothers telling their children that Allen's first husband, Rick, might turn into a ñakaq at night; but the women assured her that it was nothing personal. All white men, however benign their usual behavior, possess this capacity to feed their own strength through the consumption of Indian flesh (1978:69–71; 1988:62, 111). Rick, however, had not (yet) become a pishtaco because he had been trying to act like an Indian; his white masculinity remained unactivated.

Robert Ellis elucidates the theme of a white masculinity that must be brought into existence through acts of sexualized violence as a recurrent element in recent Peruvian fiction and autobiography (1998). Mario Vargas Llosa traces the origins of his own antipathy toward the bodies of impoverished Peruvians to the brutal teachings of his father. The latter, possessor of a fragile whiteness that he desperately wished his son to inherit, and simultaneously afraid that the boy might grow up a *"maricón"* (faggot, feminine man), literally beat the lessons of white masculine privilege into his son. Television personality Jaime Bayly's first novel also depicts a young man subjected to repeated beatings by a father intent on teaching him how to be a white man.

These fathers believe that whites are inherently superior to cholos, just as being a man is infinitely better than being a woman. Both men insist that their sons should feel an innate desire, born of inherited prerogative, to dominate the women and lesser men around them. Yet Ellis notes that in fact, they desperately fear that their sons might actually lack these violent impulses, and so fail to achieve their racial and sexual potential. This anxiety causes both fathers to resort to oddly ritualized acts of violence, in which they force their sons into the roles of Indians, homosexuals, and women—for these, of course, are the names they cry out as they beat their children. Thus in Ellis's account, the Hispanic patriarchal family is created through violence that is misogynist and racist—even though inflicted by white fathers upon their own sons.

Just as these boys have had their racial and sexual identity brutally inscribed upon their bodies in humiliating rituals of domination and submission, so they too repeat the lesson through acts of brutality against others. And just as they have been shown that their own bodies contain Indianness and femininity within them, so too they find this despicable race and sex in everyone they victimize, including other men and other whites.

Vargas Llosa consolidates a possibly shaky adolescent sexual identity through a brutal group attack on a male transvestite. Arguedas's protagonist is surprised to discover that the woman raped in the latrine *"[n]o era india; tenía los cabellos claros y su rostro era blanco"* [was not an Indian; she had light-colored hair and her face was white (1958:77, my trans.)]. The power of violence to inscribe race on its victim is made most apparent in an incident in Bayly's novel. Returning from a nightmarish hunting trip in which he had failed to kill any game—or to force his son to act like a man—the father cheers up after running over a pedestrian. The trip was not a total failure, he tells his son: we "bagged an Indian after all." But the victim, left behind on the road, had been invisible in the darkness, his racial identity as unknowable as whether he was alive or dead.[38]

Money defines masculinity as well. In the Brazilian conversations recorded by Kulick, gender pronouns are context sensitive. In recounting their life stories, *travestis* used masculine pronouns and adjectival endings to describe themselves as children, but switched to feminine forms when discussing their present-day lives (1997a: 579). When they recounted tales of their adventures with their clients, specific sex acts changed the johns' gender: if the "he" who picked up a prostitute asked to be penetrated, he quickly became a "she"—indeed, the client began to speak of himself in feminine forms from that moment on (1998: 157–66). But this changed when the sex act was over and it became time to pay up: money, too, mans and unmans. At the moment when a client pulled out "her" wallet to pay for the services rendered, "she" became a "he" again; in describing a struggle between the travesti and her client over money, gender follows the cash (1997a: 579). Like the act of sex, the act of monetary exchange is an inherently gendered exchange in which "he" buys "her"—but not the other way around.

The parallel between race and sex is very clear here. The destructive masculinity epitomized by sexual triumph is also expressed in commercial interactions that force the subaltern party to accept terms that are disadvantageous and degrading—and leave the winner exulting in his masculine prowess. So, too, whiteness gives the advantage in either sex or commerce—and the partner who takes advantage, marks himself as white.

Colombian critic Adelaida López Mejía explores this link between masculinity, exchange, and race in her study of García Márquez's *Cien años de soledad* (1995). Unlike the indigenous victims in Sonqo stories, who met their deaths through entering a store full of "mestizo" goods, José Arcadia Buendía is white, bourgeois, himself a colonist and the local patriarch. Nonetheless, he too falls victim to the fatal allure of manufactured goods, and especially of imported commodities. It is "a dementia unleashed by the unbearable 'flows of desire' within capitalism . . . [as] trade with the outside world ensnares the town of Macondo in the web of a progressively aggressive imperialism" (1995: 3–4).

López Mejía, like Bayly, sees South American men struggling to consolidate a power that is both racial and sexual in nature. But absolute masculinity, like unimpeachable whiteness, eludes Buendía, who finds himself doubly undermined through the conjunction of colonial dependence with an insecure masculinity. "The (phallic) privilege which none of us totally possess becomes, for José Arcadia Buendía, synonymous with Western (metropolitan) technology and science," she writes (5). Her reading of the novel finds the same themes we saw in *Los ríos profundos:* the obsessive drive to gain power by the acquisition of imported goods destroys both the man and the South American landscape itself. Buendía cedes control over his once-Edenic community to the anonymous forces of development, and he eventually loses his mind as well.

The violent inequalities of local hierarchies of race and sex in these South American tales take shape through a flow of commodities that itself symbolizes much larger systems of power and violence. Much of the brutality in Andean exchanges, sexual and commercial, stems from the ambiguous location of local elites, who define themselves in relationship to global systems of power that both bolster and undermine their position. In *Huasipungo,* Icaza's unconvincing claim that the Indian woman being raped sees in her white attacker's face the visage of God (1953:62) is illuminated by the hacendado's own pathetic fantasies. When North Americans investors want to deforest and mine his hacienda, he puts himself and all he possesses at their disposal, imaging that these mysterious and powerful men represent financial salvation. The hacendado is wrong in thinking that his own victim misperceives her assailant as an all-powerful deity. She does not; rather, it is he who mistakes his ravishers for saviors (10–13).

Money circulates endlessly, but its ceaseless movement disguises a hundred thousand unidirectional flows of goods, labor, and capital that fuel ever-accelerating processes of accumulation. The victories of the poor are temporary, relative, and easily reversed, while those of the wealthy build upon past triumphs. Kulick's travesti prostitutes, for example, find it amusing to unman their clients by picking their pockets. It is a theft of sexuality as well as of money: with their wallets empty, these clients, who had allowed themselves to be temporarily feminized by their desire for passive sex, are without the cash to transform themselves them back into men in their own and their partner's eyes. But sweet though those moments of symbolic triumph may be for these impoverished Brazilian sex workers, they cannot consolidate that money into real economic security. Nor can they escape the risk of being kicked and beaten—perhaps killed—by men like the young Vargas Llosa when they go back out on the street. And while market women may momentarily lord it over Indians, they are increasingly unlikely to become "reinas del tomate."

In this section, we found that race and sex inhere less in individual bodies than in the forms of exchange through which they engage each other. In the Andean produce market, fleeting transactions give rise to momentary racial and sexual identities, which knowing actors can don and shed almost at will as they engage different interlocutors. But although individuals may shift from one position to another, the structures of inequality themselves—racial, sexual, and economic—are fixed far more firmly in place. And as we shall see in the next section, each individual exchange contributes to a more permanent form of identity that accumulates in the person, consolidating a race and a sex that are not so easily altered. For those fortunate enough to secure an identity that is both masculine and white, these exchanges can result in substantial material accumulation as well.

Part Three

ACCUMULATION

CHAPTER 5

White Men

The postcard rack stocked with brightly colored cards is a fixture in every shop that caters to tourists. In the United States, the cards may show well-known buildings and monuments, or anonymous-looking freeways and skylines; in the Andes, almost all the pictures are of people or mountains. When I first began traveling to South America in the early 1980s, the postcards I saw were cheaply made. These three-by-four-inch cards, offset printed in colors a little off register, showed scenes of everyday life. I had a minor fascination with these pictures, some of which, in their attempts to make the ordinary appear folkloric, accidentally achieved surreal or even ludicrous results. I still own a postcard of Ipiales, Guayaquil's famous outdoor market, which in those days was filled with contraband manufactured items from Colombia. In the picture, a tired-looking fat woman is dwarfed by the goods piled beside her—a veritable mountain of identical black plastic shoes. Another card is labeled "*Indígenas de Chimborazo pescando truchas*" [Indians from Chimborazo fishing for trout]. It shows a half dozen indigenous men and women standing waist-deep in a river, their ponchos and shawls sodden, eyes closed and hands clasped. Unknowingly, the photographer captured an Evangelical baptismal ceremony, one brief instance of the massive indigenous conversion to Protestantism in the province of Chimborazo.

These amateurish but poignant efforts have since been swept off the racks by larger-format cards that are professionally photographed and lavishly reproduced. There is a beautiful Saraguro woman, her shawl held closed by an enormous silver *tupu* pin in the shape of a sunburst; another shows a bare-breasted Colorado girl in a striped cotton loin-cloth, her hair shiny with red dye; here we see a Salasaca man seated at his loom, improbably wearing his heavy black poncho and magenta scarf as he works. The new cards are more polished, but no less stereo-typical than the old. As an ensemble, they are the perfect complement to the ethnographic maps found in museums. Black folk from the coastal region are shown playing music and cavorting happily on the beach, while in the Amazonian rainforest scantily clothed natives glare ferociously at the camera; their highland counterparts, wrapped in lay-ers of wool, toil industriously at agricultural or artisanal tasks, their eyes averted from the lens.

This new generation of photographers tightly controls the frame: vistas of snowcapped mountains are unmarred by power lines, and the markets have been mysteriously emptied of plastics. By removing the products of industrial technology, the postcard makers create a fantasy of premodern social life that is immensely appealing to tourists. And in the process, they also confer a race upon the people photographed. Manufactured goods—especially those expensive and imported ob-jects fetishized as the epitome of technological sophistication—bestow whiteness upon the people around them; their absence performs the operation in reverse. Without wristwatches, radios, and blenders (ob-jects that are, in fact, commonplace in indigenous homes) the people in the photographs are immediately recognizable as nonwhites. By sub-stituting handmade props, the photographer seals the racial boundary between viewer and viewed.[1]

Most tourists are unreflective about the racial paradigm that under-lies what they see in picture postcards. But for those who share some sense of identity with the people in the photographs, the experience of looking at them can be unsettling.[2] Should one respond to these ra-cial caricatures with amusement, cynicism, or rage? The well-to-do, equipped with all the high-tech trappings of tourism—video cameras, cell phones, sunglasses—need only consider these questions if they wish: a wealthy descendant of Africans is far more welcome here than a fair-haired shoeshine boy. But imagine what would happen if some-one whom tourists could readily identify as being "like" the people in the pictures—an Amazonian native carrying a blowgun, or even an Indian maidservant on her way to the bus—were to walk into a souvenir shop and begin thumbing through the cards. The immediate effect on white tourists would be one of incongruity: the picture has stepped out of the frame. Other shoppers, suddenly made aware of the invisible but unbreakable racial segregation that underwrites their position, might dissolve into nervous laughter at the sight.

Picturing such an intrusion reveals something about the nature of the postcard display, which offers potential purchasers the sensation of seeing without being seen. This illusory power is a defining characteristic of tourism (MacCannell 1976)—and of racial and sexual privilege as well. The Andean tradition of representing cholas in paintings, photographs, novels, and poems was easily appropriated by the tourist industry, for it, too, offers images of nonwhite women for the delectation of an audience whose invisibility grants them a putative white masculinity. The genre of pishtaco stories, by contrast, invites listeners to inspect the white male body. In thus inverting the race (and sex) of the viewer and the object of vision, it skewers the white fantasy of invisibility—and gives whites, rather than nonwhites, the odd sensation of peeking at a display not intended for their eyes. By inventing the ñakaq, Andean nonwhites have produced a racial-sexual scopophilia all their own.[3]

LOOKING AT WHITENESS

The ñakaq is a white man: *"un gringo bien alto y cuerpudo"* (a white foreigner, really tall and with a big body). Refugees in the Lima shantytowns described the pishtacos who pursued them out of the highlands as big, plump gringos with beards, "tall, white . . . with green eyes."[4] The whiteness of the ñakaq, however, does not necessarily imply a white skin. Morote Best recounts a tale of a ñakaq with a dreadful "purple-colored face" surrounded by abundant hair of the same color (1951–52:69), while Figueroa and Carrasco were told about an encounter with

> *un negro de pelo largo . . . bien alto . . . con vaquero y botas de cabito* [sic]. *En su lado había una matraca. Caminé más rápido pensando que podría ser de verdad pishtaco.*[5]

> [a black man with long hair . . . really tall . . . with chaps and leather boots. By his side was a machine gun. I started walking faster thinking this could be a real pishtaco.]

In twelve pishtaco tales from the 1950s, most of them collected by José María Arguedas, the pishtacos were similarly described as "black."[6]

One might think that these black-skinned pishtacos are not white. But unlike the contemporary United States, where pigmentation is assumed to be the most basic and the most intransigent of racial indices, skin color is not always accorded primary importance in Andean racial discourse. Even in the United States, racial ideologies do not always focus on the skin: hatred of blackness can translate into an obsession with the shape of the lips or the texture of hair, just as anti-Semites select the nose or brow for stigmatization.[7] So too with the ñakaq in the Andes: the color of his skin is a less important sign of racial alterity than other features shared by many white and black Americans, such as light-colored eyes, a hirsute torso, and especially great height or fleshiness. Storytellers like to dwell upon these aspects of the pishtaco body, knowing that their audience will find these details fascinating, repellent—and indicative of racial whiteness.

The Whiteness of the Ñakaq

In the Andes, short stature and small size are seen as Indian traits, so much so that in Otavalo, the tall, well-fed offspring of successful indigenous entrepreneurs constitute a palpable challenge to received racial categories (Colloredo-Mansfeld 1998:195). The pishtaco, in contrast, is repeatedly described as "big"; indeed, a miner from Julcani describes him as a "blancón," combining the notion of whiteness and that of enormous size in a single word (Salazar-Soler 1991:17).

Hair is also an index of racial difference. In Cotopaxi Province, where white men are expected to be hirsute, every upwardly mobile man sports a moustache if he can, regardless of the reigning fashion regarding facial hair elsewhere. Young people in Zumbagua found both titillation and revulsion in the hairy arms and legs of Europeans and Euro-Americans: "My friend saw two gringos wearing short pants and he said they had pubic hair *all over their entire legs!*" chortled one adolescent in astonishment, unselfconsciously stroking his own smooth limbs. Peruvian storytellers, too, linger over the pishtaco's excessive hairiness. In Huamanga in the 1940s they commented on his "long, tangled hair and beard" (Morote Best 1951–52:69). The pishtaco who frightened a Campa migrant in 1987 was a huge man with a beard and a woolly cap (Vergara Figueroa and Carrasco 1989:131).

This fascination with hairiness ironically inverts early modern European fabulations about wild men and ape men, whose hairiness placed them on the boundary between human and nonhuman. Indeed, in thus focusing in an almost fetishistic fashion upon certain qualities of the body in question, and exaggerating these into grotesque form, ñakaq stories recall the long tradition of white studies of the nonwhite body. Photographic studies of racial types were assembled by nineteenth-century scientists and popularized in the Andes through albums of cartes-de-visites.[8] These range in tone from the cruelly satiric to the morbidly scientistic, but all exhibit a similar propensity for exaggerating minor physical traits, and then weighting them with phantasmagorical significance. So, too, at the mention of the pishtaco's big beard or his great size, audiences begin to tremble in anticipation, knowing that these bodily features signify truly horrible moral or behavioral traits.

An even more apt comparison, perhaps, might be between ñakaq tales and photography that eroticizes the female body. We are so inured to this sort of picture—the mainstay of Madison Avenue and Hollywood, and the pornographic industry as well—that it takes an effort to recognize the enormous amount of artifice required to produce the desired results.[9] Heterosexual pornography does to sex what racial pseudoscience does to race: it asserts that the differences between male and female bodies are as profound as the differences between species. Thus the lips, breasts, or buttocks of women in photographs are fantastically altered or enlarged, whether through manipulation in the studio, the darkroom, or the surgeon's office. And as with the pishtaco's race, specific secondary and even imaginary features of sexual dimorphism are also emphasized: the ear lobes are pierced and adorned; the hair removed from eyebrows, legs, and underarms.

All three genres (heterosexual pornography, photo albums of racial types, and pishtaco stories) display a particular kind of body—female, Indian, or white—in which selected characteristics have been morbidly exaggerated. The abnormal appearance that results is said to express peculiar characteristics or proclivities: the insatiable desire of the "slut," the subhuman intelligence of the "indio"—or the ñakaq's compulsion to kill. But while the pishtaco stories draw upon a predictable list of bodily characteristics (light eyes, big body, abundant hair) the specific physical traits that mark the ñakaq are sometimes oddly elusive.[10] This problem has been identified in other racial discourses as well. David Roediger, an American historian of race, illustrates this point in his reminiscences about his travels:

> In Ghana's Ashanti Region. . . . [w]e are greeted on the streets by children who chant, "*Oburoni koko maakye.*" English-speaking Ashantis often translate this as "Red white man, good morning." . . . The many Chinese, Koreans, and Japanese now in

Ghana are generally also termed *oburoni* . . . not just because they are "from across the sea" but because they "are white"—that is, they are perceived as looking and acting like Europeans and Americans. . . . British listeners to Malcolm X's talks in Ghana on his celebrated pilgrimage to Mecca tell me that Ghanaians expressed surprise to them that an *oburoni* could say such things. Indeed, one listener recalls hearing Malcolm described as a white man with astonishing ideas. . . .

In 1984, when we lived in the London borough of Brent, immigrants and descendants of many nationalities often called themselves "Blacks." . . . Asian Indians, Pakistanis, Malaysians, Turks, Chinese, Bangladeshis, Arabs and even Cypriots and some Irish so identified themselves. . . . [I]n South Africa in 1989, we noted how . . . [m]any among the "so-called coloured" population insisted that they were in fact *Africans.* (1994:4–5)

For Roediger, these phenomena demonstrate that the racial category "Black" is a "political colour" that belongs to those who are oppressed, while privilege makes one white. Although he argues forcibly for the autonomy of race as a category irreducible to class, he speaks of it as something symbolic: a metaphor for social inequality. But even when pigmentation, "blood," or genes are not at issue, and even though Euro-Americans, Asians, and African-Americans may look the same to Ghanaians, race as a category need not be disembodied, its material referents rendered purely metaphorical. In the Andes, race is indeed corporeal, but the definition of the physical self is extended beyond flesh and hair and teeth to include the clothing and objects that extend, shield, and adorn the body.

This expanded definition of a human being to include some accouterments is found in the other genres. In pornographic and racial displays, too, the body in question is not only systematically distorted, but also supplied with a predictable set of accessories. A rough-hewn tool and a homespun garment complete a plaster Indian, while absurdly high heels and thick false eyelashes help make a live model into a sex toy. The body and its additions appear indissoluble: breasts need a surgical implant to be really impressive, just as fingers require glossy pink talons to make them recognizably female. If the effect is successful, we no longer separate artifice and "nature" in appreciating the results: the cosmetically enhanced body is the "real woman," whereas the body without makeup, jewelry, and hairdo appears oddly sexless. So, too, the ñakaq carries with him objects that enhance his phallic whiteness—

and in thinking about him, it becomes quite impossible to separate the man from his tools.

The Whiteness of Things

Just as the picture postcards identify nonwhites by the absence of advanced technology, rural people read racial whiteness in the wristwatches and CD players, cars and cash with which outsiders surround themselves. When a visiting friend produced a battery-powered razor and began shaving his face one morning in 1985, the Chaluisa children were beside themselves with emotions ranging from amazement to delight to disgust to hilarity. In bringing together the hairiness of whites and their unlimited access to noisy and powerful gadgets, my guest had unknowingly enacted a whiteness perfectly in accordance with local paradigms. That he was coincidentally the tallest and largest person I had ever brought up to the farmstead, and the most heavily burdened with gear—he was a professional photographer bearing multiple cameras—made his performance all the more sensational. Finally, his colorful garb—shaved head, tiny purple-tinted granny glasses, and huge, brightly-colored Gore-Tex rain pants—and his affable demeanor brought the entire event, from the children's point of view, into the realm of the sublimely ludicrous.

Oliver-Smith, following the lead of the rural Peruvians he interviewed, unhesitatingly labels the pishtaco as white; yet his description lingers over objects, not bodies. The pishtaco, he says, is a "large, evil-looking man," whose size and ominous presence are enhanced by his "high boots . . . leather jacket, and . . . felt hat," and by the fact that he appeared "on horseback or occasionally driving a car" (1969:363). Manya, likewise, was emphatic about the racial difference between the ñakaq and his victims; his prose, too, emphasizes attire and reputation more than physiognomy. The murderer, a "mysterious, fearful, bloody, cruel and even sadistic" personage who is "much talked about and very well-known in Cuzco and Puno," communicated his race by appearing "on horseback, wearing a riding habit, elegant, resplendent, with a white cap on his head, and his horse similarly well-attired." [11]

The horse is old-fashioned now; today, pishtacos are identifiable by their cars and jeeps.[12] Indeed, expensive cars are almost invariably signs of a ñakaq. In Lima, "some gringos arrived in a Nissan Patrol; they were tall, bearded and well-dressed"; others were seen in "luxury cars, in Mercedes Benzes" (Sifuentes 1989:153); all of them later proved to be pishtacos. The employees of NGOS, who invariably travel in jeeps, their doors emblazoned with mysterious insignia, arouse similar suspicions.[13] In northern Potosí in 1982, members of the Tomás Katari Polytechnic (IPTK), which employed both Bolivians and European volunteers in its agricultural and sanitary projects, found its relationship with the local community of Ocuri deteriorating rapidly; the problem began with their bright red jeep.

> When the Institute's red jeep travelled the region, the country folk were afraid and fled; the children refused to go to school for fear of being abducted; the parents stopped sending their children out to tend the flocks; at night vigilantes were placed on the perimeter of the community, where they set off dynamite to scare away the lik'ichiri. (Rivière 1991:35)

In the rural Andes, ownership of a private automobile is unimaginable for most people. In Zumbagua, the wealthy shaman Segundo Iza was rumored to own two pickup trucks at a time—this in the 1980s when most people could not afford so much as a bicycle. Little boys fantasized about motorcycles and private vehicles, but as they grew older, their dreams focused on commercial forms of transportation—taxis, trucks, and buses—that might provide an income. For rural men, one of the only possible routes out of poverty and into whiteness is to become a *chofer,* a professional driver.

Even if it were financially feasible, the purchase of a vehicle for private use can be risky in a society where certain material privileges are supposed to be exclusively white. It was the purchase of a motorcycle—a patently nonutilitarian vehicle, designed for pleasure—that brought the wrath of local whites down upon Salasaca artesanías dealer Rudiscindo Masaquiza, sparking the incident that led to his imprisonment and subsequent precipitous descent from the prosperity he had so painstakingly achieved.[14]

The purchase of a car brings other dangers, for it marks its owner as a possible pishtaco. Rumors about the Chipaya man later killed for being a kharisiri began when his growing wealth enabled him to buy a van for use in his business. In highland Peru, a retired miner who returned to his hometown and bought a private car came under suspicion as well. People told Carmen Salazar-Soler that he "lived a normal life during the day, but spent the night driving through the community in his car looking for victims to attack," and then used their fat to lubricate the car's engine (1991:11).

Anthropologists can arouse similar fears, as Nathan Wachtel realized. Even though he did not "travel by personal airplane, like certain missionaries," he says,

I am often asked, "How much does a plane ticket from France to Bolivia cost?" What can I say? I can't lie, but telling the truth doesn't make sense either: in the context of Chipaya, the amount, translated into pesos, is astronomical, totally unimaginable. (104)

Wachtel became acutely aware that the things he brought to Chipaya with him (although they were far from luxurious compared to what he had left at home) underscored the enormous difference between himself and the local residents. "My possessions bespeak my wealth: the gas burner, the cans of Nescafé, the inexhaustible supplies of cigarettes, the candles, the sleeping bag . . ." (104). The retired miner mentioned above came under suspicion not only because he owned a car, but because of the lock on his front door. It was said that his house was filled with appliances (even though there was no electricity in the community on which to run them) and that he greased their parts with human fat (Salazar-Soler 1991 : 11).

Outsiders who visit rural communities nowadays often try to minimize these differences of wealth and status between themselves and the local population by wearing old clothes and adopting a "just plain folks" demeanor. Ethnographies, too, reiterate wonderful moments of shared emotion, fictive kinship, and cross-cultural understanding, and downplay the constant reminders of ineradicable economic difference: the shamefaced or truculent demands for loans, the incessant interrogations about how much one's airplane tickets, hiking boots, and eyeglasses cost.[15] But as Wachtel realized, it is useless to dissimulate in the face of such enormous material differences. The pretenses adopted by Peace Corps worker or tourist, agronomist or priest are as readily belied by their glossy good health and tall stature as by the shiny new vehicles they drive.[16]

I also practiced these stratagems to an extreme: while resident in the parish in 1985 and 1986, I lived in a tiny one-room building previously occupied by chickens and guinea pigs, traveled by local bus, and generally tried to live as much like the people I was studying as possible. Nevertheless, women and children walked into my little unheated house, pointed to the huge containers that held drinking water and dry goods, and asked quite sincerely if they were filled with money. In Chipaya, popular opinion held that it was right to kill the man suspected as a kharisiri: after all, they had found a cache of dollar bills in his house (Wachtel 1994 : 88).

If things acquire a race—or bestow one upon their possessor—it is because they are so intimately part of what we are. Like our bodies, our possessions reveal their history—and ours—through their appearance: a wooden handle is smooth and shiny from long contact with the hand that used it; the letters on a keyboard are worn away or soiled by our fingers; a pair of pants begins to sag at the knee. The things we use change us as well: a back takes on a peculiar posture in response to its customary chair, a pair of arms repeat a characteristic motion in response to the balance and heft of the objects they lift each day. Race is indeed socially fabricated—and the construction site is the zone of interaction between our skin, flesh, and bones, and the world around us.

David Roediger discovered that in Africa, as in the Andes, whites travel in cars:

> As we walk in Kumasi, especially in neighborhoods we have not been in before, residents sometimes cheerfully shout, in English, "Hey, you are white!" This struck me as being a puzzling . . . non sequitur until I realized that you almost never see whites walking more than a short distance there. The full thought was, "Hey, you are white and out walking around!" or "Hey, you are white and ought to have a car!" (1994:5)

The fact that whites in Ghana "seldom lack a car," he says, "makes race seem very much to matter in a hot, hilly, dusty place where walking is work." In the end, however, Roediger downplays this message in the Ghanaian salutation: because whites "are not biologically programmed to have a car or motorbike," their words, he says, "only seemed to be . . . 'about race'" (1994:5–6). His intent here is to neutralize the biological obsessions of racists, but the effect is to lose sight of something his cheerful black interlocutors certainly know: bodies that ride in cars are different from bodies that walk. Where whites ride in comfort and blacks trudge through the dust and heat, race gets written into the relative strength of each race's muscles, the abundance of their fat, and the shape of their feet.

Our hands and feet—the bodies' tools, thrust into constant and varied interaction with the world—are especially marked by the things we own and the lives we live. Colloredo-Mansfeld writes about hands as signifiers of race: he captures the interaction between Indian and white in the moment when an indigenous woman "places some grubby bills in the soap chaffed hand of a white-mestizo shopkeeper" who "recoils" from her customer (1998:187). Feet are important too. Wachtel noted wryly, "My shoes, in particular, are highly coveted" (1994:104); in Zumbagua, I too found that no other possession aroused so much uncontrollable envy as my boots.[17] And I seldom witnessed the burden of poverty so acutely as when I watched women in Zumbagua squeezing their feet into the ill-fitting, uncomfortable plastic shoes sold in the markets. Nothing so hurt me, or so disappointed my compadre Alfonso, as when I brought from the United States a nice pair of size 7 work boots for his size 8 feet.

When I solicited an essay about race in the Lake Titicaca region from Ben Orlove, he wrote about feet (among other things). There, a man unwilling to get mud between his toes is a man who has rejected his community—an unsurprising conclusion to be reached by people whom earlier census-takers had labeled as "Indian" precisely because of the absence of shoes (1998:210). Gary Urton, commenting upon Orlove's paper, describes the world of feet in Paucartambo (a community near Cuzco) as "tripartite."[18] There were mestizo feet, encased within shiny, thin-soled leather shoes designed for interior living. And there were Indian feet in open, thick-soled shoes called *ojotas;* when Urton started wearing them too, he found out things he had not known before. His toes exposed to the environment around them, he "discovered the value of having dirty feet. That is, when wearing ojotas, your feet are warmer when your feet are dirty (they're *very* warm when they are muddy)!"

He learned something about gringo feet too: big heavy hiking boots, the preferred footgear of foreigners (and the young sons of wealthy South Americans), do not allow the wearer to experience the earth—they force him to conquer it. Perhaps this is why pishtacos like boots; in any event, they are often seen wearing them: big boots, leather boots, goatskin boots—even boots, chaps, and a leather jacket, an outfit that encases the entire body in a thick and rather menacing layer of protection.

These hands and feet, so different in their textures and coverings, render the abstract concept of economic class concrete and unmistakable; and because they locate class within the body itself, they bind it yet more intimately to the concept of race. Peasant feet look like small rhinoceri with their splayed toes, horny heels, and dense soles like armor plating. In contrast, the feet of a mestiza shopgirl, who stands all day in narrow high heels, are as broken, confined, and misshapen as if she were the victim of footbinding.[19]

People use feet and shoes to talk about race and class. Many communities of poor farmers pridefully claim European rather than Indian descent. But although they may speak only Spanish, and bear European last names like Mendoza or Santos rather than Indian names like Mamani or Quispe, the sight of their broad, brown, bare feet inevitably calls their racial affiliation into question. The owners of such feet can always be said to resemble—or simply to be—Indians.

Indians in nice shoes, on the other hand, cause a different reaction.

In Otavalo, a small number of Indian entrepreneurs have successfully marketed their ethnicity to foreigners, either as textile and craft merchants or as musicians. This highly visible minority challenges the simple identity of wealth with whiteness, and poverty with Indians, which earlier political economies had rigorously enforced. When one of these Otaveleños shops for his shoes during a business trip abroad, returning home in Italian loafers or the latest Nikes, envious whites find the sight of his feet not only shocking but unnatural and immoral—even criminal. As Colloredo-Mansfeld discovered through uncomfortable conversations with local whites, these young men, like well-to-do blacks or Latinos in the United States, are assumed to fund such purchases through trafficking in narcotics (1998:199).

In contrast, Indians are unlikely to suspect that the shoes don't belong on the body; instead, they say that the body no longer belongs to the race.[20] "*Chasna purina / layachu karka*" sing the people of Colta about their upwardly mobile sons: "walking around like that / hasn't he become a white man?" (Harrison 1989:23; my trans.).[21] This focus on the physical elements of ethnicity is characteristic: when an Indian becomes white, the mouth must accustom itself to a new language, the feet to different shoes. The food that whites and Indians eat is different, too—and it produces different kinds of bodies. Indeed, Manya reports that the pishtaco prefers Indian victims not because they are more vulnerable, but because they produce better fat. The ñakaq, he says, attacks only "*indígenas*, because the Indian possesses dry fat, from feeding himself strongly with *chuño* and *kañiwa* . . . not like that of the *miste,* which is liquid and of poor quality."[22]

If tools and clothing shape our bodies, the things we ingest have a far more powerful effect. What, how, and how often we eat makes us strong or weak—even alive or dead. It is hardly surprising, then, that food makes Indians different from whites. Don Lucho, who lived in the center of town in Zumbagua, was white but considered a good man nonetheless. Parish residents knew they could always ride with him in his big, ancient "Cotopaxi" bus, whereas the shiny new minibuses that plied the same roads often refused to pick up Indians. Perhaps because he disdained such abuses, Lucho worked very hard to signal his whiteness through his bodily comportment. Despite the cold, he always sported a thin nylon windbreaker rather than the thick woolen ponchos worn by his passengers. His conversation was larded with references to his preferred diet of chicken and bottled beer, as well as to his supposed allergies to the guinea-pig meat and cane liquor fed to him at weddings and baptisms by his many Indian godchildren. By proclaiming this food inimical to his good health, he maintained a physiological separation from his neighbors: since he had married a local woman and settled in the community, he might otherwise have become an Indian himself.

Lucho's customers were more likely to attribute illnesses to eating store-bought food and to cure themselves with a homemade guinea-pig-and-potato stew. Like Indians elsewhere, older people especially were convinced that the processed foods eaten by whites result in soft, weakened bodies. In Zumbagua, the flesh of local, indigenous people is strong and healthy, it is said, because they eat mostly barley, the major crop of the area. As Tayta Juanchu had taught me, when this barley is homegrown, processed, and cooked, it has a special potency that makes local people what and who they are. Heloisa's half-sister, Clarita, and Clarita's husband, José Manuel, trying to find words to extol its virtues, said that it was "like meat. Just like meat. It makes you strong, like eating fat." [23] (Aymara used almost exactly the same words to describe chuño, the local indigenous food, to Andrew Orta [1997:9].)

Tayta Juanchu had a prosperous enough farm to be able to adopt a whole series of children into his household over the years (as well as a foreign anthropologist); feeding these strays and building their bodies with his own good, substantial crops was the first step in making them part of the Chaluisa family. Introducing me to their surprised acquaintances, family members would describe my growing relationship to them by saying happily, "She eats our barley gruel." Even the last time I saw him, when he had succumbed to the illness that would soon kill him, Tayta Juanchu summoned up enough energy to chastise me for my short stay: "How can we feed you enough if you go away so soon?" I introduced Stephen to him, and he smiled beneficently and said by way of a blessing, "Eat. My children will feed you." By arranging for him to be fed, the old man would infuse this stranger, as he had me, with a little of the vitality he associated with Indians.

It would take a very long time, however, to make Stephen an Indian—just as long as it does to make an Indian white, or the country girl we met in chapter 3 into a "very good mestiza." I had long puzzled over a seeming contradiction in attitudes toward race in Zumbagua and Salasaca, where people insisted that race was a physical reality, irreducible to ethnicity or social class—and yet spoke matter-of-factly about neighbors who had changed their race during their lifetime. It was while studying adoption that I finally grasped the underlying principle: membership in a family—and a race—is indeed rooted in bodily similarities, but this sameness is created through metabolic processes, not genetic codes.[24] The body, in Andean thinking, is an object built up over time. As it ingests, digests, and expels substances from the world around it, it provides its owner an identity drawn from worldly substances. Body and identity thus originate in the intimate physical relationship between persons and their social milieu; each human comprises a particular mix of food and drink, laughter and language, work and rest.

Pishtaco tales focus on the body with a gleeful physicality that is particularly unamenable to the nature/culture opposition that underlies scholarly debates about class and race. Contemporary racial pseudo-science holds that race is determined before birth, at the moment of conception when two sets of genes merge. Indigenous theories agree that race resides in the body, but not about how—and when—these races are made. The whiteness of the pishtaco (and the Indianness of his victim) does not precede social life but rather is formed by it, through a process that is unmistakably physical. Feet are soft or hard; skin is faded or burned: these differences cannot be shed like a suit of clothes, or papered over by the sudden acquisition of money.

I learned this way of thinking from the polite but nevertheless relentless scrutiny to which people in Zumbagua subjected my body. They noticed everything, even the altered texture of my hair when I returned from trips to Quito, where I applied conditioners in hotel bathrooms. This curiosity about my physiognomy was especially fueled by the desire to understand why gringos had so many fewer children than Indians. Women and girls tried to touch and see my sexual organs, assuming that the noticeable absence of babies among my friends, and among the European backpackers who hiked through town, must have an anatomical explanation. At first I dismissed this belief as amusing naïveté, but I found my position increasingly difficult to defend. They initiated many conversations about birth control, a topic on which I was initially vehement but became more hesitant over time. As I learned more about the outdated and unregulated medicines locally in use, and the absence of sanitary conditions in local homes, it became harder to refute their adamant assertion that the pills and devices that safely prevented white women's unwanted pregnancies could prove far riskier for Indians. And my sexual and medical history had indeed produced a (then) thirty-year-old body that was anomalous by parish standards. When much persistence enabled two teenaged acquaintances to report back to the older women that my physiognomy was roughly similar to their own, it only spurred the determination of the married women to see for themselves. They rightly assumed that my nonreproductive history must have shaped my breasts, genitals, and menstrual periods just as irreversibly as multiple childbirths had marked theirs.[25]

Excruciatingly self-conscious under their gaze, I searched in vain for the boundary between my "real" self and the social history they read so accurately in my casual familiarity with medicines, the cushioned interiors of my hiking boots, and the technological sophistication of my eyeglasses, tape player, and cameras. I arrived in Zumbagua relatively unaware of my own race, as whites often are; the loss of this innocence was a profound gift.

The ñakaq, too, knows that our social histories are not written upon our bodies like ink atop a blank page but rather woven into the very fabric of our selves. He peels away his victims' clothing and their skins, yet finds their race still marked in their fat.

INSTRUMENTAL WHITENESS

In chapter 4, race was ascribed to actors through social intercourse; in this chapter, we find it not in acts but in things: our material possessions, diet, and bodily habits. These two facets of race, which at first glance seem contradictory, are in fact connected through a single process, that of exchange. It is through exchange with others that we acquire or lose possessions; over time, the results of each successive exchange add up, creating a state of either wealth or impoverishment. In the process, new racial identities accrete around us as well, and often prove far more permanent than the fleeting roles we adopt during specific interactions.

The white body is an accumulation of things: foods, shoes, cars, and money. Although most whites pride themselves on their sophistication as consumers, and enjoy shopping and buying as forms of entertainment, they often feel as though the rapid accumulation of objects around them happens without their volition. They speak of the process as mysterious, even uncanny. And indeed, enormous global forces determine their position as consumers: the flow of goods and services into the world's centers of wealth is constant and inexorable, pushed—according to Adam Smith's phantasmagoric metaphor—by an invisible hand.

Hidden behind the magical accumulation taking place in the homes of white metropolitans is the reality of loss: an elderly *cargador* in Cuzco too frail to find work, a mother displaced from a Chicago housing project, an unlicensed vendor in Cuenca whose wares are confiscated by the police. Race does not create these unequal exchanges, but it supports them: abuse comes easier when the powerless person is of the wrong race, just as advantages flow faster toward the wealthy person who is white.

The pishtaco story is about the hidden relationship between these seemingly isolated moments of acquisition and immiseration—and it is here that any apparent similarity between these stories and the post-card display breaks down. Those displays are a kind of blind alley, from which it is difficult to arrive at any cogent historical narrative about Indians and whites. In the pishtaco stories, in contrast, each element illustrates, explicitly or implicitly, one stage of an exchange process that contributes to white accumulation. The violent climax of the narrative is the act by which one party enriches himself by killing the other. This denouement is foreshadowed in the details of the ñakaq's appearance, which offer attentive listeners a history of the acts of consumption and accumulation that signal the race of the killer. It is this pregnant narrative of social and material history, made visible in the pishtaco, that makes his body an object of fascination and disgust. Embedded in its possessions and its flesh is the record of what it has done to Indians in the past, and the threat of what it is about to do again.

The Ñakaq's Work: Butchering Indians

Like the word *chola,* which implies an occupational status—that of the urban working-class woman—the pishtaco's various names describe what he does as much as what he is. One of his names is *Degollador:* "Slasher," from the Spanish verb *degollar.*[26] This word describes killing by decapitating or cutting the jugular vein; it strongly evokes the butchering of animals—or of people.[27] José María Arguedas alludes to this connection in the following passage, in which he recalls that his fascination with the ñakaq had its origins in a frightening encounter with a butcher:

> *En cierta ocasión, un carnicero se había puesto a manera de máscara, un cuero de cabeza de carnero recién degollado; cubierta la cabeza con esta máscara sagrante nos persiguió a un grupo de niños. Estuve en cama enfermo de terror durante varios días. Tenía entonces doce años, corría por aquellos días la noticia de que (en la pequeña ciudad de Puquio) un nak'aq rondaba al pueblo.*

> [On one occasion, a butcher had taken the skin from the head of a recently slaughtered calf and put it on like a mask; he covered his head with this bloody mask and chased a group of us children. I was so terrified that I was sick in bed for several days afterwards. I was twelve years old then; around that time there had been a story that (in the small city of Puquio) a ñakaq was roaming the town.][28]

The pishtaco is a kind of tradesman, like a butcher; the things he owns, wears, and carries are the tools of his dreadful occupation. When storytellers speak of the ñakaq's big car and his heavy boots, audiences shudder to realize that these are not just the trappings of whiteness; they also number among the instruments that help the Butcher capture, subdue, and annihilate his victims.

The pishtaco has other tools too. He has been seen with a machete, a knife, a revolver, a shotgun, a machine gun, a bayonet, a "curved needle for severing the spinal cords of animals" (Gose 1994a:297), "a long pig-sticker with a sharpened blade" (Wachtel 1994:73): things that can penetrate the body and inflict a deep wound. In some stories, the appearance of the ñakaq is sketched in quickly, through a single detail like a hairy head or a leather vest; in others the physical descriptions are more elaborate. Inevitably, though, the storyteller describes this lethal weapon, for it is the key upon which the entire plot turns.

The ñakaq's job involves several procedures, and he has specialized tools for each. To subdue the victim, he sometimes resorts to magical powders—although he may simply use his powers of persuasion, or of sexual allure. Next, he tears open the body with one of the weapons described above. Then comes the most difficult part: the extraction of the victim's fat—especially the fat from the kidneys. Finally, although he has accomplished his objective, he often pauses to sew up the wounds before he disappears. As a medical anthropologist, Crandon-Malamud felt obliged to obtain details of the operation and its aftermath: "Marks remain where the kharisiri makes his incisions," she records. "Father Joe Picardi, a Maryknoll priest working in Achacachi in 1978, claimed to have seen three such cases, although he allowed that they were psychosomatic" (1991:120).[29]

For the brutal job of tearing open the body, the pishtaco uses primitive but effective tools: a knife, a machete, a gun. When it comes to the more delicate operation of removing fat, however, he prefers more sophisticated equipment. Indeed, a chronology of ñakaq stories reveals continual improvements in the instruments for extraction. In 1980, Carmen Salazar-Soler was told that the pishtaco uses a "needle connected to a pump," which allows him to "proceed as though in a surgical intervention" (1991:10). Advanced technology of this kind must be imported from the United States, Germany, or Japan, like the gadgets owned by tourists—and anthropologists. Wachtel reports that after killing the suspected kharisiri, the community of Orinoca declared its actions vindicated by the discovery of a small machine with a terrifying attachment: "a kind of syringe connected by a tube" that could be inserted into the body for the actual fat extraction. He was not amused when the lethal machine was described to him as "a box that looks like your tape recorder" (1994:69). Zoila Mendoza, who had taken her P.C. with her to a town near Cuzco in the early 1990s, was similarly taken aback to hear one countryman remark to another that it appeared pishtacos had begun using computers (e-mail comm., 1997). The people of Quirpini, Bolivia, wondered whether American anthropologist Stuart Rockefeller was using his camera to extract fat from them: perhaps the pharmacy where he took his film to be developed paid him for the fat, and then made medicines from it (1998).

Any white possession of unknown purpose arouses alarm and hostility. When anthropologist Susan Lobo and some companions put up bright orange nylon tents at dusk in a rural Peruvian area, then crawled in and went to sleep, these actions almost cost them their lives. Later that night, passersby, alarmed by the enormous cocoons and told that there were gringos inside, decided these must be pishtacos and made ready to attack the tents and their inhabitants with knives; fortunately, neighbors who knew Susan intervened and dissuaded them (Lobo, e-mail comm., 1997). In Bolivia, rumors about the Instituto Tomás Katari Polytechnic, which had first aroused suspicion through its bright red jeep, reached fever pitch as people speculated about the purposes of the institute's experimental farm. Convinced that the foreigners were "raising lik'ichiri" (pishtacos) there, "the country people invaded it, and the outsiders had to seek refuge in urban areas" (Rivière 1991 : 35). Miners in Julcani suspected that the equipment in the mine's laboratory was used for pishtaring: the test tubes, for instance, were said to be storage containers for human fat extracted from the miners (Salazar-Soler 1991 : 14).

Other kinds of technologies, too, are associated with whiteness. An older, illiterate man saw the pishtaco's deadly machine as covered with "puros numeritos letras no sé que más" ["lots of little numbers and letters and I don't know what else"] (Salazar-Soler 1991 : 10). This man, like the arithmetic students in chapter 4, realized that whites use "numbers and letters" as weapons. Watching us as critically as we do them, inhabitants of the rural Andes observe that white power and privilege are encoded in language, spoken and written. There are blatantly instrumental documents such as passports, letters of introduction, or business cards, as well as other, less tangible verbal forms—such as professional titles, which are also intended to affect the behavior of others. Affiliation with an institution or membership in a professional organization opens doors that are closed to the untitled, and can even sanction behavior that would otherwise be punished.

It is rare to meet a professional man or woman in the Andes who does not have a title: technical experts of all kinds are addressed as "Ingeniero" or "Arquitecto"; university graduates are "Professor" or

"Doctor." When I lived in Ecuador as a graduate student, it bothered other middle-class people that I did not introduce myself in this way; many urged me to call myself "Doctora" although I had not completed my Ph.D. My many years of schooling and a prestigious Fulbright grant entitled me to some such name, they insisted: it was inappropriate for a highly educated person not to use one. The clergy have titles as well, and military ranks are used as forms of address for any member of the armed forces, including the various branches of the police.

All such terms of address are racially coded. Out in the countryside, I observed that the same young professionals who were so embarrassed by older and more effusive forms of obsequiousness nevertheless expected Indians to address them by their titles, and to do so with respect. In the 1960s, rural people in Ancash routinely addressed all foreign men as "Señor Ingeniero" (Oliver-Smith 1969:365). The English language, too, is racialized: in Huaquirca in the 1970s, Gose was told that that the word *misti* is derived not from the Spanish *mestizo* but from the English "Mister" (1994b:21), while in Ecuador, Stutzman recorded *los místeres* (the misters) as a racial category along with *los blancos* and *los mestizos* (1981:79).[30]

The pishtaco, like other whites, is equipped with a profession and a title: the earliest pishtacos were priests or monks, and by the mid-twentieth century they began to appear dressed as engineers and military officers as well. In Ancash, the word *ingeniero,* so readily applied to foreigners, was synonymous with *pishtaco* (Oliver-Smith 1969:365). Some tales even describe becoming a ñakaq as a formal process like entering a profession, with its own titles and organizations. Morote Best tells of an Indian pishtaco who became "certified" in order to join the "Club de los Pistacos del Cuzco" (1951–52:138). In 1977, Bolivians in Kachitu emphasized the necessary training, which was offered (to mestizos only) by the same La Paz pharmacies who bought the fat; it must have been a profitable sideline, for they also sold their students the necessary materials to perform the extractions (Crandon-Malamud 1991:121).

In Chipaya, Wachtel was known to have corporate sponsors: the university that paid for his airplane ticket, the Anthropology Museum in La Paz that provided him with an affiliation, the immigration officials who issued his visa and stamped his passport. Similarly, the ñakaq wields papers signed by powerful patrons—even certificates that guarantee him immunity from prosecution. In 1980, a campesino from Achonga heard that the pishtacos had gotten a contract with Electroperú (the state-owned power company).[31] Paul Liffman, an American student captured in the 1970s by an angry group of farmers who said he had been "sucking blood," foolishly tried to allay suspicion by displaying his university I.D. card—an action that immediately convinced his accusers that he was, indeed, a pishtaco (1977).[32] In Ancon, Ayacucho, and elsewhere, ñakaqs were said to possess an identity card issued by the government that authorized them to commit their crimes.[33]

Indeed, the pishtaco is often an ally or employee of the state, especially in Peru. In the fifteen years of the "Dirty War," when state terror claimed thousands of lives, he began to appear dressed as a "Sinchi": a member of the dreaded Peruvian Special Forces deployed to fight terrorism in the sierra. The guerilla fighters of the Sendero Luminoso, too, became "'the new ñakaq,' a vampire-like creature that carries off . . . the flesh of peasants to feed the Sendero Army" (Isbell 1997a: 67). In an atmosphere already saturated with violence, these stories spread rapidly, far beyond their traditional rural audiences. Enrique Mayer describes the context of their wild popularity:

> Sendero slogans painted on walls proclaim that the "party has a thousand eyes and a thousand ears." Security employees, narco-traffickers, arms dealers, grave robbers, and police all operate underground. Terrorists dress up as police, while police personnel don Sendero guise to carry out acts of unauthorized violence. . . . In such a climate, terror thrives. (Mayer 1994: 152–53)

Nancy Scheper-Hughes, writing about similar stories from Brazil, Argentina, South Africa, and Guatemala, notes that such tales arise when "military regimes, police states, civil wars, and 'dirty wars'" use "abductions, 'disappearances,' mutilations, and death squad attacks against ordinary citizens" (1996: 8). In Peru, their credibility was enhanced by the activities of a growing number of professional kidnappers, some of whom were disenchanted guerillas, others corrupt policemen (Mayer 1994: 153).

When Vergara Figueroa and Carrasco interviewed refugees from the highlands, they quickly realized that the pishtaco tradition had become a means to talk about political violence. One woman, asked about ñakaqs, responded by describing actual acts of state terror that she had recently endured: brutal house-to-house searches by the Sinchis, who threatened that the guerillas would soon come and slaughter everyone; the seizing of her own husband for questioning; his subsequent disappearance and presumed death. She had been drafted against her will into the Civil Defense squads that patrolled rural areas under Sinchi direction, looking for guerillas: "If I don't go and march," she said, "they will punish me and perhaps even kill me." She had this to say of the ñakaq:

They say they are the Sinchis themselves, who come out at night
and kill anyone who goes out after dark, so they can take their fat
by cutting open their necks and chests. . . . They say the pishtacos,
too, come from the government. . . . They say they are foreigners;
they say they don't even speak Spanish.[34]

Despite the extremity of this woman's experiences, her image of the
ñakaq as an actual person is not very different from those found elsewhere. Other pishtacos, too, with their legal papers, identification
cards, and training courses, may strike outsiders as bizarre rather than
uncanny: in a horror story, we expect supernatural sources of power
rather than the prosaic products of bureaucrats. But the pishtaco is only
a man, like us: *"es mortal, como todos,"* the inhabitants of Pisac assured
Morote Best (1951–52: 72). His certificates are logical extensions of the
power vested in all whites, for whom race has long acted as a kind of
safe-conduct pass allowing all kinds of predations upon Indians.

The Indian's Labor: Losing Fat

The killer, then, carries magical powders to seduce, and a sharp tool to
penetrate; heavy clothing renders him invulnerable against his victim's
fists or nails; a fast car enables him to escape, while papers, titles, and
credentials place him above the law. And, of course, he has a dreadful
little machine for extracting the fat he obtains by "cutting open necks
and chests." It's different for the Indian in the story, who appears only
momentarily as an actor before being butchered, her body rendered
into a quantity of fat, and sometimes into other useful objects as well.
The pishtaco begins by treating the other character in the drama as a
person, then as an animal, and finally as a mass of animal products.

One of the weirdest pishtaco stories of all is from Ayacucho, where
a well-known figure of the Christ child is called the "Niño Ñakaq."
Everywhere in the Andes, certain sacred images within churches are
said to be evil, prone to destructive acts of witchcraft. Too, several stories describe pishtacos coating the faces of the saints in the church with
human fat as an offering. But only of the Niño Ñakaq is it said that he
leaves his pedestal every night to harvest fat from unsuspecting victims,
just like the humans who dedicate themselves to the same trade. The
traces of his nocturnal adventures are visible even as he stands immobile
in the church during the day: supposedly one can see grease spots stain-
ing the hem of his gown.[35]

This fear of nocturnal thieves who steal one's body fat expresses certain realities for the rural poor: peasants typically see fleshiness as the
very sign of life, beauty, and health, and abhor the skeletal thinness of

the very poor. At the same time, there is something peculiarly Andean in the preoccupation with fat that runs through these stories.[36] Fat was so prized in the pre-Hispanic period that a deity was named Wiracocha (Sea of Fat)—a title that, oddly enough, became an honorific for Spaniards and later for whites. Throughout most of the twentieth century, *wiracocha* was still widely used in the Peruvian highlands as a "courtesy title" by which Indians addressed whites, "the Quechua equivalent of *señor*."[37] This usage is only now beginning to sound anachronistic, and so to disappear from everyday speech.

This cultural emphasis upon fat is most clearly seen in medical beliefs and practices. Aymaras from Jesús de Machaqa told Andy Orta that fat is an index of well-being and strength: many illnesses have their source in the loss of fat, which first manifests itself in unexplained fatigue (1997:7–8). In Zumbagua, Tayta Juanchu Chaluisa had a good reputation locally as a healer. The application of animal fats was an important part of his cures, and the loss of fat an especially frightening diagnosis. I remember him binding a lamb's broken leg: he called for "*wira, wira!*" (fat, fat) to dress the wound before bandaging it, and grunted with pleasure to find that Olguita had anticipated his request.

But when Juanchu himself became ill, he could no longer eat the soups Olguita cooked for him, even though she butchered sheep and guinea pigs to make him broths rich with strengthening wira. Describing his illness, which the doctor thought might be heart disease, Juanchu used the words I expected to hear: "My fat is melting away. Look at how thin I am. I don't have the strength to do anything, and when I look down at my body, I see that I am losing all my flesh."[38]

Tough and strong until his last year of life, Juanchu was openly contemptuous of whites' stamina and physiques. The ñakaq, too, seeks out Indians because of the special qualities of their fat, which is rich and dense, unlike the soft, weak fat of whites. But when he finishes with it, the Indian body is no longer strong: drained of its vital substance, it weakens and wastes away. A teacher in Pisac told Morote Best that the killer puts his victim to sleep with a magical powder and then extracts the fat from the kidneys. The victim, awakening, remembers nothing, and continues on his way. Although there is no scar or wound, he soon begins to lose weight and finally dies (1951–52:71). This crime is clearly a theft, as well as a murder: one body's loss is another's gain. The stolen fat, according to this witness, is used to cure the illnesses of the wealthy.

The political meaning of this myth seems unmistakable—or at least it did to many scholars, especially in Peru in the 1980s and early 1990s. In his 1994 critique of this point of view (discussed in chapter 1), Peter

Gose questioned the economic model upon which it is based. Anthropologists, he says, have seen the ñakaq as a "metaphorical representation of a supposedly more real economic exploitation by unequal exchange," as well as of "western notions of imperialism." He is skeptical of this reading of the ñakaq as "a terse allegory of commercial exploitation [in] which grease signifies the labour-power of the Andean peasantry":

> Everything proceeds in these analyses as if grease were alienable from the body in the same way that labour-power is under capitalism, but the difference is that slaughtering is lethal, not a repeatable transaction that keeps both parties intact. (1994a: 276)

This statement underestimates the horrific nature of labor relations when viewed through the lens of race. Andean history is replete with nightmarish demonstrations of the fact that under extremely exploitative conditions, the alienation of labor power under capitalism—although it is indeed a repeatable transaction from the point of view of the employers or owners—could hardly be said to keep both parties intact. As is clear from his other writings, Gose himself is keenly aware of the economic exploitation of rural South Americans, and of the intimate relationship between structural inequality and definitions of Indians. Indeed, the history of nonwhite labor in the Americas began as a kind of massive primitive accumulation, in which colonial and neo-colonial powers literally consumed the bodies of nonwhites in order to produce wealth and build empires. Some of the most profitable enterprises of the colonial period—Caribbean slave plantations, Spanish silver mines—were initially operated as death camps from which few workers emerged alive.

Twentieth-century history, too, contains far too many examples—still ongoing—of unendurable and even lethal forms of waged (or non-waged) labor expressly designed for nonwhite workers. César Chávez's long battle for decent working conditions for migrant workers in the United States remains incomplete; Rigoberta Menchú's reminiscences of working in a Guatemalan coffee plantation, where pesticides and abusive labor practices took the lives of those close to her, are as chilling as her accounts of military atrocities (1983: 33–42). Tayta Juanchu, too, had nightmarish memories of those who died while working for the hacienda of Zumbagua in his youth; he was especially haunted by a man who bled to death after his arm was crushed between millstones.

The kharikhari extracts one's fat, leaving a person weak unto death; but so too does a lifetime of hard work and poor pay. In Jesús de Machaqa, the Aymara explained to Orta that when one performs physical labor, one's fat burns up, filling the body with steam and smoke (1997: 7–8). Old porters in the market, said Gregorio Condori Mamani, are all used up, "without the strength even to haul their own bones" through the city; long years spent hauling produce through the streets and markets of Cuzco have left them emptied of everything but a skeletal carcass and an unrelenting hunger. He speaks bitterly of market women who abandon the aging and unwell cargadores they once employed. Dragging themselves through the streets as beggars, old porters die "still walking, with their hands outstretched"; "we move through the streets and markets like the damned," he says, "our tattered clothes dragging behind us" (1977:88; 1996:103).

In the southern Andes, the pishtaco seems to have a special significance in mining communities, where stories about him are filled with the imagery derived from the ritual sacrifices to earth deities that are so important there.[39] The history of these mines epitomizes the lethal quality of the wage relationship under extremely exploitative labor conditions, for they have created vast fortunes for their owners while destroying thousands of workers in the process. June Nash, in her magisterial study of the lives of Bolivian tin miners, finds these ritual practices to be expressions of the work experience, communicated in a symbolic language that is richly and specifically Andean. Working conditions in the tin mines of Oruro during the 1960s and 1970s, she says, were "inhuman." Not only were the mines the sites of acute daily misery; they literally destroyed workers' bodies, either through long-term illness or sudden fatal accidents. The result is

> a cannibalistic quality in the relationship between the workers and the mine. "We eat the mines," one man told me at a ch'alla (rite of making offerings), "and the mines eat us." Their feelings about the mines are expressed in the names they give their work sites: Moropoto, Black Anus; Veta Dolores, Vein of Sadness; Sapo, Toad; El Tambo Mata Gente, People-Killer Inn, a work site where seven men were killed in a cave-in; Carnavalito, Carnival, or the last time to eat meat before Lent. In the smaller mines, the dried blood from the sacrifices of llamas splashed on the mouth of the mines gives an even more carnivorous look to the hills. (1979:170–71)

Carmen Salazar-Soler, who did research in the Peruvian mine of Julcani, found so many parallels between the tale of the pishtaco's fat-extracting practices and the experience of working in the mines that "it is not surprising that some workers think that the *Pishtaku* is a mining engineer recruited by the company especially to extract fat from the workers, which will serve as a lubricant for the machines, and especially for the concentration plant" (1991 : 14). She quotes one of the workers:

> *Pishtaku es ingeniero que manda los trabajos y mira, pero son falsos estos inges porque son Pishtaku son pues pagados por la compañia para chupar sebo de los runa para hacer caminar las máquinas de la planta. Yo me he informado bien señora, la compañia paga al Pishtaku 4500 soles el kilo de sebo, y yo mismo sabe señora cuanto gano? 518 soles el jornal. (14)*

> [Pishtaku is an engineer, one of those who give the work orders and watch us, but they are false, those engineers, because they're really paid by the company to suck fat from the runa to make the machines in the plant run. I have informed myself well, señora, the company pays the Pishtaku 4500 soles per kilo of fat, and I myself—do you know señora how much I earn? 518 soles a day.]

Mining offers an extreme example of difficult and dangerous work, in which underpaid laborers produce vast fortunes for others; this has made mines a flash point of labor history in many parts of the world. In the Andes, the extraction of precious metals from under the ground also calls up local systems of meaning with roots as deep as the veins of ore themselves.[40] But elsewhere in the Andes as well, the poor are intimately familiar with forms of labor, and of life, that eat Indians alive—often very slowly, through exchanges of debilitating work for poor wages that are, as Gose observes, repeated again and again. The Bolivian tin miner, the Peruvian cargador, and the Ecuadorian farm family can all testify to the power of the Andean economic system to consume the bodies of the poor while fattening the rich.

An Ecuadorian colleague, Diego Quiroga, protested the economic analysis in my first book, in which I describe the siphoning of labor power from rural communities into the city. He said ruefully, and accurately, that the problem for indigenous people today is not that the cities want Indian labor, but that they do not. Indeed, as Marx observed, the situation of the poor who form the vast reserve of labor is the most desperate of all. It is a phenomenon I have been unlucky enough to witness firsthand. When I first met my future compadre, Alfonso, in the mid-1980s, he was young and happy, a recently married man proud of his physical strength and graceful agility, and his success in finding employment building skyscrapers in Quito. This building boom was temporary, however, and as Ecuador fell into recession, jobs disappeared. In the intervening years, I have watched the toll that joblessness has taken on him, and on his wife, Olguita Quispe.

An underreported aspect of poverty in the Andes is the mental anguish it can cause; health workers are sometimes reluctant to attribute illnesses among the very poor to psychological trauma, as though such diseases were a luxury to which the latter are not entitled. Olguita's decline began while she was nursing her ailing father-in-law, Juanchu; after his death, exhausted and depressed, she took to her own bed. To the alarm of the family, she got no better, and the Catholic missionaries could find nothing wrong despite extensive medical tests. To me she seemed simply discouraged. She missed Juanchu, who taught her about herbs and healing. Too, the kind of life the old man represented no longer seems possible: beset with economic problems, she and Alfonso were farming out their children to relatives, rather than adopting other people's kids as her father-in-law had done.

When I talked to María, the Catholic hospital administrator, she surprised me by reminiscing about a similar illness that had struck Heloisa, an event that I remembered only from secondary accounts, since I had been absent from the parish at the time. "We couldn't find anything physiological then either," she recalled. "The only thing that finally got Heloisa out of bed was that we offered her a job at the church for a small wage. Then she recovered really quickly—and look at her now, the head of the whole family." Indeed, since Juanchu's death Heloisa has stepped into his role, even adopting Olguita's daughter Nancy as her own. She is a pillar of strength now, but María's story reminded me that she is not invulnerable. Olguita, too, had once impressed me with her vitality, and I had imagined that she would mature to be as strong as the older Quispe women I knew.

Like Tayta Juanchu, Olguita spoke of her illness as a loss of fat. Sitting up in bed, she held out her arm and made me palpate the slack, empty skin: where once her arm had been round and plump, with solid muscles bulging underneath a layer of fat, now the flesh hung limply from the bone. "See? See?" she demanded, crying. "There is no fat left at all." Her house, too, had shrunk: Tayta Juanchu's enormous thatched *chaki wasi,* into which she had moved as a bride, had fallen into disrepair and been abandoned in favor of a smaller concrete block house. Nor were the consumer goods Alfonso had once purchased—radios, a record player, dishes, and shoes—any longer in evidence: thrown out when broken, or tucked away in storage when they ran out of batteries, none of them had been replaced.

Their financial crisis was greatly exacerbated by bad debt; in the rural Andes, as in poor communities elsewhere, loans are readily available, but only on terms so outrageous that no one but the truly desperate—of whom there are plenty—accept them.[41] As Alfonso's temporary bouts of unemployment became permanent, and rifts over the division of Juanchu's property shattered any hope of help from his older brother, he had resorted to loans from creditors who now constantly harassed him for unpaid interest payments many times the size of the original loans. Such rapid accumulations of interest on debt are the mirror image of capital accumulation, just as Olguita's shrinking house inverts the middle-class expectation (often unrealized) of ever larger, more abundantly provisioned accommodations. The latter vision is recreated in pishtaco stories like the one told by Morote Best about an Indian man who learns how to "harvest" fat from a mestizo. Eventually, by selling the fat he collected to pharmacies, this Indian ñakaq is able to purchase a "splendid chalet" as well as an hacienda (1951−52: 138). In contrast, Olguita's home gets smaller and emptier, while her debts multiply and grow.

Of course, whites have found their resource base declining in recent years as well—and they have also witnessed the collapse of the traditional racial hierarchy that guaranteed rural elites an iron control over local economies. In the Bolivian community of Kachitu, Libbet Crandon-Malamud found that the changing political economy had sapped the once-absolute power of local whites; as a result, by the 1970s the kharisiri had lost some of his potency as well.

> Throughout the centuries of Spanish colonialism, and indeed until the 1950s, the kharisiri, often called the Kari Kari . . . was widely known throughout the Bolivian altiplano as a phantasm that brought a specific disease, diagnosable by the marks it left on the abdomen. It has traditionally been considered fatal. But in Kachitu in 1977 and 1978, it was not. . . . Perhaps because of the presence of the clinic, and perhaps because of a decrease in infant mortality since the land reform, a visitation from the kharisiri was no longer considered fatal, although still considered a serious illness.
>
> The . . . etiology of the kharisiri disease and its evolution is a reflection of Kachitu's and Bolivian history. . . . In this etiology, the loss of mestizo power is made explicit. Many mestizos reiterated this medical theory to me. Don Arturo Cruz, said Doña Antonia, died because he *was* a kharisiri. He was in desperate financial shape after the revolution and resorted to this means of

making money. She knew this because when Cruz died, his face was black and his body was swollen like that of a toad that is used to ensorcell. (1991:120–21)

In one sense, all Latin Americans, of every race and class, struggle with an enormous and unpayable debt: the crushing national indebtedness that cripples the entire region and largely determines the economic relationship between North and South. Latin American foreign debt doubled in size between 1970 and 1990; during this period, reports Peruvian economist Oscar Ugarteche, Latin America exported $375 billion to service this debt. This massive capital transfer aided in a global economic redistribution in which "the gap in income per capita between the richest and poorest countries grew from a multiple of 70 to a multiple of 430" (1999:21). Furthermore, the debt continues to erode the national sovereignty of Latin American nations, which have been forced to let the IMF dictate and even micromanage their internal social and economic policies (Green 1999).

In the abstract, the debt impoverishes all South Americans and forces the entire continent into the position of debt peon to the white North. But in reality the burden of the debt—and especially of the "structural readjustments" imposed by the IMF—does not fall equally on all citizens. If anything, the debt crisis of the 1980s and the neoliberal policies that followed have created an even closer and more mutually beneficial relationship between Latin American elites and foreign investors, increasing the indifference of both to the suffering of people like Olguita. Duncan Green writes that

> while foreign investors and local elites enjoyed most of the gains of the precrisis period, they have had to bear very little of the costs of the crash. Instead, these have fallen on the poor, in the form of recessions, accompanied by public spending cuts, job losses and falling wages. . . . All along, both lenders and borrowers are seeing that they have nothing to fear from rash decisions. . . . Foreign investors have found that they will be bailed out by the international financial institutions—i.e. Western taxpayers—when the going gets rough. . . . [National] elites have seen that debts can be socialized—passed on in turn to their own taxpayers and workers. (1999:34–35)

Thus the neoliberal revolution has solidified the whiteness of Latin American elites, whose right to accumulate at others' expense is protected by financial institutions like the IMF. When greed and malfeasance cause economic disasters, neither they nor their wealthy foreign friends will suffer. Rather, the nonwhite poor of their own countries are forced into service as whipping boys, assuming debts they did not incur and paying for them with the flesh of their own bodies.

The Ñakaq's Job: Selling Indian Flesh

Doña Antonia's story is unusual in its portrayal of the pishtaco as a desperate and impoverished man—indeed, in her tale it is Don Arturo Cruz, rather than his victims, who ends up dead. Although Arguedas recorded tales from the 1950s that end with tips on how to outwit a pishtaco, in most stories today it is the Indian who dies, while his killer acquires health, wealth, and material possessions. Rather than a blackened, swollen corpse, the pishtaco is a big, handsome man with a liking for clothes—especially ones made of leather.

Like cowboys, cattle ranchers, and hacendados—and wealthy elites from the city, when they visit their country estates—the pishtaco likes to wear leather jackets, vests, boots, and chaps. Listeners shudder at this detail, imagining that like a hunter dressed in animal skins—or the butcher who teased Arguedas—the ñakaq is wearing the by-products of his work. In the tale of Don Sittichu, the pishtaco's wardrobe of leather clothing expands as he becomes more successful in his chosen profession, until finally he appears dressed entirely in tanned skins—the product of his activities as a butcher of humans—and surrounded by his illegitimate offspring—the result of his actions as a rapist of Indians.

It is revolting to think that the pishtaco carries on his person the remnants of his victim's bodies: his leather clothing, hat, and boots, and the magical powders he manufactures out of their reproductive organs. But most repellent of all is the thought of his white flesh, which is fed by the fat extracted from the eviscerated bodies of Indians. A miner told Salazar-Soler about a roadside grill on the highway between Huancavelica and Lima run by a pishtaco, who served human flesh. If Indians ate there, they became ill; but the mine owners enjoyed the food and met there regularly to discuss which employees should be sent down into the mines, and which should be rendered by the pishtaco for their fat (1991:18). In Ayacucho, an old country woman, asked about pishtacos, told of a restaurant in faraway Lima that served "a very delicious soup" made from the bodies of infants brought from her community. Ansión and Sifuentes, who collected this tale of city folk feasting on rural bodies, comment on "the nutritiousness and high quality of the flesh"—and the low price charged for it, because it came from Indians.[42]

Pishtaco stories linger with dreadful pleasure on the pishtaco's fatness, his leather clothing, and any other fragments or residues of his victim's bodies incorporated within, on, and around his person. But if he occasionally uses some of these by-products, they do not motivate his acts. The pishtaco story, in which a man butchers other human beings and renders their fat, seems like a myth of cannibalism, and in some versions it is.[43] But in others, it is not, or at least not exactly. In most stories, and especially more recent ones, it is not the desire to eat Indians, or rape them, or wear their skins that really drives him. Indeed, a mere act of cannibalism—the pishtaco eating his victim with relish— would almost come as a relief.

What the ñakaq does with the fat of Indians is to sell it: he is moved by a lust for profit, not for flesh. He has been remarkably successful at finding markets for his product: the fat that he harvests is sold for a variety of uses, few of which are dietary. Some of the better known are illustrated in the lively visual histories of the pishtaco made by artist Nicario Jiménez. Jiménez is the greatest living maker of *retablos,* painted wooden boxes filled with small modeled figures made from paper and potato flour that are among the most popular forms of folk art produced in the region of Ayacucho (Sordo 1990). Lesser retablo makers produce clichéd images of markets and hat shops for the tourist trade, or Nativity scenes for Christmas; the execution is often as crude as the themes are trite, and the mood is relentlessly cheery. Jiménez's works, in contrast, are evocative and unsettling. The boxes are filled with small figures that gesture and grimace, compelling the viewer's attention; the crowded compositions, which layer realistic and supernatural elements, convey a sense of urgency.

Even his renditions of folkloric themes such as festivals have an undertone of violence. Jiménez likes to represent the costumed figures known as scissors dancers, whom he depicts brandishing whips and enormous shears and laughing with red-lipped, open mouths. In one such retablo, a condor presides over the scene from above. In Jiménez's hands, this conventional icon of the Andes is not a benign presence: his cruel beak and forward-thrusting neck remind the viewer that he is a carnivore. Positioned at the apex of the box, where an image of Christ or the Holy Spirit would appear on the Catholic altarpiece from which the retablo tradition is derived, this raptor could be a stand-in for the murderous Niño Ñakaq (who is, after all, an Ayacucho native like Jiménez).

Jiménez's most elaborate retablos depict a history of the pishtaco. These are enormous constructions with three separate chambers, each recounting a moment in Peruvian history as remembered in Ayacucho folk tradition. The first shows a colonial pishtaco robed as a Franciscan, who uses human fat to found church bells. In the next scene, a modern ñakaq appears as a gringo with long hair and a mechanic's overalls. This pishtaco of the 1960s uses the grease from his human victims to lubricate airplane engines and factory equipment: he is "the man who works for the modern age of machinery in a very brutal way." [44] The last compartment, depicting the ñakaq of the 1980s, shows the pishtaco in a variety of garbs and poses. Himself forced to flee his home in Ayacucho because of the escalating violence, Jiménez portrays the pishtaco as a member of the special forces who terrorized rural communities. Basing his work on tales told by his fellow refugees, he also shows the bogeyman dressed as a general, using human fat to pay off Peru's foreign debt and buy armaments.[45] This ñakaq is the paid agent of a corrupt and violent state—and of the vicious international system that profits by aiding and abetting local oppressors.

Crandon-Malamud, too, provides a short history of the commercial ends a Bolivian kharisiri has found for his product—and here we see a different regional history reflected in the business practices of a local entrepreneur. The story begins like Jiménez's:

> Until the 1950s the kharisiri was universally the image of a dead Franciscan monk. It had a broad Franciscan hat and a long beard, and it roamed about the countryside at night. . . . The kharisiri magically removed the fat from its victims' kidneys and gave it to the bishop. Out of the kidney fat of Aymara Indians, the bishop made holy oil.

By the late 1970s, however, things had changed. The parish priest had been told that the kharisiri stole kidney fat "to sell to the North Americans to run their electricity"—a tale combining industrial elements with the theme of U.S. imperialism. Crandon-Malamud also heard about cosmetic and pharmacological uses. "By the time of my arrival in Kachitu in 1977," she writes, the human kidney fat extracted by the kharisiri "was sold to factories in La Paz who used it to make colored, perfumed luxury bath soap for export, for tourists, and for the Bolivian elite" (1991:121).

An entire economic history of the Andes is written in these uses that Indians believe whites have found for the fat they rob. During the colonial period, the European religious orders were expansive global enterprises with vast spiritual, economic, and political ambitions; they competed with one another vigorously to set up extractive industries in the South American highlands. In central Ecuador, the Augustinians received hunting licenses from the Spanish Crown to capture Indians from the warmer, lower altitudes and bring them up forcibly to the sparsely inhabited grasslands of Zumbagua as shepherds; by the eighteenth century the region was producing thousands of bales of wool, raw materials for the textile sweatshops set up closer to urban areas (Weismantel 1988:60–64). It was this type of aggressive clerical entrepreneurship that Peruvians first attributed to pishtacos, who hunted Indian fat for use in the casting of bells.

For most of the twentieth century, the pishtaco usually appeared as an hacendado (or an Indian recruited by a white landowner to do the dirty work for him): this is how Arguedas and Oliver-Smith describe him. He was less interested in agriculture than in machines: he wanted Indian fat because it is an efficacious lubricant, which he could use in his sugar mill or smelting operations. These industrial themes dominated in the 1960s: when "Man" went to the moon, rural Peruvians knew immediately that although only gringos were walking around up there, the fat from Indian babies must have provided the fuel that propelled them through space (Mayer 1994:152).

Nowadays the cosmetic and pharmacological uses reported by Crandon-Malamud appear to be eclipsing the industrial theme in popularity. This seems perfectly appropriate for the current phase of late capitalism. Today the core nations of Europe, the United States, and Japan—together with elite enclaves throughout the world—are still the economic engines driving the world economy, but not as industrialists in need of labor and raw materials. Rather, it is as hyperconsumers that whites dominate, fueling world economic activity through their insatiable desire for new and luxurious personal possessions.

The cult of the body is an important aspect of this feverish consumerism; the desire to alter one's physical appearance and abilities through drugs and procedures once restricted to the medical arena is widespread, and by no means restricted to the wealthy. Recent studies of Brazil's poor, for example, have documented the rampant use of patent and prescription drugs to treat the listlessness caused by malnutrition (Scheper-Hughes 1992), and even amateur silicone implantations by prostitutes seeking to enhance their ability to attract customers (Kulick 1998:66–83).

I was surprised to discover that some of the most appreciated gifts I could bring to Zumbagua were skin lotions and cold creams. Middleclass Americans take for granted the availability of products that soften the skin and hair and mitigate the effects of pollution and weather, but not so poor Latin Americans. In the high altitudes and equatorial latitudes of Zumbagua, the effects of the sun are devastating: faces and lips are burned, swollen, and scarred from constant exposure to ultraviolet rays. The winds are relentless, too, and carry a heavy load of drying dust from the unpaved roads and eroding fields. Women's skin and hair are further roughened and scarred from the smoky cookfires over which they spend long hours, and their hands are chapped from the icy water they draw and haul from underwater springs.

Rural women who have worked as domestics report back on the contents of wealthy women's medicine cabinets and dressing tables: the oils and creams that claim quasi-magical abilities to reverse aging and erase damage—even to whiten dark skin, straighten nappy hair, or curl the straight hair of an Indian. The women in Tayta Juanchu's household did not envy the indoor lives of these pale, weak women; but they very much wished they could afford skin creams. Pishtaco stories draw a direct line between the dry, cracked skin of women like Rosita Quispe or Clarita Chaluisa, and the overstocked dressing tables of the wealthy. The tales Crandon-Malamud heard about "perfumed luxury bath soaps" are not new: as early as the 1950s, Morote Best was told that skin lotions were made from human fat, extracted by pishtacos and sold to foreign factory owners (Morote Best 1951–52:80).

The fear that whites will take what they want from Indian bodies produced a frightening new development in Lima in 1988, when rumors about a new kind of bogeymen swept the city: the *sacaojos*.[46] Although their advent coincided with that of the refugees flooding the cities, the sacaojos were a strictly urban phenomenon. They were said to traverse the shantytowns in vans, snatching up children in order to extract their eyes or other organs for use in transplant operations; indeed, their name comes from the verb *sacar* (to extract or remove) and the noun *ojos* (eyes). These tales are eerily similar to those Scheper-Hughes has collected from urban neighborhoods in Africa, Brazil, Guatemala, and the United States, stories the origins of which she traces to the fear and anger aroused by the emerging transnational market in human organs. Poor people, she says, picture the rising popularity of transplants and plastic surgery as a traffic in the blood and organs of the powerless (1996:7; 2000).

Her research into the actual practices of clinics and morgues in Brazil and South Africa suggests that while the specific bodily violations described by poor Latin Americans are mostly imaginary, the economic stratification of medical care makes their fears eminently reasonable. She documents in grisly detail the brutal treatment given to the dead bodies of the poor, and the cavalier attitudes of doctors toward impoverished patients. "At the municipal clinic in Bom Jesus Dr. Joao took a cursory look at Seu Antonio . . . and said: 'That eye of yours isn't worth anything; let's just have it removed'" (Scheper-Hughes 1996:6).

In the meantime, the wealthy enjoy access not only to lifesaving transplant technology, but also to plastic surgery, assisted reproduction, and sex-change operations. On the pages of the same Peruvian newspapers that reported mysterious kidnappings and disappearances, gossip columnists chatted about the popularity of these medical procedures among the international elite. Such stories have captured the imagination of the poor across the continent: as an old Brazilian woman living in a shantytown told Scheper-Hughes, " 'So many of the rich are having plastic surgery and organ transplants . . . that we really don't know whose body we are talking to anymore' " (1996 : 7). Here the inversion between accumulation and loss takes on ghastly proportions: the rich assemble ever more perfect bodies, while the poor lose body parts deemed worthless to begin with. When we add to this picture the outdated or harmful medicines dumped on Latin American markets by U.S. pharmaceutical companies, and Kulick's matter-of-fact descriptions of the results of prostitutes' self-inflicted breast surgeries gone awry, the fears expressed in tales of the sacaojos start to make an uncanny kind of sense.

In Zumbagua, much covert interest was aroused when I began having extensive dental work done during my occasional absences, but only the children were bold enough to question me directly. Alberto's son Andrés asked whether a new crown was carved out of pigs' teeth; when I laughed—somewhat discomfited by the idea—he said eagerly, "So they are someone else's teeth, then, aren't they? I mean, another person's?"

This picture of a gringa with someone else's teeth inside her head clearly brings us back to the terrain of Freud. The piles of body parts accumulated by the pishtaco and the sacaojos resemble the psychoanalyst's list of uncanny phenomena from German horror stories, which included eyes plucked from the head, "dismembered limbs, a severed head, a hand cut off at the wrist." The German tales horrify because these fragments of the body talk, open their eyes, or move about: things that are (or should be) dead exhibit signs of life. The ñakaq, in contrast, is a living person, large and fat and full of strength and purpose, whose powerful body is made from—or nourished by—the dismembered bodies of the dead. Thus rather than an inanimate object that appears to be alive, he is a living thing animated by the remnants of the dead.

What makes the pishtaco most uncanny—and most white—is the indirect nature of the relationship between his body and that of his victims. He opens up their bodies in order to feed others, enriching himself in the process: his surgical operations suture the flesh of all three people—victim, killer, and consumer—into the circulatory system of the global economy. Between the pishtaco and his white business partners, this flow may take the form of a mutually beneficial exchange; but from the Indian point of view, there will be only losses.

The Whites' Job: Buying Fat

When I talk about pishtacos to middle-class audiences in Chicago or Los Angeles, someone in attendance invariably expresses rueful amazement that there are places in the world where the loss of one's body fat inspires terror rather than enthusiasm. Whites, it seems, have too much fat, and too much food: the problem for the American consumer at century's end is not the lack of sustenance but the unavoidable superabundance of it. If Indians dread being seduced by a man who takes their fat away, whites seem to have an almost equal horror of an economy that continually lures them into buying and eating it.

One might make too much of this apparent symmetry: seen from the other side, do the actions of wealthy whites actually bear any resemblance to the work of the ñakaq? If so, we seem curiously unknowing bogeymen. To us, the harm we do occurs without our volition; we resemble the African witches of classical anthropology, who killed without realizing it, rather than the consciously evil creatures of this particular Andean myth. From either side, it is difficult to grasp the system of global exchange in its entirety. Stories of ñakaqs and pishtacos offer glimpses of the relationship between Indians and whites, and between local suffering and the global economy, but the picture is sketchy and offers few solutions for reversing the trend of Indian impoverishment. White Americans, despite incomparably greater access to information, money, and power, are even more mystified than the Indians by the economic and political processes that sustain them. And many whites express total ignorance of the sources of their own desires as consumers, as well.

At the same time, whites take their role as consumers completely for granted, so much so that it becomes an implicit but crucial aspect of identity, most salient when contrasted to the less perfect relationship to commodities attributed to others. On picture postcards, an absence of commodities makes people into Indians. Whites, in turn, are surrounded—and defined—by a profusion of purchases, large and small.

In conservative white mythologies, this observed relationship is given a positive moral dimension. Blacks are routinely stigmatized as perverse consumers, fashion-conscious but prone to excess and to cheap display, and hence unable to accumulate; Indians are imagined to be naïve and inept where money is concerned, reluctant to spend and easily cheated. "White Bolivians say that the Indians of the Altiplano eat nothing but potatoes yet have thousands of dollars buried in their floors; they piss all the money away on wild drinking bouts," says Shukman (1989:46). In contrast, Ruth Frankenberg found that liberal white women considered their role as global consumers distasteful, and a source of white guilt. They spoke of racial whiteness not only as "linked with" capitalism, but as "spoiled by" it, and thus as a cause for "alienation" from one's own racial identity (1993:199–200).

When Frankenberg asked these women to describe what whiteness is, they responded by naming "commodities and brands: Wonder bread, Kleenex, Heinz 57" (Frankenberg 1993:199). For the most part, however, Frankenberg found that whites had a hard time envisioning their racial identity at all: as the taken-for-granted absence of a stigma, it is hard to see. This privilege presents a problem: others may have a culture, an identity, a sense of pride, but whites do not. In an image reminiscent of the ethnographic museum, where whites stand on the darkened side of the displays, staring at the brightly lit and costumed figures across the velvet ropes, women told Frankenberg that their race placed them in a void from which they looked out longingly at others. Like the ñakaq, who finds white flesh flavorless and insubstantial, these whites described their own culture as "bland" or "blah," like "white bread" or "mayonnaise" (1993:122).

They pictured nonwhites as the possessors of a genuine identity, something intangible but deeply satisfying: a kind of inheritance, a birthright, which their own ancestors had somehow sold for a mess of Wonder bread and electronics equipment. But as Jane Hill found in her study of white linguistic practices in Arizona, whites do not take this state of affairs lying down. If nonwhites have what they lack, whites simply use their own far greater financial resources to appropriate it— or at least its outward manifestations (Hill 1994).

Whiteness, in short, is not the passive state that whites themselves imagine it to be: it is constituted through a set of specific processes, one of which Hill labels "incorporation." Through incorporation, she says, whites combat the perceived blandness of their own culture and attempt to sate their appetite for the strongly flavored products of colored bodies. She recalls her own childhood as a succession of incorporative events: visits to museums to learn about Indians, a "romance with things Hispanic" (such as bullfighting), a Girl Scout troop "big on 'Negro spirituals'" (12–14). White identity, says Hill, only feels empty; in reality, it is chock-full of dismembered and re-appropriated cultural traits that originally belonged to someone else. She summarizes her own enculturation into whiteness as a process whereby "family and schools carefully helped me build an identity out of thousands of fragments of 'others'" (14). White privilege, in her retelling, lies in the power to pick and choose among all these imaginary nonwhites, and so to create oneself.

Tourism, of course, is predicated upon just such practices, which can lead to frenzies of acquisitiveness when traveling in countries with a favorable exchange rate. In the Andes, the process of incorporation is most visible among the younger and less affluent foreigners who travel the "Gringo Trail," a string of inexpensive guest houses and restaurants dotting the Andes that cater to European backpackers. Since they must wear or carry everything with them, each purchase these travelers make is immediately added to their eclectic costumes, which become a material record of their progression through the Americas. Arriving in the Andes wearing jeans from New York and a Guatemalan shirt, they add a sweater from Otavalo, a knitted hat from Taquile, a vest made of old Bolivian textiles.

Even college students who cannot afford the luxury of foreign travel can indulge in this form of accumulation. Micaela di Leonardo provides a glimpse of the commercial district in Evanston, Illinois, where both she and I now live, which she describes as "a white-bread, Midwestern college town" where small stores merchandise "the charm of the unfamiliar."

> Crowded cheek by jowl up against Navajo and Pueblo pots, rugs and jewelry are tarot cards and crystals, Southeast Asian guardian figures, Mexican *santos*. . . . Store names celebrate Otherness: Nomads, Ltd., Primitivo, East Meets West . . . fabric covers vaguely evoke Indonesian batik . . . curbside cars sport "Native American" dream catchers. (1998 : 1)

Complex class, regional, and generational relationships determine the movement of items from fringe subcultures, such as the devotees of the Gringo Trail, into mainstream white society:

> College towns across the nation since at least the 1950s have been staging grounds for selling the offbeat . . . not just for students and hangers-on eager to display sophistication through the consumption of the exotic, but for outlying suburbanites as well. Particular commodities—folk music, Indian import women's wear, Balinese jewelry—succeeded first in college town test markets before becoming standard American mall merchandise. (1998 : 2)

The products that meet the incorporative urge, like the ever-changing market for the pishtaco's goods, are not stable over time. The bearded backpacker with a woven sash threaded through his belt loops has become a laughable anachronism. In the 1980s, the Body Shop found a lucrative market for bars of soap and jars of lotion packaged as products of rainforests and Indians;[47] in the 1990s, electronic dance music blended Amazonian shaman's songs and the voices of whales. As each borrowed item crosses the racial barrier, it loses its exotic appeal and is rapidly discarded, leaving its purchasers still voraciously in need of what the other has and they lack: they are left, in other words, as perfect consumers.

White behavior thus seems to passively conform to the needs of the market, but Frankenberg suggests that consumers connive in their own incompleteness, preferring the fragmented and essentialized pieces of race—and even their own "blahness"—to anything that might threaten their comfort. Her informants loved to show off their carefully acquired knowledge of particular aspects of nonwhite culture, but they persistently evaded discussion of race relations. This avoidance, which she calls "power evasiveness" or "race evasiveness," defines a racial privilege the more luxurious for being unexamined; it emerges in her study as the defining quality of whites. As we saw in the opening of this chapter, a similar evasion of racial self-knowledge is intrinsic to the racial displays constructed for white audiences. We are invited to enjoy a spectacle of nonwhiteness but are protected from perturbing scenes of racial interaction such as those enacted by the ñakaq. This evasiveness underwrites the insatiability of consumer demand, ensuring that nonwhites remain a distant, essentialized, and unattainable source of fantasy, as in the estranged vision of the chola produced by Andean whites discussed in chapter 2.

White consumers, then, are guaranteed invisibility and unaccountability: they do not know about the people who made the things they eat, wear, and accumulate, and those people do not know them either. Commodity fetishism and white privilege coincide in protecting this safe position; the scopophilic vision of the pishtaco story thwarts it. A listener to one of these stories, or a viewer of Nicario Jiménez's retablos, is invited to scrutinize the white male body as though it belonged to an Indian in a display, or a prostitute showing her wares; but this probing gaze is only the beginning. The inventory of white possessions in these stories catalogs white consumption and accumulation, and makes each commodity bear the full weight of its accumulated history. It also reveals the instrumentality of the things whites own, and so underscores the responsibility for our actions that we seem so anxious to avoid.

By relating the beauty and vitality sought by white consumers to the theft of Indian sustenance, these tales give the lie to the global market's apparent ability to magically generate wealth out of thin air. Money circulates endlessly, but the market is not really a perpetual motion machine: hidden behind the fattening but pleasurable fantasia of late capitalist consumer culture are the workers, whose invisible labor in fields and factories, homes and businesses creates the wealth that belongs to others. For the very poor in peripheral economies, such labor eats up their bodily health and strength, leaving them thin and broken. The cycle of exchange rarely permits reciprocity; rather, goods and capital accumulate around the white body, while the Indian sees her possessions devoured by ever-accumulating debt.

Inheritance

Part 2 of this book emphasized the fluidity of racial and sexual identities, which inhere less in specific bodies than in unequal relationships and forms of exchange. This chapter followed the results of those exchanges over time: as profits accumulate, the once-fluid identity of the white partner solidifies into a permanent association between whiteness, goods, and an endless appetite to consume. This accumulation is not only a matter of individuals, however, but of families, communities, and generations. When one generation passes its accumulated wealth on to another, the economic position—and the racial identity—of the group is solidified, and a new round of accumulation can commence. Other groups, in contrast, inherit only poverty and indebtedness, and so begin life already locked into a negative cycle of loss in which their labor, like that of their parents, vanishes and takes their health and well-being with it.

Because people in places like Zumbagua think of racial inheritance in terms of accumulation, they have contradictory responses to those accidents of genetic inheritance, such as blue eyes or blond hair, which receive such intense attention elsewhere. They have clear evidence at hand that the physical traits of racial whiteness do not always lead to wealth or privilege. Everyone knows that the children of Zumbagua women raped or forced into concubinage by white overseers of the now-defunct hacienda have been unable to gain financial or social recognition from their fathers, or any wider acceptance from Ecuadorian society because of white facial features or coloring. The obvious poverty that shows itself in their broken teeth and dirty clothing, their peasant bodies and the Quichua-flavored singsong in which they speak their hesitant Spanish, is far more salient than the green eyes or curly hair that is their only paternal inheritance. The social, cultural, and economic inheritance of these individuals comes to them from their mothers alone—as does their race.

At the same time, people in the parish are highly cognizant of the fact that, in Cheryl Harris's words, whiteness is property: a set of economic and political privileges passed down from generation to generation (C. Harris 1993). When strangers appear, their inherited traits are scrutinized together with the other physical and material features of whiteness described in this chapter, as people try to assess these new people and the risks they may represent. Someone who has inherited features suggestive of European ancestry is also likely to have been born and raised in a community endowed with racial privilege—and to act like other whites. Even if that person is a racial orphan, deprived by circumstances of those material benefits that accrue to most members of the dominant group, he may nonetheless on occasion manage to gain temporary access to those privileges, simply by looking as though such assets ought to be his.

The presence of a truly white body, in which these genetic endowments are matched by material assets, is never an innocent fact. The story of the pishtaco links the wealth enjoyed in the present to invisible atrocities committed far away, both now and in the past. The long and violent history of racial oppression is written onto the descendants of Europeans whether we like it or not, for our bodies represent the destruction of other, Indian bodies: those killed in the past, and their absent descendants. North American individualism finds the notion that a person bears responsibility for the acts of his ancestors repugnant. In Latin America, where a person is more often evaluated as a product of one's family, it is easier to conceive of race as a collective inheritance that cannot be disavowed.

Inheritance leads us to reproduction, the theme of the final chapter. Pishtaco stories embed a moral about capitalism within a story about fat—a preoccupation shared by anorexic American teenagers and Andean native healers. Ñakaqs steal more than fat, however, and even more than health and money. They also steal sex, as we saw in chapter 4—and sometimes they steal one's sexual organs as well. Chapter 6 takes up the theft of testicles and fetuses—and contrasts the ñakaq's destructive sexual proclivities with those of the Mama Negra, a fictitious chola whose body is very different from the white flesh investigated here.

....

CHAPTER 6

The Black Mother

It was September 1983. I had just arrived in Ecuador and would shortly move to Zumbagua, where I planned to live for at least a year. In the meantime, I was staying in Latacunga at an inexpensive hotel with the exotic name "Estanbul": four stories of salmon-colored walls around a central courtyard occupied by overgrown plants, women washing clothes, and a loud-mouthed parrot in a cage. The owners lived on the bottom floor; at the very top were bright, cheerful rooms with windows and private baths. On the two middle floors, the rooms were windowless, dark, and cavelike, with one rather unpleasant bathroom at the end of each hall. I lived on the second floor and was lonely and apprehensive. I had one friend, a Swiss girl named Katrina whose room was near mine; she spoke only a little more English than I French. One afternoon, she stuck her head in my door and said there was some kind of fiesta going on, come and see.

We went outside and walked toward the church, where we were immediately overwhelmed by crowds filling the narrow streets. I could only catch glimpses of a long, raucous procession of costumed dancers, but one figure towered above the others, riveting my attention. In the notes I later scribbled to myself, I summarized the experience with these words: "It's the 'Return of the Mama Negra'—she is big."

The Mama Negra was indeed big, an enormous costumed woman on horseback who danced in her saddle and laughed uproariously as she sprayed the crowd with liquor from a baby bottle. She had enormous breasts and buttocks, and a plastic baby doll that she waved in the air as though it were a flag. This fantastic mother, who appears every September to lead a procession in honor of the Virgen de la Merced, is emblematic of the market women who sell fresh food and dry goods at El Salto, the largest market in the city. These vendors sponsor the Fiesta of the Mama Negra: it is their celebration. They employ the performers, rent their costumes, hire the bands, pay for masses to the Virgin, and buy the candies, fruit, cookies, liquor, and other treats that are handed out to the crowd. The other residents of the city, and the many visitors who come for the festival, attend as the market women's guests.

The Mama Negra represents the vendors in their happiest self-invention: as big generous mothers, who provide sustenance like mother's milk to the entire populace of the city in which they live. This fantasy of maternal abundance is the antithesis of the pishtaco, who embodies instead Freud's castrating father.

ÑAKAQ: THE CASTRATING FATHER

The sexual symbolism of the pishtaco's tool is hard to miss. He always has something big, hard, and dangerous in his hand or hidden beneath his clothing: a knife, a machete, or a gun. Often it dangles ominously from his belt. This terrifying thing is overtly phallic, the sign and instrument of a vicious masculinity. Even the pishtaco's genitals are said to be a weapon—not only does he use them to rape his victims, as we saw in chapter 4, but to kill as well. William Stein, rumored to be a pishtaco, was taken aback by tales of his own monstrously large and weirdly shaped penis, capable of inflicting great pain or fatal injury (1961:x); a livestock rustler in Julcani, tried and condemned for crimes that included pishtaring and having sex with his own sister, as well as stealing cows, was given the sobriquet "*Pishtaku pene loco,*" the Crazy Penis Pishtaco (Salazar-Soler 1991 : 19).

To young Indian boys, white masculinity is frightening and antipathetic—and highly desirable. Everything about the ñakaq, including his possessions, epitomizes this dreaded, longed-for, and unattainable state. The automobile in which pishtacos travel is not only emblematic of whiteness; it also carries the powerful allure of masculine sexuality. In the 1980s, boys in Zumbagua too poor to own even a bicycle papered the walls above their beds with magazine advertisements gleaned from roadside trash heaps. The crumpled photographs, carefully smoothed, showed scantily clad women caressing the bodies of automobiles, motorcycles, and even car batteries.

A series of calendars distributed by a car parts manufacturer were even more popular as wall ornaments in rural homes. They depicted enormous spark plugs emerging from between the white thighs of curvaceous blondes; the captions were double entendres about performance and emissions. These glossy photomontages, with their surreal juxtaposition of tiny women and big electrical parts, projected a highly instrumental masculinity: those rapacious spark plugs were charged up and ready to act upon the soft feminine flesh that surrounded them. Like the spark plugs, the pishtaco's masculinity is an active force: his penis and his possessions do things to others against their wills. In this, he exemplifies an ideal of masculinity found in much of Latin America. Roger Lancaster writes of Nicaragua that

> Violence in whatever form is assigned a masculine character. The threat *Te voy a hacer verga*—which is used to mean "I'm going to punch you"—could be translated literally as "I'm going to do you a dick" or "I'm going to dick you" or even "I am going to put my dick into you."

When "the physical subordination of another is equated with penile intromission," he concludes, the penis (*verga*) is defined as "necessarily a violent organ" (1992:41). In the system of thought outlined by Lancaster, the destruction of another man's sexual organ is the most masculine act of all—and indeed, castration is a constant theme in humor and verbal jousting among Latin American men. But the very ubiquity of this motif requires that each case be carefully interpreted: Andean pishtaco stories are both like and unlike stories about male violence told elsewhere.

José Limón, in his classic essay "Carne, Carnales and the Carnivalesque," portrays mexicano men who declare their friendship through constant teasing and horseplay in which they pretend to attack one another's genitals (1994). Pisthacos, too, evince an appetite for attacking the sexual organs of other men. But here, the underlying theme is not reciprocity but racially motivated battery, mutilation, and theft. Billie Jean Isbell watched a Yarqa Aspiy festival in the village of Chuschi, where dancers dressed as "caricatural white men" pantomimed the castration of audience members. The name of these dancers, she was told, is "naqaq"; they "castrate men, steal fat, and eat babies" (1978: 141, 144). Stein endured many jokes about his "role as a castrator"; he was also rumored to rape other men painfully and violently. He heard stories alleging that he placed little pills that prevented erections in his drinking canteen, which he then offered to the unsuspecting. "No Hualcaino," he says, "ever accepted water from me" (1961:x). Peruvian miners told Carmen Salazar-Soler that one of the company's engineers was really a pishtaco, who "*con picota no más anda para hacer hueco . . . en los huevos de runa y para chupar bonito no más el sebo*" [goes around with a little pick to make holes in . . . Indians' balls (lit., eggs) and so he can just suck out all the fat] (1991:14).[1]

Freud suggested that the many motifs of dismemberment found in stories, dreams, and European folktales of the uncanny—the severed limbs that creep along the floor, the decapitated head that opens its eyes and speaks—are all displacements of castration anxiety. In the image of the ñakaq, this theme is omnipresent. At times, as in Chuschi, it is not disguised or repressed, but rather mimed in the public square, with much hilarity, clowning, and drunkenness. In other versions of the tale, however, there are more subtle motifs that a post-Freudian interpreter must nevertheless recognize as metaphors for castration. For example, the creepy pishtaco in an unusual variant recounted by Gose first attracts his victims' attentions by pulling his own rotting fingers off his hand and letting them drop (1994b:306). This ñakaq, who points down to his own severed members "squirming like fat worms" on the ground, is evidently making a ghoulish joke about his predilection for cutting off penises.[2]

To Freud, uncanny stories of this sort ultimately reveal a universal male obsession with "the dreaded father at whose hands castration is awaited" (1963:36–37); this broad insight is helpful in thinking about the ñakaq, although fathers are not everywhere the same. In one "terrifying scene" from *The Sandman,* Nathaneal remembers an episode from his childhood in which his father's mysterious friend Coppelius "had screwed off his arms and legs as an experiment; that is, he had experimented on him as a mechanician would on a doll" (Freud 1919: 37–39). This is a striking image of powerlessness: the child fears that an adult male could make of him a plaything, to be taken apart on a whim. While such anxieties clearly animate tales of the pishtaco, the fear these stories express is not of one's own father but of strange white men, any of whom may be a secret "mechanician," intent upon forcing adult Indians into the passive position of a child or a toy in order to dismember them.

The image of the white man as castrating father is historically apt, for under the economic regime of the hacienda highland Latin America was long haunted by a racial paternalism that infantilized Indians. One elderly man who grew up on an hacienda near Latacunga, searching for something that would make a young Peace Corps volunteer understand the emotional destruction wrought by the region's racial history, recounted the following anecdote from his own childhood.[3]

As a boy, he said, when he misbehaved, his mother would tell him, "Wait until Saturday!" On Saturdays, the owner arrived from Quito to inspect the hacienda, ordering all the Indian mothers to line up their children for punishment; he then proceeded to beat each one in turn. His own father, the man said, never raised his hand to him—and was sometimes beaten himself by the hacienda foreman. Years later, the man looked back on his father's passivity with a mixture of love and shame, uncertain how to interpret his lack of violence toward his son.

In this tale, race forces open the family structure and burdens the emotionally fraught relationship between a boy and his father with an additional weight. The situation recalls Freud's memories of his own father. In a famous passage from *The Interpretation of Dreams,* Freud recalls:

> I may have been ten or twelve years old, when my father began to take me with him on his walks and reveal to me in his talk his views upon the world we live in. Thus it was, on one such occasion, that he told me a story to show me how much better things were now than they had been in his days. "When I was a young man," he said, "I went for a walk one Saturday in the streets of your birthplace; I was well dressed, and had a new fur cap on my head. A Christian came up to me and with a single blow knocked off my cap into the mud and shouted: 'Jew! Get off the pavement!'" "And what did you do?" I asked. "I went into the roadway and picked up my cap," was his quiet reply. This struck me as unheroic conduct on the part of the big, strong man who was holding the little boy by the hand. (1999:286)

This memory haunted Freud for years: he introduces the story as "the event in my youth whose power was still being shown in all these emotions and dreams." His own compulsive reworking of this incident in dreams was the key that revealed to him the very topography of the unconscious and the existence of the Oedipus complex. And yet, as Daniel Boyarin has recently commented, elements of the story—the city in which it took place, the clothes his father was wearing—are as emblematic of a particular moment in the history of Jews in Europe as the tale is revealing of Freud's individual psychology (1997:33–34).

Freud saw in the story of the Sandman—and in castration anxieties more generally—a boy's fear that his father will prevent him from becoming a man. Racism and anti-Semitism confuse and heighten these anxieties by denying adulthood—and masculinity—to the nonwhite or the Jew. Both the young Jew in Europe in the 1880s and the young Indian in South America in the mid–twentieth century resented their fathers for failing to demonstrate the manhood they themselves desired—and both hated and admired the white men who stood in their fathers' way. In the Andes, the Latin American hacienda system forced Indians to live out their lives under a cruelly abusive white "father" who never allowed his Indian "children" to escape his regime. "We don't know how to be fathers here," the man from the hacienda told the young American: "The hacienda took that away from us. I don't want to play the hacendado to my own children, but I won't be weak like my father either."

Unwilling to be as passive or childlike as they perceive their fathers to have been, a new, politically active generation has changed the very meaning of the word *indio*. But the image of hacienda paternalism—and of the pishtaco—continues to thrive. Isbell alternated her field research site between the highlands and Lima, because so many Chuschinos had migrated to the capital city.[4] The first time she saw the Lima version of a Chuschi festival, in 1970, the ñakaq dancers were absent, as were other caricatures of white authorities—the priest and the military—that had been part of highland ritual. At the time, Isbell interpreted the change to mean that the "migrants' experiences have been such that they do not see the world as foreign and threatening. . . . They are upwardly mobile and desire integration into the national culture" (1978:188). By 1974, however, few Chuschinos had realized the upward mobility—and the ñakaq had staged a dramatic reappearance.

"Four or five" families out of sixty migrant households had experienced some modest financial success and moved out of the poor barrio where the others lived. They returned, however, to celebrate the Yarpa Aspiy festival with their fellow Chuschinos—with a difference. These families reintroduced some long-defunct traditions, originally performed when Chuschi had been an hacienda—and thus quite self-consciously placed themselves, as festival sponsors, in the position of hacendados vis-à-vis their fellow migrants. Affronted, the other organizers responded by dressing several of their dancers as ñakaqs, who clowned and cavorted in front of the nouveaux hacendados. The performers pretended to castrate impoverished Chuschinos from the audience with a wooden sword, and so provided a caustic commentary on the behavior of their more fortunate ex-neighbors (Isbell 1978:244).

Fourteen years later, in 1988, the situation of migrants such as these had worsened. The debt crisis of the 1980s greatly immiserated poor Latin Americans, and Lima was filling up with thousands of new migrants—some of them from Chuschi—fleeing political violence (Isbell

1997a). The city responded with a flood of rumors about a new kind of pishtaco, far more frightening than any rustic dancer with a wooden weapon: the sacaojos. Eudosio Sifuentes interviewed students, secretaries, seamstresses, and maids about these mysterious medical technicians in dark suits ("like Mormon missionaries"), who were said to roam poor neighborhoods and snatch little children (1989:152). One young woman told him about "some gringos dressed in dark clothing" who

> stole a child and took him into their truck; once they had him inside, they took out his eyes; in the vehicle they have a series of instruments and apparatuses for performing these extractions. They took the eyes and the kidneys from this stolen child and he showed up dead on a street in the Villa María with fifty thousand *intis* [Peruvian currency] tucked inside his clothing.[5]

A university student reported that the children were abducted from "large, poor families" by men who "form part of an international mafia that traffics in organs." The thieves were expensively dressed and drove Mercedes-Benzes, and they left the eyeless children on their parents' doorstep with "fifty [American] dollars in their pocket."[6]

The theme of eyes torn from children's heads is familiar from psychoanalysis, where patients often tell of a "morbid anxiety connected with the eyes and with going blind" that obsessed them as children (Freud 1963:36). Descriptions of the sacaojos recall an especially vivid episode in *The Sandman*. On "certain evenings," Nathanael was sent upstairs early because "the Sandman was coming"; from his bed, he would hear "the heavy tread" of his father's visitor. When he asked his nurse about the Sandman, she replied with a lurid description of

> a wicked man who comes when children won't go to bed, and throws handfuls of sand in their eyes so that they jump out of their heads all bleeding. Then he puts the eyes in a sack and carries them off to the moon to feed his children. They sit up there in their nest, and their beaks are hooked like owls' beaks, and they use them to peck up naughty little boys' and girls' eyes with. (Freud 1963:32)

Freud readily interprets this tale, and his patients' worries, as "a substitute for the dread of castration" (36), and so it may be in Lima as well. But when Limeños talk about sacaojos, this fear also expresses a quite different kind of terror, unfamiliar to Nathanael or to Freud's patients. The castrating ñakaq, or the technician who steals childrens' eyes, is not just any man: he is a white man. These tales are about race, as well as sex. Behind mexicano men's verbal play, too, Limón heard a shared but unspoken awareness of the nation's power structures. With one another, the men played at *chingaderas* ("fuck-you games"), but it was only members of "the dominant Mexican-American and Anglo upper classes," including powerful men like then-president Ronald Reagan, who were referred to as the real "*chingones*" (the big screwers) (1994: 131–32).

In the Andes, the racial critique expressed through the symbol of the penis is much more explicit, and it encompasses more than inequality between men. Unlike the sexual humor of Limón's Texans or Lancaster's Nicaraguans, in which all social strata accept the phallus as the sign of violent domination, these Andean stories contrast the pishtaco's brutality with other models of masculinity, derived from the region's rich indigenous traditions.[7]

For Indians as well as whites, fears about castration, paternity, loss of life, and bodily dissolution coalesce to create a sense of the uncanny. But race bifurcates this symbolic complex, suffusing male sexual organs with two different sets of social and political meanings. The ñakaq exemplifies phallic power: his entire being is a masculine weapon, Lancaster's "violent organ" in the shape of a man. But this insatiable appetite for violence is presented as a specifically white form of masculinity. The male organ he severs from an Indian body, in contrast, carries a different set of meanings.

In white phallic ideology, the loss of male sexual organs symbolizes personal weakness and the violation of bodily integrity; for Indians, sexual mutilation means something different, and something more. Among members of the white middle class in the United States, masculine prowess is primarily invoked in competitions between adults; the power of the phallus is not strongly associated with paternity. Indeed, fathering often denotes weakness and the feminine role of caregiver, while the man who uses his penis for sex and competition without becoming "trapped" into paternity retains an unadulterated masculinity. In Zumbagua, in contrast, masculine sexuality and social status are closely linked to being a good father. Youthful sexual escapades are expected and tolerated, but they earn no one any respect. The only accomplishment that matters in this regard is social reproduction: not just the begetting but the raising of children. Powerful older men of the past had many younger dependents: sons and daughters (whether biological or adopted), godchildren, nieces, nephews, and foster children. Such a man had a future: his influence extended beyond his own lifetime. More than just a man, he was a father, a godfather, an uncle, eventually a grandfather. These were the roles represented by the honorific "Tayta," a word that represented an earned status not unlike a professional's title. Within this system of meaning, the penis is a condensed symbol of reproductive potency, and of social fatherhood in general.

Thus the story of the pishtaco who castrates an Indian involves two different masculinities. The destructive virility of the killer is enhanced when he emasculates another man, who is thus rendered symbolically female. This is white masculinity in action—even when the pishtaco himself is an indigenous man. The bloody wound of the Indian, however, can signify in a different register. This loss represents more than just one man's humiliation: it stands for the community's collective loss of children, and so of a part of the future—a social death larger and more final than the immediate bodily destruction of the individual.

These meanings infuse a brief story recorded by Carmen Salazar-Soler, in which the pishtaco utters an ominous salutation: "Buenos días tayta," he says to his victim (1991 : 10). There is a double signification here. First, many whites, when addressing Indians, adopt the Quichua-speaker's habit of addressing mature women and men as "Tayta" and "Mama": in effect, they make a term of respect in one language into a racial label in another, just as Indians do with white titles. Thus the pishtaco's apparently innocuous greeting announces that the killer, previously described as "seeking out only runas" has found his mark. Secondly, the Quechua meaning of these words amplifies the impending loss, for they presage the death not only of a man (a "runa") but of a father (a "tayta") as well.

Because nonwhite populations have so often been threatened with extirpation, many of their cultural traditions speak—as does the tale of the castrating pishtaco—to an acute anxiety about reproduction. It is perhaps for this reason that ñakaq stories emphasize the cutting away of the testes, not the penis: the former may be more directly associated with reproduction, the latter with pleasure. Slavery, said Orlando Patterson, is social death; nowhere is this more evident than when a slave becomes a parent, for the pregnant slave carries her master's child, not her own. For Indians, forced assimilation denies parents their children: the loss of language and culture makes the generations strangers to one another. In Zumbagua today, Quichua-speaking mothers raise Spanish-speaking children and try to plan futures for them outside the dying agricultural life of the parish: it is a form of voluntary social death, in order to ensure mere physical survival for the next generation. Whether these children—or these children's children—will be Indians is desperately uncertain. This sense of loss animates stories about sacaojos: the well-dressed white men who steal children from Quechua and Aymara immigrants in Lima, leaving their mothers only corpses and little piles of money.

This alienation is repeated on a larger scale when Latin Americans look toward the domineering culture of the North—and see the seductive power of that alien society at work in their own Americanized children. Indian and South American anxieties overlapped in 1961, when the Alliance for Progress introduced development projects designed to halt the spread of communism, which were denounced by Latin American intellectuals as imperialist ventures cloaked in humanitarian guise. In Bolivia, rumors began to spread that Peace Corps volunteers were performing involuntary sterilizations on Aymara women as part of a racist policy of covert genocide—a story that gained a wide audience through Sanjines' film *Blood of the Condor* (*Yawar Malku*). As late as 1978, rural Bolivians warned Crandon-Malamud "not to eat Alliance for Progress food lest it make me sterile" (1991 : 120).

In the United States, too, real and reported cases of involuntary sterilization have horrified minority women; this issue has special resonance for Native Americans, who previously suffered the loss of children through forced adoptions and boarding schools,[8] and for Puerto Ricans, who have been subjected to involuntary sterilizations.[9] Among African-Americans, the image of castration—a form of torture frequently practiced upon lynching victims—likewise arouses historical memories of the most devastating kind. In the context of race, then, sexual torture is more than an individually terrifying act. For those who are not white, such acts also signify the killing of children, and call up the specter of forms of white racial violence that specifically targeted their ability to reproduce.

Race changes the meanings of male and female as well. In the Sandman story, Freud sees the incident in which Coppelius dismembers Nathanael "as though he were a doll" as one in which the boy is forced into a feminine position vis-à-vis his father. As Lancaster says of Nicaragua, the object of violence is feminized when one man subdues another with his penis (1992:41). In these ideologies of the violent and dominating phallus, women are (rather famously) lacking, and so the man deprived of his penis becomes female. In raping or castrating men, the ñakaq treats them like, or makes them into, women. But this symbolism is understood to be part of white sexual ideologies, rather than posing as a universal truth. According to Indian ways of thinking, both men and women are active sexual agents; thus to lose one's sex is not to become female but to become sexless—a neuter.

In Freud's world, fertility was as gendered—or more so—as sexu-

ality. Women's urge to become mothers was an indication of their biological destiny as producers of men; in fulfilling those desires, women
consigned themselves to a private life of submission. These meanings
still bedevil us today, when career and motherhood are assumed to be
contradictory goals.[10] Thus to deprive a woman of a child or of her
reproductive potential could never mean the same thing as cutting off
the phallic organ of a man, the guarantor of his success in the world. In
some Indian ways of thinking, in contrast, the paternity encoded in the
testes is analogous to motherhood, rather than symbolizing masculine
superiority.[11] For men and women alike within the agrarian community, parenthood was a powerful metaphor for a position of achieved
influence—and the actual means to its achievement. The womb, like
the penis, thus signified a road toward economic and political success.
In Andean cities as well, motherhood can be a powerful—and a very
public—status, as even a glimpse of the Mama Negra reveals.

In this regard, the ñakaq thinks like an Indian. He finds the reproductive organs of women as desirable as those of men: the same knife
that removes the testes also rips open women's wombs. Rather than
making a man into a woman, both these acts treat humans like animals.[12] Male domestic animals are routinely castrated to control reproduction and to fatten them for later consumption; during butchering,
the testes of intact males are removed and eaten as a delicacy. Similarly,
the fetus is removed from the bodies of female llamas—an act of special
significance, for it is used (or sold) for medicinal and magical purposes.[13]
The pishtaco treats human fetuses in the same way: he extracts them
and then either sells them whole to American pharmaceutical companies or else dries and grinds them up into a powder for his own use, or
for sale.

These powders are the magical medicines with which the ñakaq be-
witches future victims.[14] And like the sacaojos, the ñakaq also targets
the eyes: those are the organs into which he tosses a powder made of
reproductive matter extracted from his previous victims. This acceler-
ating cycle of destruction, in which a dead woman's aborted womb
produces first a dead child, and then the castration and death of others
from the same community, reflects a dominated people's fears. The reproductive cycle that should be set in motion by having sex and feeding children is perverted instead into a negative cycle in which deaths,
rather than new births, are what accumulate. The killer's people, in the
meantime, fatten themselves on the body parts of Indians, like the baby
owls in the Sandman story who "peck up" and eat the bloody eyeballs
stolen for them by their terrible father.

The Mama Negra is a strong antidote to the pishtaco. Unlike the terrible white father, who kills Indians and destroys families, the black mother is an emblem of wholeness.

MOTHER'S MILK

After that first tantalizing sight of the Mama Negra, I returned later, alone, and managed to see her more clearly. She was definitely a "Negra," a black woman—that is, the person playing her wore thick shiny blackface and big red lips, a heavy black wig, and huge gold earrings. She was obviously a "Mama," a mother, surrounded by her children. When she wasn't waving her plastic baby doll around, she clasped it to her breast with one enormous hand; two real children, also painted in blackface and wearing earrings, sat behind her in saddlebags.[15]

The other immediately apparent thing about the Mama Negra was that she was a he. Her femininity was as fabricated as her race: her enormous breasts and buttocks, like the glossy jet-black paint of her mask, or the wig worn *over* her headscarf, were obviously phony. The man chosen to play the part was muscular and broad-shouldered, almost grotesquely male; even hung with all her female appendages—breasts and buttocks, skirts and earrings, babies and bottles—the body of the Mama Negra was unmistakably masculine.

This surprising figure, the symbolism of which baffles even the Latacungueños who grew up with her, gives us a chance to revisit the many contradictory images that surround market women. El Salto, which straddles the entrance into Latacunga from the Panamerican Highway, is an enormous roofed and open-air market complex that completely dominates the neighborhood that bears its name. We have seen that the produce vendors who work in this market and others like it are maligned as dirty and disreputable, both because of their hybrid race and their putatively deviant sex.

Market women resent these vicious stereotypes. And yet in the Mama Negra they seem to have re-created the very grotesque and lascivious image they detest. Individually, each of this fantastic figure's traits—her dark skin, her sexualized body, her ludic behavior—corresponds to a negative quality associated with cholas. When combined into the figure of an enormous, manly mother, however, their significance changes. By wedding the stigmatized characteristics of a non-white woman to the positively valued traits of motherhood and masculinity, the festival of the Mama Negra constructs a mythic chola body that challenges racist and misogynist assumptions. Rather than weakness and dependency, this body, like the white male body examined in the previous chapter, exudes power, wealth, and self-confidence. And in its exuberant fertility, it also expresses an Indian sense of what both women and men can be.

Latacunga's *gente de bien* find this big black mother a troubling and unsuitable emblem of their city; recently, they have invented a more appropriate Mama Negra of their own. The festival that I witnessed in September takes place on a Catholic feast day for the Virgin, and it has a long local history. Tourist guidebooks, however, list the annual Return of the Mama Negra in November, as part of the city's Fiestas Patrias, or civic festival. On this latter date, elites stage a sanitized version of the Mama Negra; the city's mayor and its historians speak of this new event with pride. "We have cleaned up the market women's disorderly celebration," one said. "The new Mama Negra is secular and modern, not like the old." [16]

In November, the Mama Negra is played by a well-known politician or businessman (annually selected by a blue-ribbon commission) rather than by an anonymous actor, as in the market women's festival. When this wealthy and powerful man rides by on horseback, wearing a costume that denigrates the poor and nonwhite women of the city, while dozens of women dance in attendance, the effect is a chilling reinforcement of the city's structures of power. Indeed, the mayor explained this reorganization as designed specifically to focus the crowd's attention on the man portraying the Mama Negra, in contrast to the chaotic—one might say demotic—market women's fiesta.

In the mayor's fiesta, everyone looks up to the man beneath the false breasts and the black makeup, acknowledging his power. His funny costume tells us that the city is on holiday, but there is no doubt that he is the only legitimate representative of the polis—and especially of the wealthy white men who control it. The market women's Mama Negra celebrates an ideal city of a different kind.

For although the November civic event is the one televised nationally, the women of El Salto continue to put on their own Mama Negra in September. On this occasion, the big black mother is only nominally the center of attention. Dozens of other women, castles made of meat and cigarettes, Indian dancers, deer skulls, men in blackface, and bottles of booze all compete for the crowd's eyes, ears, and minds; to the women of El Salto, this is as it should be. Cuenca's Paso del Niño is, if possible, even more democratic. People construct their own floats—some large enough to cover a school bus, others as small as a child's wagon—and parade with them whenever they are ready, so that little autonomous fragments of the parade appear on city streets days before and days after the main event.

A comparison of these different kinds of parades, and of another

festival involving cross-dressing and racial drag in Oruro, Bolivia, reveals the radically different political visions that lie behind such playful
acts as putting on a pair of false breasts, or a little black face paint.

Wawandi: Women Carrying Babies

Men dress as women for many different reasons; their performances
are not always flattering, nor do they necessarily undermine gender
and sex stereotypes.[17] Cross-dressing has often been noted in traditional
Andean festival costume; Blenda Femenias, possibly the only anthropologist to study this phenomenon in the light of contemporary gender
theory, finds the sexual politics of this practice ambiguous at best (n.d.).
Elsewhere in the Americas, some performances are explicit expressions
of a male right to define femininity. In the words of a heterosexual
Brazilian man who performs in drag annually for Carnaval,

> the women of Brazil have forgotten how to be real women. We
> are setting ourselves up as a model of how we want women to
> behave. We want them all to be . . . like us—sweet, demure,
> pleasing, and teasing. Our [performance] is a kind of school, and
> we, the dames, are teachers. (Scheper-Hughes 1992:494–95)

When this kind of sexual performance is combined with racial drag,
the results can be even more repressive. In the last few decades, the
white professional classes in the Andes have begun taking over popular
festivals, seizing the opportunity to dress up like Indians and cholas
while edging out the working people who once ruled the day. In
Oruro, Bolivia, for example, the professional classes have developed a
passion for staging elaborate processions during Carnaval, in which
wealthy women dress up as sexy "cholitas" who seem to suggest that
they have more than just fruits and vegetables for sale. These make-
believe cholas, sanitized of their working-class appearance and sexualized into whorish coquettes ripe for masculine conquest, offer a star-
tling contrast to actual market women (Abercrombie 1992:302).[18]

These performances take a further bawdy turn later in the year,
when college students put on an anti-Carnaval. Here, it is men who
dress up as cholitas in a burlesque of both the market women themselves and the respectable society matrons of the Carnaval parades. In
these performances, which combine racial and sexual cross-dressing
with political satire, young male bourgeoisie feel emboldened to indulge in outrageous antics far more risqué than the matrons' sedately
seductive behavior.

Like the cholitas of anti-Carnaval, the Mama Negra is flamboyantly
lascivious. She may be a man underneath, but on top she is all woman.

She is enormously, bulbously, monstrously female, with overblown breasts and buttocks pendant from her body, and babies and fruits draped across her saddle. Her big bosom, especially, recalls the erotic image of the chola, whose breasts are fetishized in male fantasy. In the poem "Chola Cuencana," Ricardo Darquea pictures them as "two doves held prisoner" within a cage of lace, "restless, fluttering" (Lloret Bastidas 1981::276). On a more vulgar note, Bolivian men describing a chola to Rob Albro began by listing "her braids, pollera . . . and stove-pipe hat"—upon which others broke in, laughing, to add "'and her milk cows!' (*vacas lecheras*)—a reference to her breasts." [19] Indeed, the chola's breasts are both sexy and lactating, as befits the mother of the nation. Uriel García enthused about "her abundant and maternal breasts," which nurture the Peruvian "race."

García's chola is more Indian than white, "smelling of chicha, and with a *huayno* in her throat." [20] The Mama Negra, with a baby at her breast and two more behind her, also evokes images of the Indian woman, who is often depicted with a child clinging to her breast or tied onto her back. Indeed, she is strikingly reminiscent of descriptions of market women from nineteenth-century travelers. Willis Baxley wrote in 1865 that the chola of Lima "is seen riding astride a mule with an infant in her arms taking its primitive meal"—a sight so nauseating that "[t]he dainty stranger should not visit the market before breakfast," for the "indecency, immodesty, and immorality" of such women and children will surely take away his appetite. [21]

Then and now, these representations switch back and forth between the grotesque and the erotic. Watching women get on the bus, a Latacunga bus driver said, "Those cholas are always *wawandi* [a Quichua phrase for a woman with a baby tied to her back], just like an Indian. It's definitely a drawback, because of course you want to fuck a woman like that from behind, standing up; otherwise it's not worth the bother. But the damned baby gets in the way."

His companion laughed and rejoined, "Ahh, you've just got to bend 'em over farther, that's all."

In misogynist fantasy, the chola is available for the taking, as she is evidently a woman without virtue, already sullied by the sexual experiences that resulted in a baby, but no husband. The Mama Negra, smiling her red-lipped smile, her breasts falling out of her clothes, caricatures these caricatures—but with her big, burly shoulders and masculine laugh, she does not resemble Oruro's dainty cholitas.

Many single mothers do indeed live on the border between Indian and white society. But Carol Smith finds the notion of them as passive victims of male desire misleading. Unlike the whore of masculine fantasy, who is powerless to reject anyone, Smith argues that it is women who insist upon making their own sexual choices who find themselves rejected by both Indian and white society—and thus branded as racially anomalous (1996).

Certainly the women I knew became mothers for reasons that had little to do with male desires. My first landlady in Zumbagua, Helena, had two boys: one of them had been born to her brother, the other to her. She raised them together, as brothers, and worried about them incessantly; intricate financial plans for their futures, and her own, occupied most of her waking hours. Her friend Heloisa was childless; neither had ever been married. In 1991, after Helena finally left the parish for good (fed up, as she put it, with "the cold and the Indians"), Heloisa consoled herself by bringing her small niece Nancy de Rocio to live with her—and to become her daughter. When I visited in 1991, Nancy was living with Heloisa but called her "tía" [aunt]; two years later, the child was calling her "Mami."

These two women became mothers deliberately, because they wanted children, and remained unmarried because they did not want—or need—a spouse. This independence is rooted in economic self-confidence, in the knowledge that, like poor women of color elsewhere in the Americas, they can depend upon other women for support[22]—and in a corresponding skepticism about the fathers of their children. Helena and Heloisa got their babies from brothers and lovers—and little else; in fact, both these women provide substantial financial assistance to their male kin, even while raising some of these men's offspring.

I have since watched the same pattern repeat itself in the next generation, with a young niece of Heloisa's who has a semiprofessional job as a nurse's aide—a rarity among rural women. As a teenager, I watched this girl flirt with the good-for-nothing white boys who hung around Zumbagua drinking up their mothers' earnings, and I wondered if she contemplated marrying one of them. I needn't have worried. Today, she is a proud single mother who expends her salary only on her two precious children and herself, and extends an occasional helping hand to her parents and her younger brothers.

Child Labor

This kind of motherhood defies the values upheld by the gente de bien—and not only because there is no man in the picture. Neither the movement of women and children between households nor their relations within households conform to white expectations. The ease with which Helena and Heloisa took responsibility for their brothers' children has its roots in the rural Andes, where adoption, fosterage, and multiple parents are common (Weismantel 1988, 1995). Nancy's move from her mother's house to her aunt's is perfectly congruent with practices among Zumbagua's Indian farmers.

Movement from one household to another is common among market women as well. Barbara Faniquina of La Paz, for instance, was glad to leave her rural home. "'My stepmother was very abusive,'" she recalled to Leslie Gill. "'She was always humiliating me. My godmother saw how I was suffering and that's why she brought me to La Paz.'" The godmother was a merchant who regularly visited Faniquina's community after the harvest to buy potatoes and sell goods such as sugar, rice, soap, and cooking oil to the peasants (Gill 1994:67). Julia Yapita, another woman interviewed by Gill, changed households several times. She left her home to come to La Paz with female cousins at the age of twelve. Then she moved in with an older sister, who sold food on the street and knit sweaters for tourists. But she was unhappy because "'[m]y sister bossed me around a lot.'" Female relatives helped again: "'my aunts, who lived next door . . . knew of a chola . . . who wanted a maid and took me to meet her. She wore a pollera . . . and sold salteñas. I started working for her that day'" (68–69). Julia moved restlessly between women: cousins, sisters, aunts, and finally an unrelated "chola"—whom she also left, still dissatisfied with what she felt was bad treatment. Unlike a woman trapped in a patriarchal setting, she felt free to contest the authority of every adult, and to keep moving until she found the autonomy she sought.

By American middle-class standards, the treatment Julia received was abusive: her relatives treated her like an employee, not a child. But within the social geography of the markets, this distinction is not very meaningful. Chola mothers and their children do not inhabit a private, inner world devoted only to consumption and affective relations: in their expanded social universe, the domestic world of the home has been exploded into the public sphere of work and money.

Indeed, if we compare chola family life to that of gays and lesbians in the United States, we can see that market women's domestic arrangements challenge not only heteronormative and patriarchal norms for family life, but even more deeply held class assumptions as well. Kath Weston's popular ethnography *Families We Choose* documents loosely knit families of young gay and lesbian adults, who provide one another with affective relations no longer available from the birth families who have rejected them (1991). These fictive kin ties are based upon a modern bourgeois ideal of voluntary emotional association between independent adults. Basic physical needs, whether sexual or economic, are deemed inappropriate reasons for long-term partnership, and perfect egalitarianism is a strongly held ideal. Some of these women and men want children, but like their heterosexual peers, they understand this desire to be purely psychological and affective. The acute physical dependence of children fits awkwardly within this picture, and the notion that children might provide substantial material assistance to their parents in return, through domestic or even commercial labor, is completely unimaginable.

Market women are different. They want children badly, for their labor as much as for their love, and consider any woman's life not only emotionally incomplete but materially more difficult without them. The families *they* choose are built upon structural inequality and economic interdependence. When Sofía Velasquez wanted a domestic helper to care for her aging mother, she tried to adopt a poor child, whom she planned to treat as a daughter and eventual heir—and as a servant who must work to earn her daily keep. Similarly, she proudly recites the work her own daughter does for her, finding in it a material demonstration of love:

> Rocio . . . gets up at 4:30, dresses warmly and goes out to light the kerosene stoves and prepares the food. . . . I get up at 5:00 just to see what she has done. At 6:30 she packs up the food and has it transported with the stevedore to my sales site on the street . . . at 7:30 she leaves for school. (Buechler and Buechler 1996:210–11)

Here, the bourgeois convention of cooking as an expression of female affection is translated into a commercial proposition. In Sofía's experience, when mothers and daughters cook for each other, they don't make intimate, lovingly crafted meals to be shared in a context insulated from the brutality of the capitalist world. They produce them in bulk, as cheaply and efficiently as possible, because they are business partners hoping to turn a profit.

In Cuenca in the late 1990s, young women helped older ones in relationships that were either actually or fictively the kin relations of mother and daughter, or aunt and niece—but were also those of employer and employee, banker and debtor, investor and fledgling entrepreneur. The relationships between older and younger, richer and poorer women are unequal—and affectionate. In typical chola fashion, love (and inequality) takes physical form as plates of food that move between stalls. Established vendors—big women with rolls of flesh— sit behind their piles of merchandise and watch while younger, thinner women approach them with plates of food. "*Por si acaso . . .*" the young women offer timidly, "If perhaps this might please you a little . . ." Grudgingly, the older woman accepts, and begins to eat while her younger associates wait on customers. In the Saquisilí market in July 1998, I watched a prosperous-looking merchant sitting on a stool pushed back from her merchandise, eating noodle soup from a big shallow bowl. A younger woman served her like a waitress, bringing her a glass of cola and waiting for the empty glass, even offering her a paper napkin to wipe her mouth and then accepting it back again.

Sofía began her working life helping her mother as a little girl and then graduated to her own small business, run under her mother's supervision. Heloisa, too, has started Nancy doing some selling on her own. When her aunt Clarita opens up the trago shop for business on Saturdays, Nancy sets up a little table outside, on which she piles up a mound of big, pretty apples. It is a small business, as befits a young vendor just establishing herself; but anyone walking by would know that those luscious, rather pricey pieces of fruit, brought up by bus from the warm valleys below, represent an investment from a loving— and moneyed—older relation.

Sofía's career began when her mother gave her forty pesos as capital; during her long life, the little hoard of "capital" to which she constantly refers is like a living embodiment of that initial gift, carefully nurtured over the years. But this gift was not unencumbered: it was a loan, which she had to repay with interest. Remembering her initial forays into marketing, she says fondly and with pride, my mother "made a really good profit from me in those years." She recounts mutually beneficial financial arrangements, pleased that she was able to return her mother's love—with interest: "my mother must have earned [double] the capital. She made easy money. And so did I. We would go together to sell and when we arrived at home my mother would say, "This much is yours" (Buechler and Buechler 1996:17–18).

Sofía sees no contradiction between loving a child and using her labor, and no shame in the expectation of immediate economic return on the relationship. This definition of mother love contrasts jarringly with the Latin vision of the endlessly self-sacrificing mother.

The vivandera's notion of motherhood deviates from expectation in another way too: when market women talk about themselves as mothers, they could just as easily be describing fathers. A sixty-two-year-old potato seller told de la Cadena, "I have stood up to anyone who failed to respect me . . . I have chased them out with knife in hand . . . if I have defended myself and insulted them, it is for my children" (1996: 131). The potato seller is a married woman; single vendors are even more likely to define a good mother as one who nurtures her babies with abundant food and milk, defends them with sharp words and a sharper knife—and supports them like the male parent they neither have nor need. But then, we already knew that there was something masculine about the chola.

THE CHOLA'S MALE ORGAN

According to Alison Spedding, rural Bolivians think of market vendors, as they do of white men, as potential kharisiris (n.d.*b*:5). She mentions an infamous "*verdulera del mercado de Chulumani que tiene fama de ser kharisiri*" (a vegetable seller in the Chulumani market who was reputed to be a kharisiri).[23] Because she encountered so many tales of women kharisiris, Spedding criticizes authors like Molinié Fioravanti (1991) for describing the pishtaco as "*un ser cuya virilidad es muy marcada*" [a being of exceptional virility] (Spedding 1998a:6). But market vendors do display a very marked virility, both as women and as mothers. We need only remember Heloisa Huanotuñu's trousers, Sofía Velasquez's tomboy youth, or the Cuzco vendor who raised her daughters to be "machas" like her. Market women, it seems, have appropriated some of the power of the virile member for themselves; indeed, the chola might seem even more masculine if we were to peek under her skirts.

In addition to her ample bosoms and buttocks, the Mama Negra has a few male reproductive organs as well. There is, of course, the actual penis and testes presumably belonging to the man who plays the part. He teases us with this knowledge, showing off his corpulent body, deep laugh, and forceful gestures while manhandling the baby doll in a fashion that elicits laughter from the crowd. Among the dancers that follow, too, are the "camisonas," a troupe of men dressed like women (Naranjo et al. 1986:122). But the Mama Negra doesn't stop there. Along with her round fruits, balloons, and other spherical objects, she is also hung with objects of phallic shape or association: her big bananas, especially, recall Josephine Baker. In 1983, the hand that didn't hold the baby carried an enormous water pistol with a barrel in the form of a fruit. (These pistols, imported from China, had been popular toys all that year; the Mama's costumers appropriated one as a perfect stage prop. In other years, she carries a big baby bottle.)

With a gun in her hand, the Mama Negra is more masculine than ever. Like the pishtaco, she wields a weapon with which she acts upon the people around her. Her gun (or bottle) is phallic in shape and has a nozzle with which she sprays the audience. However, her tool does not deal out death and castration, but something entirely different. When she turns it on the crowd, what comes out is trago (cane liquor), that very male substance that lubricates Andean festivities.[24]

Drinking trago is an activity that is gendered male—in the ambivalent fashion of the Andes. In other words, while it is difficult to imagine anything that denotes Indian masculinity as strongly as getting drunk in public, these gender associations do not prevent Indian women from doing it too, frequently and publicly.[25] When I got extremely drunk at a Zumbagua baptismal party and ended up in a ditch on the side of the road with three teenaged girls, total strangers congratulated me for weeks afterwards. "We thought you were a missionary, or a teacher," they would say warmly, "but then we saw you drinking with the other girls." By getting drunk with other women, I had inadvertently completed a rite of passage into indigenous society.[26]

Even among Indians, women's freedom to indulge in such behavior is more circumscribed than men's. Not only do they drink less often and in smaller amounts than men, but they are less prone to leisure activities more generally. During rest breaks from agricultural work, men typically lie down in positions of total repose, while women "rest" by engaging in various small tasks. Among whites, this gender distinction is far more marked: self-indulgence, especially "bad" behaviors such as drinking, gambling, spending money—not to mention extramarital sex—are condoned in men, but unforgivable for women. The explicitly hedonistic behavior of the Mama Negra—her dancing, laughing, trago-guzzling exhibitionism—makes oblique reference to one of the most striking aspects of market women's public behavior on ordinary days: for like her—and unlike other women—they do not hesitate to indulge their senses.[27]

The casual ease with which market vendors satisfy their physical appetites and bodily needs in public is one of the characteristics that makes them seem masculine. A minor example is that, like Latin American men—and Indian women—they urinate in public when they need to, using their full skirts to hide their genitals. (Of course, they themselves would be the first to decry the absence of clean restrooms in the markets that necessitates such behavior; but white women go to extreme and self-abusive lengths to avoid revealing their bodily functions when in the same circumstances.)

More significant is their fondness for eating—in public, and with gusto. A list from my notes on Saquisilí is headed: "What market women do while selling"; the first entry is: "Eat." (The second: "Take care of their kids.") Older women, especially, display a ribald indulgence in the physical pleasures of eating that is more reminiscent of *Tom Jones* than of white consumption habits today. Important vendors eat with relish and a sense of drama: they suck on ripe mangoes or succulent bones, throw away the residues, and lick their fingers when they're done. In one memorable scene glimpsed from a Quito taxi, a woman stood pensively at her corner stall, eating the brains out of a boiled goat's head with a spoon while watching the cars and buses go by.[28]

White women have long been told to curb their appetite: well-brought-up girls once ate meals before going out to dinner, so as not to appear gluttonous, and some still do; for anorexics, it becomes literally impossible to eat anything in public at all.[29] To display too much pleasure while eating is seen as a gross and sexually provocative act, and as for drinking large quantities of alcohol or taking recreational drugs, such behavior is widely considered an invitation to rape. In Latin America, especially, self-gratification is a defining quality of masculinity, and self-abnegation marks the virtuous woman. In this context, the market vendor's eating style is an even more striking appropriation of male privilege.

By extension, the vendors' entire approach to their work is ill-suited to their gender. Women are supposed to *be* commodities: beautiful things that a man wishes to acquire. Accordingly, when they sell things, whether as sales clerks, cashiers, or models, their role is to project the allure of attractively packaged goods from themselves onto the products they display. They should arouse desire in others while disavowing their own: the unnaturally thin body of the model proclaims her self-denial. As consumers, too, women should buy in order to give pleasure to others; if they acquire things for themselves, it is only in order to perfect their own commodification as objects of beauty.

A corpulent, well-dressed market woman, in contrast, offers something else to satisfy her customers. She is not a commodity herself, but rather someone who knows a tasty tidbit when she sees one. So too the Mama Negra, who squeezes her own breast with a little pleasurable squeal and then gives it to her baby, or squirts the crowd with the bottle and then takes a quick nip herself. These actions confound the distinction between giving pleasure and taking it—and blur the boundaries between male and female, Indian and white as well.

The Mama Negra, then, is a radically different kind of drag queen from Oruro's sexy cholitas, whose feminine displays are clearly intended for male consumption. But then, the difference between these two performances is written into the structure of the events. The students act up for their own amusement and to scandalize their fellow bourgeoisie, while the man who plays the Mama Negra is hired help. The fact that his employers are women changes the gender dynamic dramatically—especially since these are women who know something about how to act manly in a pollera.

Latacunga market women sometimes do a little cross-dressing of their own. In chapter 3, we caught a glimpse of them in the 1980s, with their work boots and men's pants under a skirt and an apron—an outfit topped off with earrings, a baseball cap, and an Indian man's poncho. In hiring a man to be their representative and dressing him in women's clothing, the vendors of El Salto playfully invert this kind of quotidian transvestism—and make reference to their own masculinity as well.

But the politics of drag performances are slippery. Men dressed as women do not necessarily admire the female body; instead, like the travesti studied by Kulick, they may extol the superiority of the penis, and adhere to the belief, as deeply held as any racial prejudice, that the female genitalia are repugnant. Kulick recalls the day when

> Tina suddenly turned to me and shouted, "Don, have you ever sucked a buceta [cunt]?" She and everyone else burst into laughter, and she continued, "I've sucked one, Don, and it's horrible, horrible, it's horrible, Don, it's horrible. All this slime. It's a really slimy thing . . ." (Kulick 1993 : 194)

Heterosexual men, too, despite their desire to penetrate the vagina, nonetheless find the female genitalia uncanny—a reaction that Freud saw as the very definition of estrangement: they call this place "unheimlich," he says, and yet it is "the entrance to the former heim [home] of all human beings."

In applauding market women for their audacious appropriation of the penis, we may have unwittingly joined in this denigration of the pudenda, and hence reinscribed the figure of the Mama Negra with misogynist meaning. In intimating that women de pollera are to be admired only to the extent that they replace their own sexual physiognomy with a fantasied male member, this analysis resembles the ideologies of mestizaje critiqued earlier. Like a man celebrating his mestiza lover's beauty by extolling her pale skin, we have applauded the Mama Negra for her penis. But the connection goes beyond mere analogy between race and sex. In the celebration of the Black Mother, like the castration scene in ñakaq stories, when race intersects with sex it changes the meaning of both.

We can find in the undiluted blackness of the Mama Negra as fierce a response to misogyny as to racist sexual fantasy. In rejecting so absolutely the almost-white attractiveness of the chola, she suggests something about the sex of the pollera as well. Rather than the pretend woman of masculinist drag, who promises to reveal a nice satisfying penis instead of something nasty and smelly, the de pollera is a physiological woman who has appropriated the penis for her own purposes. Just as she finds no need to shed her pollera when donning a pair of trousers, so too the market vendor may take on a roll of cash, a knife, or any other phallic tool she needs—but without repudiating the female sexual organs that allow her to become a mother. To poor farmers, the frightening masculinity of the market woman is inseparable from her whiteness; but as a manly mother, she projects an androgynous fertility more reminiscent of Indian men.

Her White Masculinity

Pishtaco stories encourage a close scrutiny of the white male body—and represent that body as big, powerful, and loaded with money and goods. The Mama Negra, too, looks big and imposing: her large body, mounted on a tall horse, towers over her male attendants. But unlike the figures found at other festivals, she is still human in size and proportions. Año Nuevo (New Year's) celebrations feature human effigies (often of politicians), which are paraded through the streets and then immolated; these can be far larger than life-size. Cotopaxi Province is known for its harvest festival, Corpus Christi, when the famed *danzantes* appear in their resplendent costumes. They wear a huge headdress and flat panels over the legs and torso. Every surface is covered with gold paper and encrusted with mirrors, costume jewelry, and pieces of broken glass, which refract the light, dazzling onlookers as the danzante performs his slow, spinning dance.[30] This costume obscures and alters the human form, replacing its round contours with rectangles, and flattening its three-dimensionality into two planes, front and back. In contrast, the body of the performer provides the basic frame for the Mama Negra costume; she is just a man dressed like a very big (and very black) woman.

She thus resembles market vendors themselves, for they too have big bodies. Their legs, arms, and backs are strong and muscular, accustomed to hauling sacks of potatoes, animal carcasses, and cooking stoves. But no one would call them "athletic": they tend to be round and fleshy. Henry Shukman, repulsed, says they "are invariably plump and waddle about in their puffed-out skirts" (1989:32). In a more analytical mode, the Buechlers comment that obesity is "the traditional hallmark of the successful chola" (1996:224). Market women's abundant flesh is a sign that they eat well, unlike the poor; and that unlike farm women, they eat lots of meat, fried foods, and sugary things. Other urban women eat their meals at home, but the vendors buy theirs in restaurants, or in the markets. (They also, it appears from Sofía's account, go out drinking like men.) As Sofía says smugly of her daughter, "Rocio and I like to eat *salchipapas,* that's why Rocio is fat" (1996: 204). Salchipapas (greasy little mounds of fried potatoes and sausages wrapped up in a twist of waxed paper) are street food par excellence—and they are rather expensive.[31]

The result of such a diet, as can be seen in Martín Chambi's photograph of the woman drinking chicha, is an imposing physical presence. Chapter 5 described the material manifestations of whiteness—boots and documents, cameras and cars—as tools with an instrumental value, as well as possessions that signify status and identity. So too for market women, who find it useful to be big. Seligmann observed that vendors "occupy crucial space" in the crowded outdoor markets, forcing passersby to give them ample room simply by the way they arrange themselves as they sit.[32] In *Los ríos profundos,* the vendors use their large bodies to make space during political protests, just as they do in the market square: "The crowd made way. . . . The senior women, who were also the fattest, such as the owners of the chicherías, formed a sort of front line to the left and right of the leader."[33]

Like the Mama Negra, women in polleras augment their already noteworthy bulk with a lot of clothes. Layers of heavy gathered skirts and aprons cover limbs and torso; as can be seen in Chambi's photograph, these fabrics have weight and substance. Arguedas, too, portrays a monumentality that is both vestimentary and corporeal. Doña Felipa, the leader of the protesters in *Los ríos profundos,*

> was a well-known chicha bar owner; her stout body completely filled the arch; her blue silk bodice, trimmed with beads and velvet ribbons, shimmered. The ribbon on her hat shone even in the shade; it was satin and stood out in high relief from the extreme whiteness of her hat, which had recently been painted with white lead. The woman had a broad face, pitted all over with smallpox scars. Her plump bosom, rising like a rampart, was moving; its bellows-like rhythm, from her deep breathing, could be seen from afar.[34]

Responding to Felipa's exhortations, the market women leave the plazas and taverns where they usually work and descend upon the masculine space of the main plaza, where they crush the feminine flower beds that decorate its peripheries. The women's shoes, shawls, and earrings, as well as their voices and bodies, are described as having a destructive power more commonly associated with men in uniform:

> a great crowd of clamoring women extended from the church steps to beyond the center of the square. They wore shawls of Castilian cloth and straw hats. . . . There were no men in sight. With their bare feet or high-heeled boots the women crushed the delicate park flowers, breaking off rosebushes, geraniums, lilies, and violets. . . . The women were sweating; earrings made of silver and of gold coins glittered in the sunlight.[35]

Here, sexed body and gendered clothing are indistinguishable: the women's bare feet inflict the same damage as their boots, and the smell of the sweat exuding from their bodies strikes the onlookers with the same force as the metallic glint of their earrings.

In 1983, the vendors of El Salto walked the parade route alongside the Mama Negra, dressed in their finest de pollera outfits. A few were accompanied by husbands, brothers, or sons; many more marched in pairs or trios of mothers and daughters, sisters, or partners; just as many walked alone. (Not all the women were from El Salto, or even from Latacunga: a large phalanx of women marched behind a banner announcing them as "merchandisers of the markets of Pichincha.")[36] They made an impression: my notes describe them in almost as much detail as the costumed dancers. They were stout, self-assured women, wearing a lot of clothes.

Unlike the exuberant Mama Negra, the vendors walked rather stiffly, arms at their sides, bestowing dignified glances on the crowds at either side. They looked pleased and self-confident, and why not? Their appearance in the company of the frolicking dancers announced that these were the city's wealthiest and best-known dealers in fresh produce and comestibles. Although the crowd's attention was drawn to the figures in costume, everyone knew that it was these women who collectively paid for the party.

On a daily basis, the big vendors signify their material success through their ample physical presence. Not only are they well-nourished in a region where many are not, but their clothing itself represents a substantial investment. Today only the most prosperous of vendors—like Sofía, who stockpiled twelve high-quality polleras before making the change from de vestido—can afford to dress as a "true" chola. According to Sofía,

> Even Sra. Judith [Buechler] must not be spending as much money on clothing. The best polleras cost two thousand pesos (U.S.$100) and a vicuña manta costs eight hundred pesos (U.S.$90). That makes thirty-eight hundred. . . . A Borsolino hat costs fifteen hundred pesos (U.S.$75), adding up to say, five thousand (U.S.$250).

Then come the earrings. I had a pair made for three thousand pesos (U.S.$400). Now, while a pair of street shoes costs only 120 (U.S.$6) or so, a better pair of shoes costs 350 (U.S.$17.50). . . . I figure that to dress well, a woman has to spend between eighteen thousand pesos (U.S.$900) and twenty thousand (U.S.$1000), or perhaps, fifteen thousand (U.S.$750). In contrast, a de vestido woman doesn't spend that much . . . only five hundred (U.S.$25). (Buechler and Buechler 1996:173–75)

To dress in this fashion is one's ability to accumulate wealth. Market women store their wealth on their bodies in the form of shoes, cloth, jewelry—as well as fat and gold teeth. By age fifteen, with her mother's help, Sofía invested some of her accumulated earnings in having her front teeth "rimmed with gold" (19). In Cuenca, too, we saw women with gold insets in their front teeth—including one beautiful young campesina, come to sell in the markets illegally, without a formal booth, who nonetheless had made enough of a profit to have a twinkling gold star set into the center of each incisor. As with whites, then, the boundary between the chola body and its possessions is impossible to draw. Market women and their peers recognize this fact when they use the expression "a woman de pollera": one article of clothing metonymically describes a whole person.

This chola form of accumulation baffles the middle classes. In later years, Sofía learned how to successfully apply for development loans intended to help the poor; she chuckles over the young men who interrogated her about whether she has a bank account. They were oblivious to the wealth that she brought into the bank with her—her gold-rimmed teeth, the earrings in her ear lobes, and the valuable shawls and skirts draped around her ample torso—enough to disqualify her, were they but able to see it (1996:110).

In Bolivia, a "real" chola (not a farm girl imitating the style, nor a "chota chola," an "almost chola," who lacks the financial means to assemble the entire costume) is an impressive sight. Physically large and visually eye-catching, she announces herself as a person of financial substance—a message that is not lost on her peers. As Sofía says, "When I see them [cholas] in their outfits, my mouth drops open because I know how much it costs" (175).

If Sofía is impressed, men from the countryside are absolutely dazzled—and intimidated. Andrew Orta recalls a conversation he had with a rural Aymara man who was butchering a sheep:

As I was asking my interminable questions about fat, he held up the lliklla: the membrane of fat that covers the stomach. He re-

marked upon the patterns evident in the lliklla, where thicker
patches of fat formed shapes that stood out against the thinner,
translucent background of the membrane. The lliklla, he said,
looked precisely like the expensive embroidered shawls worn by
"señoritas" in La Paz. He referred, I think, not to white upper
class Bolivians . . . but rather to "cholas": a class of successful
and powerful Aymara women residing in La Paz. Among the
more striking aspects of the chola Paiceña is her . . . very expensive . . . dress comprising skirts, embroidered blouses, sweaters
and shawls . . . fine derby hats, jewel encrusted earrings, and
shoes. . . . From the points of view of rural men (whose migrant
experiences in La Paz often entail working for cholas as cargadores) these women are very powerful indeed. They are also
sexualized. . . . These various potencies are embodied in their
dress, and it is little wonder my consultant sees them as draped
with fat. (1996:15–16)

And little wonder, either, that rural men suspect such women of
robbing them by supernatural means—even of being kharisiri. A body
draped in a layer of fat obtained through butchering is an image that
immediately calls to mind the nocturnal activities of the pishtaco; it
thus likens the wealth embodied by these women to the bogeyman's
ill-gotten gains.

If whites enjoy thinking of the chola as a ripe fruit fresh from the
country, Indians associate her large body more readily with a big,
frightening roll of cash. Market vendors, like bus drivers, are known to
carry enormous quantities of money on their persons. When I first
began traveling in the Andes, I was astonished by these big wads of bills,
most of it in very small denominations; before long, though, I began to
accumulate one myself.

Money has its own rules in the produce market. Cash cannot be
taken for granted as a medium of exchange, for it is itself a scarce commodity.[37] No one is willing to make change for a stranger: if you want
to buy a small amount of bananas in a strange town, you had better
have a small amount of change in your hand. Big bills are useless, even
dangerous. When people in Zumbagua asked me for a loan, they were
appalled if I tried to give them a thousand-sucre bill (then, about five
dollars). "Break this for me when you go to the city, can't you?" they
would plead. "I can't let anyone see me with a bill this big."

Small change, however, brings other hazards. Since the government
never recalls old money, the markets are flooded with torn and faded
bills, which everyone tries to pawn off on one another in a constant

game of monetary musical chairs.[38] It takes only a few experiences with
women who make change reluctantly, and then hand over small bills
so dirty and damaged that not even beggars will accept them, to begin
to appreciate the value of possessing a large quantity of good-quality
money in all denominations.

Small-time sellers are short not only on merchandise but also on
cash. Young women have to ask their older relatives to break large bills
for them—and often receive less than the full amount of change in
return. The big roll of cash carried by older women is a powerful symbol, for it indicates a vendor successful enough that she need not dig
into her daily profits to buy herself dinner or bus fare home. It is a tool
of her trade as well: she can make her own change—and earn a little
money by making change for others.

The interactions that occur between large and small vendors over
big bills make compelling little dramas. The younger woman approaches hesitantly, holding out the big bill that a customer has just
given her; despite her deference, she is in a hurry, for fear the buyer
might take her business elsewhere. The older woman is under no such
pressure: slowly she puts down her plate of food, turns from a conversation with another vendor, or seems to waken from a moment's nap.
Finally she relents, pulls her wad of money from beneath her skirts and
peels off the change requested. Customer and seller alike watch in some
anxiety, afraid she is reaching deep into her roll for the oldest and most
worn of her stock of bills. Sometimes the action takes place within
a single stall, where an older vendor employs younger helpers. They
stand and sell, while she sits back and watches, moving forward on
occasion to greet an old customer, to hear some gossip—or to make
change.

When *comerciantes* go out into the countryside to buy peasant goods,
these fat wads of cash are displayed to even greater effect. The money
may remain hidden until the transaction is completed, only then making an all-too-brief appearance beneath the farmer's fascinated eyes;
during a tough negotiation it may be shown earlier, whetting the
seller's appetite. In the end, the seller watches unblinkingly as each bill
is peeled off and counted out into his waiting hands—but the payoff is
small, and the big roll looks intact as it disappears again into the buyer's
clothing.

As with the pishtaco's tool, the sexual symbolism here is hard to
avoid. When Sofía tells a story about being robbed on a city bus, she
plays upon the elision between this hidden cache of money and genitalia. "The other day there was a fellow who pushed me and lifted my
skirt up. 'What's wrong with you?' I asked. But he just continued, leav-

ing me naked below." By the time she realized that it was her money he was after, it was too late: he had gone, taking not only her bankroll but the bus driver's as well (Buechler and Buechler 1996:91). He knew she was carrying a big roll, she says, because "He had smelled the odor of the money." The old, much-handled money rolled up under her skirt gives off its own distinctive smell of decomposing ink and paper, human skin oils, and dirt.

Of course, he may have lifted up her pollera simply because she looks like the wealthy vendor that she is. The pishtaco hides a weapon under his clothes, or hanging from his belt; descriptions of actual chola costumes often mention something carried in a similar position. But what lurks beneath the layers of voluminous skirts, unseen but known to all, is not a weapon, a banana, or a bottle of alcohol, but money. According to Seligmann, as the Cuzco vendors walk around the market, one can see the "money purses bulging beneath their skirts" (1989:703).

The money purse makes a fitting phallus for these women, for it is the source of their power. If the wad of dough that hides beneath the pollera exerts such a fascination on rural men, it isn't just because they don't have one. They also recognize in it the reason why the market woman can treat others like Indians. Her bankroll not only enables her exploitative behavior, it also motivates it: she needs to protect her money, to keep it intact and to make it grow, even at others' expense.

Like the pishtaco, this phallus has both a sex and a race. As successful sellers convert each exchange into another layer of bills on their bankrolls, they build a white identity into their wad. Their interactions are like those described by Colloredo-Mansfeld, who says that race becomes visible every time an Indian "places some grubby bills in the soap chaffed hand of a white-mestizo shopkeeper." The woman in the outdoor market is far more able to capture those Indian bills than the shopkeepers, but as the roll tucked under her skirts grows, so too does the perception of her as a racial alien—maybe even a pishtaco. Indians see in her accumulated profits the record of their own exploitation in the past—and a visible sign of her willingness to cheat them again.

Her Indian Masculinity

From the perspective of whites, however, this big roll of money fails to impress. It looks vulgar, even laughable. Real wealth—the kind that can bring down a president, a neighborhood, or a forest—is invisible; it cannot be seen or touched, but sits quietly in a bank generating interest or flows unobserved between transnational corporations and agencies.

So too with bodies. Bankers and investors, the servants of capital, attract customers by their very discretion, which bespeaks a certain kind of power. Market women, however, use their physical presence and their voices, their layers of enormous skirts and their tall imposing hats, to call attention to themselves and thus to catch a customer's eye. Ironically, their very bigness and fierceness is necessitated by their vulnerability: they must fend for themselves on the crowded and dangerous streets and are always susceptible to robbery or assault. Big money need never run such risks. Every bank and commercial building in the Andes is guarded by a bored and angry-looking young man in a uniform, his shiny boots heavy on his feet and his hand restless against his submachine gun. His face is black or Indian, unlike the people he serves: the "ones in the offices," we recall, is a definition of the word "white" in Cotopaxi.

From the perspective of rural farmers and the desperately poor, or even the precariously situated middle classes, established vendors look big and prosperous—draped with fat, in Orta's felicitous phrase. But their financial position is intrinsically insecure. Sofía recalls many occasions during which her precious "capital"—the money she reinvests in new merchandise—disappeared because of inflation, bad luck, or a run-in with the police. Even the most successful women are vulnerable to sudden downturns in their fortune, when the very fat melts from their bodies. The economy in which they operate consumes them almost as readily as it does Indians. The unstable economies of the 1980s and 1990s forced most women to hock their jewelry and their hats; the mighty polleras have been sold to a tourist shop and replaced with a pair of sweatpants and a baseball cap. Produce vendors do not have the consolidated wealth or the layers of legal and political protections that protect the elite, as a class, from catastrophic losses. Nor do they have the sense of inalienable privilege that belongs to those who are very white, and unquestionably male.

According to Sofía, in the mid-1970s Bolivian president Banzer said on television that

> he didn't want to see women wearing chola outfits any longer. . . . He felt that they were spending too much on their outfits, that they had too much money, and that he didn't know where they were getting all that money from. That's why he has declared war on the vendors using the police. (Buechler and Buechler 1996: 174–75)

Like the Otavaleño entrepreneurs believed to be drug dealers, cholas who succeed in accumulating visible wealth are perceived as criminals or bloodsuckers: their race renders their profits illegitimate. And in fact, although it is not illegal, the vendors' relationship to money is fundamentally different from that of whites—and more primitive.

In the white world, the most powerful kinds of money have ceased to take material form at all. The biggest transactions are conducted electronically, and what is moved is only a line of code. Lacking a body, this money circumnavigates the globe at lightning speed. For Sofía, in contrast, money is a burden: heavy and awkward, it is hard to disguise from thieves not only because of its size but even because of its smell. During Bolivia's period of hyperinflation, she complained about the difficulties: "I wrap the [stacks of devalued banknotes] with this carrying cloth and with these rags. . . . [W]hen I go to Doña Betsa and she pays me . . . She gives me bundles this big. I have to wrap them carefully and enter a taxi" (Buechler and Buechler 1996:91).

By the same token, the physical presence of money also provides material and even aesthetic pleasure. In the festival of the Mama Negra, and in Cuenca's Paso del Niño, market vendors invite the crowd to enjoy looking at money—and at food. For the Return of the Mama Negra, and even more so for Cuenca's famed Paso del Niño, the vivanderas construct enormous "castles" of food, drink, and money, which are marched down the parade route. These elaborate geometrical tableaux feature whole roasted chickens, their feet and beaks extended in decorative protrusions; atop them are layers of fruits. The whole is adorned with liquor bottles, garlanded with brightly colored Chiclets packages, garnished with money and Ecuadorian flags, and finished off with big shooting-star formations composed entirely of roasted guinea pigs (*cuyes*), their little clawed feet curled up and their mouths open in manic grins. The largest constructions are mounted on trucks; I saw one topped by an entire roasted pig raised upright on a pole, his mouth stuffed with paper money. Just below, guinea pigs were impaled upon a horizontal stick. A curtain made of long strings of packaged cookies and candies interspersed with fajas (woven sashes) hung from the stick.

There were women of all ages; some were children of five or six, carrying miniature displays. Younger market women carried big tin trays mounted atop their hats; bananas and cigarettes, chickens and flags, beer bottles and pineapples cavorted riotously above their heads, evoking Carmen Miranda in a way that their broad figures, stiff postures, and solemn faces did not.[39] Older women hired bearers to carry their fabrications while they marched alongside. Some of these were vertical constructions: tall poles held roasted chickens, which sported money or cigarettes in their mouths, their bodies wrapped with textiles, banners, and flags; strings of brightly colored hard candies and balls of *guayusa* tea leaves were then tacked like bunting around the whole. Other designs were horizontal, with bottles of trago, piles of fruit, and platters of meat, lavishly adorned, nailed to tables borne aloft by sweating men. Unlike the highly visible bodies of the women, the cargadores' faces and torsos were obscured by the tablecloths, garlands, and decorations. The heavily laden table, groaning with provender, thus appeared to have sprouted legs to march of its own volition in the parade beside its mistress.

This Rabelaisian display of abundance, stocked not with everyday foods like potatoes and noodles—the staples of highland diet and the bulk of market sales—but rather with liquors, cigarettes, roasted meats, candies, and money, is a physical manifestation of wealth, just like the market women's own amply fleshed bodies. Indeed, all those animal bodies on display, shiny with fat and draped in clothing, make the analogy with an alarming literalness. This notion of comestibles as wealth, like the desire for clothing that functions as an actual investment of capital rather than a simple display of conspicuous consumption, appears to be a naïve and outdated conception that reveals the market women as peasants, ill-equipped to deal in the modern marketplace. Even the paper bills and coins that decorate the displays are too vulgar; tourists are amused and fascinated by the vendors' display of wealth, which in their eyes only reveals the women's poverty—and their lack of whiteness. Who but a poor Indian could think that a pile of coins, a carton of cigarettes, a box of chewing gum—or even a hundred of them—constituted wealth?

Even without these displays, the market women's party has a very Indian character: among the dancers are costumed figures long familiar to anthropologists from rural festivals. The parade begins with the *curiquingues*—a highland bird often depicted in ritual and song, here portrayed by "happy dancers" dressed in paper plumes. Next comes the Angel of the Star and the Ambassador (children dressed in white mounted on horseback, reciting poems of praise to the Virgin), next the Mama Negra and her two attendants. Following her are "las cholas," a dance troupe of men and women, all dressed identically as women; then the yumbos or "wild men"; and last a pair of men called "huacos," whom Ecuadorian scholars identify as "brujos": shamans.[40]

As a relative newcomer, I did not then know the names of the costumed figures I was watching, but I recognized the shamanic activities of the huacos, which resembled descriptions I had read in old books. I scribbled a description:

One pair danced separately . . . 2 men with white masks, painted
with stripes and spots (later I saw more of them, six in a group).
They had batons in one hand and deer skulls with horns in the
other, both of these also painted white, with colored bars and
rows of spots. They wear pants made of crocheted lace from the
knees down, and a woman's shawl tied neatly across the shoulders. . . . They had big backboards with all kinds of stuff sewn or
fastened on, and lots of paper flowers attached on top of everything else. . . . They whistle, and clack the deer head and baton
together. They danced together in a circle, going up and down
and waving the skulls and batons. Then, they got a nursing
mother—in the act of nursing—with another babe clutching her
skirts, out there, and started dancing in front of her, honoring/
menacing her with baton and skull and chanting "*A ha ha*—*A
ha ha*" as they thrust the baton and skull forward. Next they chose
a small child. The child's father didn't want to, but the crowd said
"let them soplar him" . . . the child crouched terrified, while his
dad held him out towards the dancers, not letting him escape—
but also providing comfort—while this whole thing of thrusting
forward while chanting was repeated. Next, they did it to a market woman's 5 gallon container (I couldn't see contents)—she was
delighted, smiling. Then the military band, just behind, decided
to start playing again and the two went back to just dancing.[41]

These dancers enacted a magical, undomesticated Indiannesss that walks
the boundaries between animal and human, male and female, sacred and
profane. Terrifying and fertilizing, they whistled and grunted, incapable
of human speech but possessed of the shaman's power to *soplar,* or blow,
well-being and abundance onto people and things. Using a baton and
a wild animal's skull as tools, these men wrapped in women's shawls
represent an Indian notion of power utterly alien to capitalist society.
They called upon a fertilizing wind that emanates from just those places
denigrated by South American whites as the source of their nations'
poverty: the bodies of Indian women and of wild animals, and a landscape both mountainous and tropical.

Latacunga's elites have been quick to eliminate these types of players
from their version of the festival: unable to whiten the famous Mama
Negra herself, they have surrounded her with troupes of dancing white
cholitas, like those in the Oruro Carnaval, and sent the Indians home.
The market women, in contrast, are at ease with the shamanic dancers,
whom they invite each year. Indeed, many of the symbols associated
with the Mama Negra—and with market women—are more Indian

than white. The money purse is her white phallus, but pollera masculinity has an Indian dimension as well. The men with the huacos paid attention to a nursing mother, a child held by his father, and a vendor's bucket of drink; these are the places where market women count their wealth, too, and in this they resemble Indians, not white men. For in Indian terms, a man proves his virility not by his fat wad of money, but by his fat and healthy children.

The Mama Negra endows market women with some of that Indian virility, for she is not only doubly gendered and doubly sexed, but also doubly reproductive. Her many appendages suggest both male and female organs; they also promote a confusion between the two. If the incongruity between clothing and body invites us to imagine the penis beneath the Mama Negra's skirts, the squirting baby bottle and the gun filled with milk call attention to her breasts—and invest them with a certain sexual ambiguity. In one hand she holds a tube with which she sprays the crowd; with the other, she presses her tiny plastic baby to her enormous breast, as though giving it milk to drink. Her two hands, one holding a breast and the other her male tool, both flowing with liquid to be drunk, condense the meaning of breasts, penis, and testes (the latter, in Spanish and Quichua, "eggs") and suggest that the reproductive organs of women and men produce the same fertilizing substance.[42]

Rather than a reproductive neuter like the Native American berdache, the Mama Negra resembles Plato's androgyne, the self-fertilizing creature with both male and female generative organs. In these androgynous reproductive capacities, the Mama Negra mimics the self-fertilizing abilities that market women claim for themselves. Not only are single mothers common, but vendors speak of having babies as though men were unnecessary to the task. When Linda Seligmann, then a single woman, was doing fieldwork among the Cuzco placeras, they did not urge her to marry, but "to have children, man or no man in my life" (1995). They were simply baffled when she told them of unmarried women in the United States who wanted to have children but could not because they had no male partners. Heloisa and Helena became mothers without visible male partners, and like the domestic servant mentioned in chapter 4, Helena never mentioned the biological father of her birth child. She took total credit for the boy as absolutely as if he had sprung spontaneously from her body in an act of auto-reproduction.

The excessive, emphatic maternity of the Mama Negra raises an interesting problem for the anthropological investigation of "third sexes" or "third genders."[43] Andean market women do not sit easily within this pantheon, although they live in a public, homosocial world, and dress and act in ways that cause others to recognize them as a gender set apart from other women. They are certainly not mirror images of well-known male figures such as the berdache or the Polynesian mahu; and there are few women to whom they can be compared, for the cross-cultural search for third sex/third gender phenomena has uncovered few examples of biological females. The question that emerges from this poor match is whether the problem is with cholas, or with inadvertently masculinist definitions that render the transvestism—and even the sexuality—of women with babies invisible.

Market women do resemble berdaches to a degree. Sexually, berdaches enjoyed some freedoms: they might take many lovers, or become the wife of another man; there are a few reports of marriage to a woman.[44] Occupationally, they did women's work—and sometimes men's. As described by contemporary gay writers, they seem to have had the best of both gender worlds: like the Carnaval dancer quoted above, they gloried in their ability to outperform women at being feminine, while still retaining an admirable masculinity. The latent masculinity of the berdache, in sum, does not lessen her womanhood: it enhances it. Market women do not occupy as distinctly gender-neutral a position as the berdache, but they, too, have appropriated something of the phallic power of the white male, without ceasing to be Indian women.

When we turn to reproduction, though, the chola and the berdache part company. The only tragedy of a berdache life, we are told, was social and physical infertility: she could never become a father—or a mother. The chola, in contrast, is depicted—even vilified—as a masculine woman unable to get or keep a husband, but her ability to become a mother (and even a father) is never called into doubt. The man who crosses over into femininity becomes reproductively neutered, then, but not so the woman who appropriates masculinity. In the Andean context, this chola virility, with its enhanced emphasis on reproductive powers, is more Indian than white; and so, too, is the market woman's expectation that if she feeds her children, they will feed her in return.

Unlike the bourgeoisie, chola mothers expect their children to contribute to their parents' accumulation of wealth, rather than expending it. But these women also turn their own profits into children: these, rather than gold teeth or polleras, are the investments that they expect to grow and increase. Market women accumulate money like a white man—or try to—but when we factor reproduction into the equation, their exchanges invert those of the pishtaco. The white bogeyman takes body fat, releases it into circulation on the world market, and so turns it into profit; market women, in contrast, take their money and turn it into Indian fat. And rather than the pishtaco's deathly reuse of fetuses, they transform their accumulated food and money into living children. Like the Mama Negra, they are not just big women; they are big mothers, whose own size and power is extended by the children with whom they surround themselves.

The Virgin's Black Wet Nurse

The Mama Negra's breasts and their abundant milk, her most apparent attributes, have much in common with the magic of the dancing shamans who surround her. Everyone in the crowd hopes to catch a few drops from her, or from the liquor sprayed by her attendants, in order to increase their own bodily strength and reproductive powers. And no wonder: if the bodies of ordinary men and women generate this liquid, the Mama Negra's body, with its large, multiple organs, has a super-abundance. Spraying the entire city with milk from her phallic flask, she has reproductive power to spare.

She thus nurtures her own children, and all Latacunga as well. This lactating woman echoes the imagery of nationalist mestizaje, as when Uriel Garcia declared the chola "the rejuvenated organic force" whose breasts nurtured the Peruvian nation "like a mother or a wet nurse." But this image of the all-embracing mestiza who satisfies every need too easily becomes a masculinist and colonizing ideology, not far distant from the rape fantasies to which market women are ordinarily subjected. The Mama Negra and her children enact a different scenario.

The chola of fantasy is desirable because she is almost white: she has few of the nonwhite physical features that disgust. What her color adds is the exhilarating knowledge that, unlike white women, she is there for the taking: hence her heady erotic appeal. The Oruro cholitas—whether played by men or women—foster this fantasy, for these fictitious cholas have not only been sexualized, they seem to have been whitened as well. Their little outfits—the minipolleras, the pinned-on braids, the big earrings—identify them as cholas, but the audience knows that the bodies beneath their faux-folkloric clothes are white. Their bouncy breasts, narrow waists, tiny feet, and reddened lips derive from the gender ideology of white Andean culture, and are at odds with both the appearance of actual market women and the erotic aesthetic of indigenous Andean culture. The use of similarly sexualized cholitas by Bolivian populist politicians has aroused some indignation, but the chola in makeup and miniskirts is becoming more familiar even among the working classes nevertheless. Peruvian television watchers, meanwhile, have become accustomed to a different chola, who is also white: La Chola Chabuca, a cross-dressing male television personality who dons the outfits—and the saucy attitudes—of the chola.

In Latacunga, the new Mama Negra has replaced her Indian companions with dance troupes of white girls drawn from the wealthy neighborhoods of the city, all dressed in matching cholita costumes. As in Oruro, these dancers' clothing identifies an exotic and accessible sexuality, while the body underneath remains safely white, bourgeois, and feminine.

The Mama Negra herself, however, destroys this tantalizing racial vacillation. Actual market women are diverse in appearance and thus racially ambiguous as a group. The Mama Negra, in contrast, is clearly and uncompromisingly black—this in a part of the Andes where extremely few Afro-Ecuadorians live, so that blackness is most familiar as a racial fiction, the imaginary opposite of what is white. If every Oruro bourgeois likes to imagine that they have a secret chola alter ego, who dances down the street fluttering her long eyelashes, the vendors of El Salto have a different fantasy. They represent themselves as grotesquely big, masculine, and black: the nonwhite woman as an elite's nightmare.

The powerful effect of the Mama Negra's race on educated Latacungueños can be seen in the endless, almost obsessive debates about how and why a black woman could come to symbolize the city—debates that have eclipsed discussion of other aspects of the festival's history and iconography.[45] But if elites profess themselves at a loss, the market women themselves have an explicit exegesis. The Mama Negra, they say, is the Virgin's wet nurse, and the baby she holds to her breast is Jesus.

At this point, the Mama Negra's reiteration of racial and sexual stereotypes seems finally to collapse under its own weight: surely in this image of the black Mammy serving the white Virgin we have finally arrived at an utterly retrograde picture of racial submission. And yet even here, the market women have the last word.

Although I did not know it at the time, three anthropologists from the Universidad Católica in Quito, Marcelo Naranjo, Lilian Benítez, and Carmen Dueñas, had come to Latacunga to observe the festival of the Mama Negra on September 23, 1983—the day before I saw it. Better informed than I, they had arrived for the official date of the festival: the Virgin's feast day. According to their report, the plastic baby doll that the Mama Negra holds in her hand is blond and white, like many other representations of the baby Jesus (Naranjo et al. 1986:121).

The Mama Negra, then, seems to be in the position of other nonwhite women who take care of white babies: she must feed not only her own, black children, who ride behind her, but the more privileged Child who gets her full attention. She thus resembles the black Mammy of plantation fantasy, or the Indian wet nurse in Icaza's *Huasipungo,* who nurses a white baby during the day and must submit to the baby's grandfather at night.

This symbolism, provided by the women of El Salto themselves, seems to acquiesce to an unchanging racial hierarchy in which nonwhite women forever act as body servants to the powerful. But as I was later to learn in Zumbagua, Andean festivals often have two halves: an officially sanctioned set of rituals, in which the established values of white society are observed; and a second, unbridled performance, later in time, in which very different things can happen. By pure happenstance, I witnessed the festival on its second, rowdier day—and by then the doll had received a coat of black paint, just like the Mama's older children and the gigantic woman who fed Him.

The Mama Negra's breast milk, it appears, had colored the white Child black. This transformation conforms to Indian ideas about motherhood, in which feeding, rather than insemination or birth, is the act that determines who a child's parents are, and so gives it a social identity. In this vision of the lactating woman, the nonwhite nurse gradually becomes not the white Child's servant but its Mother; her other black children will then be its brothers and sisters. The Mama Negra, and the women who create her, are happy to claim the status of generous mother—even of wet nurse—to Christ, and by extension to all of Latacunga. They thus resemble the mestiza mothers of nationalist ideology, from whose ample wombs whole nations were born. Unlike those women, though, the Mama Negra is neither a complacent rape victim who passively submits to the nation's aggressive masculinity, nor a servile Indian nursemaid whose racial degradation props up its whiteness. When a white boy drinks from this woman's tits, he becomes as black as her, though he be Christ Almighty and she but a lowly slave. In a nation nourished by *her* body, whiteness vanishes.

It is not only through her black breasts, but also through her white phallus that the Mama Negra threatens the social hierarchies of Andean society. By claiming the white penis as her own, the Mama Negra discards as unnecessary and undesirable the white phallic fathers of Andean history: the Spanish conqueror who raped the Indian mother; and his descendants, the rapacious hacendado and the castrating pishtaco. She challenges male superiority, too, by hiring men to do her work for her: to carry the castles, wear the costumes, and dance in the parade, while she rides above it all, drinking and partying with the crowd. But despite the mythology of chola matriarchies, the effect is not to invert patriarchy but simply to dissipate it into a radical democracy that over-turns sex and gender oppression as well as that of race and class.

....

Strong Smells

At the produce market, strong smells from the country fill the city air: the aroma of garlic and fresh corn, the reek of pig's blood and sheep shit. Florence Babb remarks with pleasure upon the unforgettable "mélange" of smells that accompanied her days talking to produce vendors (1989:1–2). My nose remembers too: potatoes frying in hot oil, chili peppers and cilantro chopped fine, mangoes liquefying in a blender. But not everyone finds this olfactory assault pleasant. Hernán Montes, a white Bolivian, told Leslie Gill, "Of the one hundred odors that one encounters in the street, ninety-nine of them are bad" (1994:53).

Delightful fragrances impel us irresistibly toward some things, while foul odors repel us more strongly from others. Not surprisingly, then, smell figures often in stories about strangers in the Andes—especially when sex and race figure in the tale. A short tour of these olfactory reminiscences provides an opportunity to revisit some of the themes of this book, and so to bring it to a close.

SICKENING SMELLS

Of all the nightmarish experiences Shukman suffered in his encounters with Andean market women, perhaps the worst occurred on a bus trip.

Already sick with a bacterial infection that made his stomach "swell and ache" and his forehead "as hot as a branding iron," he found himself without a seat on a crowded bus, forced to "slump on the steps by the door."

> When the bus stopped . . . all the passengers climbed out while I lay where I was, too ill to move. One after another the women's skirts brushed over my face. The stench was horrifying: they never have baths. I almost retched. (87)

On the surface, this unpleasant experience of uncleanliness and body odor has a simple explanation: "they never have baths." And certainly we can sympathize with this weary traveler, sick and feverish, jostled by strangers. But as Mary Douglas found in British notions of hygiene, the "horrifying" sensation a young man feels when inadvertently looking up women's skirts may have more than one cause.

Whites are taught to feel something akin to horror at coming into contact with a nonwhite body. A long intellectual tradition links this fear to that of contagious disease; even Mariátegui, the founding father of Peruvian political philosophy, whose views on race were far more progressive than most of his contemporaries, wrote that mestizaje produces "a sordid and unhealthy stagnation" (1952 : 232).

The idea of race as rot is readily expressed through metaphors of body odor: self-avowed racists across the Americas enjoy talking about how nonwhites—whether Koreans, Indians, or Mexicans—stink. At some white fraternity parties, party-goers sing along with bootleg CDs featuring raunchy or racist lyrics; according to a *New York Times* article about country singer David Allan Coe, one nationally popular refrain asserts that some blacks "never die / They just smell that way." [1]

Sex, too, brings its share of horrors. Shukman's position on the floor of the bus, weak and prone beneath strong Indian women who stride over him, immediately recalls his fear that among "cholos," women rule over men. In his brief account, the actual source of the stench is unstated but apparent: as the women's skirts brush over his face, they open, releasing an emanation from the genitalia. Here, too, he has chosen an image with long and deep roots. The notion that an odor that can sicken men exudes from the pudenda is ancient in the West and can be found elsewhere as well. Fears that masculine purity would be contaminated by contact with the female body reached an extreme among the protofascist Freikorps in Weimar Germany; among the Kaulong of New Guinea, men allegedly become ill if a menstruating woman steps over them or even over their possessions. [2] Abhorrence, fascination, and humor are closely connected: the travestis who prided themselves on creating the realistic appearance of a "buceta" or cunt underneath their clothes nevertheless made fun of its odor:

> Once, in her room, Tina took it upon herself to inform me and two travestis who were smoking a big joint with her that "cunts, even if they're washed really well, have a smell like codfish (bacalhau)." (Kulick 1993 : 194)

All these themes—bad hygiene, noxious smells, nonwhite bodies, and women's genitals—come together in the following narrative, told by a well-to-do Bolivian woman about a recently hired Aymara woman:

> I have an extremely well-developed sense of smell and was absolutely disgusted by the mortal odor of this maid. I made her take a shower immediately and then the next day I took her for a medical examination. . . . [I]t turned out that she had venereal disease. I came home, disinfected everything, and threw out a lot of things that she had touched. Unfortunately, a high percentage of this kind of people have venereal diseases. They are ignorant and don't take care of themselves and that's why they spread diseases. (Gill 1994 : 116)

Here, racial fear and loathing cause one woman to experience revulsion toward another. In early twentieth-century Vienna, sexual fears divided members of the same race: Freud reported that his male patients "often declare that they feel there is something uncanny about the female genital organs" (1963 : 51).

In suggesting a link between an idea (that a woman's sex can make men ill, or that "a high percentage" of Aymara carry a communicable disease) and a sensation (a strong smell), whether real or imagined, these narratives exemplify Victor Turner's theory about how symbols work. Like Mary Douglas, he observed the ubiquity and importance of body imagery in myths and rituals across cultures. Borrowing his language from Freud, he argues that symbols based in our physical experience charge the normative with the visceral power of the orectic, and thus render a culture's core principles unassailably convincing. The notion that the white male body is inherently clean, while other bodies are not, seeps into our minds from a multitude of sources, legitimate and otherwise; even when we refuse it as avowed principle, it clings to our perceptions of others like a faint but penetrating smell.

Claims about smells are compelling not only for the reasons Turner adduces, but also because of the value we place on knowledge gained through the senses. When Shukman calls the market women "witches," we read it as a flight of fancy, not a literal accusation of black magic.

But when it comes to the foul odor that nauseates him when forced to look up a pollera, we may be persuaded that this stench really exists—not simply in his own mind, but in the actual bodies of the women who step over him.

Many whites in the Andes say that Indians smell bad; indigenous people who live like, or among, whites tend to agree.[3] Ambitious young Otavaleños repeatedly told Rudi Colloredo-Mansfeld that they wanted to live "clean" lives, like "mistis" (1998:196); after she began working for a white household in La Paz, Ema Lopez disliked going back to her home community because "in the countryside nobody pays attention to the filth. That's just how it is. People change their clothes only if they're really dirty" (Gill 1994:102).

In the contentious political debates over race in Ecuador, members of the indigenous parties angrily accuse bus drivers and white passengers of making racist statements about smelly Indians (Colloredo-Mansfeld 1988). These comments are undoubtedly reprehensible, intended to belittle and shame; but I myself, traveling on rural buses, could not help but notice that some passengers brought with them odors unmistakably associated with country life. When the bus stops on the *páramo* in the early hours of the morning, flagged down by an Indian woman, the doors swing open to a whole sequence of smells. First, there is a burst of cold mountain air. Then, the strong and distinctive odor of a body encased in wet woolen shawls. Faint but unmistakable is the scent of straw—the broken and crushed strands upon which the woman slept and the ash from the *ichu*-grass fire that kept her warm and cooked her breakfast. At first these smells were a surprise; later, as I moved up to in the high grasslands myself, they became familiar, even comforting. Sometimes I could even recognize the aroma of warm barley gruel, hastily swallowed on the way out the door, lingering on an adult's breath or spilled across the shirt of a sleepy child.

The scents of cooking fires and breakfast foods, of draft animals and small children that cling to adult bodies speak of Indian poverty. They evoke the intimacies between humans and animals living together on small family farms and in one-room houses, their bodies forced into constant contact. But they also embody a moral economy based upon the sharing of substances between living bodies—not only humans but animals, as well as the mountain environment itself, conceptualized as animate and sentient.

After death, indigenous homes are traditionally scoured for all the little traces left by the deceased: the few hairs stuck between the teeth of a comb, dried sweat or sloughed skin clinging to the inside of a shirt, the invisible but still-remembered residues of sex on the body of the spouse. Death renders these aftereffects of human contact frightening; the ritual attention to these substances, suddenly turned harmful because of their intimate attachment to the corpse, indicates an everyday awareness of the house and its inhabitants as constantly engaged in organic and mutual processes of ingestion and exhalation, growth and decay.

ALIENATING ODORS

On the Cotopaxi bus, whites from the lower-altitude towns pulled away distastefully from those aromatic passengers: they found such smells repulsive, discouraging intimacy rather than recalling it. After all, a moral order based upon interdependence is incompatible with a modern life; indeed, according to the foundational theorists of the social sciences, estrangement is inherent to modernity.[4] Marx, especially, found estrangement (Entfremdung) inescapable in capitalist society, where class difference creates a world "of estranged labor, of estranged life, of estranged man" (1964:117).[5] The owners of capital appear "alien, hostile, powerful" to workers, who see the bosses enriching themselves at their employees' and customers' expense (1964:114). The wealthy, in turn, refuse to recognize in their employees a common humanity, reserving their sympathies for members of their own class (119). Sex and race exceed and exacerbate the alienation produced by class, resulting in a still more extreme alterity, which ultimately alienates us not only from others but from our own bodies as well. This state of utter estrangement is embodied in the ñakaq, who looks at the bodies of his fellow humans and perceives only a stock of raw materials to be turned into a profit. But we may also find it in certain characteristic smells; for like Indian life, white existence has a distinctive olfactory quality of its own.

Stephen remarks that all his memories of visits to white homes, hotels, and businesses throughout the Andes are clouded by the smell of kerosene, a substance applied liberally to nearly every available surface as a disinfectant. These odors, too, convey racial and sexual meaning. Leslie Gill writes that white La Paz in the 1950s upheld "rigid standards of cleanliness, which were closely connected to notions of moral superiority that whites associated exclusively with themselves." Women not only required their maids to mop and scour kitchens and bathrooms daily "from floor to ceiling," but even enforced such practices as "ironing laundered underwear to kill lingering germs." "Smells," says Gill, "delineated social hierarchies" (1994:53).

In this context, we can read the contemporary La Paz housewife's reference to her "well-developed sense of smell" (in the narrative about venereal disease) as an insignia of respectable white femininity. Women of her mother's generation believed strongly that "noxious odors . . . signified health and moral hazards." Like fairy-tale princesses, their ability to detect even the faintest unclean smell demonstrated their refined sensibilities, as well as their competence as "gatekeepers of domestic virtue." In Ecuador today, the enthusiastic sterilization of rooms and buildings with buckets of kerosene has a corollary in the maintenance of the human body, which is similarly scrubbed and disinfected. As in other poor nations, the ability to purchase imported deodorants and douches, soaps and shampoos is a mark of elite status. Perhaps no other products so perfectly symbolize the United States, whose commercial exports reflect our national preference for bodies that look and smell as though they are neither dead nor entirely alive. Relentless advertising in foreign markets has gone far in convincing members of far smellier cultures—those of Europe, for instance—to follow our deodorized example.

In the Andes, these grooming habits also express the gendered geographies of urban life. The residues of domestic activities—whether the scent of nighttime embraces lingering on adult skin, traces of morning breakfast still visible on a child's face, or even the hairs from the family dog on pants and socks—all must be thoroughly removed from urban bodies before they leave the house. The latter, after all, is a private emotional space, dedicated to consumption; effluvia from the messy relationships that abound there must not leak into the impersonal public sphere. It's different in indigenous communities where homes are workplaces, and where families, not individuals, are the basic units of political and economic life: there, all signs of domestic life need not be cleansed from the body to render it ready for work.

This white cultural obsession with eliminating smells not only helps create a particular geography of gender, but also an alienated knowledge of one's own bodily sex, especially for women. Capitalist culture offers an arsenal of chemicals and paper products designed to hide the female genitals—their smells, their warmth, their wetness. As they grow up, girls learn to fear any accidental failure to disguise odors and stains with an intense, even anguished anxiety reinforced by brushes with brutal male humor on the topic. Racism provides white women an opportunity to displace some of this self-hatred onto the imagined strong-smelling bodies of nonwhites. But this strategy, too, backfires on those who employ it, as racial fears compound the discomfort with which women confront their own uncontrollably odorous sex.

The deodorized body is perfectly suited to capitalist culture: like the fetishized commodity it has been groomed to resemble, it presents itself to potential buyers cleansed of history. In fact, of course, bathroom rituals do not really empty a body of odors, but rather replace one set of olfactory messages with another. (As a poet friend who teaches college in Los Angeles remarked to me, "My students all smell like shampoo.") In short, like the other evasive strategies associated with whiteness, hygienic practices reveal as much as they conceal. In South America, the smell of expensive pharmaceuticals indicates substantial financial wherewithal and more generally a life sustained through anonymous economic exchanges with strangers. These substances come from the clean, cool aisles of a supermarket, not from the dirty hands of a market woman.

Sanitized bodies seek out nourishment that is similarly cleansed. My undergraduates tell me that they love fast food, not so much for its convenience but because they find it reassuring to ingest substances so completely denuded of their biological origins. In one memorable classroom discussion, students reminisced happily about the moment when the objects slide down little metal chutes, individually wrapped in opaque paper and looking perfectly sterile.

Like Indian habits, these practices generate their own morality. The thought that the meat they ate was once part of an animal body disgusted these students, who glared resentfully at me for forcing this awareness upon them. Fast food venues do not cater to vegetarians, however: these consumers felt no compunction about the actual deaths of cows and chickens, so long as they need not witness them. In a similar vein, they did not want to be told that their food or clothing had been touched by others—and especially by poor, nonwhite, non-American people laboring in fields, factories, and warehouses under insalubrious conditions. This notion, too, aroused a physical unease bordering on nausea—but not any political sentiments.[6] Indeed, the group was quite vehement about their own total lack of responsibility as consumers for the labor practices of the companies whose products they buy. This, then, is the white dream of the bourgeoisie: that wants should appear to be met without social intercourse—indeed without interaction with other living things, still less the incursion of responsibility.

The figure of the ñakaq brings to light what the bright clean surfaces of the fetishized commodity try to hide: the multiple unequal exchanges that feed the white body and drain the Indian one. Taste and smell do not figure often in pishtaco stories, and when they do, they produce an exceptionally terrifying reaction: the idea of the bogeyman sniffing out fat in the dark is not a pleasant one, nor are stories of the wealthy dining upon Indian-baby soup. These appeals to the senses are too vivid, calling to mind unbidden pictures of just exactly what the pishtaco does to the body of his victim. This is what this book has tried do with race: to break out of the well-rehearsed dichotomy of nature and culture, and materialize whiteness as social fact. The first section explored the geography of race and sex that shapes the Andean cities and countryside; the second detailed the processes of exchange through which race is enacted and daily re-created. The third and last section turned to accumulation, a process at once social and physical, internal and external. Here—in the interactions between bodies and the substances they ingest, the possessions they accumulate, and the tools they use to act upon the world—we can really see race being made, and making the society around it. This kind of race is neither genetic nor symbolic, but organic: a constant, physical process of interaction between living things. Little surprise, then, that it has a distinct smell.

And yet white culture encourages its members to misrecognize these smells, what they are, where they come from, and what they might mean—a form of self-delusion riskier than it seems.[7] Consider the tale of venereal disease told above, in which the medical rationale offered for the maid's abrupt dismissal unravels to reveal the hallucinogenic logic of race. The speaker claims preternatural powers of smell and insists upon the "fact"—all the more vehemently defended when Gill demurred—that venereal disease can be contracted through touching inanimate objects. Missing entirely from her account are the factors public health workers recognize in the spread of sexually transmitted disease: the confluence of economic, racial, and sexual inequality that breeds coercive acts of sex in which the most vulnerable partner is least able to negotiate the degree of risk. "Mortally" offended by an Indian woman whom she perceives as a threat, the only person the narrator need actually fear is a white man—her husband. Her servants cannot infect her directly, for she does not have sex with them. And in her bedroom, for all her class privilege, this woman may be as little able to protect herself as an Aymara maid.

This domestic drama is recapitulated in the continent's geopolitics, for when residents of the Andes embrace the ideology of whiteness, they inadvertently conspire with foreigners in the continued degradation of their nations and their region. Attempts on the part of South Americans to shore up their own racial privilege by dissociating themselves from Indians inevitably backfire, as outsiders use the same distorted lens to look at them. The imaginary racial distance imposed between Indian villages and Andean cities, or between the produce markets and the interiors of upper-class homes, is re-created between the Andean nations and the Southern Cone, between South America and the NAFTA nations, and between Latin America and the United

States. Each pairing makes one partner play Indian to the other's white, thus enforcing a unidirectional flow of people as well as of capital.

Freud taught us to look for something hidden wherever an uncanny figure such as the pishtaco appears. "The prefix 'un-,' " he said, "is the token of repression" (1963 : 51). The first repressed secret was the hidden intimacies between Indian and white, linked over five hundred years by a thousand forms of exchange. The last secret to be disinterred is that white masculinity is more vulnerable than it pretends—and less able to secure the boundaries between itself and the noxious qualities of the lesser race and the weaker sex. We followed the ñakaq to uncover the secret history of whiteness; now we can turn to his ludic antithesis the Mama Negra for a final resolution to the story.

As a white father, the pishtaco cuts a frightening figure; like many an elite Latin American child, we might well run away from him to take refuge in the protective embrace of the nonwhite women who feed and care for us. The Mama Negra is certainly motherly, but guzzling liquor and fondling her own tit, she is neither saintly nor self-sacrificing. Instead, in keeping with the ethos of Indian reciprocity, she is simultaneously generous and selfish. Erotic, productive, and nurturing, her body is also self-serving, self-satisfying, and even self-fertilizing. This is an apt enough metaphor for the strategies by which poor women, to whom so little is offered, survive in the hostile cityscapes of late capitalist Latin America. And it also carries a message—both threatening and comforting—to those who unthinkingly depend upon nonwhite and female labor every day.

The Mama Negra suckles a white child—in striking counterpoint to the pishtaco, a white man who sucks the life out of Indians. But in return for her abundant milk, she takes away the child's whiteness; or is she giving it a gift, that of her own blackness? Either way, she threatens to destroy the false security promised to those who cling to their white masculinity. This makes her a frightening figure indeed—but unlike the ñakaq, an absurd rather than an uncanny one. She encourages us to reject the pishtaco's seductive offer, in which estranged desires are satisfied through commodified corpses, and to reach out instead for something that smells a little less dead. The destruction of whiteness, she claims, might finally enable us to create a more generous and all-inclusive democracy than we have yet enjoyed—not only one that ceases to discriminate against women and Indians, but that also puts an end to the seemingly endless reciprocities of accumulation and impoverishment. In this delirious vision of the Americas, thefts and rapes would be replaced with forms of exchange so mutually enriching as to destroy not only the vicious forms of intercourse we have visited here but the very difference between taking and giving, between the giver and the gift.

This is pure fantasy, of course, more so than any tale from Andean folklore. This book has explored a social landscape so inexorably shaped by the dystopian mythologies of racial and sexual inequality that escape seems impossible. But if these alienating myths have such instrumental power, we should not then discount the ability of other images and narratives to help create a different reality. We begin the new century bereft of revolutionary vision; it may be from such collective fantasies as the Mama Negra and the pishtaco, products of the struggles of the last five hundred years, that we will forge a new symbolic language with which to articulate social ideals for the future.

Notes

269

Introduction

1. Zumbagua is located almost exactly one degree south of the equator, at perhaps the narrowest part of the Andes. Altitudes vary from 3,200 meters to above 4,000 meters; the agricultural economy mixes the farming of barley, fava beans, and potatoes with sheep and camellid husbandry. Wage labor outside the parish provides an important if unreliable source of income. In the neighboring parish of Tigua (also called Guangaje or Quilatoa), young families have begun a successful enterprise selling paintings to tourists; these have erroneously come to be identified as painters from "Zumbagua." Zumbagua and Tigua are bisected by the Latacunga-Quevedo Highway; they are within the canton of Pujilí, province of Cotopaxi. For more information, consult Weismantel 1988; Hess 1997; Costales and Costales 1976.

2. Weismantel 1988. In Ecuador, as in Louisiana, a parish is a civil jurisdiction.

3. Salasaca is located in Tungurahua Province, on the road between the capital city of Ambato and the spa town of Baños. Like the much larger city of Otavalo in the northern province of Imbabura, Salasaca is known to tourists for its textile production. The community, which retains a striking degree of cultural and aesthetic autonomy from surrounding areas, is often said to have been founded by Bolivian *mitimaes* forcibly transplanted by the Inca. For information on Salasaca textiles, consult Rowe et al. 1998: 126–144.

4. All translations are mine unless otherwise indicated.

5. Open-air markets can be found throughout much of the Americas, Africa, and Asia; in several areas of the world, including Haiti, West Africa, and parts of Mexico and the Mediterranean, the small-scale selling of food, both cooked and raw, is a peculiarly female occupation (see for example Babb 1989, 1996; Behar 1993, Cazamajor D'artois 1988; Chiñas 1992; Clark 1994, 1988; Kapchan 1996; Klump 1998; Mintz 1971, 1972, 1978; Robertson 1984; Sudarkasa 1973). In South America, markets dominated by women are especially associated with the Andean region: the cities, towns, and rural areas of highland Ecuador, Peru, and Bolivia (and areas of southern Colombia and northern Argentina and Chile as well). This area is roughly coterminous with the extent of the Inca empire at the time of European conquest; although it

has since been fragmented into parts of five distinct nations, it retains a certain cultural unity.

6. Other urban working-class women, such as domestic servants, waitresses, butchers, chicha-brewers, and washerwomen are also called cholas.

7. Recounted in his 1993 book, *Cuencanarías: Tomo II* (77–122).

8. The geographical distribution of names is roughly as follows: *kharasiri* among Aymara-speakers, *pishtaku* among Quechua-speakers of central Peru, *ñakaq* in southern Peru, and *pishtaco* throughout Spanish-speaking Peru. Both ñakaq and pishtaco have become familiar terms in the anthropological literature; I will use the two interchangeably here. For further discussion of the orthography, distribution, variations, and meanings of these terms, see Ansión 1989; Morote Best 1951–52:69; Wachtel 1994:72. Regional differences in dialect and vocabulary lead to many variations on these terms, and many different orthographies as well; I will use only *ñakaq, pishtaco,* and *kharisiri,* except in direct quotes from other authors. Molinié Fioravanti reminds us of a Spanish version of the pishtaco, the "sacamantecas" or "tío mantaquero" of Andalucia (1991:84).

9. This version (the secret cave, the victim upside down) is very common, but there are endless variations. The pishtaco appears to be growing in popularity and geographical reach; a recent search of the Internet turned up several hits, primarily in international or Latin American collections of ghost stories. The heartland of the tales is clearly southern Peru and highland Bolivia; in Cuzco, for example, it has a long history indeed, whereas in Ecuador it appears to be unknown. In a discussion following an American Anthropological Association meeting session on the Andes, Peter Gose and Stuart Rockefeller suggested that there is a correlation between regions where there was mining in the colonial period, and areas where pishtaco stories are told today (November 1998). The exact limits of the story's reach have never been systematically documented and are not stable over time.

10. *Degollar* means to slash the throat, or to decapitate; like the Quechua *ñakaq, degollador* refers especially to the man who slaughters animals, while the verb form has connotations of massacre. (On the origins of the Quechua word, see Morote Best 1951–52:69). It is noteworthy that, according to Luise White, the Swahili word for a similar African bogeyman, *kachinja,* similarly derives from a verb meaning "to slaughter animals by cutting their throats" (1999:7), although the modus operandi of the two evildoers is otherwise somewhat different.

11. A department is a geopolitical unit in Peru and Bolivia, similar to a state in the United States or a province in Ecuador.

12. "[La víctima] comienza a temblar de miedo, le salen de los ojos chispas de fuego, la cabeza comienza a crecer, luego automáticamente se dirige hacia el Ñak'aq" (Manya 1969:136)

13. See, for example, Gose 1994a; Stein 1961; Wachtel 1993. As we shall see, the list of those who are commonly suspected of being pishtacos includes not only anthropologists but development workers, medical technicians, hacendados, soldiers, catechists, translators, and even market women and a statue of the infant Christ.

14. A few authors, notably Deborah Poole (1988, 1994, 1997), have long insisted that race is a salient category in the Andes.

15. This was true both in the English-speaking world and in Latin America, although for somewhat different reasons: Latin American academies were profoundly influenced by Marxist theory, and turned to analysis of class, while in the United States, liberal rather than radical thinking predominated. Nonetheless, Latin Americans and Anglophone scholars influenced each other in the turn away from race as an analytical category.

16. Rasnake 1988 : 43–48; Mitchell 1991 : 8; Gose 1994b : xi–xii.

17. This is an enormous literature; critical authors include Paul Gilroy (1993, 1987) and David Roediger (1991, 1994), among many others. For further sources, see the bibliography of Weismantel and Eisenman 1998. Since we wrote that essay, anthropologists have increasingly turned to the question of race as well; see, for example, the 1998 special issue of the *American Anthropologist,* and the yearlong debate on the pages of the AAA newsletter as well.

18. In a recent book on indigenism in Brazil—the Latin American country best-known in the United States for its multiple racial categories—Brazilian anthropologist Alcida Ramos makes a case for the necessity of the category "white" that is very similar to my own. (Although interestingly, while I worry about how my words will sound to Latin American readers, she worries about readers in the United States) She writes,

   > I am aware of the problems the terms *Whiteman* and *whites* bring to the minds of a North American audience. But considering the ethnographic reality of the interethnic relations in Brazil, I cannot avoid it. . . . [I]n Brazil brancos encompasses all non-Indians—Brazilians and foreigners, regardless of racial features. Moreover, branco is used by both Indians and non-Indians and thus constitutes a "native" category of Brazilian society in general. As a polar category to Indio, branco is [a] necessary . . . element in the Brazilian model of interethnic relations. . . . Any ethnographic analysis devoted to the interpretation of this model must conform to it. (1998 : 8)

19. See, for example, C. Harris 1993 : 1768–9; Frankenberg 1993 : 14.

20. Dozens of ethnographies make passing reference to these terms. Among them, de la Cadena stands out for her critical discussion of the racial meanings of terms like "decent" and "educated" (see especially 1996 : 116–18, 1998). Crandon-Malamud 1991 : 16 mentions the use of *vecinos* as a synonym for *mestizos*—a group that she defines in turn as "those who dominated the Aymara in the canton socially, juridically, politically and economically. They form a group that they consider to be racially distinct." Stutzman 1981 : 79 discusses *culto,* "cultured" as a synonym for *blanco.* Isbell 1978 : 67 defines *vecinos* as a synonym for *qalas,* while van den Berghe and Primov describe it as a synonym for *mestizo* (1977 : 127) and as the opposite of "Indian"; see also Gose 1994b : 18, who discusses the origins and current usage of *vecino.* Abercrombie says that *mestizo* is not heard in Canton Culta, Bolivia, where *vecino* is the preferred term of address (1998 : 46 and passim).

21. Quechua is one of the most important indigenous languages spoken in the Americas today; its speakers number in the millions, although the number of

monolingual Quechua-speakers continues to decline precipitously. For an insightful history of the language, see Mannheim 1991. Its range extends from southern Colombia through Peru and Ecuador, and into northern Bolivia. There are many different dialects, of which it is conventional to refer to Ecuadorian variants as "Quichua" and Peruvian/Bolivian variants as "Quechua." For simplicity's sake I will use "Quechua" to refer to both "Quechua" and "Quichua" dialects, with apologies to Quichua-speakers.

22. This meaning shows up most often in nationalist discourses of mestizaje. This is a topic too large and too important for me to address adequately here; see Gould 1998, Whitten 1981, Stutzman 1981, and the 1996 JLAA special issue on mestizaje 2(1) for some significant contributions.

23. This is true even when neither or both parties would appear "white" according to dominant racial schemes. See Brackette Williams 1989 on racial politics in Guyana, which, she argues, are predicated upon a colonialist racial schema even in the absence or relative weakness of whites. For the shifting definitions of whiteness, see Sacks 1994; Theodore Allen 1994, 1997; Roediger 1991, 1994.

24. I do not address the multiple other racial and ethnic identities—black, Asian, Arab, and Jewish, to name only the most obvious—that are also important and highly visible in the Andean social landscape. Their absence impoverishes the book, but it allows us to focus attention on the Indian/white binary, which, like the black/white binary in the United States, defines a fundamental racial paradigm that is, in itself, a defining problem for other minorities. There is a well-established and rapidly growing literature on Afro-Latin cultures, and on racism against blacks in South America. Recent and excellent publications on blacks and blackness in Latin America and the Caribbean include the two-volume Whitten and Torres 1998; and Wade 1993b. Orlove 1997 is a beautifully written essay about doing fieldwork in the rural Andes as an American Jew; it discusses perceptions of Jews and Arabs in rural Peru.

25. This book is a collection of essays by Ecuadorian social scientists (and also including an essay by indigenous political leader Luis Macas) about the indigenous uprising of 1990 and the *"avivamiento de atávicas pasiones segregacionistas y racistas en los mestizos y citadinos"* (revival of atavistic segregationist and racist passions among mestizos and urbanites) that ensued ("Prólogo," Cornejo Menacho 1992:11).

26. He continues: "During the early 1900s, Boaqueno ladinos in polite conversation referred to the region's Indians by the terms 'indigena,' 'natural,' and 'indio.' But they had an ample supply of other terms as well: indigesto, indino, jincho (jinchería for a large quantity of them), napiro, natucho (natuchada). Although the etymological origins of [some terms] are obscure, the other derogatory expressions have a distinctly physical quality to them" (Gould 1998: 71–72).

27. For the classic description of life under this system, see Icaza 1953.

28. See, for example, Colloredo-Mansfeld 1998:197.

29. See, for example, Colloredo-Mansfeld 1998; Orlove 1998:209; Harrison 1989:12.

30. On the notion of *habitus,* see Bourdieu 1979; further discussion of this point in Weismantel 1988:159–67.

31. See Weismantel 1991 for a more detailed discussion of this point.

32. Allen 1988, 1978. Norman Whitten's writings about the Canelos Quichua of Amazonian Ecuador contain subtle and nuanced discussions of the dimensions of the word *Runa,* which in Amazonia play off not only white/Indian dichotomies, but highland/lowland contrasts as well (Whitten 1976, 1985; Whitten and Whitten 1985).

33. 1988:22. Like Norman Whitten (see citations in previous note), Allen uses the capitalized *Runa* to distinguish this use of the word from more negative usages.

34. On Otavalo and its surrounding area, see especially Colloredo-Mansfeld 1998. See also Salomon 1981a; Casagrande 1977; Harrison 1989:12.

35. I would like to thank the Buechlers for a personal comment several years ago confirming my sense that this is the case; see also Casagrande 1980 about the central Ecuadorian sierra in general.

36. This situation may be changing somewhat due to the strong presence of indigenous political activism in the province in the 1990s; for example, Luis Macas, the current president of CONAIE, the largest and most active indigenous party, is from Cotopaxi.

37. *Shimi* means "tongue," or "language."

38. See Roediger 1991:3 for a discussion of the word "nigger" among white Midwesterners; he apparently grew up in a town close to where I went to high school. Our experiences are different because of gender and generation, but the racial milieu he describes is all too familiar to me.

39. Still unmarried, she lived with her older brother and his wife but slept in a small storage building that she had turned into a dormitory for herself.

40. Not only do gringos have a race—mishu—but the word "gringo" itself does not translate as a racial category so much as a description of foreigners or outsiders. The first weeks that I lived in the parish, I was terrified at night when crowds carrying burning torches, guns, and machetes marched around town shouting "Gringos get out or we will kill you!" By day, local people were bemused by my fears: didn't I realize that those slogans had nothing to do with me? The marchers were a group of activists trying to oust the Catholic priests from the parish. I found this even more puzzling, since most of the priests were Ecuadorian. "They are calling the priests 'gringos' to say that they don't belong here. They're not talking about you—no one cares if you come or go, why should we?" explained one man frankly. "But I'm a gringa." "Yes, obviously, you come from another country. But the priests are not from here either, and they are trying to run the whole parish."

41. See, for example, Freyre 1946; Amado 1966.

42. 1971:223–45 and passim.

43. See de la Cadena 1998 and 2000. Unfortunately, her book came out too late for me to incorporate it into this text, which is based solely on her earlier articles.

44. See, for example, Fontaine 1985.

45. See, for example, Malik 1996; Wade 1993.

46. *Zambo/a* is difficult to translate. It is often translated as "mixed African and European," "mixed African and Indian," etc., but my own experience suggests that, at least in some parts of the Andes, it is a simple descriptor of physical appearance. My own hair is dark brown and very curly, and I have often been called "zamba," although in the United States I am always considered white. My daughter, a light-skinned African-American child from the United States, was also called "zamba." The term seems to have little to do with skin color, since I was always "blanca" or "mishu" and she was considered "morena"; indeed, in these contexts, it seemed to indicate little more than a specific kind of hair, with no particular imputation of African descent.

47. See Smith 1997, 1996; Ramos 1998.

48. See Weismantel 1995 for a longer discussion of this process.

Chapter 1

1. Wolf 1955, 1957; his own review of the ensuing debate can be found in Wolf 1986.

2. See, for example, Clifford 1992; Blunt and Rose 1994.

3. Cotopaxi is one of the poorest, most rural, and most indigenous provinces of Ecuador, despite its location just south of Pichincha Province, where the capital city of Quito is located. Cotopaxi Province is the site of my own research in Zumbagua and Tigua, and in the market towns of Pujilí, Saquisilí, and Latacunga (the provincial capital).

4. See also Orlove 1993; Whitten 1981.

5. I am indebted to Denise Arnold for bringing Alison Spedding's unpublished work on the kharisiri to my attention.

6. "They say that the president, that Alan (Garcia), sends them" (Vergara Figueroa and Ferrúa Carrasco 1989:131).

7. In her book *The Female Thermometer,* Castle suggests that one might productively treat certain themes and metaphors in Freud's "Uncanny" "as a mode of historical assertion. . . . Might one argue . . . [t]hat the uncanny itself has a history, originates at a particular historical moment, for particular historical reasons . . . ?" (1995:7). She goes on to discuss the presence of specific objects (mechanical dolls, optical instruments) in Hoffman's novel, and the relationship between scientific discoveries and horror stories in the eighteenth century. Her notion of the uncanny as a specifically *modern* phenomenon is suggestive in relation to pishtaco stories as well.

8. Kramer's understanding of mimesis also echoes that of the art historian E. H. Gombrich, whose formula "making comes before matching" was elucidated in *Art and Illusion* (1960).

9. See, for example, Arguedas 1953; Morote Best 1951–52; LaTorre 1984.

10. Other scholars who have interpreted the pishtaco as a representation of exploitative Indian-white relations include Molinié Fioravanti 1991; Ansión and Sifuentes 1989; Oliver-Smith 1969; Rivière 1991; Sifuentes 1989.

11. The paintings are actually produced in the parish of Tigua/Guangaje, rather than in the parish of Zumbagua, but the entire region is known as "Zumbagua," and so the painters, previously known as the "Tigua painters," are increasingly referring to themselves as "from Zumbagua."

12. Cervone 1999, 1998 discussed similar incidents, reporting that they have become extremely common throughout the Ecuadorian highlands.

13. Whitten 1976: 10–12; see also Stutzman 1981 : 45.

14. Anthropologists and historians have done much to document the active and important presence of indigenous people in Andean cities during the last five hundred years. For example, see Abercrombie 1996; and Larson and Harris's excellent edited volume *Ethnicity, Markets and Migration in the Andes* (1995).

15. As early as 1560, the produce markets were already racially heterogeneous; Karen Spalding discusses an anonymous protest to the Crown by a Spanish merchant, asking that Indians be banned from selling "bread and foodstuffs" to the residents of Potosí (1984 : 152–53; also discussed in Tandeter et al. 1995 : 197–98).

16. Seligmann perceptively uses Sartre's classic 1948 essay on anti-Semitism in her discussion of the Andean chola (1993 : 199–200).

17. 1988:xxv–xxvi; cited in Montrose 1993 : 182.

18. It is interesting to note the use of the English word "supermarket" in Condori Mamani's Quechua text, recorded in the 1970s, which is otherwise bereft of English terms (Condori Mamani and Huamán 1996).

19. "El alma quechua alienta en los cuadros de un artista vernáculo," interview with Martin Chambi published in *Hoy* (Santiago), March 4, 1936. Cited in López Mondéjar 1993 : 24.

20. The first title is found in Chambi 1993 : 52; the second from a 1998 Web site on Martin Chambi (socrates.berkeley.edu/~dolorier/Chambidoc.html). All the Chambi photographs discussed here are illustrated in Chambi 1993.

21. For an overview of the changing culture of drinking in the Andes, see Orlove and Schmidt 1995.

22. In Andean communities today, cans of large sardines in tomato sauce (which are caught and canned in Peru) are an affordable luxury food for rural people—not something that can be eaten every day, but a special-occasion food that can be doled out in spoonfuls over plates of potatoes, rice, or noodles (or a combination thereof) as a tasty sauce.

23. López Mondejar 1993 : 16.

24. Quoted in Vargas Llosa 1993b : 7. Chambi shared the indígenistas' love of the chicheria; out of the tens of thousands of photographs he made between 1919 and 1940, one of the photographs he himself most treasured was a single shot taken in the courtyard of a chichería: *Sapo y Chicha* (1931) (Ranney 1993 : 11). One of a series of photographs documenting life in the tavern, it reveals his ties to the movement by its similarity in theme and title to indígenista paintings of the time (and demonstrates his artistic independence by its freedom from the cloying sentimentality and predictability that has consigned most of the latter to oblivion).

25. Sáenz 1933:175; cited in de la Cadena 1996:140.

26. The fact that chicheras serve male customers, while produce vendors largely sell to women, explains much of the special appeal of the chichera; see chapter 2.

27. Abercrombie 1992:299–301; Albro 1997:14 (the latter gives an initial publication date of 1929 for parts of the novel).

28. These excerpts are from a lovely message titled "Desde flushing, NY" (from Flushing, N.Y.) written by Luis Franco and posted on Friday, May 30, 1997, on the listserv "echarla," which serves expatriate Ecuadorians.

29. For a discussion of comparable themes in Bolivia, see Albro 2000.

30. Miles 1989:55 records similar sentiments on the part of women whose husbands have migrated to the United States.

31. For comparable figures from Bolivia, see Buechler and Buechler 1996:173–75, quoted at length in chapter 6 of this book.

32. 1996:49, 183; quoted partially in chapter 6 of this book.

33. Since republished as *Andean Lives,* in a new translation from Quechua to English by Paul Gelles and Gabriela Martínez Escobar (1996).

34. 1977:48; 1996:55. In this and subsequent quotes from Condori Mamani, I have consulted both versions and modified the Gelles/Martínez Escobar English as seems appropriate.

35. See note 13.

Chapter 2

1. For a well-illustrated discussion of Salasaca costume, see Rowe et al. 1998: 126–43.

2. Women dressed in the indigenous manner, in a wrapped skirt known as an anacu and a wide woven sash or *chumbi,* usually carry valuables tucked inside their blouses or sashes, rather than in a purse.

3. See, for example, Denich 1974; Friedl 1967; Harding 1975; Reiter 1975; Silverman 1967.

4. See, for example, Cook and Diskin 1976.

5. See Low 1997 for an insightful discussion of Spanish re-appropriation of Native American plazas in Mesoamerica and the Caribbean.

6. See Weismantel and Eisenman 1998.

7. But see Rivera Cusicanqui 1996:260.

8. On novels, see Ellis 1998. A joke circulating among professional men in the 1990s:

   A little kid is talking to his mommy. He asks, "Mommy, Mommy, can we humans eat the lights—the ones that we turn on and off?"

   "Oohh son, but of course not, we can't eat light. Why are you asking me this?"

   "Because when I got back from school my father was talking to our maid upstairs in your room, and he said . . .'Just turn the light off, and put it in your mouth.'"

9. A town near Cochabamba.

10. Bolton and Mayer 1977; Rivera Cusicanqui goes so far as to maintain that a supposed Andean culture of heterosexuality is a reproof to "radical lesbianism" (in THOA 1990:181), but see Paulson 1996 on the prevalence of woman-headed households in one region of rural Bolivia.

11. As a nun, of course, Mother Chantal has also chosen a vocation that precludes marriage.

12. Vallarnos 1962:65, cited in de la Cadena 1996:140, n. 26.

13. The references are to García Lorca's play *La casa de Bernarda Alba* (1983), which has no male characters, and to García Marquez's novel *Cien años de soledad* (1987).

14. Hot toddies made with trago (cane liquor), a traditional drink of the highlands.

15. On Cortázar, see Schmidt-Cruz 1998; on Vargas Llosa, see Ellis 1998.

16. For a very interesting discussion of this term as it is used in the markets, see Morales 1995:34–35.

17. The worsening economy has lengthened the days and hours that these women work, a subject of much bitter commentary among them. They envision a proper workweek as one in which they rise early, but finish early, and in which most women can take Sundays and holidays off; but since the late 1980s, they have worked endless long days, afraid to miss out on a single purchase.

18. Shukman would undoubtedly consider Velasquez to be of a different race than himself: a mestizo, even a cholo, rather than a white man. Velasquez might counter that he himself is white—but he would perceive Shukman's gringo whiteness as quite different from his own.

19. Weismantel and Eisenman 1998:136; Arizpe 1990:xix. See also Weismantel 1997b,c for a fuller discussion.

20. An especially horrible case from Guatemala is that of Alaskan tourist June Weinstock, an apparently harmless soul who had told a friend she wanted to "fight poverty and human rights abuses." Anxious to get off the beaten track, she attended the market at San Cristobal Veracruz, where rumors began that she was a "gringo robaniños," a ghoulish creature believed to snatch children in order to harvest their organs. A mob gathered, and further rumors developed that she was a "man who has turned into a woman"; eventually, she was beaten into a coma, her vagina penetrated with sticks (Adams 1998:118).

21. He distinguished between estrangement (*Entfremdung*) and alienation (*Entäusserung*); the former originates in—but is not identical to—the latter, more fundamental process (Milligan and Struik in Marx 1964:58–59).

Chapter 3

1. Drinking vessels.

2. On these shawls, see Miller 1990 and Rowe et al. 1998:254–62. See especially the illustrations on the title page, plate XIV, and pp. 257 (no. 244) and 259 (no. 246).

3. The same observation has recently been made by Rebecca Tolen (1999:22–23), who highlights the special significance given to clothing in these displays.

4. On the religious history and iconography of the shrine itself, and the relationship between Baños and the Oriente, see Vargas 1983.

5. I am entirely indebted to Stephen F. Eisenman for all the material concerning the nineteenth century presented here, much of which he originally wrote, and all of which can be found in expanded form in the article on race that we wrote together (Weismantel and Eisenman 1998).

6. Disraeli 1927:153; Stocking 1974:413.

7. De Lanessan 1897:60, cited in Todorov 1993:257.

8. Saco 1938, cited in Rout 1976:128–29.

9. Humboldt 1840:268; quoted in Poliakov 1974:174.

10. On the meanings and history of the word *cholo* in Mexico and among Mexican-Americans, see, for example, Valenzuela Arce 1997, 1999.

11. For an interesting example of the frequently overlooked phenomenon of nonindigenous individuals adopting an Indian identity, see Belote 1978.

12. See discussion by Rebecca Tolen in Rowe et al. 1998:167–229.

13. In Cuenca, thirty-two of Brownrigg's thirty-four informants identified an Afro-Ecuadorian woman from Esmeraldas as a chola (1972:71). In her book about race in the Andes, Deborah Poole quotes nineteenth-century travel writers who describe the vendors in Lima as both "mulatas" and "cholas" (1997:96).

14. 1989:696n. 1; 703–4.

15. 1975:234, cited in Seligmann 1989:704.

16. See note 12.

17. I have simplified her categories for clarity. The actual categories are costumed groups (Indians, costumed cholos); and uncostumed urban groups (urban lower class, true middle class, status ambivalent upper class, and *nobles*) [Brownrigg 1972:xiii and passim]. Thus there are two cholo categories, one "costumed" and one "uncostumed" ("urban lower class").

18. The use of racial terms between lovers, a common phenomenon throughout Latin America, merits further study.

19. On the capulí, see Weismantel 1988:111–12; Gade 1975:161.

20. The quote is from 1978:46 (Barraclough's translation); the original reads: "Ellas sabían solo huaynos del Apurímac y del Pachachaca, de la tierra tibia donde crecen la caña de azúcar. . . . Cuando cantaban con sus voces delgaditas, otro paisaje presentíamos: . . . La lluvia pesada y tranquila que gotea sobre los campos de caña" (1972:69).

21. If nothing else, the passage of time exposes cultural limits on authors' claim to objectivity, as when once *au courant* language—van den Berghe's "chick" as a translation for chola, for example—now makes us wince (1977:128).

22. There is an element of historical slippage in de la Cadena's use of late-twentieth-century opinions to attack writers from mid-century: the women to whom she spoke in the 1990s wish to be called "mestizas," not "cholas";

therefore their mothers and grandmothers must have felt the same. However, there is at least indirect evidence to support this assertion. Martín Chambi, although working at the height of the neo-indígenista love affair with real and imagined "cholas" and chicheras, did not label the woman at the chichería "a chola": she is, instead, a "Mestiza de Cuzco." Chambi, an intimate of intellectuals but himself of humble rather than elite origins, was undoubtedly more aware of the women's own point of view than were the young men who composed poems in their honor. Likewise, Condor Mamani and his wife Asunta Quispe, working-class Cuzqueños, never use the word *chola* to describe market women, chicheras, or any other working-class women. As two older residents of Cuzco speaking during the 1970s, they provide a historical bridge between the writers de la Cadena criticizes and the interviews she herself conducted.

23. The term *scopophilia,* which derives from Freud's *Three Essays on Sexuality,* was popularized by Laura Mulvey (1975:6–18).

24. See illustrations in Rowe et al. 1998:114, 191 (nos. 101, 171, 172).

25. For a similar example from Bolivia, see Paulson's description of a woman changing her appearance from "rural Indian" to "urban vendor" through, among other things, rebraiding her hair (this chapter).

26. See Ackerman 1990 for a similar discussion from Peru.

27. At one point, I took a taxi in Guayaquil with my friend and fellow American, archaeologist Tom Aleto. He and his wife had been doing fieldwork on an island off the coast and had picked up the strong coastal accent of the fishermen who lived there. When the two of us started giving him directions— me talking like a Quichua-speaking Indian from the mountains, Tom like a montubio from the islands—the taxi driver started laughing so hard he had to pull off the side of the road. "La gringuita longuita y el gringo montubio," he kept saying incredulously.

28. This comment surprised me, for I found the language of Cuenca's market women to be free of Quichua cadences or syntax. Whether this difference reflects changes in the region, the shorter time that I spent in the area, or the implicit comparisons we may have been making (Brownrigg to middle-class Spanish, me to the heavily Quichua-inflected Spanish of the central highlands), I cannot say.

29. De la Cadena 1996:126–26; Sáenz 1933:275, quoted in de la Cadena 1996: 140. The Cuenca references are from Darquea's "Florista Cuencana" and "Chola Cuencana," Lloret Bastidas 1981:272–76.

30. See for example the unidentified illustration on the cover of Larson and Harris 1989, and the wonderful Bolivian illustrations in Rivera Cusicanqui et al. 1996.

31. Canavesi de Sahonero 1987, cited in Gill 1994:105.

32. See note 2 of this chapter.

33. In earlier decades, cholas are described as wearing high heels—perhaps because in those days, white women did not. Then and now, the stereotype of the chola is of a woman willing to spend money on her shoes.

34. When cooked, lupins resemble beans, except that they do not disintegrate.

Boiled and salted, they are a popular street food, especially when eaten with toasted corn kernels and/or a fresh hot sauce prepared with cilantro.

35. This is an enormous literature; see especially Tyler 1991, 1998 for thorough overviews and incisive discussions of the theoretical literature on passing and crossing; Garber 1992 for a lively study of cross-dressing; and Newton 1979 for an important early study of drag by an anthropologist.

36. In Quichua, the word *chagra* refers to an agricultural plot: like "hayseed" in English, the suggestion is of someone right off the farm.

37. The literature on the berdache (or two-spirit person) and two related debates about nomenclature and the question of feminine equivalents is enormous and growing. A recent account that surveys most of the previous literature is Lang 1998; Walter Williams 1986 was an important landmark, as were Jacobs 1968; Blackwood 1984; and P. Allen 1986. See also Jacobs, Thomas, and Lang 1997; Medicine 1983; and Roscoe 1994.

38. Brecht 1989–98, 16:135, quoted in Jameson 1998:69; translation by Jameson.

39. See, for example, Isbell 1978. The original passage in Lévi-Strauss is found in *The Savage Mind* 1966:16–29.

40. Babb 1989:25. Ackerman 1991:234, in an interesting discussion of "mestiza" dress from Abancay, Peru, comments on the division of the body into an upper and a lower field; it is unclear whether the "mestizas" she describes would include market women.

41. On stigmatized "white" behavior, see Weismantel 1988:82, 147.

42. Women do participate importantly in festivals as sponsors, a role that does give them great visibility.

43. On the Corpus Christi bullfight in Zumbagua, see Weismantel 1988:201–7, 1997b, 1997c.

Chapter 4

1. The family's gift of hospitality has underwritten my scholarly career, although the books and articles that I have written are the products of my own labor. But even leaving that fact out of the accounting, their generosity has been, and continues to be, overwhelming.

2. In 1988, I spoke of this as the "articulation of two modes of production" (29–32), an idea based upon the work of French anthropologist Claude Meillassoux (1981), as well as economists Carmen Diana Deere (1976) and Alain de Janvry (1981).

3. See, for example, Allen 1988; Isbell 1977a, 1977b; and Harris 1978, 1980. The notion of complementarity remains important but has also become, in Denise Arnold's words, a "sacred cow" that has been both attacked and significantly reconfigured (1997a:23). See Arnold 1997b for an excellent survey of contemporary work on gender; several of the articles, including Isbell's own, take up the question of complementarity. Rivera Cusicanqui et al. 1996 also provides a good sampling of contemporary writing about women in Bolivia.

4. See, for example, Silverblatt 1987; Isbell 1978.

5. On the flexibility of gender roles, see especially C. Allen 1988.

6. See Weismantel 1989.

7. From the archaic Spanish, "Dios se le pague," may God repay you—but in Zumbagua today, the reference to the deity is completely forgotten.

8. For an examples of work skeptical of gender egalitarianism in the Andes, see de la Cadena (1993).

9. On *tinkuy*, see Platt 1987; Earls and Silverblatt 1978; C. Allen 1988:205–7; Abercrombie 1998:66 and passim. The *tinkuy*, writes Allen, is "simultaneously a dance, a fight, and a love affair" (206).

10. Arguedas 1972:69.

11. On the symbolism of white rice and racial whiteness, see Weismantel 1988: 144–49 and passim.

12. See the more recent discussion in Enloe 1989.

13. Vallarnos 1962:65, cited in de la Cadena 1996:140n. 26.

14. The baking of breads in anthropomorphic and other shapes is part of All Souls' Day custom in the Andes. For a nice photograph of these *tanda wawas* or bread babies, see Bastien 1978:184.

15. The passage about the saqras follows immediately after her explanation of the ñakaq; both are described as negative representations of outsiders in local folklore, whose appearance can be explained by recent history (1988:110– 11). She does not directly elucidate the connection between ñakaqs—far more widely reported in the ethnographic literature—and the saqra, but I think I am following her lead in making an explicit connection between the two.

16. This translation, and all others followed by a 1978 citation, are by Frances Barraclough. In other cases I have retranslated the text myself.

17. These field notes were written by Harold Skalka, a student in the Colombia-Cornell-Harvard-Illinois Universities' Summer Field School, 1961; some of them make reference to earlier notes, including those by Humberto Ghersi. However, Florence Babb, who participated in the Cornell-Peru project as a student, tells me that Ghersi too was citing an earlier researcher, Norman Pava. (See Babb's own comments on Pava's notes in her master's thesis [Babb 1976], an important and overlooked work on Andean gender and the masculine biases of anthropological work on the Andes.) I can only conclude that a project culture of collaboration and unattributed borrowings makes it difficult to trace the origins of various observations made during the course of the project. The notes come from the Archives of the Cornell-Peru Project, Olin Library, Cornell University, and I use them with the kind permission of William Stein, to whom I am greatly indebted not only for the use of these notes, but for his sustained encouragement and support for my inquiries into the pishtaco, as well as for having written the introduction to *Hualcan* (1961) that first started my ruminations into the pishtaco's odd and unpleasant sexual habits. The notes reproduced here have been slightly edited for clarity. I am also very grateful to Florence for the clarification—and for introducing me to Bill Stein.

18. Stuart Rockefeller makes a similar observation about the need to preserve gender neutrality in translating kharisiri tales from Spanish to English (1998).

19. . . . entre los cuentistas de la masa campesina, se ha podido captar, que el Ñak'aq, tiene dos formas de presencia ante las víctimas, unas veces camina con una túnica, otras veces va a caballo, con pantalones de montar, bien elegante, reluciente, con capuchón blanco en la cabeza, asimismo el caballo bien ataviado . . . Cuando aparece la gente señalada, por el camino silencioso, estando cerca a unos 50 metros, el Ñak'aq resa una oración mágica, luego sopla un polvillo hipnotisante hacia la víctima y, al recibir éste el impacto, comienza a temblar de miedo, le salen de los ojos chispas de fuego, la cabeza comienza a crecer, luego automáticamente se dirige hacia el Ñak'aq. Llegando a su lado, so pone de rodillas y cae en un profundo sueño; de inmediato el Ñak'aq procede con unas palmaditas en las nalgas, luego inyecta una aguja que conecta con un pequeño aparato, que se cree que es el depósito de los cebos que extrae con mucha maestría. Y en cuanto ha concluido, reze otra oración, se despide con otra palmadita en la cabeza y de unos cinco minutos que se ha separado el Pistaco, la víctima resucita sin sentir síntomas de dolor, ni huellas en el cuerpo. Pero si alguna persona ha visto el deguello, morirá instanteamente, porque es mala suerte, y casa contrario, irremediablemente la víctima muere dentro de unos 15 a 20 días, sin saber la dolencia (1969:137).

20. Doña Satuca . . . cuenta muy graciosamente de . . . Sitticha y Jasikucha . . . al primero de ellos degollador de varones, especializado en muchachos, el segundo, degollador de mujeres; . . . Don Sitticha, excelente seguidor de Pistaco, ha aspirado con armaña vivir en la ciudad, donde sigue decapitando a los muchachos, . . . En cambio Don Jasikucha, monstruo, gordo, astuto, a la vez cobarde y tacaño, sigue degollando a las mujeres, especialmente a las indígenas, pese a que lo han descubierto en las provincias altas haciendo chacra con las humildes pastorcitas, con vestido de jerga, por la aparición de dos Pistaquitos, producto ilegal que por esta mala suerte abandona, luego se ha perfeccionado en la técnica de degollar de día, de noche, en la ciudad y en el campo; como fiera ambiciosa y hambrienta tiene víctimas conquistadas, bajo la capa de amor y amistad; en caunto ha extraido el cebo busca pretextos para exportar a las pobres mujeres lejos de la tierra donde mueren el el olvido (138).

21. 1961:11, quoted in Degler 1971:190.

22. Rowe et al. 1998:260 identifies men in ponchos from Azuay province as "cholo men" in traditional garb. However, this seems to me to be an instance of artificially pairing women and men together into a single ethnic category. Older rural men throughout the Andes wear ponchos, but not all rural women wear costumes similar to the distinctive "chola" clothing of rural Azuay.

23. From the extensive literature on this topic, see particularly Galeano's brilliant evocation (1985:49–50); Montrose 1993; Chabram-Dernesesian 1997:127; and Alarcón 1989, 1983.

24. I am very grateful to Robert Ellis for having introduced me to this book, for *his own insightful* writings about it (Ellis 1998) and for our conversations on this subject and many others, which have greatly increased my understanding

of the interconnections between mandatory heterosexuality and other forms of oppression.

25. For a discussion and definition of gamonalismo, see Poole 1988.

26. See, for example, Amado's *Shepherds of the Night,* especially pp. ix–11.

27. Nieto 1942, cited in de la Cadena 1996:126–27.

28. See, for example, C. Allen 1988:183–86; Isbell 1976:119.

29. Evidence is starting to accumulate about adults in the rural Andes who practice same-sex relations throughout life, whether by remaining single, through extramarital sex, or by setting up same-sex households in which one partner assumes the male, and one the female, role. To date, this information remains fragmentary and largely unpublished. An exception is Spedding n.d.*b* on sexual variation in the Yungas region; in a few years' time, it may be possible to generalize her findings to areas in the highlands.

30. See note 17, this chapter.

31. Baudelaire 1970. This example comes from Stephen Eisenman.

32. Chicana writers have had a lot to say on this subject recently; see, for example, Alarcón 1983, 1989.

33. Indeed, almost all the words for pishtaco originate in verbs—which then become transformed into different verbs, such as "pishtar." This flexible productivity is typical of Quechua and Aymara, and of colloquial Andean Spanish as well.

34. See Chabram-Dernersesian 1997.

35. This discussion owes an intellectual debt to the journal *Race Traitor* (see, for example, the selected articles in Ignatiev and Garvey 1996).

36. Women pishtacos appear to be more common in older stories, such as those collected by Arguedas.

37. See also Kulick 1998, 1997b.

38. This tale reflects common themes of running over pedestrians as a form of "hunting Indians" or "hunting cholos" in elite humor in the Andes.

Chapter 5

1. On reading race in Orientalist postcards, see Nochlin 1989.

2. I do not claim such an identity, having enjoyed white privilege my entire life. Nevertheless, the more time I have spent in indigenous communities, the odder the experience of viewing photographs of the highlands has become for me. An apparently timeless depiction of a "Salasaca youth at his loom" in a coffee-table book makes me do a double take: it's my old friend Rudi Masaquiza, some twenty years younger than he is today, grinning as he pretends to make a product that he really only sells. A series of Abya Yala books—not intended for tourists, but for academics—about bilingual education in Cotopaxi Province are illustrated with photographs of unnamed children and teachers whose faces (and names) I know well. Even a picture of a brooding and craggy mountain peak on a postcard causes me to laugh uneasily. The maker had taken what is for me a familiar sight, glimpsed on every bus ride to and from the parish, and made it into something pretentiously ominous

and—since the highway has been carefully cropped from the picture—apparently remote and inaccessible.

3. See chapter 3, note 23. The word *scopophilia,* which describes the pleasure of viewing, was coined by Laura Mulvey (1975).

4. "Eran así altos, gordos, eran gringos, gringos con barba"; "Los pishtacos son altos, blancos, . . . de ojos verdes" (Ansión and Sifuentes 1989:91).

5. Vergara Figueroa and Carrasco 1989:133; see also Gose 1994a:296 and Mayer 1994:153.

6. Salazar-Soler 1991. In a verbal commentary on an oral presentation of this paper, R. T. Zuidema suggests that the prominence of people described or portrayed as "black" in Andean ritual and myth need not refer to either Afro-Peruvians, Africans, or "Moors," as is usually assumed. Instead, their color may be related to mythic forms of blackness that have nothing to do with race, but rather with calendrical, astronomical, or other symbolism (Urbana, 2000). This is a salutary reminder of how easily our own obsessions can easily lead us astray in our interpretations.

7. See Weismantel and Eisenman 1998.

8. Gilman 1985; on cartes-de-visites, Poole 1997:107–41.

9. For a very educational demonstration of this point, see Annie Sprinkle's "Anatomy of a Pinup Photo," reproduced in Straayer 1993:160 and Sprinkle 1991.

10. See Rivière 1991:25 on this point, which leads him to draw a conclusion almost identical to Roediger's.

11. "a caballo, con pantalones de montar, bien elegante, reluciente, con capuchón blanco en la cabeza, asimismo el caballo bien ataviado" (1969:136).

12. Although Salazar-Soler was told of pishtacos on horseback in Huancavelica in 1980 (1991:10).

13. This aspect of pishtaco and sacaojos stories are reminiscent of rural white Americans' fears about the insignia of the United Nations, and the rumors about secret U.N. missions to the United States.

14. This violent policing of the racial restrictions on who can own cars sheds some light on the prevalence of jokes and stories told by whites about killing Indians with their cars. In the Andean republics, the private car is literally a vehicle for white privilege, hence its fascination as an actual lethal weapon that kills nonwhites.

15. There are noteworthy exceptions; in the South American literature, Dumont's *The Headman and I* (1978) especially stands out.

16. It is not my intention to belittle the democratic impulses of foreign aid workers and researchers; we have too often been targets for facile criticism. The willingness of North American and European researchers to sit in the dirt and eat with their hands, to live in small unheated homes without electricity, and to work with a hoe or a machete in the fields or spend hours in a smoky kitchen peeling potatoes has genuinely startled and moved many poor people throughout Latin America. But few foreigners have really forgone their per-

manent access to forms of economic and political privilege denied those whom they study, nor would anyone expect them to do so. Thus the discomfort that those same anthropologists evince at any mention of these obvious differences between themselves and the people among whom they have temporarily taken up residence causes understandable bemusement—or suspicion.

17. Abercrombie also notes that "One of the most oft-asked questions was the price of my hiking boots" (1998:66).

18. These comments are excerpted from a response to a draft of Orlove's paper, solicited by the author, and later circulated via e-mail.

19. A similar point about peasant and bourgeois bodies is eloquently made by John Berger in "The Suit and the Photograph" (1991).

20. In calling this subaltern vision of race "indigenous," and labeling various other visions of race as "white," I do not intend to reinscribe a biological determinism in which ideologies adhere to specific populations. In some places entire Andean communities of Quechua or Aymara-speakers have adopted the language of blood or of genes, naturalizing it into something of their own. Colloredo-Mansfeld finds race deployed as a class weapon within Imbabura: wealthy Indians can now deride poor ones as "dirty" and pride themselves on having become "clean"; their impoverished neighbors respond by expanding their critiques of racism to include these Quichua-speaking snobs.

   If European racisms operate within Indian communities, indigenous attitudes have migrated to the white Andes as well. In our own travels in the Andes, Stephen and I find that side by side with the ubiquitous, often flamboyant racists live many whites who have, to a greater or lesser degree, adopted indigenous ways of thinking about race unselfconsciously and seemingly without great personal or political difficulty.

21. Harrison accurately translates these lyrics as "Acting like that, he became a 'white.'" The word "purina," which literally means "to walk," carries the larger meaning of "to habitually act" or "to behave" in a particular way. The Quichua phrase thus conveys a specific physicality of racial socialization— walking in a certain kind of way, even perhaps having a certain kind of feet— within the more general notion of how one "acts." Other verbs of action, such as "to sit" or "to stand," similarly relate physical behavior to social identity, but in reference to domains other than the very public self-presentation emphasized by this reference to how one "walks."

22. . . . indígenas, porque el indio posee cebo seco, por alimentarse duramenta a base de chuño y kañiwa . . . , no así del miste, porque de él es líquido y de mala calidad (Manya 1969:136). Salazar-Soler was told the same thing in Julcani in 1980; she also learned that whites and Indians, because of these different constitutions, sicken from different illnesses (1991). The notion that Indian and white bodies are made of different kinds of fat is an old one: colonial witchcraft required making a doll out of llama fat mixed with cornmeal to ensorcell an Indian, while a white victim required pig fat and wheat flour (Arriaga 1968 [1621]:210–11, cited in Molinié Fioravanti 1991:82).

23. For an extended discussion of barley in Zumbagua, see Weismantel 1988.

24. This biological theory produces a kinship system based less in consanguinity than in cooking, feeding, and eating (see Weismantel 1995).

25. For a similar experience by a woman fieldworker in a very different setting, see Faithorn 1986:281.

26. See footnote 10 in the introduction.

27. Etymologically, the other names do too, but Spanish-speaking listeners may not always recognize these roots.

28. Arguedas 1953:215; also cited in Kapsoli 1991:76.

29. In other versions, the operation is said to leave no mark whatsoever; see, for example, Manya 1969:137 (quoted in previous chapter).

30. Membership in an Indian community or ethnic group is denoted by a different kind of sobriquet: mature Indian men and women are called "Tayta" and "Mama" ("Father" and "Mother"), even by whites who do not know them. Quichua-speakers use these titles routinely, as a matter of respect, especially when referring to someone in the third person; unlike white titles, these terms are used with the first name rather than the family name: "Mama Rosa"; "Tayta Alberto." In this, they resemble the archaic "Don," today used in jocular fashion to refer to skilled blue-collar workers like auto mechanics and drivers. (See the further discussion in chapter 6.)

    In Zumbagua, the stratification between whites and Indians was clearly demarcated by titles: Indians were inevitably called "Tayta So-and-So," "Mama So-and-So," while local whites were "Don" or "Señora." Once I realized this, I tested it by deliberately making mistakes, such as asking about a neighbor whom I referred to as "Señora Helena" instead of "Mama Helena." The response surprised me: rather than merely correcting me—which people did all the time, for my mistakes were numerous—my interlocutor never for a moment imagined that I could be talking about her neighbor. Although it should have been obvious by the context of my question that I was referring to a woman standing only a few hundred feet away from us, Berta looked at me in puzzlement and said, "Señora Helena? [referring to a white woman who once lived in town] Don't you remember that she moved to Pujilí years ago? She's never come back, and what would she be doing up here, anyway?"

31. "*Dicen mamay que ha sabido tener contrata con Electroperú dicen como será*" (They say the pishtacos usually have a contract with Electroperú [the state-owned power company], yes, that's what they say) (1991:10).

32. The situation was complicated by the fact that the word "hospital," which appeared on his I.D., was one of the few English words comprehensible to the men, who deduced from it that he was an employee of an American hospital that had sent him to obtain the human products he was extracting from local people.

33. Oliver-Smith 1969:368; Ansión and Sifuentes 1969:99; Kapsoli 1991:71.

34. Dicen que son los mismos sinchis que de noche salen y matan a los que andan de noche para sacar su grasa cortándole su cuello y su barriga. . . . Dicen que el pistaco es también del gobierno. Con papel del gobierno, matando gente anda, por eso el gobierno no le dice nada, aunque mate a la gente. . . . Dicen

que son gringos, no hablan ni castellano, dicen (Vergara Figueroa and Carrasco 1989:129−30).

35. Morote Best 1951−52:79−80; Ansión and Sifuentes 1989:81.

36. Many authors have written of the significance of body fat in Andean cosmology and religion. See, for example, Bastien 1978; Orta 1997; Abercrombie 1998.

37. The quote is from Van den Berghe and Primov 1977:127, but many other authors mention the same kind of usage.

38. Fifty years earlier, Elsie Clews Parsons, too, had returned to an Andean community to find a friend and informant wasting away.

> On my return to Peguche in 1941, I found Rosita lying bundled up in bed, weaker than just after the birth of the baby eighteen months before. She was listless. . . . The expression of her face was quite altered; . . . I might not have recognized her. For a year, she said, she had been sick, on and off.

Parsons believed her to be severely anemic; certainly Rosita had lost almost all of her body fat, and like Juanchu, she never regained it—or her health. Parsons makes no specific mention of Rosita's anxieties about losing fat, but refers slightingly to the latter's "superstitions" about her illness (1945:166−69).

39. On the southern Andean sacrifice complex, see, for example, Abercrombie 1998; Gose 1994b; O. Harris 1995, 1982.

40. See, for example, the very interesting discussion by Olivia Harris of "The Sources and Meanings of Money" among the Bolivian Laymi (1995).

41. On loans and race in the United States, see Brett Williams 1994.

42. "el restaurant es de lujo y de mucha fama, lo que indica el valor y la exquisitez de esa carne, pero se cobra muy barato, hecho que muestra lo poco que vale la vida de esos niños" (1989:76).

43. See especially Kapsoli 1991, who summarizes the findings of Peruvian folklorists Arguedas, Pedro Monge, and Sergio Quijano, many of which differ in quite a few details from other stories.

44. Oliver-Smith 1969:366; many other authors describe the sale of human fat to lubricate machinery, including Ansión and Sifuentes 1989:74; Gose 1994a:297; and Kapsoli 1991:71.

45. This element crops up in pishtaco stories collected by Vergara Figueroa and Carrasco (1989:129−34) and Sifuentes (1989:151−54).

46. Mayer 1994; Rojas Rimachi 1989; Sifuentes 1989; Zapata 1989.

47. Shades of the pishtaco! But the Body Shop claims to be returning profits to the people, although it was embarrassed by a lawsuit brought by an Amazonian elder, whose photograph had been used to promote Body Shop products without his permission.

Chapter 6

1. In a fascinating passage, Peter Gose relates the pishtaco's desire to castrate to the process of mining, which Andeans describe as emptying the mountain's

testicles; this observation seems especially apt in relation to Salazar-Soler's research on the pishtaco, conducted among miners (Gose 1994b: 303).

2. This interpretation in no way contradicts Gose's own, which involves the bodily decomposition of those condemned as condenadus for having committed incest.

3. I heard this story at the Estanbul, sitting on the rooftop at night with other Americans.

4. In the 1980s, the area where she had done fieldwork became a center of violent conflict between the Peruvian army and Sendero Luminoso, sending thousands of refugees into Lima.

5. En Villa María, unos gringos vestidos de oscuro llegaron en una camioneta; estuvieron dando vueltas y despúes se robaron a un niño, lo subieron a la camioneta; y en su interior le sacaron los ojos; dentro del carro tenían una serie de instrumentos y aparatos que servían para hacer esas extracciones. Al niño robado, le sacaraon los ojos y los riñones y apareció muerto en una calle de Villa María con 50 mil intis guardados dentro de su ropa (Sifuentes 1989: 151–52). Other descriptions of the sacaojos can be found in Zapata 1989 and Rojas Rimachi 1989.

6. Mi prima dice que roban niños para quitarles los ojos . . . después los devuelven vivos, pero sin ojos. Los que roban son extranjeros y se supone que han estudiado medicina. La mayoría de los niños son de cuatro a catorce años, de familias numerosas pero pobres, de escasos recursos económicos. Al hijo del vecino de mi prima lo dejaron sentado en la puerta de su casa con 50 dólares en el bolsillo. Los que roban dicen que forman parte de una mafia internacional que trafica con órganos; andan bien vestidos; se movilizan en carros lujosos, en Mercedes Benz (Sifuentes 1989: 152–53).

7. Racism is an important theme in Lancaster's book, but he does not specifically link it to sexual imagery in his analysis.

8. Indigenous South Americans, too, are far too familiar with involuntary adoptions, in which well-to-do whites simply take Indian children to raise as servants. During my first summer in the Andes, I stayed with Rudi Masaquiza and Pancha Jerez in Salasaca, who were acting as foster parents to several young people. One young woman never spoke. Pancha told me that they had rescued her from a white couple who had stolen her; she had been living with them for six months, but she was still too traumatized by the experience to tell them her name or where her family lived.

9. In 1937, for example, the Puerto Rican legislature created a "Eugenics Board" to oversee the sterilization of women deemed "unfit" for reproduction. This legislation was an outgrowth of earlier efforts by private American capitalists such as the heir of Procter and Gamble, who found the island a convenient place to exercise an enthusiasm for eugenic experimentation (Pérez 2000; see also López 1993, 1987; and Ramírez de Arellano and Seipp 1983).

10. See Clark 1999 for an African context in which this equation is entirely absent.

11. Indigenous societies are not without forms of gender inequality, notably in

the exclusion of women from male political spheres; however, the rationales for these practices do not connect power differentials to bodily and sexual differences in the same fashion as in Euro-American sexual ideologies. Absent any sustained research into masculine sexual ideologies among indigenous men, however, it is difficult to go far in this analysis.

12. Spedding observes that metaphors of butchering are stronger in Peruvian pishtaco stories than in Bolivian kharisiri tales. A systematic analysis of regional and temporal variation in these tales has yet to be done.

13. See, for example, Orta 1997; Abercrombie 1998; and Bastien 1978.

14. In some stories, this powder is made from ground-up bones rather than dried fetuses (for example, Salazar-Soler 1991:10).

15. Each child was attended by an anxious man, also in costume and blackface, who ran alongside to make sure the kids came to no harm during the riotous festivities.

16. I am grateful to Aaron Bielenberg for his assistance in providing me with videos of the Mama Negra parade.

17. Not all forms of drag perform in this misogynist and sexually conservative fashion; indeed, some analysts would argue that all homosexual performances of cross-dressing are by definition subversive. For an excellent overview of this debate, and of the theoretical literature about drag in general, see Carol-Anne Tyler 1991, 1998.

18. This material is taken from a rich interpretive article by Abercrombie, which appeared together with insightful commentary from Bolivian and other scholars; I am unable to do justice to either the article or its commentaries here.

19. Albro 2000:22; see also Abercrombie 1992 on the breasts of the *Chaskinawi*.

20. Quoted in de la Cadena 1996:126. A huayno is a traditional folk song, sung by Indian women.

21. Baxley 1865:142–43, quoted in Poole 1997:96.

22. The kinship strategy of these women resembles those of poor women of color throughout the Americas, which have variously been called "matrifocality" or "Othermothering." When Sofía Velasquez refers to her friend Yola's plural mothers, and her "second mothers," too, her speech reflects these social practices, in which women depend upon one another's assistance in raising their children.

23. Spedding n.d.*a*:3; see also Orta 1997:14–15. Spedding goes on to say that since kharisiris are especially associated with the altiplano town of Achacachi and its surrounding rural areas, merchants selling products from that region are immediately suspect, as are any highland merchants who come to the low-lying Yungas region to sell (Spedding n.d.*a*:2).

24. Naranjo, Benitez, and Dueña report that she doused the faces of spectators with "a mixture of water and milk," while the "brujos" or shamans sprayed (spit) trago, like shamans do during healing ceremonies. These observations were made during the first, Church-sponsored day of the festival. My notes indicate trago, jokingly called "Mother's milk"; whether members of the crowd humorously misled me, or whether the Mama Negra used milk the

first day and trago the second, there is a double entendre of milk/trago. Andean shamanic and festival culture is full of such double meanings: between trago and holy water, cigarette smoke and breath, holy water and urine.

25. The best discussion of the strict symbolic gendering and very flexible actual behavior in indigenous Andean culture is Allen 1988 : 67–86.

26. Drinking stories as rites of passage are something of a trope in Andean ethnography; see, for example, Isbell 1978.

27. For all the declarations in the literature about the chola's erotic appetites, no one—myself included—has studied the actual sexual behavior and attitudes of market women, chichería employees, or any of the other kinds of women who are described as "cholas." Rob Albro attended folkloric events staged in Bolivian chicherías by populist political parties, at which women dressed as cholas were encouraged to perform lewdly: singing dirty songs, telling dirty jokes, dancing lasciviously, and swinging on a high swing designed to let the crowd look up their skirts (Albro 2000 : 22–24). He has much to say about the men present, but he does not seem to have ever spoken to any of the women who attended wearing polleras and engaged in all the sex play that made the event such a success in male eyes. He can only speculate about their motivations, or even about whether they were, in fact, market vendors as he was told.

   His reticence—or theirs—is far from unique. Sofía Velasquez is elusive in her descriptions of her brief sexual encounters with men, even the man who fathered her child. And in her many descriptions of intimate friendships between women, she never hints at sexual behavior. Heloisa and Helena never engaged in physical intimacies in my presence—in fact, they were far less likely to touch each other than schoolgirls, who hold hands and embrace one another constantly, or farm girls, who liked, when they sat with me, not only to hold my hand or put their arms around my waist, but also to touch my nipples and stroke the inside of my thigh. But their rectitude was exactly like that of the married couples around them and did little to quash popular opinion that they were lovers. In earlier years I was too intimidated by Heloisa to ask intimate questions, and in recent years she has deflected any discussion of Helena, which I think makes her unhappy, onto other topics.

28. My thanks to Joyce Kohl for noticing this woman and pointing her out to me.

29. I have been startled and dismayed by classroom discussions with students on this topic; middle-class white women, especially, often described strategies for curbing their appetites before going out on dinner dates—a behavior that many of their minority and working-class female classmates found incomprehensible. These "normal" behaviors made the painful admissions by anorexic students about their inability to eat in the company of other people more comprehensible.

30. Weismantel 1997b; Cerny et al. 1996; there is also a rich literature on Corpus Christi rituals in the Andes more generally, especially in colonial Peru (see, for example, Dean 1999).

31. Salchipapas are also less countrified than boiled fava beans or lupins, or toasted corn—snacks that people make at home, and which don't require expensive oils. And while other fried foods, such as sweet fried bread dough or

Latacunga's famous llapingachos, a potato-and-cheese pancake, are prepared by women on enormous skillets over charcoal fires, salchipapas are sold from specially manufactured deep-fryers mounted on mobile carts. Unlike other foods, too, these are often sold by men: Sofía thus presents herself and her daughter as women who are regularly served by members of the male sex.

32. Seligmann 1993 : 194.

33. Las mujeres mayores, que eran también las mas gordas, como las dueñas de las chicherías, formaron una especie de primera fila, a la izquierda y derecha de la cabecilla (139).

34. The translation is by Frances Horning Barraclough (1978 : 91). Here is the original: "La mujer que ocupaba el arco de la torre era una chichera famosa; su cuerpo gordo cerraba completamente el arco; su monillo azul, adornado de cintas de terciopelo y de piñes, era de seda, y relucía. La cinta del sombrero brillaba, aún en la sombra; era de raso y parecía en alto relieve sobre el albayalde blanquísimo del sombrero recién pintado. La mujer tenía cara ancha, toda picada de viruelas; su busto gordo, levantado como una trinchera, se movía; era visible, desde leojos, su ritmo de fuelle, a causa de la respiración honda."

35. From the translation by Barraclough (1978 : 91). Here is the original: "una gran multitud de mujeres vociferaba, extiéndose desde el atrio de la iglesia hasta más allá del centro de la plaza. Todas llevaban mantas de Castilla y sombreros de paja. . . . No se veían hombres. Con los pies descalzos o con los botines altos, de taco, las mujeres aplastaban las flores endebles del 'parque,' tronchaban los rosales, los geranios, las plantas de lirios y violetas. Gritaban todas en quechua" (1958 : 137).

36. Pichincha, the wealthiest highland province (its capital, Quito, is also the nation's capital), is directly to the north of Cotopaxi (its capital is Latacunga), one of the poorest provinces.

37. Mayer 1971.

38. Unlike the United States, Andean nations make many bills in small denominations—the equivalent of a penny, a nickel, or a dime.

39. Indeed, her costume is based upon the Brazilian market vendors from the Afro-Brazilian region of Bahia.

40. The information on these figures is from Naranjo et al. 1986. On the yumbo dancer, see Salomon 1981b.

41. These words are almost verbatim from my field notes, slightly edited for grammar and coherence.

42. The notion that these two substances are the same is widespread in tribal societies and has been repeatedly documented in the anthropological literature, especially from Oceania.

43. For an overview of the literature on third sexes and third genders, see Herdt 1994; for a critique of the notion, see Kulick 1996 : 226–30.

44. See chapter 3, note 37.

45. See, for example, Paredez Ortega 1980. These debates are mentioned in Naranjo et al. 1986 (120–21).

Afterword

1. According to the article, Coe originally wrote and produced several albums of "X-rated" songs; today, as he has gained a more mainstream audience, he would like to distance himself from these earlier efforts and their blatant racism and misogyny. But circulated nationally as bootleg tapes, these songs have taken on a life of their own as fraternity party songs—and Coe continues to profit from their sales through his Web site (Strauss 2000).

2. On the Kaulong, see Goodale 1980:129–31; other writers on Melanesia have observed similar ritual observances designed to protect men from women's genital fluids. (See, for example, Herdt 1981, in which the excellent analysis of male self-protective ritual is often overlooked in favor of the attention-getting descriptions of fellatio.) On the Freikorps, see Klaus Theweleit 1987. He analyzed a series of texts—novels, letters, and autobiographical writings—by the men of this right-wing volunteer army, which fought communists in Germany between the World Wars. The result is a brilliant study of misogyny, which begins with the author's reminiscences about his own father, "a good man and a pretty good fascist." Like Ellis, in this passage Theweleit finds that men, too, suffer within misogynist families because of the domestic violence meted out by fathers against sons. He also connects this kind of violence—and misogyny more generally—to larger political ideologies, asserting, "The blows [my father] brutally lavished as a matter of course, and for my own good, were the first lessons I would one day come to recognize as lessons in fascism" (1987:xx).

3. See chapter 2, note 21.

4. Freud's essay on the uncanny is an exploration of estrangement, as is Durkheim's concept of anomie (1951).

5. See chapter 2, note 21.

6. I would be remiss to suggest that no college students react with political insights about this particular dilemma. The fast-food enthusiasts who predominated in that particular seminar represent only one subculture among university students; I also know vegetarians and animal rights and living-wage activists, as well as young women and men struggling with anorexia and bulimia. It is far beyond the scope of this book to unravel the interconnections between these various positions, but all express different kinds of abhorrence in the face of an onslaught of advertising exhorting unceasing consumption. Some of these responses are thoughtful and farsighted, others not; most are somewhere in between.

7. In his essay on the pishtaco, Michael Taussig offers a surprising reading of these tales, which he sees as able to erase white guilt. Pishtacos are our "fetishized antiselves"; when we retell their story, we convert their ability to suck fat into a "power slippery and magical that can exorcise from the colonizing self the evil of having more" (1987:240–41). This vision of the pishtaco performing metaphysical liposuction reveals a white subjectivity at work. Like my students, he appropriates others' labor—in this case, that of Andean storytellers—for his own use, alienating it from the political context of its production. Furthermore, Taussig concludes that "We are all ñakaqs." But there are two characters in the pishtaco story, not one. In ignoring the Indian

victim, he falls prey like Julio Cortázar to a narcissistic fascination with his own guilt—even as he attempts to dissipate it.

These racial politics bear a curious relationship to those found in his earlier book, *The Devil and Commodity Fetishism* (1980). My own analysis of the pishtaco owes a great deal to that book, in which Taussig argued that the myths, rituals, and symbols produced by nonwhite South Americans constituted a critique of capitalism. What no longer rings true, however, is his representation of the black and Indian peoples of South America as purely and wholly anticapitalist in their thoughts and actions. Today, when many an Indian's greedy profit-taking has caused his neighbors to accuse him as a kharisiri, this vision is hard to sustain. But even when the book was written, the Bolivian tin miners and Colombian farmers who are its subjects were involved in the cash economy—indeed, their critique of capitalist exchange displays an intimate knowledge of its workings. Taussig later abandoned his belief in the native's innocence, but only to embrace its mirror image: a postmodern cynicism in which everyone is equally culpable. Here, I have argued for a more dialectical understanding of the interplay of capitalist and anticapitalist moralities in the Andes. Every member of Andean society inherits the dream of indigenous reciprocity and the reality of capitalist exchange; and each person, in each of the many exchanges in which they take part, positions themselves in a variety of ways.

Works Cited

Abercrombie, Thomas. 1998. *Pathways of Memory and Power: Ethnography and History among an Andean People*. Madison: University of Wisconsin Press.

———. 1996. "Q'aqchas and la plebe in 'rebellion': Carnival vs. Lent in Eighteenth-Century Potosí." *Journal of Latin American Anthropology* 2(1):62–111.

———. 1992. "La fiesta del carnaval postcolonial en Oruro: clase, etnicidad y nacionalismo en la danza folklórica." *Revista Andina* 10(2):279–352.

Ackerman, Raquel. 1991. "Clothes and Identity in the Central Andes: Province of Abancay, Peru." Pp. 231–260 in *Textile Traditions of Mesoamerica and the Andes: An Anthology*. Austin: University of Texas Press. Blum Schevill, Margot, Janet Catherine Berlo, and Edward B. Dwyer, eds.

Adams, Abigail E. 1998. "Gringas, Ghouls and Guatemala: 1994 Attacks on North American Women Accused of Body Organ Trafficking." *Journal of Latin American Anthropology* 4(1):112–133.

Alarcón, Norma. 1989. "Traddutora, Traditora: A Paradigmatic Figure of Chicana Feminism." *Cultural Critique* 13:57–8.

———. 1983. "Chicana's Feminist Literature: A Re-vision through Malintzin/or Malintzin: Putting Flesh Back on the Object." Pp. 182–190 in *This Bridge Called My Back*. Cherrie Moraga and Gloria Anzaldúa, eds. New York: Kitchen Table Press.

Alberti, Giorgio, and Enrique Mayer, editors. 1974. *Reciprocidad e intercambio en los Andes peruanos*. Lima: Instituto de Estudios Peruanos.

Albro, Robert. 2000. "The Populist Chola: Cultural Mediation and the Political Imagination in Quillacollo, Bolivia." *Journal of Latin American Anthropology* 5(2):30–88.

———. 1997. "Engendering the Chola: Populist Exchange in Quillacollo, Bolivia." Paper presented at the Annual Meetings of the Latin American Studies Association, Guadalajara, Mexico.

Allen, Catherine J. 1988. *The Hold Life Has: Coca and Cultural Identity in an Andean Community*. Washington: Smithsonian Institution Press.

———. 1978. "Coca, Chicha, and Trago: Private and Communal Rituals in a Quechua Community." Ph.D. dissertation, University of Illinois.

Allen, Paula Gunn. 1986. *The Sacred Hoop: Recovering the Feminine in American Indian Traditions*. Boston: Beacon Press.

Allen, Theodore W. 1996. *The Invention of the White Race*. Volume 2, *The Origin of Racial Oppression in Anglo-America*. London: Verso.

———. 1994. *The Invention of the White Race*. Volume 1: *Racial Oppression and Social Control*. London: Verso.

Almeida, Ileana, et al. 1992. *Indios: una reflexión sobre el levantamiento indígena de 1990*. Quito: ILDIS and Abya-Yala.

Amado, Jorge. 1966. *Shepherds of the Night*. Translated from the Portuguese by Harriet de Onís. New York: Avon Books.

Ansión, Juan, ed. 1989. *Pishtacos: de verdugos a sacaojos*. Lima: Tarea, Asociación de Publicaciones Educativas.

Ansión, Juan, and Eudosio Sifuentes. 1989. "La imagen popular de la violencia, a través de los relatos de degolladores." Pp. 61–108 in *Pishtacos: de verdugos a sacaojos*. Juan Ansión, ed. Lima: Tarea, Asociación de Publicaciones Educativas.

Anzaldúa, Gloria. 1987. *Borderlands/La Frontera: The New Mestiza*. San Francisco: Aunt Lute Books.

Arguedas, José María. 1985. "The Novel and the Problem of Literary Expression in Peru." Introductory essay in *Yawar Fiesta*. Translated by Frances Horning Barraclough. Austin: University of Texas Press. Pp. xii–xxi.

———. 1978. *Deep Rivers*. Translated by Frances Horning Barraclough. Austin: University of Texas Press.

———. 1958. *Los ríos profundos*. Buenos Aires: Editorial Losada.

———. 1953. "Cuentos mágico-realistas y canciones de fiesta tradicional del valle del Mantaro, provincias de Jauja y Concepción." *Folklore Americano* 1(1):101–293.

Arizpe, Lourdes. 1990. "Democracy for a Small Two-Gender Planet." Foreword to *Women and Social Change in Latin America*. London: Zed Books. Pp. xiv–xix.

Arnold, Denise Y. 1997a. "Introducción." Pp. 13–52 in *Más allá del silencio: las fronteras de género en los Andes*. La Paz: CIASE/ILCA. Denise Y. Arnold, editor.

———, editor. 1997b. *Más allá del silencio: las fronteras de género en los Andes*. La Paz: CIASE/ILCA.

Athey, Stephanie, and Daniel Cooper Alarcón. 1993. "Oroonoko's Gendered Economies of Honor/Horror: Reframing Colonial Discourse Studies in the Americas." *American Literature* 65(3):415–443.

Babb, Florence. 1996. "Market/places as Gendered Spaces: Market/women's Studies Over Two Decades." Unpublished ms.

———. 1989. *Between Field and Cooking Pot: The Political Economy of Marketwomen in Peru*. Austin: University of Texas Press.

———. 1976. *The Development of Sexual Inequality in Vicos, Peru*. Buffalo: State University of New York. Special Studies Series, Council on International Studies.

Balibar, Etienne. 1991. "Is There a 'Neo-Racism'?" Pp. 17–28 in *Race, Nation, Class: Ambiguous Identities*. Chris Turner, trans. London: Verso.

Barthes, Roland. 1973 [1957]. "Myth Today." Pp. 109–159 in *Mythologies*. London: Granada Publishing.

Basso, Keith H. 1979. *Portraits of "the Whiteman": Linguistic Play and Cultural Symbols among the Western Apache*. Cambridge University Press.

Bastien, Joseph W. 1978. *Mountain of the Condor: Metaphor and Ritual in an Andean Ayllu*. St. Paul: West Publishing Co.

Baudelaire, Charles. 1970. *Paris Spleen*. Translated by Louise Varese. New York: New Directions.

Baxley, H. Willis. 1865. *What I Saw on the West Coast of South and North America and at the Hawaiian Islands*. New York: D. Appleton and Co.

Bayly, Jaime. 1994. *No se lo digas a nadie*. Barcelona: Seix Barral.

Behar, Ruth. 1993. *Translated Woman: Crossing the Border with Esperanza's Story*. Boston: Beacon Press.

Belote, Linda. 1978. "Prejudice and Pride: Indian-White Relations in Saraguro, Ecuador." Ph.D. dissertation, University of Illinois, Urbana-Champaign.

Berger, John. 1980. "The Suit and the Photograph." Pp. 31–40 in *About Looking*. New York: Vintage.

Berlo, Janet Catherine. 1991. "Beyond Bricolage: Women and Aesthetic Strategies in Latin American Textiles." Pp. 437–479 in *Textile Traditions of Mesoamerica and the Andes: An Anthology*. Blum Schevill, Margot, Janet Catherine Berlo, and Edward B. Dwyer, eds. Austin: University of Texas Press.

Bielenberg, Aaron. 1998. "Painting Tourists: Indigenous Art and Tourism in the Ecuadorian Andes." Video.

Blackwood, Evelyn. 1984. "Sexuality and Gender in Certain Native American Tribes: The Case of Cross-Gender Females." *Signs: Journal of Women in Culture and Society* 10:1–42.

Blanco, Hugo. 1972. *Land or Death: The Peasant Struggle in Peru*. New York: Pathfinder Press.

Blumberg, Rae Lesser, and Dale Colyer. "Social Institutions, Gender and Rural Living Conditions." Pp. 247–266 in *Agriculture and Economic Survival: The Role of Agriculture in Ecuador's Development*. Morris D. Whitaker and Dale Colyer, eds. Boulder: Westview Press.

Blum Schevill, Margot, Janet Catherine Berlo, and Edward B. Dwyer, eds. 1990. *Textile Traditions of Mesoamerica and the Andes: An Anthology*. Austin: University of Texas Press.

Blunt, Alison, and Gillian Rose, eds. 1994. *Writing Women and Space: Colonial and Postcolonial Geographies*. New York: The Guilford Press.

Bolton, Ralph, and Enrique Mayer, eds. 1977. *Andean Kinship and Marriage*. Washington, D.C.: American Anthropological Association. Special Publication Number 7.

Bourdieu, Pierre. 1979. *Outline of a Theory of Practice*. Richard Nice, trans. Cambridge: Cambridge University Press.

Bourke, L. Nicole. 1997. "Making Space: Social Change, Identity and the Creation of Boundaries in the Central Ecuadorian Andes." *Bulletin of Latin American Research* 16(2):153–167.

Boyarin, Daniel. 1997. *Unheroic Conduct: The Rise of Heterosexuality and the Invention of the Jewish Man*. Berkeley: University of California Press.

Brecht, Bertolt. 1989–98. *Grosse kommentierte Berliner und Frankfurter Ausgabe*. Werner Hecht, Jan Kopf, Werner Mittenzwei and Klaus-Detlef Müller, eds. Gerlin: Aufbau/Suhrkamp.

———. 1966. *Mother Courage and Her Children: A Chronicle of the Thirty Years' War*. English version by Eric Bentley. New York: Grove Weidenfeld.

————. 1963. *Brecht on Theater: The Development of an Aesthetic.* John Willet, editor and translator. New York: Hill and Wang.

Bromley, Ray. 1981. "Market Center and Market Place in Highland Ecuador: A Study of Organization, Regulation, and Ethnic Discrimination." Pp. 233–259 in *Cultural Transformations and Ethnicity in Modern Ecuador.* Norman E. Whitten, Jr., editor. Urbana: University of Illinois Press.

Brownrigg, Leslie Ann. 1972. "The 'Nobles' of Cuenca: The Agrarian Elite of Southern Ecuador." Ph.D. dissertation, Columbia University.

Brush, Stephen B. 1977. *Mountain, Field and Family: The Economy and Human Ecology of an Andean Valley.* Philadelphia: University of Pennsylvania Press.

Buechler, Hans, and Judith-Maria Buechler. 1996. *The World of Sofía Velasquez: The Autobiography of a Bolivian Market Vendor.* New York: Columbia University Press.

Bunster, Ximena, and Elsa M. Chaney. 1985. *Sellers & Servants: Working Women in Lima, Peru.* New York: Praeger.

Butler, Judith. 1993. *Bodies That Matter: On the Discursive Limits of "Sex."* New York: Routledge.

————. 1990. *Gender Trouble: Feminism and the Subversion of Identity.* New York: Routledge.

Casagrande, Joseph B. 1980. "Strategies for Survival: The Indians of Highland Ecuador." Pp. 260–277 in *Cultural Transformations and Ethnicity in Modern Ecuador,* Norman E. Whitten, Jr., ed. Urbana: University of Illinois Press.

————. 1977. "Looms of Otavalo." *Natural History* 86(8):48–59.

Castle, Terry. *The Female Thermometer: Eighteenth-Century Culture and the Invention of the Uncanny.* Oxford: Oxford University Press.

Catlin, George. 1867. *O-kee-pa: A Religious Ceremony; and Other Customs of the Mandans.* London, Trübner and Co.

Cazamajor D'Artois, Philippe. 1988. "La red de mercados y ferias de Quito." Pp. 175–185 in *Nuevas investigaciones antropólogicas ecuatorianas,* Lauris McKee and Silvia Argüello, eds. Quito: Abya-Yala Press.

Cerny, Charlene, Suzanne Seriff, and John Bigelow Taylor. 1996. *Recycled Re-Seen: Folk Art from the Global Scrap Heap.* New York: Harry N. Abrams.

Cervone, Emma. 1998. "The Return of Atahualpa: Ritual, Power and Justice in the Ecuadorian Andes." Lecture, Latin American Studies, University of Illinois at Chicago, September 21.

————. 1997. "Los desafíos de la etnicidad: las luchas del movimiento indígena en la modernidad." *Journal of Latin American Anthropology* 4(1):46–73.

Chabram-Dernersesian, Angie. 1997. "On the Social Construction of Whiteness within Selected Chicana/o Discourses." Pp. 107–164 in *Displacing Whiteness: Essays in Social and Cultural Criticism.* Ruth Frankenberg, ed. Durham: University of North Carolina Press.

Chambi, Martín. 1993. *Martín Chambi: Photographs, 1920–1950.* Introductions by Edward Ranney and Públio López Mondéjar. Translation from the Spanish by Margaret Sayers Peden. Washington: Smithsonian Institution Press.

Chiñas, Beverley Newbold. 1989. *The Isthmus Zapotec: A Matrifocal Culture of Mexico.* Second edition. Forth Worth: Harcourt Brace Jovanovich College Publishers.

Clark, Gracia. 1999. "Mothering, Work, and Gender in Urban Asante Ideology and Practice." *American Anthropologist* 101(4):717–729.

———. 1993. *Onions Are My Husband: Survival and Accumulation by West African Market Women*. Chicago: University of Chicago Press.

———. 1988. *Traders vs. the State*. Boulder: Westview Press.

Clifford, James. 1992. "Traveling Cultures." Pp. 96–111 in *Cultural Studies*, edited by Lawrence Grossberg, Cary Nelson, and Paula Treichler. New York: Routledge.

Clifford, James, and George Marcus, eds. 1986. *Writing Culture: The Poetics and Politics of Ethnography*. Berkeley: University of California Press.

Colloredo-Mansfeld, Rudi. 1998. " 'Dirty Indians,' Radical Indígenas, and the Political Economy of Social Difference in Modern Ecuador." *Bulletin of Latin American Research* 17(2):185–206.

Collier, John, Jr., and Aníbal Buitrón. 1949. *The Awakening Valley*. Chicago: University of Chicago Press.

Condori Mamani, Gregorio, and Asunta Quispe Huamán. 1996. *Andean Lives: Gregorio Condori Mamani and Asunta Quispe Huamán*. Ricardo Valderrama Fernández and Carmen Escalante Gutiérrez, original editors; Paul H. Gelles and Gabriela Martínez Escobar, trans.

———. 1977. *Gregorio Condori Mamani: Autobiografía*. Ricardo Valderrama Fernández and Carmen Escalante Gutiérrez, editors and translators. Cuzco: Centro de Estudios Rurales Andinos "Bartolomé de las Casas."

Cook, Scott, and Martin Diskin, eds. 1976. *Markets in Oaxaca*. Austin: University of Texas Press.

Cordero Palacios, Alfonso. 1985. *Lexico de vulgarismos Azuayos*. Cuenca: Casa de la Cultura.

Cornejo, Marcela. 1997. "The Chicha in Lima." *Abya Yala News* 10(3):14–16.

Cornejo Polar, Antonio. 1995. "Condición migrante y representatividad social: el caso de Arguedas." Pp. 3–14 in *Amor y fuego: José María Arguedas 25 años despues*. Lima: Centro de Estudios para la Promoción y el Desarrollo.

Costales, Alfredo, and Piedad de Costales. 1976. *Zumbagua-guangaje: Estudio socio-ecónomico*. Quito: Instituto Ecuatoriano de Antropología y Sociología.

Crandon-Malamud, Libbet. 1991. *From the Fat of Our Souls: Social Change, Political Process, and Medical Pluralism in Bolivia*. Berkeley: University of California Press.

Cuvi, Pablo. 1988. *In the Eyes of My People: Stories and Photos of Journeys through Ecuador*. Quito: Dinediciones Grijalbo.

Dean, Carolyn. 1999. *Inka Bodies and the Body of Christ: Corpus Christi in Colonial Cuzco, Peru*. Durham: Duke University Press.

Deere, Carmen Diana. 1976. "Rural Women's Subsistence Production in the Capitalist Periphery." *Review of Radical Political Economics* 8(1):9–17.

Degler, Carl N. 1971. *Neither Black nor White: Slavery and Race Relations in Brazil and the United States*. New York: Macmillan.

de Janvry, Alain. 1981. *The Agrarian Question and Reformism in Latin America*. Baltimore: Johns Hopkins Press.

Denich, Better S. 1974. "Sex and Power in the Balkans." Pp. 243–262 in *Women, Culture, and Society*. Michelle Z. Rosaldo and Louise Lamphere, eds. Stanford: Stanford University Press.

de la Cadena, Marisol. 2000. *Indigenous Mestizos: The Politics of Race and Culture in Cuzco, Peru 1919–1991*. Durham: Duke University Press.

————. 1998. "Silent Racism and Intellectual Superiority in Peru." *Bulletin of Latin American Research* 17(2):143–164.

————. 1996. "The Political Tensions of Representations and Misrepresentations: Intellectuals and Mestizas in Cuzco (1919–1990)." *Journal of Latin American Anthropology* 2(1):112–147.

————. 1995. "'Women Are More Indian': Ethnicity and Gender in a Community Near Cuzco." Pp. 328–348 in *Ethnicity, Markets, and Migration in the Andes: At the Crossroads of History and Anthropology*. Brooke Larson and Olivia Harris, editors. With Enrique Tandeter. Durham: Duke University Press.

————. 1991. "Las mujeres son mas indias": etnicidad y género en una comunidad del Cusco." *Revista Andina* 9(1):7–29.

de la Torre, Carlos. 1998. "Racismo y vida cotidiana." *Ecuador Debate* 38:72–87.

di Leonardo, Micaela. 1998. *Exotics at Home: Anthropologies, Others, American Modernity*. Chicago: Unversity of Chicago Press.

Disraeli, B. 1927 [1847]. *Tancred, or the New Crusade*. London: Peter Davis.

Doughty, Paul L., with the collaboration of Mary F. Doughty. 1968. *Huaylas; an Andean District in Search of Progress*. Ithaca: Cornell University Press.

Douglas, Mary. 1966. *Purity and Danger: An Analysis of the Concepts of Pollution and Taboo*. London: Routledge and Kegan Paul.

Dumont, Jean-Paul. 1978. *The Headman and I: Ambiguity and Ambivalence in the Fieldworking Experience*. Austin: University of Texas Press.

Durkheim, Emile. 1951. *Suicide, A Study in Sociology*. Translated by John A. Spaulding and George Simpson. Edited by George Simpson. Glencoe, Ill.: Free Press.

Earls, John, and Irene Silverblatt. 1978. "La realidad física y social en la cosmología andina." *Actes du XLIIe Congrès Intenational des Américanistes* (Paris) 4: 299–325.

Ellis, Robert. 1998. "The Inscription of Masculinity and Whiteness in the Autobiography of Mario Vargas Llosa." *Bulletin of Latin American Research* 17(2): 223–236.

Enloe, Cynthia H. 1989. *Bananas, Beaches & Bases: Making Feminist Sense of International Politics*. Berkeley: University of California Press.

Enock, C. Reginald. 1908. *Peru: Its Former and Present Civilization, History and Existing Conditions, Topography and Natural Resources, Commerce and General Development*. London: Unwin.

Faithorn, Elizabeth. 1986. "Gender Bias and Sex Bias: Removing our cultural Blinders in the Field." Pp. 275–288 in *Self, Sex, and Gender in Cross-Cultural Fieldwork*, edited by Tony Larry Whitehead and Mary Ellen Conoway. Urbana: University of Illinois Press.

Feal, Rosemary Giesdorfer. 1995. "Reading against the Cane: Afro-Hispanic Studies and Mestizaje." *Diacritics* 25(1):82–98.

Feminias, Blenda. 1990. "Regional Dress of the Colca Valley, Peru: A Dynamic Tradition." Pp. 179–204 in *Textile Traditions of Mesoamerica and the Andes: An Anthology*. Austin: University of Texas Press.

————. n.d. "Dancing in Disguise: Cross-Dressing and Performance in a Peruvian Festival." Unpublished ms.

Ferreira, Mariana Kawall Leal. 1997. "When 1 + 1 = 2: Making Mathematics in Central Brazil." *American Ethnologist* 24(1):132–147.

Field, Les W. 1994. "Who are the Indians? Reconceptualizing Indigenous Identity, Resistance, and the Role of Social Science in Latin America." *Latin American Research Review* 29(3):237–238.

Fontaine, Pierre-Michel, ed. 1985. *Race, Class, and Power in Brazil*. Los Angeles: Center for Afro-American Studies, UCLA.

Frankenberg, Ruth. 1993. *White Women, Race Matters: The Social Construction of Whiteness*. Minneapolis: University of Minnesota Press.

Friedl, Ernestine. 1967. "The Position of Women: Appearance and Reality." *Anthropological Quarterly* 40:97–108.

Friedlander, Judith. 1975. *Being Indian in Hueyapan: A Study of Forced Identity in Contemporary Mexico*. New York: St. Martin's Press.

Freud, Sigmund. 1999. *The Interpretation of Dreams*. Translated by Joyce Crick. Oxford : Oxford University Press.

———. 1963 [1919]. "The 'Uncanny.'" Translated by Alix Strachey. Pp. 19–62 in *Studies in Parapsychology*. New York: Collier Books.

Freyre, Gilberto. 1946. *The Masters and the Slaves: A Study in the Development of Brazilian Civilization*. Translated from the Portuguese by Samuel Putnam. Second English-Language Edition, Revised. New York: Alfred A. Knopf.

Gade, Daniel W. 1975. *Plants, Man and Land in the Vilcanota Valley of Peru*. The Hague: W. Junk.

Galeano, Eduardo. 1985. *Memory of Fire: Genesis*. New York: Pantheon Books. Cedric Belfrage, trans. Originally published as *Memoria del fuego, I. Los nacimientos*. Spain: Siglo Veintiuno de España.

———. 1973. *Open Veins of Latin America: Five Centuries of the Pillage of a Continent*. Translated by Cedric Belfrage. New York: Monthly Review Press.

Garber, Marjorie. 1992. *Vested Interests: Cross-Dressing and Cultural Anxiety*. New York: Routledge.

García Lorca, Federico. 1983. *La casa de Bernarda Alba,* edited by H. Ramsden. Manchester: Manchester University Press.

García Márquez, Gabriel. 1987. *Cien años de soledad*. Barcelona: Mondadori.

Geertz, Clifford. 1973. "Thick Description: Toward an Interpretive Theory of Culture." Pp. 3–32 in The Interpretation of Cultures. New York: Basic Books.

Gill, Leslie. 1994. *Precarious Dependencies: Gender, Class and Domestic Service in Bolivia*. New York: Columbia University Press.

Gilman, Sander L. 1985. *Difference and Pathology: Stereotypes of Sexuality, Race, and Madness*. Ithaca: Cornell University Press.

Gilroy, Paul. 1993. *The Black Atlantic: Modernity and Double Consciousness*. Cambridge: Harvard University Press.

———. 1987. *"There Ain't no Black in the Union Jack": The Cultural Politics of Race and Nation*. Chicago: University of Chicago Press.

Godelier, Maurice. 1977. *Perspectives in Marxist Anthropology*. Translated by Robert Brain. Cambridge: Cambridge University Press.

Gombrich, E. H. (Ernst Hans). 1960. *Art and Illusion; A Study in the Psychology of Pictorial Representation*. New York: Pantheon Books.

Goodale, Jane. 1980. "Gender, Sexuality and Marriage: A Kaulong Model of Nature and Culture." Pp. 119–142 in *Nature, Culture, and Gender*. Carol MacCormack and Marilyn Strathern, editors. Cambridge: Cambridge University Press.

Gose, Peter. 1994a. "Sacrifice and the Commodity Form in the Andes." *Man* 21: 296–310.

———. 1994b. *Deathly Waters and Hungry Mountains.* Toronto: University of Toronto Press.

Gould, Jeffrey L. 1998. *To Die in This Way: Nicaraguan Indians and the Myth of Mestizaje, 1880–1965.* Durham, N.C.: Duke University Press.

Gould, Steven J. 1980. *The Mismeasure of Man.* New York: W. W. Norton.

Green, Duncan. 1999. "The Failings of the International Financial Architecture." NACLA Report on the Americas 33(1):31–36.

Guillet, David. 1979. *Agrarian Reform and Peasant Economy in Southern Peru.* Columbia: University of Missouri Press.

Hale, Charles R. 1996. Mestizaje, Hybridity, and the Cultural Politics of Difference in Post-Revolutionary Central America. *Journal of Latin American Anthropology* 2(1):34–61.

———. 1993. "Between Che Guevara and the Pachamama: Mestizos, Indians And Identity Politics In The Anti-Quincentenary Campaign." Critique of Anthropology 14(1):9–39.

Harding, Susan. 1975. "Women and Words in a Spanish Village." Pp. 283–308 in *Toward an Anthropology of Women*, Rayna R. Reiter, ed. New York: Monthly Review Press.

Harris, Cheryl I. 1993. "Whiteness as Property." *Harvard Law Review* 106(8): 1710–1791.

Harris, Marvin. 1974. *Patterns of Race in the Americas.* New York: Norton Library.

Harris, Olivia. 1995. "The Sources and Meanings of Money: Beyond the Market Paradigm in an Ayllu of Northern Potosí." Pp. 297–398 in *Ethnicity, Markets, and Migration in the Andes: At the Crossroads of Anthropology and History.* Larson, Brooke and Olivia Harris, eds. Durham: Duke University Press.

———. 1982. "The Dead and the Devils among the Bolivian Laymi." Pp. 45–73 in *Death and the Regeneration of Life.* Maurice Bloch and Jonathan Parry, eds. Cambridge: Cambridge University Press.

———. 1980. "The Power of Signs: Gender, Culture, and the Wild in the Bolivian Andes." Pp. 70–94 in *Nature, Culture, and Gender.* Carol P. MacCormack and Marilyn Strathern, eds. Cambridge: Cambridge University Press.

———. 1978. "Complementarity and Conflict: An Andean View of Women and Men." Pp. 21–40 in *Sex and Age as Principles of Social Differentiation.* J. S. La Fontaine, ed. London: Academic Press.

Harrison, Regina. 1989. *Signs, Songs, and Memory in the Andes: Translating Quechua Language and Culture.* Austin: University of Texas Press.

Hartigan, John, Jr. 1995. "Establishing the Fact of Whiteness." *American Anthropologist* 99(3):495–505.

Herdt, Gilbert. 1994. *Third Sex, Third Gender: Beyond Sexual Dimorphism in Culture and History.* New York: Zone Books.

———. 1981. *Guardians of the Flute: Idioms of Masculinity.* New York: Columbia University Press.

Hess, Carmen G. 1997. *Hungry for Hope: On the Cultural and Communicative Dimensions of Development in Highland Ecuador.* New York: Stylus.

hooks, bell. 1995. "Representing Whiteness in the Black Imagination." Pp. 165–179 in *Displacing Whiteness: Essays in Social and Cultural Criticism.* Ruth Frankenberg, ed. Durham: Duke University Press.

Hill, Jane H. 1994. "The Incorporative Power of Whiteness." Paper delivered at the American Ethnological Society meetings, Santa Monica, California.

Humboldt, A. von. 1840. *Cosmos, a Sketch of a Physical Description of the Universe.* Translated by E. C. Otté, vol. 1. London: Bohn Press.

Icaza, Jorge. 1953. *Huasipungo.* Buenos Aires: Losada.

Ignatiev, Noel, and John Garvey, eds. 1996. *Race Traitor.* New York: Routledge.

Isbell, Billie Jean. 1997a. "Time, Text, and Terror." Pp. 57–76 in *Structure, Knowledge, and Representation in the Andes.* Vol. 2: *Studies Presented to Reiner Tom Zuidema on the Occasion of His 70th Birthday. Journal of the Steward Anthropological Society* 25(1 and 2).

———. 1997b. "De inmaduro a duro: lo simbólico femienino y los esquemas andinos de género." Pp. 253–301 in *Más allá del silencio: las fronteras de género en los Andes.* Denise Y. Arnold, editor. La Paz: CIASE/ILCA.

———. 1978. *To Defend Ourselves: Ecology and Ritual in an Andean Village.* Austin: University of Texas Press.

———. 1976. "La otra mitad esencial: un estudio de complementaridad sexual en los Andes." *Estudios Andinos* 5(1):37–56.

Jacobs, Sue-Ellen. 1968. "Berdache: A Brief Review of the Literature." *Colorado Anthropologist* 1:25–40.

Jacobs, Sue-Ellen, Wesley Thomas, and Sabine Lang, eds. 1997. *Two-Spirit People: Native American Gender Identity, Sexuality, and Spirituality.* Urbana: University of Illinois Press.

Jameson, Fredric. 1998. *Brecht and Method.* London: Verso Press.

Jones, Gareth A. 1994. "The Latin American City as Contested Space: A Manifesto." *Bulletin of Latin American Research* 13(1):1–12.

Jones, Gareth A., and Ann Varley. 1989. "The Contest for the City Centre: Street Traders versus Buildings." *Bulletin of Latin American Research* 13(1):27–44.

Kapchan, Deborah. 1996. *Gender on the Market: Moroccan Women and the Revoicing of Tradition.* Philadelphia: University of Pennsylvania Press.

Kapsoli, Wilfredo. 1991. "Los pishtacos: degolladores degollados." *Bulletin de l'institut français d'études Andines* 20(1):61–77.

Klump, Kathleen. 1998. "Black Traders of Highland Ecuador." Pp. 357–376 in *Blackness in Latin America and the Caribbean,* edited by Norman E. Whitten Jr. and Arlene Torres. Bloomington: University of Indiana Press.

Kramer, Fritz. 1993. *The Red Fez: Art and Spirit Possession in Africa.* Malcolm R. Green, trans. Orig. published in German 1987. London: Verso.

Kristal, Efraín. 1987. *The Andes Viewed from the City: Literary and Political Discourse on the Indian in Peru 1848–1930.* New York: Peter Lang.

Kulick, Don. 1993. *Travesti: Sex, Gender and Culture among Brazilian Transgendered Prostitutes.* Chicago: University of Chicago Press.

———. 1998. "A Man in the House: The Boyfriends of Brazilian Travesti Prostitutes." *Social Text* 52–53: 133–160.

———. 1997. "The Gender of Brazilian Transgendered Prostitutes." *American Anthropologist* 99(3):574–585.

Lan, David. 1985. *Guns and Rain: Guerillas and Spirit Mediums in Zimbabwe.* Berkeley: University of California Press.

Lancaster, Roger N. 1992. *Life Is Hard: Machismo, Danger, and the Intimacy of Power in Nicaragua.* Berkeley: University of California Press.

Lang, Sabine. 1998. *Men as Women, Women as Men: Changing Gender in Native*

American Cultures. Translated from the German by John L. Vantine. Austin: University of Texas Press.

Larson, Brooke, and Olivia Harris, eds. 1995. *Ethnicity, Markets, and Migration in the Andes: At the Crossroads of Anthropology and History.* Durham: Duke University Press.

LaTorre, Roberto. 1984. "El nákaj." In *Narradores cusqueños,* Rubén Sueldo Guevara, editor. Cuzco: Librería Studiu, pps. 195–197.

Lawlor, Eric. 1989. *In Bolivia: An Adventurous Odyssey through the Americas' Least-Known Nation.* New York: Vintage Press.

Lehmann, David, editor. 1982. *Ecology and Exchange in the Andes.* Cambridge: Cambridge University Press.

Lévi-Strauss, Claude. 1966. *The Savage Mind.* Chicago: University of Chicago Press.

———. 1963. "The Effectiveness of Symbols." In *Structural Anthropology.* New York: Basic Books.

Liffman, Paul. 1977. "Vampires of the Andes." *Michigan Discussions in Anthropology* 2 (winter):205–226.

Limón, José E. 1994. *Dancing with the Devil: Society and Cultural Poetics in Mexican-American South Texas.* Madison: University of Wisconsin Press.

Lloret Bastidas, Antonio. 1993. *Cuencanarías.* Tomo II. Cuenca, Ecuador: Casa de la Cultura.

———. 1982. *Antología de la poesía cuencana.* Tomo II: *época del romanticismo.* Cuenca, Ecuador: Consejo Provincial del Azuay.

———. 1981. *Antología de la poesía cuencana.* Tomo II: *Época del romanticismo.* Cuenca: Consejo Provincial del Azuay.

López, Iris. 1993. "Agency and Constraint: Sterilization and Reproductive Freedom among Puerto Rican Women in New York City." *Urban Anthropology* 22(3–4):299–323.

———. 1987. "Sterilization among Puerto Rican Women in New York City: Public Policy and Social Constraints." In *Cities of the United States: Studies in Urban Anthropology.* Leith Mullings, editor. New York: Columbia University Press.

López Mejía, Adelaida. 1995. "Debt, Delirium and Cultural Exchange in Cien años de soledad." *Revista de Estudios Hispánicos* 29(1):3–25.

López Mondéjar, Públio. 1993. "The Magic of Martín Chambi." Pp. 13–28 in *Martín Chambi: Photographs, 1920–1950.* Introductions by Edward Ranney and Públio López Mondéjar. Translation from the Spanish by Margaret Sayers Peden. Washington: Smithsonian Institution Press.

Low, Setha. 1997. "Indigenous Architecture and the Spanish American Plaza in Mesoamerica and the Caribbean." *American Anthropologist* 97(4):748–762.

MacCannell, Dean. 1976. *The Tourist: A New Theory of the Leisure Class.* New York: Schocken Books.

Malik, Kenan. 1996. *The Meaning of Race: Race, History and Culture in Western Society.* New York: New York University Press.

Malinowski, Bronislaw. 1987 [1929]. *The Sexual Life of Savages in North-Western Melanesia.* Introduction by Annette Weiner. Boston: Beacon Press.

Mannheim, Bruce. 1991. *The Language of the Inka Since the European Invasion.* Austin: University of Texas Press.

Manya, Juan Antonio. 1969. *Temible ñakaq?* Cusco: Allpanchis 1. Pp.135–138.

Maríategui, José María. 1952. *Siete ensajos de interpretación de la realidad peruana.* Lima: Amauta.

Martin, Emily. 1985. *The Woman in the Body: A Cultural Analysis of Reproduction.* Boston: Beacon Press.

Martínez Escobar, Gabriela, and Daniel Aizenstat. 1993. "Ñakaj: fabula andeium." Videorecording. Berkeley: Taruka Films and University of California Extension Center for Media and Independent Learning.

Marx, Karl. 1964. *The Economic and Philosophic Manuscripts of 1844.* Edited by Dirk J. Struik; translated by Martin Milligan. New York: International Publishers.

Mauss, Marcel. 1987. *The Gift: The Form and Reason for Exchange in Archaic Societies.* W. D. Halls, trans. Originally published as "Essai sur le don," 1950. New York: W.W. Norton.

Mayer, Enrique. 1994. "Patterns of Violence in the Andes." *Latin American Research Review* 29(2):141–177.

———. 1991. "Peru in Deep Trouble: Mario Vargas Llosa's 'Inquest in the Andes' Reexamined." *Cultural Anthropology* 6:466–504.

———. 1971. "Un carnero por un saco de papas: aspectos del trueque en la zona de Chaupiwaranga, Pasco." *Actas y memorias del XXXIX Congreso Internacional de Americanistas, 1970.* Vol. 3.

Medicine, Beatrice. 1983. "'Warrior Women'—Sex Role Alternatives for Plains Indian Women." Pp. 267–280 in *The Hidden Half: Studies of Plains Indian Women,* ed. Patricia Albers and Beatrice Medicine. Washington, D.C.: University Press of America.

Medinaceli, Carlos. 1981 [1929]. *La chaskañawi.* Sucre: Editorial Tupac Katari.

Medlin, Mary Ann. 1990. "Ethnic Dress and Calcha Festivals, Bolivia." Pp. 261–282 in *Textile Traditions of Mesoamerica and the Andes: An Anthology.* Austin: University of Texas Press. Blum Schevill, Margot, Janet Catherine Berlo, and Edward B. Dwyer, eds.

Meillassoux, Claude. 1981. *Maidens, Meals, and Money: Capitalism and the Domestic Community.* Cambridge: Cambridge University Press.

Meisch, Lynn. 1990. "We Are Sons of Atahualpa and We Will Win: Traditional Dress in Otavalo and Saraguro, Ecuador." Pp. 145–178 in *Textile Traditions of Mesoamerica and the Andes: An Anthology.* Austin: University of Texas Press. Blum Schevill, Margot, Janet Catherine Berlo, and Edward B. Dwyer, eds.

Menchú, Rigoberta. 1983. *I, Rigoberta Menchú: An Indian Woman in Guatemala.* Edited and introduced by Elisabeth Burgos-Debray; translated by Ann Wright. New York: Verso.

Meyerson, Julia. 1990. *Tambo: Life in an Andean Village.* Austin: University of Texas Press.

Miles, Ann. 1989. "The High Cost of Leaving: Illegal Emigration from Cuenca, Ecuador and Family Separation." Pp. 55–74 in *Women and Economic Change: Andean Perspectives.* Ann Miles and Hans Buechler, eds. Volume 14: Society for Latin American Anthropology Publication Series. Washington, D.C.: American Anthropological Association.

Miles, Ann. 1994. "Helping Out at Home—Gender Socialization, Moral Development, and Devil Stories in Cuenca, Ecuador." *Ethos* 22, no. 2: 132–57.

Miller, Laura Martin. 1990. "The Ikat Shawl Traditions of Northern Peru and Southern Ecuador." Pp. 337–358 in *Textile Traditions of Mesoamerica and the*

Andes: An Anthology. Austin: University of Texas Press. Blum Schevill, Margot, Janet Catherine Berlo, and Edward B. Dwyer, eds.

Miller, Tom. 1986. *The Panama Hat Trail.* New York: Vintage Books.

Mintz, Sidney. 1978. "Caribbean Marketplaces and Caribbean History." *Nova Americana* 1:333–344.

———. 1972. "The Contemporary Jamaican Market System." Pp. 214–224 in *Caribbean Transformations.* Baltimore: Johns Hopkins Press.

———. 1971. "Men, Women and Trade." *Comparative Studies in Society and History* 13:247–269.

Mitchell, William P. 1991. *Peasants on the Edge: Crop, Cult and Crisis in the Andes.* Austin: University of Texas Press.

Molinié Fioravanti, Antoinette. 1991. "Sebo bueno, indio muerto: la estructura de una creencia Andina." *Bulletin de l'institut français d'études Andines* 20(1): 79–92.

Montrose, Louis. 1993. "The Work of Gender in the Discourse of Discovery." Pp. 177–217 in *New World Encounters.* Stephen Greenblatt, editor. Berkeley: University of California Press.

Moore, Henrietta L. 1988. *Feminism and Anthropology.* Minneapolis: University of Minnesota Press.

Morales, Edmundo. 1995. *The Guinea Pig: Healing, Food, and Ritual in the Andes.* Tucson: University of Arizona Press.

Mörner, Magnus. 1967. *Race Mixture in the History of Latin America.* Boston: Little Brown.

Morote Best, Efraín. 1951–52. "El Degollador (Nakaq)." *Cusco: Tradición* 11(4): 67–91.

Mulvey, Laura. 1975. "Visual Pleasure and Narrative Cinema." *Screen* 16(3):6–18.

Murra, John V. 1975. *Formaciones económicos y políticas del mundo andino.* Lima: Instituto de Estudios Peruanos.

Museo Crespo Toral. 1917–18. "Oficios a varias autoridades y particulares. Años de 1917–1918." Archivo del Museo Crespo Toral, Cuenca.

Naranjo V., Marcelo, coordinador de la investigación, et al. 1986. *La cultura popular en el Ecuador.* Tomo II: *Cotopaxi.* Con Lilían Benítez y Carmen Dueñas. Quito: CIDAAP (Centro Interamericano de Artesanías y Artes Populares).

Nash, June. 1978. *We Eat the Mines and the Mines Eat Us: Dependency and Exploitation in Bolivian Tin Mines.* New York: Columbia University Press.

Nelson, Diane M. 1998. "Perpetual Creation and Decomposition: Bodies, Gender and Desire in Assumptions of a Guatemalan Discourse of Mestizaje." *Journal of Latin American Anthropology* 4(1):74–111.

Newton, Esther. 1979. *Mother Camp: Female Impersonators in America.* Chicago: University of Chicago Press.

Nochlin, Linda. 1989. "The Imaginary Orient." Pp. 38–42 in *The Politics of Vision: Essays on Nineteenth-Century Art and Society.* Boulder: Westview Press.

Núñez del Prado, Oscar. 1973. *Kuyo Chico: Applied Anthropology in an Indian Community.* Chicago: University of Chicago Press.

Offerhaus, Manja, and Júlio Cortázar. 1984. *Alto el Perú.* México, D.F.: Editorial Nueva Imagen.

Oliver-Smith, Anthony. 1969. "The Pishtaco: Institutionalized Fear in Highland Peru." *Journal of American Folklore* 82:326–363.

Orlove, Benjamin. 1998. "Down to Earth: Race and Substance in the Andes."
  Bulletin of Latin American Research 17(2):207–222.
———. 1996. "Surfacings: Thoughts on Memory and the Ethnographer's Self."
  Pp. 1–29 in *Jews and Other Differences: The New Jewish Cultural Studies,* Jonathan Boyarin and Daniel Boyarin, eds. Minneapolis: University of Minnesota Press.
———. 1993. "Putting Race in Its Place: Order in Colonial and Postcolonial Peruvian Geography." *Social Research* 60(2):301–336.
———. 1974. *Alpacas, Sheep, and Men: The Wool Export Economy and Regional Society in Southern Peru.* New York: Academic Press.
Orlove, Benjamin, and E. Schmidt. 1995. "Swallowing Their Pride—Indigenous and Industrial Beer in Peru and Bolivia." *Theory and Society* 24(2):271–
  298.
Orta, Andrew. 1997. "Seductive Strangers and Saturated Symbols: Fat Stealing,
  Catechists and the Porous Production of Andean Locality." Unpublished ms.
Page, Helán A. 1997. "'Black' Images, African American Identities: Corporate
  Cultural Projection in the Songs of My People." *Identities* 3(4):557–607.
Paredez Ortega, Eduardo. 1980. *Tradiciones de Cotopaxi.* Latacunga: Litografías
  Andrade Hno.
Parsons, Elsie Clews. 1945. *Peguche, Canton of Otavalo, Province of Imbabura, Ecua-
  dor: A Study of Andean Indians.* Chicago: University of Chicago Press.
Paulson, Susan. 1996. "Familias que no 'conyugan' e identidades que no conju-
  gan: la vida en Mizque desafía nuestras categorías.'" Pp. 85–162 in *Ser mujer
  indígena, chola o birlocha en la bolivia postcolonial de los años 90.* La Paz: Ministerio de Desarollo Humana.
Paulson, Susan, and Pamela Calla. 2000. "Gender and Ethnicity in Bolivian Politics: Transformation or Paternalism?" *Journal of Latin American Anthropology*
  5(2):112–149.
Pérez, Gina. 2000. "The Near Northwest Side Story: Gender, Migration and Everyday Life in Chicago and San Sebastián, Puerto Rico." Ph.D. dissertation,
  Northwestern University Department of Anthropology.
Platt, Tristan. 1987. "Entre cháwxa y muxsa: para una historia del pensamiento
  político Aymara." Pp. 61–132 in *Tres reflexiones sobre el pensamiento andino.*
  Thérèse Bouysee-Cassagne, Olivia Harris, Tristan Platt, and Verónica Cere-
  ceda, eds. La Paz: HISBOL.
Poliakov, L. 1974. *The Aryan Myth — A History of Racist and Nationalist Ideas in
  Europe.* Translated by Edmund Howard. London: Basic Books.
Poole, Deborah. 1997. *Vision, Race, and Modernity: A Visual Economy of the An-
  dean Image World.* Princeton: Princeton University Press.
———. 1994. "Introduction: Anthropological Perspectives on Violence and
  Culture—A View from the Peruvian High Provinces." Pp. 1–30 in *Unruly
  Order: Power, Violence and Cultural Identity in the High Provinces of Peru.* Boul-
  der: Westview Press.
———. 1988. "Landscapes of Power in a Cattle-Rustling Culture of Southern
  Andean Peru." *Dialectical Anthropology* 12(3):367–398.
Preiur, Annick. 1998. *Mema's House, Mexico City: On Transvestes, Queens, and
  Machos.* Chicago: University of Chicago Press.
Quijano, Aníbal. 1980. *Dominacion y cultura; Lo cholo y el conflicto cultural en el Peru.*
  Lima: Mosca Azul Editores.

Radcliffe, Sarah, and Sallie Westwood. 1996. *Remaking the Nation: Place, Identity and Politics in Latin America.* London: Routledge.

Ramírez de Arellano, Annette, and Conrad Seipp. 1983. *Colonialism, Catholicism and Contraception: A History of Birth Control in Puerto Rico.* Chapel Hill: University of North Carolina Press.

Ramos, Alcida. 1998. *Indigenism: Ethnic Politics in Brazil.* Madison: University of Wisconsin Press.

Ranney, Edward. 1993. "The Legacy of Martín Chambi." Pp. 9–12 in *Martín Chambi: Photographs, 1920–1950.* Introductions by Edward Ranney and Públio López Mondéjar. Translation from the Spanish by Margaret Sayers Peden. Washington: Smithsonian Institution Press.

Rasnake, Roger Neil. 1988. *Domination and Cultural Resistance: Authority and Power among an Andean People.* Durham: Duke University Press.

Reclus, E. 1895. *Nouvelle géographia universelle. La terre et les hommes.* Vol. XVIII. Paris: Librarie Hachette.

Reiter, Rayna R. 1975. "Men and Women in the South of France: Public and Private Domains." Pp. 252–282 in *Toward an Anthropology of Women,* Rayna R. Reiter, ed. New York: Monthly Review Press.

Rivera Cusicanqui, Silvia. 1996. "Prólogo: Los desafíos para una democracía étnica y genérica en los albores del tercer milenio." Pp. 17–84 in *Ser mujer indígena, chola o birlocha en la bolivia postcolonial de los años 90.* Silvia Rivera Cusicanqui, editor. La Paz: Ministerio de Desarollo Humana.

Rivera Cusicanqui, Silvia, et al. 1996. "Trabajo de mujeres: explotación capitalista y opresión colonial entre las migrantes aymaras de La Paz y El Alto, Bolivia." Pp. 163–300 in *Ser mujer indígena, chola o birlocha en la bolivia postcolonial de los años 90.* Silvia Rivera Cusicanqui, editor. La Paz: Ministerio de Desarollo Humana.

Rivière, Gilles. 1996. "Lik'ichiri y kharisiri. a propósito de las representaciones del 'otro' en la sociedad aymara." *Bulletin de l'Institut Français d'Etudes Andines* 20(1):23–40.

Robertson, Claire C. 1984. *Sharing the Same Bowl: A Socioeconomic History of Women and Class in Accra, Ghana.* Bloomington: Indiana University Press.

Rockefeller, Stuart. 1998. "The Gaze Sucks: On Looking, Stealing Grease and the Play of Difference in Quirpini-Bolivia and Elsewhere." Unpublished ms.

Roediger, David. 1994. *Towards the Abolition of Whiteness: Essays on Race, Politics, and Working-Class History.* London: Verso.

———. 1991. *The Wages of Whiteness: Race and the Making of the American Working Class.* London: Verso.

Rojas Rimachi, Emilio. 1989. "Los 'sacaojos': el miedo y la cólera." Pp. 149-154 in *Pishtacos: de verdugos a sacaojos.* Juan Ansión, ed. Lima: Tarea, Asociación de Publicaciones Educativas.

Rosaldo, Renato. 1988. *Culture and Truth: The Remaking of Social Analysis.* Boston: Beacon Press.

Roscoe, Will. 1994. "How to Become a Berdache: Toward a Unified Analysis of Gender Diversity." Pp. 329–372 in *Third Sex, Third Gender: Beyond Sexual Dimorphism in Culture and History,* Gilbert Herdt, ed. New York: Zone Books.

Rout, L. B. 1974. *The African Experience in Spanish America. 1502 to the Present Day.* Cambridge: Cambridge University Press.

Rowe, Ann Pollard, Lynn A. Meisch, Laura M. Miller, et al. 1998. *Costume and Identity in Highland Ecuador.* Ann Pollard Rowe, editor. Seattle: University of Washington Press.

Rubin, Gayle. 1975. "The Traffic in Women: Notes on the 'Political Economy' of Sex." Pp. 157–210 in *Toward an Anthropology of Women,* Rayna R. Reiter, ed. New York: Monthly Review Press.

Saco, J. A. 1938. *Historia de la esclavitud de la raza africana en el Nuevo Mundo y en especial en los países américo-hispanos,* 4 vols. Havana: Cultural, S.A.

Sacks, Karen Brodkin. 1994. "When Did Jews Become White Folks?" Pp. 78–102 in *Race,* edited by Steven Gregory and Roger Sanjek. New Brunswick N.J.: Rutgers University Press.

Salazar-Soler, Carmen. 1991. "El pishtaku entre los campesinos y los mineros de Huancavelica." *Bulletin de l'Institut Français d'Etudes Andines* 20(1):7–22.

Salomon, Frank. 1981a. "Weavers of Otavalo." Pp. 420–449 in *Cultural Transformations and Ethnicity in Modern Ecuador,* Norman E. Whitten, Jr., ed. Urbana: University of Illinois Press.

———. 1981b. "Killing the Yumbo: A Ritual Drama of Northern Quito." Pp. 162–208 in *Cultural Transformations and Ethnicity in Modern Ecuador,* Norman E. Whitten, Jr., ed. Urbana: University of Illinois Press.

Sanday, Peggy. 1990. *Fraternity Gang Rape: Sex, Brotherhood and Privilege on Campus.* New York: New York University Press.

Sartre, Jean-Paul. 1948. *Anti-Semite and Jew.* George J. Becker, trans. New York: Schokcen Books.

Scheper-Hughes, Nancy. 2000. "The Global Traffic in Human Organs." *Current Anthropology* 41(3):191–224.

———. 1996. "Theft of Life: The Globalization of Organ Stealing Rumors." *Anthropology Today* 12(3):3–11.

———. 1992. *Death without Weeping: The Violence of Everyday Life in Brazil.* Berkeley: University of California Press.

Schmidt-Cruz, Cynthia A. 1998. "Cortázar's Working Women: Maids and Prostitutes in His Short Stories." Paper presented at the Annual Meetings of the Latin American Studies Association, Chicago, Illinois.

Seligmann, Linda J. 1995. "My Little Vices: The Life Story of a Peruvian Marketwoman." Unpublished ms.

———. 1993. "Between Worlds of Exchange: Ethnicity among Peruvian Market Women." *Cultural Anthropology* 8(2):187–213.

———. 1989. "To Be In Between: The Cholas as Market-women." *Comparative Studies in Society and History* 31(4):694–721.

Sharpe, Jenny. 1991. "The Unspeakable Limits of Rape: Colonial Violence and Counter-Insurgency." *Genders* 10:25–46.

Shukman, Henry. 1989. *Sons of the Moon: A Journey in the Andes.* New York: Charles Scribner's Sons.

Sifuentes, Eudosio. 1989. "La continuidad de la historia de los pishtacos en los 'robaojos' de hoy." Pp. 149–154 in *Pishtacos: de verdugos a sacaojos.* Juan Ansión, editor. Lima: Tarea, Asociación de Publicaciones Educativas.

Silverblatt, Irene. 1987. *Moon, Sun, and Witches: Gender Ideologies and Class in Inca and Colonial Peru.* Princeton: Princeton University Press.

Silverman, Sydel F. 1967. "The Life Crisis as a Clue to Social Functions." *Anthropological Quarterly* 40:127–138. (Reprinted in *Toward an Anthropology of*

Women, Rayna R. Reiter, ed. New York: Monthly Review Press." Pp. 309–321.)

Skalka, Harold. 1961. "Notes from the Colombia-Cornell-Harvard-Illinois Universities' Summer Field School." Archives of the Cornell-Peru Project, Olin Library, Cornell University.

Skar, Harald O. 1982. *The Warm Valley People: Duality and Land Reform among the Quechua Indians of Highland Peru.* Oslo: Universitetsforlaget.

Smith, Carol A. 1997. "The Symbolics of Blood: Mestizaje in the Americas." *Identities* 3(4):495–522.

———. 1996. "Myths, Intellectuals, and Race/Class/Gender Distinctions in the Formation of Latin American Nations." *Journal of Latin American Anthropology* 2(1):148–169.

Smith, M. G. 1965. *The Plural Society in the British West Indies.* Berkeley: University of California Press.

Sordo, Emma. 1990. "Del cajón San Marcos al retablo testimonio." *Cuadernos de arte y cultura popular* 1:9–14. Taller-Gráfica Retablos Ayacuchanos.

South and MesoAmerican Indian Rights Center (SAIIC). 1997. "Indian City: Indigenous Survival in the Latin American Megacity." *Abya-Yala News* 10(3).

Spalding, Karen. 1984. *Huarochirí: An Andean Society under Inca and Spanish Rule.* Stanford University Press.

Spedding, Alison. n.d.*a* "El Kharisiri." Unpublished manuscript.

———. n.d.*b* "El Kharisiri: un enfoque epidemiológico." Unpublished manuscript.

Sprinkle, Annie. 1991. *Annie Sprinkle: Post Porn Modernist.* Amsterdam: Torch Books.

Starn, Orin. 1992. "Rethinking the Politics of Anthropology: The Case of the Andes." *Cultural Anthropology* 35(1):13–39.

———. 1991. "Missing the Revolution: Anthropologists and the War in Peru." *Cultural Anthropology* 6:63–91.

Stein, William W. 1961. *Hualcan: Life in the Highlands of Peru.* Ithaca: Cornell University Press.

Stepan, Nancy Leys. 1989. *"The Hour of Eugenics": Race, Gender and Nation in Latin America.* Ithaca: Cornell University Press.

Stocking, George. 1974. "Some Problems in the Understanding of Nineteenth Century Cultural Evolutionism." Pp. 407–425 in *Readings in the History of Anthropology,* edited by R. Darnell. New York: Harper and Row.

Straayer, Chris. 1993. "The Seduction of Boundaries: Feminist Fluidity in Annie Sprinkle's Art/Education/Sex." Pp. 156–175 in *Dirty Looks: Women-Pornography-Power,* Pamela Church Gibson and Roma Gibson, eds.

Strathern, Marilyn. 1991. *After Nature: English Kinship in the Late Twentieth Century.* Cambridge: Cambridge University Press.

———. 1988. *The Gender of the Gift: Problems with Women and Problems with Society in Melanesia.* Berkeley: University of California Press.

Strauss, Neil. 2000. "Songwriter's Racist Songs From 1980s Haunt Him." *New York Times,* Monday September 4, p. B1.

Streicker, Joel. 1995. "Policing Boundaries: Race, Class and Gender in Cartagena, Colombia." *American Ethnologist* 22(1):54–74.

Stutzman, Ronald. 1981. "El Mestizaje: An All-Inclusive Ideology of Exclusion."

Pp. 45–94 in *Cultural Transformations and Ethnicity in Modern Ecuador.* Norman E. Whitten, Jr., editor. Urbana: University of Illinois Press.

Sudarkasa, Niara. 1973. "Where Women Work: A Study of Yoruba Women in the Marketplace and the Home." *Museum of Anthropology Anthropological Papers* no. 53. Ann Arbor: University of Michigan Press.

Tandeter, Enrique, Vilma Milletich, María Matilda Ollier, and Beatríz Ruibal. 1995. "Indians in Late Colonial Marekts: Sources and Numbers." Pp. 196–223 in *Ethnicity, Markets, and Migration in the Andes: At the Crossroads of Anthropology and History.* Brooke Larson and Olivia Harris, eds. Durham: Duke University Press.

Taussig, Michael. 1987. *Shamanism, Colonialism, and the Wild Man: A Study in Terror and Healing.* Chicago: University of Chicago Press.

———. 1980. *The Devil and Commodity Fetishism in South America.* Chapel Hill: University of North Carolina Press.

Theweleit, Klaus. 1987. *Male Fantasies.* Vol. 1: *Women Floods Bodies History.* Minneapolis: University of Minnesota Press.

THOA (Andean Oral History Workshop). 1990. "Indigenous Women and Community Resistance: History and Memory." Compiled by Silvia Rivera Cusicanqui. Pp. 151–183 in *Women and Social Change in Latin America,* ed. Elizabeth Jelin; translated by Ann Zammit and Marilyn Thomson. London: Zed Books.

Todorov, Tzvetan. 1993. *On Human Diversity: Nationalism, Racism and Exoticism in French Thought.* Cambridge: Harvard University Press.

Tolen, Rebecca. 1998. "Receiving the Authorities in Chimborazo, Ecuador: Ethnic Performance in an Evangelical Andean Community." *Journal of Latin American Anthropology* 3(2):20–53.

Tschirley, David, and Harold Riley. 1990. "The Agricultural Marketing System." Pp. 193–224 in *Agriculture and Economic Survival: The Role of Agriculture in Ecuador's Development.* Morris D. Whitaker and Dale Colyer, eds. Boulder: Westview Press.

Tschudi, J. J. von. 1847. *Travels in Peru During the Years 1831–42, on the Coast, Across the Cordilleras and the Andes, into the Primeval Forests.* Translated by Thomasina Ross. D. London: Bogue.

Turino, Thomas. 1993. *Moving Away from Silence: Music of the Peruvian Altiplano and the Experience of Urban Migration.* Chicago: University of Chicago Press.

Tyler, Carole-Anne. 1998. "Passing: Narcissism, Identity, and Difference." *Differences* 6:2 and 3:212–248.

———. 1991. "Boys Will Be Girls: The Politics of Gay Drag." Pp. 32–70 in *Inside/Out: Lesbian Theories, Gay Theories.* Diana Fuss, ed. New York: Routledge.

Ugarteche, Oscar. 1999. "The Structural Adjustment Stranglehold: Debt and Underdevelopment in the Americas." *NACLA Report on the Americas* 33(1): 21–23.

Urton, Gary. 1980. "The Ambiguity of the Serpent." Paper presented at the conference "Heritage of the Conquest," Cornell University.

Valenzuela Arce, José Manuel. 1999. *Impecable y diamantina: la deconstruccion del discurso nacional.* Mexico: Instituto Tecnologico y de Estudios Superiores de Occidente.

————. 1997. *El color de las sombras: Chicanos, identidad y racismo*. México, D.F.: Universidad Iberoamericana: Plaza y Valdes Editores.

Vallaranos, José. 1996. *El Cholo en el Perú: Introducción al estudio sociológico del hombre y un pueblo mestizo y su destino cultural*. Buenos Aires: Imprenta López.

van den Berghe, Pierre, and George Primov. 1977. *Inequality in the Peruvian Andes: Class and Ethnicity in Cuzco*. Columbia: University of Missouri Press.

Vargas, José María O.P. 1983. *Nuestra Señora del Rosario en el Ecuador*. Quito: Goberieno Eclesiástico de la Arquidiócesis.

Vargas Llosa, Mario. 1993a. *A Fish in the Water: A Memoir*. H. Lane, trans. New York: Farrar, Straus, and Giroux.

————. 1993b. *El pez en el agua: memorías*. Barcelona: Seix Barral.

————. 1993c. "Martín Chambi." Pp. 7–9 in *Martín Chambi: Photographs, 1920–1950*. Introductions by Edward Ranney and Públio López Mondéjar. Translation from the Spanish by Margaret Sayers Peden. Washington: Smithsonian Institution Press.

Vergara Figueroa, Abilio, and Freddy Ferrúa Carrasco. 1989. "Ayacucho: de nuevo los degolladores." Pp. 123–136 in *Pishtacos: de verdugos a sacaojos*. Juan Ansión, ed. Lima: Tarea, Asociación de Publicaciones Educativas.

Wachtel, Nathan. 1994. *Gods and Vampires: Return to Chipaya*. Originally published in Paris as *Dieux et vempires: Retour à Chipaya*, 1992. Carol Volk, trans. Chicago: University of Chicago Press.

————. 1977. *The Vision of the Vanquished: The Spanish Conquest of Peru through Indian Eyes, 1530–1570*. Originally published in Paris as *La vision des vaincus; les Indiens du Pérou devant la conquête espagnole, 1530–1570*, 1971. Ben and Siân Reynolds, trans. New York: Barnes and Noble.

————. 1973. *Sociedad e ideología: ensayos de historia y antropología andinas*. Lima: Instituto de Estudios Peruanos.

Wade, Peter. 1993a. *Race and Ethnicity in Latin America*. London: Pluto Press.

————. 1993b. *Blackness and Race Mixture: The Dynamics of Racial Identity in Colombia*. Baltimore: Johns Hopkins University Press.

————. 1993c. "'Race,' Nature and Culture." *Man* 28:17–34.

Weismantel, Mary. 1997a. "White Cannibals: Fantasies of Racial Violence in the Andes." *Identities* 4(1):9–44.

————. 1997b. "Corpus Christi: Masculinity, Ecology and the Calendar in Andean Ecuador." Pp. 96–122 in *Structure, Knowledge, and Representation in the Andes*, Vol. II: *Studies Presented to Reiner Tom Zuidema on the Occasion of His 70th Birthday. Journal of the Steward Anthropological Society* 25 (1 and 2).

————. 1997c. "Time, Work-Discipline, and Beans: Indigenous Self-Determination in the Northern Andes." Pp. 31–54 in *Women and Economic Change: Andean Perspectives*. Ann Miles and Hans Buechler, eds. Volume 14: *Society for Latin American Anthropology Publication Series*. Washington, D.C.: American Anthropological Association.

————. 1995. "Making Kin: Kinship Theory and Zumbagua Adoptions." *American Ethnologist* 22(4):685–709.

————. 1992. "Embedded Catholics, Foreign Priests: Cultural Autonomy and Religious Identity in Zumbagua, Ecuador." Paper presented at the Annual Meetings of the American Anthropological Society, San Francisco, Calif.

————. 1991. "Being Catholic: Religious Practice and Imagining Indians in the

Andes." Paper presented at the Annual Meetings of the American Ethnological Society, Charleston, S.C.

————. 1989. "Making Breakfast and Raising Babies: The Zumbagua Household as Constituted Process." Pp. 55–72 in *The Household Economy: Reconsidering the Domestic Mode of Production*. Richard R. Wilk, editor. Boulder: Westview Press.

————. 1988. *Food, Gender and Poverty in the Ecuadorian Andes*. Philadelphia: University of Pennsylvania Press. Reprinted 1998 by Westview Press.

Weismantel, Mary, and Stephen F. Eisenman. 1998. "Race in the Andes: Global Movements and Popular Ontologies." *Bulletin of Latin American Research* 17(2):121–142.

Weiss, Wendy. 1985. "Es El Que Manda: Sexual Inequality and Its Relationship to Economic Development in the Ecuadorian Sierra." Ph.D. dissertation, Bryn Mawr College.

Weston, Kath. 1991. *Families We Choose: Lesbians, Gays, Kinship*. New York: Columbia University Press.

White, Alan. 1982. *Hierbas del Ecuador/Herbs of Ecuador*. Quito: Ediciones Libri Mundi.

White, Luise. 1999. "Blood and Words: Writing History about (and with) African Vampire Stories." Workshop paper presented at the Alice Berlan Kaplan Center for the Humanities, Northwestern University, Evanston, May 13, 1999.

Whitten, Dorothea S., and Norman J. Whitten, Jr. 1985. *Art, Knowledge and Health: Development and Assessment of a Collaborative Auto-Financed Organization in Eastern Ecuador*. Cambridge, Mass: Cultural Survival, Inc. and Sacha Runa Foundation.

Whitten, Norman E., Jr. 1985. *Sicuanga Runa: The Other Side of Development in Amazonian Ecuador*. Urbana: University of Illinois Press.

————. 1981. Introduction (pp. 1–44) to *Cultural Transformations and Ethnicity in Modern Ecuador*. Norman E. Whitten, Jr., ed. Urbana: University of Illinois Press.

————. 1976. *Sacha Runa: Ethnicity and Adaptation of Ecuadorian Jungle Quichua*. Urbana: University of Illinois Press.

Whitten, Norman E., Jr., and Arlene Torres, eds. 1998. *Blackness in Latin America and the Caribbean: Social Dynamics and Cultural Transformations*. Vols. 1 and 2. Bloomington: Indiana University Press.

Williams, Brackette. 1989. *Stains on My Name, War in My Veins: Guyana and the Politics of Cultural Struggle*. Durham: Duke University Press.

Williams, Brett. 1994. "Babies and Banks: The 'Reproductive Underclass' and the Raced, Gendered Masking of Debt." Pp. 348–365 in *Race*, edited by Steven Gregory and Roger Sanjek. New Brunswick, N.J.: Rutgers University Press.

Williams, Raymond. 1976. *Keywords: A Vocabulary of Culture and Society*. New York: Oxford University Press.

————. 1973. *The Country and the City*. New York: Oxford University Press.

Williams, Walter. 1986. *The Spirit and the Flesh: Sexual Diversity in American Indian Culture*. Boston: Beacon Press.

Wolf, Eric R. 1986. "The Vicissitudes of the Closed Corporate Peasant Community." *American Ethnologist* 13(2):325–329.

———. 1957. "Closed Corporate Peasant Communities in Mesoamerica and Central Java." *Southwestern Journal of Anthropology* 13(1):1–18.

———. 1955. "Types of Latin American Peasantry: A Preliminary Discussion." *American Anthropologist* 57(3):432–471.

Wolf, Eric R., and Edward C. Hansen. 1972. *The Human Condition in Latin America*. New York: Oxford University Press.

Zapata, Gastón Antonio. 1989. "Sobre ojos y pishtacos." Pp. 137–140 in *Pishtacos: de verdugos a sacaojos*. Juan Ansión, ed. Lima: Tarea, Asociación de Publicaciones Educativas.

Zuidema, R. T. 1977. "The Inca Kinship System: A New Theoretical Overview." Pp. 240–281 in *Andean Kinship and Marriage,* Ralph Bolton and Enrique Mayer, editors. Washington, D.C.: American Anthropological Association, Special Publication no. 7.

Name Index

Abercrombie, Thomas, 161, 232, 271n20, 274n14, 276n27, 285n17, 287nn36, 39, 289nn13,19

Alarcón, Norma, 282n23, 283n32

Albro, Rob, 33, 63, 276nn27,29, 289n19, 290n27

Aleto, Thomas, 48

Allen, Catherine, xxix–xxx, 139, 150, 171–2, 273 nn32, 33, 280n3, 281nn5,9, 283n28, 290n25

Ansión, Juan, 270n8, 274n10, 284n4, 286n33, 287nn35,44

Anzaldúa, Gloria, xxxiii, 155

Arguedas, José María, xvi, xxvii, 20, 63, 99, 100, 121, 127, 141, 150–1, 159–60, 164–5, 168, 172, 182, 194, 207, 210, 243–4, 274n9, 283n36, 286n28, 287n43

Arizpe, Lourdes, 49, 71, 75

Arnold, Denise, 274n5, 280n3

Babb, Florence, 38, 39, 68, 70, 100, 259, 280n40, 281n17

Baker, Josephine, 238

Balibar, Etienne, xxvi

Banzer Súarez, Hugo, 39, 61, 249

Barthes, Roland, 22, 28, 43–4

Bastides, Roger, 164, 166

Baudelaire, Charles, 163, 283n31

Bayly, Jaime, 97, 158, 172, 173

Belote, Linda, 278n11

Berger, John, 34, 285n19

Berlo, Janet Catherine, 123–4

Bielenberg, Aaron, 13

Blanco, Hugo, xxvii, xxix

Bolívar, Simón, 89

Bolton, Ralph, 277

Bourdieu, Pierre, 273n30

Boyarin, David, 8, 223

Brecht, Bertolt, xxxvi, 116–27, 132–5, 141, 160, 167, 170, 280n38

Brownrigg, Leslie, 90, 91, 97, 105, 278nn13,17

Buechler, Hans and Judith-Maria, 38, 57, 69, 106–7, 113, 145, 236, 244, 248, 250, 273n35, 276n31

Buitron, Anibal, 51, 109

Bunster, Ximena, and Elsa Chaney, 59

Butler, Judith, xxxiv, xxxvi, 110–4, 132–3

Calla, Pamela. *See* Susan Paulson

Candler, Kay, 73

Cárdenas, María Cristina, 25

Casagrande, Joseph, xxiii, 273nn34,35

Chaluisa, Alfonso, 138, 189, 203–5

Chaluisa, Clarita, 191, 211, 237

Chaluisa, Juanchu, Tayta, 64, 78, 138, 191, 200, 201, 204, 211, 287n38

Chaluisa family, xxviii, 13, 64, 131–2, 137–8, 191, 212

Chaluisa Quispe, Nancy de Rocio, xxxv, 204, 234, 237

Chambi, Martín, xxxv, 29–34, 42–3, 243, 275nn20,24, 279n22

Chaney, Elsa. *See* Ximena Bunster

Chávez, César, 201

Clifford, James, 103, 274n2

Collier, George, 51, 109

Colloredo-Mansfeld, Rudi, xxix, xxx, xxxii, 14, 182, 187, 190, 248, 262, 272nn28,29, 273n34, 285n20

Condori Mamani, Gregorio, 41–2, 55, 62, 117, 119, 202, 275n18, 276n34, 278n22

Cordero Palacios, Alfonso, 166, 169

Cornejo Polar, Antonio, xvi–xvii

Subject Index